U0593676

闽文化

郑立宪　主编
MIN CULTURE

译著者　何绵山　郑立宪　谢燕华

厦门大学出版社
XIAMEN UNIVERSITY PRESS

目 录

英 文 部 分

中 文 部 分

PREFACE

With the increasing favor for regional culture, the treasure of Fujian culture is being dug up and the specific charm and profound connotation of the culture is arousing the interest of more and more people.

Fujian is a province of songs and dances. Because of the cultures of mountains, rivers and sea, songs of farmers and fishers occupy a very important place in the Fujian folk songs. In addition, the rural and regional songs, such as work songs, poem singing, canzonet, songs of dance, children's songs and the tunes of life, are active and popular in different regions. For example, the children's song *The Cloudy Sky*, popular in South Fujian, describing an old couple who don't agree with each other on the flavor of the dish of loaches—to add more salt or not and who argue and break the pan, is very interesting and amusing. There are more than twenty kinds of folk songs in Fujian, of which *nanqu* (also called *nanyin*, the South Music) has the longest history and the greatest influence. *Nanqu* is not only the fading sound of the Yan music of the late Tang Dynasty and the Five Dynasties, but the echo of the South Opera of the Song Dynasty. *Nanqu* is a major kind of music in China, with the richest and the most complete musical culture of the old times, being regarded as living music history and musical fossil.

Fujian is also a province of opera. There are five operas, *Puxian* Opera, *Liyuan* Opera, *Gaojia* Opera, *Min* Opera and *Xiang* Opera, which are famous at home and abroad with rich patrimony. Take *Puxian* Opera for example, it has more than 5000 traditional plays and more than 8000 copies, which conserves more plays of South Opera and the old plays of the Central Plains than any other kind in the country and which is also a library and a museum collecting opera the most and the richest works worldwide. The traditional plays, music and roles of *Puxian* Opera and *Liyuan* Opera have great relation to the South Opera, and their music and music playing somewhat succeed the music of the Tang Dynasty and the Song Dynasty, so they are referred to as the fading sound of the South Opera and the living fossil of the traditional plays of the mid-land.

The calligraphy and painting of different generations in Fujian are abundant and colorful, which greatly enrich the treasury of arts of the country. Fujian painters have been syncretizing the strong points of different styles of drawing, presenting a strong creativity. Hui Chong, from Jiangle in the Song Dynasty, his paintings were idyllic of the scenery of the south of Changjiang River, and people called them *Huichong pastorals*. Chen Rong, from Futang (now Fuqing), his painting, *Cloud and Dragon Picture*, created a precedent after the Yuan Dynasty, harmonizing poem, calligraphy and drawing in one picture. Zheng Sixiao, from Lianjiang, drew *Molan Picture* of orchids rootless and without touching the soil, which made drawing orchids exposing root a style of painting popular until the end of the Qing Dynasty. Shangguan Zhou, from Changting in the Qing Dynasty, focused on the vividness of persons in his drawings and started the drawing style of Min (Fujian). Huang Shen, from Ninghua and one of the Eight Eccentrics in Yangzhou, was the first one who inosculated calligraphy with portrait painting.

There were quite a few famous calligraphers in Fujian such as Cai Xiang, from Xianyou in the Song Dynasty, who learnt writing skills from different styles and then created his own, Huang Daoshu, from Zhangpu in the Ming Dynasty, whose calligraphist style were considered coherent to his character and Yi Binshou, from Tingzhou in the Qing Dynasty, were regarded as the pioneers. of the *Lishu style* in epigraphy carving in the Qing Dynasty. The tradition of calligraphy and Chinese painting in Fujian has been going down from generation to generation up to now and the Ministry of Culture named successively the counties of Longhai, Tong'an, Jinjiang, Putian, Zhao'an, Jian'ou and the town in Zhangping *The Home of Calligraphy and Painting*.

The folk arts in Fujian are various and colorful. Pictures for the New Year here are mainly woodcuts, the content covering almost all the aspects of people's life. In Zhangzhou old style of such pictures always give their way to new ones, embodying both the characters of straightforwardness as in the North of China and the gracefulness as in the South. The pictures in Quanzhou always depict the folkcustoms, widely accepted by the overseas Chinese in South of Asia. Those in Fuding have a u-

nique style. For example, the picture *The Eight Hammers Fight
in Zhuxian Town* mingles pretty ladies and fighting soldiers together, which is rare in such paintings. Fujian's stone engraving
is famous at home and abroad, the most remarkable kinds of
which are that of Huian's and of Shoushan's. Of Huian's there
are four sub-classes, circular engravings, basso-relievos, deep
engravings and shadow engravings, works of which people can
see everywhere in the world, such as the *Huabiao* in Zhongshan
Tomb in Nanjing, the eight pairs of dragon columns in Longshan
Temple in Taiwan, the seats of the columns in the People's
Great Hall of Beijing, the garden of Monk Jianzhen of Japan,
and so on. And of Shoushan's there are five sub-classes, circular
engravings, bassorelievos, throughengravings, filmcarvings and
signet carvings, which include nearly a thousand designs. Folk
wood carvings are also popular in Fujian. The twenty-four wood
carvings, *Flying Musicians*, on the bucket arch of the Kaiyuan
Temple in Quanzhou are precious treasures. The famous puppet
image maker Jiang Jiazou has merged the skills of wooden image
carving and facial makeup in opera and made quite a lot of art
treasures. Paper-cut is one of folk arts in Fujian that countryside women love very much. Zhangpu County was once named
the *Home of Paper-cut by* the Ministry of Culture, and twice
edited and published *Album of Paper-cut of Zhangpu, Fujian,
China.* The books and thousands of paper-cuts have been sold a-
broad. Fujian has a long history in ceramic making. The black
glazed porcelains from Jian Kiln in Shuiji, Jianyang County in the
Song Dynasty were marvelously attractive, the typical of which
was *Jian Zhan* that was once brought to Japan as a Japanese na-

tional treasure collected in a well-known library of Tokoy. In the
Yuan Dynasty, the white glazed porcelains from the kilns in Dehua County were commonly called *Jian Bai* which was white and
light yellow, crystalloidally bright, smooth and strong. In the
Ming Dynasty and the Qing Dynasty, the blue and white porcelains were mostly produced from the kilns in Dehua County and
Anxi County, and they were all precious.

The writers in Fujian were famous for their argumentation.
There were no other provinces whose literary theory was as
flourishing as in Fujian. The real notes on poets and poetry began in the Song Dynasty and the *Cang Lang Notes* by Yan Yu in
the Song Dynasty was the most remarkable and onwards the
most influential book of the notes. The *Poet's Notes* by Wei
Qingzhi was an indispensable collection of the notes on studying
the poetic theory in the Song Dynasty. The *Hou Cun Notes* by
Liu Kezhuang and the *Ao Qizhi Notes* by Ao Taosun were representative works of the remarkable popular poetic theory. The
Poet Rules, *The Right Resources of Poetics and Rules of Rhyme*
by Yang Zai in the Yuan Dynasty were important works of the
notes at that time. The *Collection of Comments on the Poems of
the Tang Dynasty* by Gao Bing in the Ming Dynasty began the
debate on the poems of the Tang Dynasty and the Song Dynasty,
leading the tendency of the literature of that time. Wang Shen
zhong's theory of poems was looked up to as the standard. Li
Zhi's *On the Childlikeness* and his other literacy theories were
taken as the creed of the new literacy thoughts in the late Ming
Dynasty. Xie Zhaozhe's incisive statements on the story and the
opera enhanced their importance in the literacy history. In the

Qing Dynasty and in the modern times, the literacy critique in Fujian was by no means inferior. Lin Changyi's *Comments on Poems in Sheying Mansion*, Liang Zhangju's *Notes of Poems Beyond the Southeast Bridge*, Chen Shiyi's *Remarks on Poets and Poetry in Shiyi's Room*, Yan Fu's and Lin Xu's argumentations, etc. played a very important part in the Chinese history of literacy critique.

Fujian has been paying great attention to education since the Tang Dynasty when Fujian was in the exploitationperiod. When Li Yi, a member of the Tang imperial family, was an inspector in Fujian, he carried out the policy of "building schools and brightening the custom". When Chang Yan was an inspector in Fujian, he "built schools in the towns and invited good teachers to teach the local people". Chen Yuanguang, the prefectural governor of Zhangzhou, encouraged the local people as well as his followers to study more and hard. In the Five Dynasties, Wang Shenzhi, the King of Fujian, built many schools, requiring that all the school-age children should go to school. In the Song Dynasty, there were eight prefectures and each had a prefectural school, and many counties also ran local schools. You Zuo, from Jianyang, and Yang Shi, from Jiangle, went to the Central Plains to search for teachers and they stood deep in the snow, waiting for the master to accept them. In the Song Dynasty, Fujian had so many schools with such high quality and such great affect that it was rare in the country. Free schools, public schools and private schools were also popular. Reading became a common practice. Not only in Fuzhou "one remembered the light and silence of the street and bridge, hearing the sound of reading aluoud in the

lanes and alleys", but also in the remote county Taining "sound
of music and reading aloud could be heard from house to house".
The flourishing of education made miracles in the history of imperial examination. In the Five Dynasties Fujian only had a population of about 700 thousand, but there were 74 learners obtained the *Jinshi* degree. In the Northern and Southern Song Dynasties, in Fujian, there were 5987 learners received Jinshi degree and 22 won the title of *Zhuangyuan* , which was on the top
in the country according to the proportion of population.

Education in Fujian was still on the top in the Dynasties of
Yuan, Ming and Qing. In the Yuan Dynasty, there were subjects of Mongolian Character, Medicine and Technology (also
called Yinyangology). In the Ming and the Qing Dynasties,
there were more than thousand free schools and in the Qing Dynasty, there were Official Pronunciation Schools to rectify the local accent, and there were also Official Schools for the Eight
Banners. And in the Dynasty, the westernizing party set up a
Fujian Shipping Affair School in Fuzhou.

In the Dynasties of Song, Yuan, Ming and Qing in Fujian,
dominating in the field of the academic ideology was the Minnology, which was born in the Northern and Southern Song Dynasty and developed up to the height in the South Song Dynasty
with Zhu Xi as the representative the core of whose ideology was
moral principles. In Chinese history, there were few academic
schools that had such profound influence as the Minnology did.
The kernel of the Minnology was Zhu Xi's ideology which was
gradually taken by the rulers as official philosophy controlling
the national social ideology after the rulers recognized its theoret-

ical value. The Minnology has also been introduced into Japan,
Korea, Vietnam, Singapore and some other Southeast Asian
countries and merged into the society and the reality of the countries producing Zhuziology in Japan, Tuixiology in Korea and so
on. And the Minnology has brought into Europe and the Unitied
States and the study of Zhuzi's theory is very active in the West.
The Minnology has gradually become a universal theory. In the
ancient times, technology in Fujian was also flourishing. Just
take the two Song Dynasties for example, there were Su Song,
who was an astronomer and the writer of *The Summary of Newly Discovered Astronomic Signs*; Song Ci, who was the pioneer
of the medical jurisprudence in the world and the writer of *A
Collection of Justified Cases* and Zeng Gongliang, who was the
editor in chief of *An Outline of Wushu*.

Religion in Fujian occupied a special place in the religious
history of the country. Buddhism in Fujian has developed since
the Tang Dynasty and the Five Dynasties where there appeared a
great number of dignitaries who were closely related to the five
zens. For example, the second founder of the Zen of Cao Dong o-
riginally came from Putian, the founder of the Zen of Yu Men,
Wenyan, was a disciple of Yi Cun (from Nan'an) of Fuzhou
Xuefeng Temple, the founder of the Zen of Fayan, Wen Yi was
one of the second generation of the disciples of Xuansha Shibei's
(from Fuzhou), whom Wang Shenzhi respected, the founder of
the Zen of Wei Yang, Ling You, was from Changxi (now Xiapu), and the founder of the Zen of Lin Ji, Yi Xuan, was the
heir of Huang Bo of Fuqing. The printing of Buddhist Scripture
was also well developed in Fujian. In the Song Dynasty, there

were altogether five editions of the *Dazang Scripture* privately
or officially printed in the country, of which two were in Fujian,
Congning Wanshou Dazang in the Dongchan Temple and *Pilu
Dazang* in the Kaiyuan Temple. Dignitaries in Fujian had a close
relation with those abroad. In 1654, Yinyuan, a dignitary from
Huangbo Temple of Fuqing, brought a score of followers over to
Japan, setting up the Zen of Huangbo in Japan. Almost all the
known temples in Fujian had agencies abroad. Taoism was also
flourish in Fujian. It is said in *Yunji Qiqian* that Wuyi Mountain
in the North Fujian was regarded as the 16th spot of the 36 ones
of Taoism and Mount Zhiti (Mount Huotong) in the East Fujian
was another one. And in the florescence of Taoism, there were
ninety-nine Taoist abbeys. Islam in Fujian was in rather big a
scale in the Song Dynasty. At that time, Muslims came to
Quanzhou by way of the Silk Road, settling there and building a
huge mosque, the Saint Friend's. And in the Yuan Dynasty,
they constructed some more mosques there. Christianity was introduced into Fujian as early as in the Wuzong period of the Tang
Dynasty, but he who had the greatest influence was the missionary Aleni from Italy, who got to know all the famous scholars in
Fujian, and who was regarded as *Confucius from the West*. And
the folk religions in Fujian were quite popular. The sailing guard
goddess Ma Zu, the water goddess Chen Jinggu, the childbearing
protecting god Immortal Wu were believed in not only by Fujian
folks but also by those in Taiwan and the overseas Minnanese in
Southeast Asia.

The architecture in Fujian has a special value in the history
of that of the country. The "Three Alleys and Seven Lanes" of

Fuzhou was first shaped in the late Eeastern Jin Dynasty, which is typical of lane style in the construction of historical cultural cities in China, which is one of the rather complete existing ancient lane blocks in the South of China and where a number of houses of well-known historical persons and of buildings of the Ming and the Qing Dynasties, regarded as Museum of Architectures of the Ming and the Qing Dynasties. Zhaojiabao Village of Huxi Town of Zhangpu County has kept undamaged structures of Kaifeng, the capital city of the Song Dynasty. Tulou scattered in the Southwest of Fujian is the most typical and fascinating of the folk buildings in Fujian, which is "a great marvel in the the historical development of architecture" in China, even in the world and which can be "compared beauty with the Great Wall".

Fujian is one of the areas that has the most ancient temples. Located in the Xi Street of Quanzhou, Kaiyuan Temple is the oldest and the greatest of the wooden structures in the South Fujian and it embodies a great number of break-through innovations dexterously combining the art of engraving and the techniques of structuring that have special cultural values in the history of architecture in the country. Situated in the Tumen Street of Quanzhou, Qingjing Temple, a treasure of architecture, is the oldest Islamist temple in China with its architectural typical of Islamist temple of the Middle Ages modified with Chinese traditional crafts. Bridges in Fujian are also well known: Luoyang Bridge and Anping Bridge are two out of the ten great bridges in Quan zhou. There is a saying that goes that bridges in Fujian are top in the country and bridges in Quanzhou are top in Fujian.

Although it lies in the southeast corner of the country far

from the political and cultural center, Fujian has produced a great number of brilliant persons from generation to generation like bright stars in the sky, among whom there have been quite a few that have had a great effect on China's history, not to mention such outstanding persons as Zhu Xi in the old times. In modern times in this tiny coign there emerged in a very short period scores of important persons like Lin Zexu, a national hero who was the first claiming prohibition of opium and resistance against western capitalist invasion, and who was regarded as the first one of the modern China "opening the eye toward the world" and whose patriotic verses, "to the benefit of the nation devoting the life and from the danger the country is in never shunning" quoted from his *Words to Family on setting off to Defend the Border*, have become a motto to the politicians dedicating their lives to the nation. Yan Fu was a well-known bourgeois enlightener and translator in the modern times, who was the first one systematically translating and introducing western bourgeois academic thoughts and who was praised as "top in studying both the west and China". Besides, there were some other outstanding figures as Lin Shu, Shen Baozhen, Lin Changyi, Guo Bocang, Chen Yan, Liu Buchan, Lin Yongsheng, Sa Zhenbing, Fang Shengdong, Lin Juemin, Lin Xu, etc. They were politicians, militarists, educators, writers, thinkers and translators who, to our surprise, covered various fields and played a very important part in Chinese modern history. The excellent traditions, such as the strong patriotic spirit, the determined truth pursuit, hearted aspiration for the strength of their motherland, have lasted to the present days.

Chapter One
History of the Min Culture

Ⅰ. In Remote Antiquity Period and Shang-Zhou Period

According to the general cultural relic investigation before 1960s, there are as many as 1100 ancient relics in Fujian. The representative ones are as follows:

1. Zhangzhou Culture in the Paleolithic Age, the Neolithic Age and the Shang-Zhou Period

The Paleolithic Age cultural sites of Zhangzhou are scattered on Lianhuachi Mountain and Zhulin Mountain in the northern suburb of Zhangzhou, which were discovered in a highway construction project in 1989. Gathered from the protophyte layer, are 27 pieces of the stoneware made in the Old Stone Age, with 23 pieces from Lianhuachi Mountain and 4 pieces from Zhulin Mountain. The stoneware can be cataloged into four kinds—kernels, slices, cutters and sharpeners. The Neolithic Age cultural .sites of Zhangzhou are in Fuchuang Mountain in the suburb, Wangbao Mountain in Longhai County, Xiangshan in Zhangpu County, Damao Mountain in Dongshan County and Lazhou

Mountain in Zhaoan County, etc. Most of the discoveries are pottery slices, stoneware, stone pieces, animal bones and seashells. From these relics we can imagine the busy lives of the primitives who dwelt here around 7000 to 3000 years age. Because of the natural effect, they usually chose bay areas and top of isles and mounds as living quarters where they could possibly avoid strong winds and face sea and lived on fishing, hunting, picking shells and gathering fruits. (*The Prehistory Culture of Zhangzhou*, edited by You Yuzhu, Fujian People's Publishing House, 1991). According to the textual researches, there are 274 sites of the Shang-Zhou Periods' cultural relics discovered across Zhangzhou, mainly distributing on low hills, plateaus, slight slopes along the river, and slopes on seashore, top of isles and delta areas. Principally, the reliquiae are of three species: stoneware, pottery ware, bronze ware. (*The Prehistory Culture of Zhangzhou*)

2. Pingtan Keqiutou Cultural Relics

Located in Keqiutou, Nanlong Village, Pingyuan Town of the Pingtan Island, the biggest island in Fujian, the Neolithic cultural relic is about 5500 to 6000 years of age. The unearthed tools of production are mainly stoneware, bone object, such as forging tools, polishing adze, axe, hatchet and arrowhead, and large amount of sea shells and beast bones that indicate a primitive living chiefly on fishing and hunting; the unearthed pottery are mainly hand-made granulated round-bottom pottery, such as kettles, various jars, stemmed cups, plates, bowls and spinning wheels.

3. Minhou Tanshishan Culture

Located in Ganzhe Town of Minhou County, the relics belong to the late Neolithic Age, more than 5000 years ago. The unearthed one thousand pieces are cataloged into six classes, 33 species made from pottery, stone, bone, jade, tooth and shell. The production tools are mostly polishing implements such as stone adze, stone arrowhead, bone arrowhead, pottery net weight. Pottery kettles account for a large proportion, and stemmed cups, jars, mugs, bowls, pots and *qie* (a round mouthed food vessel with two or four loop handles) are also great in numbers. The people at that time had engaged in fairly developed primitive agriculture, fishery, hunting and animal husbandry, textile, and sewing techniques as are inferred and concluded from the discoveries. The statistics provided by the archaeologists show that some other ancient cultural relics of the remote ancient time and the Shang-Zhou Period in Fujian can be found on the upper reaches of the Min River, the eastern coastal areas such as Zhuangbian Mountain of Minhou, Xitou and Huangtulun of Baisha, Xindian Fu Village of Fuzhou, Dongzhang of Fuqing; and on the northwest of Fujian mountain areas such as Shipaixia of Pucheng, Tieshan of Zhenghe, Zhanghuban of Nanping, Nanshan Tower of Mingxi; in the Ting River Valley and the west of Fujian mountain areas such as Wuping, Longyan, Liancheng, Changting; also along the Jiulong River, Jin River Valley and the southern coastal areas such as Shizi Mountain of Quanzhou, Kengbei of Dongshan, Meili Reservoir of Zhangpu, Fuyoudun of the Jinmen Island. (Lin Gongwu, *Conspectus on Fujian's Prehistory Cultural Remains*). From the above mentioned sites, we find that during the Neolithic Age, the ancestors in Fujian had a close relationships with rivers, seas and mountains. Their traces spread all over the Min River, the Ting River, the Jiulong River, the Jin River, the coastal areas as well as mountain areas.

The suspended coffin burial of Wuyi Mountains is typical of Fujian culture during this period. The suspended coffins are spread out over the sheer precipice and overhanging rocks along the both sides of the Jiuqu Stream in Wuyi Mountains or placed in grottos, generally 70 meters above stream surface, in the cliffs and peaks towering to the skies. About 1500 years ago, an historical book about Wuyi Mountains said that there were several thousands of coffins suspended in the middle of the cliff. *The History of Wuyi Mountains* written in the Qing Dynasty estimated that 16 coffins still remained there. According to the investigation implemented in August of 1979 by relevant departments, the suspended cliffs that had boat coffins (i. e. suspended coffins) or coffin remains were named the Shengzhen Cave of Dawang Peak, Douao Peak, Zhenwu Cave, Baiyun Rock, Jinji Cave and Jike Rock of Dazhang Peak, Huanggu Rock, Guzi Peak, Bai Peak, Beidong Cave of Mangting Peak, the north crack of the Dawang Peak, the east side of the Xianguang Rock, Xianji Cave of the Minguan Peak, Beipi Cave of the Guanying Rock, Changke and the east side of the Xiabin Rock and so on, altogether more than twenty, of which few remained in good condition. In September 1978, a study group sent by Fujian Museum took out a complete boat coffin from a cave in the Bai Rock, 51 meters above the ground surface. It is found that the boat coffin was made 3445 years ago(±150 years), and the tags of the textile comprise 4 kinds of materials: hemp, tawny daylily, silk and cotton. The arts and crafts displayed in the hemp fabrics slightly exceeded that of the Middle Period of the Shang Dynasty; the silk fabrics were from natural silk and techniques used in silk textile equaled that of the Shang Period; but the cotton fabrics belong to the earliest cotton substances that have been discovered in China. Thus it can be seen that the ancient people had a very high level of spinning and weaving skills. The ship coffin takes the form of a ship, which speaks out the indissoluble bond between the ancient people and boats on the streams and valleys. People lived across Fujian during this period of time were called Seven Minsas in the book *Zhou Etiquette— Yu Tribute*. Some think that the Mins probably means seven small states while others think that it only means seven tribes. Around 334 BC, the Yue State to the north part of the Mins was defeated by the Chu State and therefore collapsed. So parts of its people came to Fujian and integrated with the Min people whom were consequently called Min-Yue.

Ⅱ. The Min Culture in the Qin-Han Period

The *History: Dong Yue Biographies* records that Wuzhu, the King of Min Yue and Yao, the King of Yue Donghai are both the offsprings of Goujian, the King of the Yue State···. After the Qin conquered the land, the Emperor disthroned the kings of the states and nominated the Mins the District of Central Min.

This is the first time that Fujian was formally brought into the territory of a unified China. However, the Qin did not send forces into Fujian after the establishment of District of Central

Min. At the early Han Dynasty, Wuzhu was the king of Min Yue who built up his capital city in Fuzhou. On October 29, 1996, Ou Tangsheng, Huang Rongchu, together with some other experts, inspected the ancient town in Xindian Village of Fuzhou. From the excavation of the middle section of the west city walls, they found that the city was built up in the period between the late Warring States Period and the early Han Dynasty. The second phase wall supplementary construction was done at early Han period. The city wall was 23 metres wide. Excavated at the same time were rope-veined grey and red bricks and broken pieces of tiles made during the late Warring States or the Qin Period, and thousands of pottery pieces with check, string-veined, rope-veined, wave-veined, mat-veined patterns. Experts even succeeded in reconstructed four pieces of pottery wares from the remains: two big ckecked urns, one grey hard pottery box and one yellow hard pottery cup. The archaeologists believe the ancient town in Xindian was constructed by Wuzhu when he was the king of the MinYue, i. e. City of Min Yue Kingdom, also called Mid-City. Then and there, Fuzhou was the center of politics and economics. The Min Yue Country existed for 92 years before it was destroyed by Wu Emperor of the Han Dynasty when Yushang tried a rebellion. In order to conquer the Min Yue residents, the Emperor removed the residents and ruined the land. Parts of the residents were moving to Jianghuai, but subsequently the scattered people came back little by little and finally set up a county by themselves. At the same period, the Han people came down south and began to mix up with The Min Yues. Pottery wares made at this period such as cooking vessel,

stemmed cup, pot and jar display strong cultural features typical
of the Central Plains culture taste.

With regard to the culture of the Min Yue Country, very
few written historical records are available. But by the relics that
are unearthed continuously, people have become to formulate a
rich cognition about the Min Yue Country culture: the most valuable one being the Han relic site in Wu Yi Mountains that was
dug out in 1958, and where there have been more discoveries recently. The ancient town covered 480 thousand square meters
with 850 meters from the south to north in length. The Chongy-
ang Stream surrounds its three sides—the east, the west and the
north. The town wall was 2896 meters in length with rammed
earth blanks as building materials. It is the earliest and most
complete ancient walls ever discovered in the south of China and
still preserved in good condition. Judged from the dimensions of
the site, the broken pieces of tile and the burn charcoals all over,
the town is believed to have been built before the Han Emperor
dispersed local settlers and was left behind. But there are other
explanations which believe that it was set up by the Min Yuers
who came together after the town was abandoned. Despite of the
different opinions, the excavation of the ancient town has filled
in the gaps in the culture studies on Qin-Han Period in Fujian.
The development of architecture, ceramics and metallurgy at
that period are reflected.

Ⅲ. The Min Culture in the Period of the Wei, Jin and Nan
    Dynasties

One of the characteristics of the Min culture in this period is

that large groups of northern Han people came into Fujian ming-
ling with the local dwellers. After a long time congregation, the
Central Plains culture and the Min Yue culture became melted.
The more advanced Central Plains culture became dominant
gradually while the Min Yue culture subsided into historical relics.

At the end of Eastern Han, the northern Hanese surged into
Fujian in large quantities who were mostly running-aways,
travelers, exiles, peasant rebels, officials or even criminals, etc.
The thousand tombs of the Wei, Jin and Nan Dynasties discovered in Fujian by now show evidence of the Central Plains people's entrance. For example, in December 1986, a tomb·built in
the 6th year of Xianhe of the Eastern Jin Dynasty was found in
Yangze Village of Jianou County with earthen bowls and cups
without handles. The relics and the construction of the tomb
make it evident that the owner of the tomb had been an immigrated landlord of the Central Plains. In 1990s, there were tombs
built in Eastern Jin period discovered in the countryside of Jianou
County, Jiangle County, Pucheng County. Their posy bricks,
burial customs and burial articles reflect a close relationship between the owners and the Central Plains. Numerous means of
livelihood and means of production discovered in the counties in
Fujian tincture the strong color of the Central Plains. The immigration of the northern people led to the increase in population.
In the year AD 260 (the 3rd year of Yonghe), Fujian comprised
Jianan prefecture, under which there were 9 counties; in the Jin
Period, Fujian comprised two prefectures, i. e. Jianan prefecture
having 7 counties with Jianou as its capital, and Jinan prefecture

having 8 counties with Fuzhou as its capital. In the Nan Dynasty, Jinan prefecture expanded. Therefore, the comparatively advanced Central Plains culture, production skills and managerial
experience greatly promoted the development of Fujian's economics and culture.

The shipbuilding in the Wei, Jin and Nan Dynasties in Fujian was under development. As early as in the Three Kingdoms
(220—265), Sun Wu regarded Fujian as a shipbuilding base and
set up administrative positions (Dian Chuan Official, taking
charge of shipbuilding), and Wenma Shipyard in today's Xiapu
County, to be engaged in shipbuilding. Thus Fujian was a center
of shipbuilding with its spacious shipyard, various types and
good facilities. By the end of Jin Period, folk shipbuilding took
the place of government. In the Nan Dynasty period, Fujian was
able to make wooden ocean-going ships sailing to India and the
South Oceans (an old name for the Malay Archipelago, the Malay Peninsula and Indonesia or for the southeast Asia). The contemporary ceramic industry was also well developed: Fujian
mainly produced celadon that was famous for its manifold shapes
such as flat-round-short ones of the West Jin Period, fate-round
ones of the East Jin Period, the tall-round ones of the Nan Dynasty Period, and even elliptical ones of the late Nan Period (*On
Fujian's Celadon in Six Dynasties*, Lin Cunqi, *Fujian Culture*
1~2, 1993). The fine arts and crafts show that Fujian's celadon
manufacture has possessed a very important historical position.
At the same period, hemp and arrowroot fabrics were improved
which showed the development in the textile industry.

Ⅳ. The Min Culture in the Sui-Tang Period

Throughout the Sui-Tang period, immigrants entered Fujian in large quantities. These new comers that mostly composed of refugees, army entourages and government officials increased the population steadily. Many unearthed tombs give evidence to the history of northerners' southbound immigration. For example, in February 1966, by the early Tang tombs dug out in Jinfeng Mountain of Yongchun County, experts speculated that "Jinfeng tomb cluster is probably the family grave yard the owner of which is an offspring of the Central Plains officials who came down to live in Taolinchang (today's Yongchun) on the Jin- jiang valley between the end of the Sui Period and the early Tang Period". (*On Tang Tombs in Jinfeng Yongchun Fujian*, Lin- cunqi, *Fujian Culture*, 1,1983).

In 21st year of Kaiyaun of the Tang Dynasty (733), a Jin- lueshi (a commander in that time) was sent to Fujian which took the first syllables of both Fuzhau and Jianzhou. This is the first time that the name "Fujian" appeared. During the Tang Dynas- ty, there established in succession five prefectures — Fuzhou, Jianzhou, Quanzhou, Zhangzhou and Tingzhou; in AD 771, i. e. the 6th year of Daizhong Dali, the Fujian Observer, the highest regional chancellor was appointed, and thereafter an embryo of an administrative province came into being.

The characteristics of Fujian culture during the Sui-Tang manifest themselves in the following aspects. Prosperity of learning institute boosted the imperial examinations that owed a great deal to the support from the government officials. When Li

Yi, a family member of Tang imperial clan was appointed Fujian
Observer, he encouraged the promotion of higher learning institutes and enrollment of the Min people, and so did Chang Gun.
Chen Yuanguang, Zhangzhou prefecture governor, believed that
setting up schools was just as important as setting up state government, which resulted in the establishment of state institution. Lu Changyuan, then Jianzhou governor, also paid attention
to creation of learning institute and encourage study. Development of education gave rise to the imperial examination system.
According to imperfect statistical figures, there were 56 successful candidates in higher imperial examinations in Fujian in the
Tang Dynasty who contributed to the prosperity of Fujian culture in the Song Dynasty despite the fact that there were much
fewer candidates in Fujian than in the Central Plains. Ceramics,
textile industry and shipbuilding experienced development in succession. A majority of ceramics gathered in the north of Fujian or
along the coastal areas possessing features typical of the times as
can be seen in a kiln site of the Tang Dynasty found in 1988 in
Zhutanyao Village, Shibei Town, Pucheng County. Zhao
Hongqing describes the unearthed wares like this: "the blue and
grey, fairly crass nature of celadon, clumsy shapes, simple and
brief intaglio scores, vigorous ceramic glaze and burning techniques all typical of the Tang's style, remarkably presenting the
local arts and crafts as well as assimilating and inheriting the
Tang and Yue's ceramics techniques, displaying a historical relationship. " (*Investigation in Pucheng Tang Dynasty Kiln Site*,
Zhau Hongqing, etc. , *Fujian Culture* 1, 1990). According to
the records in *New Tang History*, *Geographical Records*, tex-

tile industry was represented by Quanzhou. At that time Quanzhou's native tributes were composed of silk floss, silk, Manila hemp and arrowroot etc. including 200 blots of silk floss. Fuzhou and Jianzhou presented separately 20 blots of Manila hemp cloth. Shipbuilding industry was centered in Fuzhou and Quanzhou. In Tian Bao period, Quanzhou produced a passel of large and gorgeous sea boats, 18 yards in length, 4.2 yards in width, 2 yards wide at the bottom, with sharp and round shape and 15 silver bordered cabins, capable of storing 20 to 40 thousand piculs of goods. At that time Buddhist monks who wanted to travel across the sea to Japan had tried to come to Fujian to purchase this kind of ships.

V. The Culture of Min Kingdom in the Five Dynasties

The Min Kingdom was one of the Ten Kingdoms in the Five Dynasties, set up by Wangchao and Wang Shenzhi, Fuzhou being its capital. In its flourishing age, it administered Fuzhou, Jianzhou, Tingzhou and Zhangzhou, a territory equivalent to to-day's entire Fujian. In the First Year of Guang Qi (885), Wang Chao, Wang Shengui and his brother Wang Shenzhi launched a mutiny in Nan'an of Fujian for independence. The following year they took Quanzhou by storm. Fujian Observer Chen Yan declared Wang Chao to be the prefectural governor of Quanzhou. In the 2nd Year of Jingfu (893), the Wang brothers captured Fuzhou and occupied Tingzhou, Jianzhou and Zhangzhou. The Tang Dynasty offered Wang Chao Fujian Observer and mighty force officer successively. Wang Chao passed away in the 4th year (898) of Qian Ning of the Tang Dynasty (898) and Wang

Shenzhi took over the post. When Wang Shenzhi on position,
the Min Kingdom was at its golden age. Wang Shenzhi adopted a
national policy to protect the kingdom and appease the people —
outwardly to contribute to the central court and accept leadership, inwardly to be diligent in political affairs and economic development. He made a great contribution to the promotion of
land and water transportations, domestic and foreign trade, agricultural production, handicraft industry and commercial business. Wang Shenzhi attached great importance to culture and education, eager to get talented personnel. He had organized intel-
lectuals to write and compile biographies, which was commented
in *The Stone Tablet of Benevolence of Lang Ya Emperor like*
this "to sign the papers one by one and there are so many of
them" and "again to set up another four subjects to educate excellent learners of the Min".

Consequently, education was very popular and the state, the
county and the township had their own learning institutions respectively. At a time when wars broke out constantly in the Central Plains, the Min Kingdom turned out to be a peaceful oasis,
so quiet as to be rated as an Xanadu. Thereby, the remote Min
Kingdom's culture flourished for a period of time. Wang Shenzhi
actively explored overseas traffic and expanded foreign trade. He
constituted special policy to treat foreign businessmen and free
trade and set up Gantang Foreign Port in Fuzhou with goods
handling department that specialized in shipping and cargo transactions. Quanzhou port was turned into a direct foreign trade
port from the original transfer port. The Min Kingdom had a direct and frequent contact with overseas governments. All these

indicate that the Min had possessed an unprecedented free independent right to foreign trade. Direct participation and sparkplug
of the ruler was precipitous for the formation of free trade that
supplemented the internal trade impeded by poor traffic. There
were instances that individuals undertaking foreign business finally immigrated to the overseas and the Court ordered goods
from the overseas. The Min Kingdom linked with Xinluo (today's Korean Peninsula) in the north, with the southeast Asia
and Indonesia, Saudi Arabia countries in the south by the communications of businessmen and envoys. Exotics such as ivory,
rhinoceros horn, natural pearl and spice were provided to satisfied needs. Relics unearthed show evidence. For example, in the
tomb of Liu Hua, wife of Wang Yanjun who was the king of the
Min Kingdom, there was a peacock blue ceramic vase that must
have been a Persia product brought into the land by Arabian or
Persia businessmen according to the textural research by Chen
Cunxi. The tomb was discovered in February 1965 in the Dong-
bao Mountain, on the northern side of Lianhua Peak in the suburb of Xindian of Fuzhou.

Ⅵ. The Min Culture in the Song Dynasty

In the Northern Song period, Fujian was administratively
divided into six prefectures: Fu, Jian, Quan, Zhang, Ting,
Nanjian and two military areas: Shaowu and Xinghua. In the
Southern Song period, there was one governmental state, five
prefectures, two military areas — eight units in all so Fujian has
been known as "Eight Mins" — all belonging to the same level of
administrative organization. As the northern Hanese came to the

Min constantly for a long period of time, Fujian did not suffer any serious disasters in the Sui-Tang and the Five Dynasties, and as the imperial families of the Song Dynasty moved southwards, the center of politics transferred to the south and the east. Consequently, in the Song period Fujian experienced a leap forward in economic and cultural development as is depicted by Zhang Shou in the Volume Six of *Pilin Collections*, "only a remote and dangerous mountainous terra in the past, a most powerful state in the southeast nowadays".

In the Northern Song period, there were 2503 Jinshi (successful candidates in the higher imperial examinations) of Fujian origin, in the Southern Song period, there were 3482 Jinshi, ranking first across the nation; in the Yuanfeng Period of the Northern Song Dynasty, the number of family household ranked eighth in the nation, only next to Jianxi and Two Zhe's, ranking third in the Jiading period of the Southern Song Dynasty. There had been 18 persons of Fujian origin holding high position like prime minister, which ranked number three in the nation. 'The Teachings of Tao' and 'the Biographies of Confucians' of the *Song History Records* says that there had been seventeen prime ministers of Fujian's origin, which ranked first in the history of the nation. In regard to the Min's cultural development, we can find that Fujian came on to its most flourishing phase in the Song Dynasty, the characteristics of which fell into the following fields.

The Min study and its development: In the Ren Zhong period of the Northern Song, the study pursued by the Min learners was still in bud stage. A group of scholars focused their researches on the classics of the Confucianism, concentrating on the righteousness argumentation without paying too much attention to the teaching, advocating the Confucius morality, spreading the Confucius theory of 'making the best of a human's nature' that lay emphasis on the Confucius moralities and general moral guiding principals. These scholars attached a great attention to personal qualifications and were keen on accepting followers and discoursing on an academic subject. Generally speaking, the late Northern Song period and the early Southern Song period are regarded as the beginning phase of the Min study, especially remarked by the arrival of the Two Chen's who introduced the Li School (one of Confucian Schools emphasizing on the ideological philosophy) to Min and made it spread and develop in Fujian.

Between Shaoxing and Chunxi of the Southern Song, the Min study reached its maturity while Zhuxi's theory came into being. Zhuxi established an ideological system of objective idealism based on a complete study on the Confucian schools since the Northern Song Dynasty. The birth and growth of studies in Min produced a significant influence far and wide over the Chinese cultural history. This valuable inheritance belongs to China as well as to Fujian. It is inevitably a priceless treasure to the world.

Fujian was the third biggest center of block printing in the country. There are four points about Fujian's block printing in the Southern Song Dynasty. Firstly, wide distribution. Every prefecture, quarters of district administrative authority, even remote county could undertake block printing; especially almost everywhere in Fuzhou and in Jianyang, the printing was so pre-

vailing that they were known as block printing centers in the
whole country. Secondly, large production quantity. For example, in the Northern Song period, Fuzhou engraved the Great
Buddhist Scriptures and the Taoist Scriptures, filling up 18
thousand volumes in all, which either of the other two printing
centers— Zhejiang and Sichuan could not match. Ye Mengde of
the Southern Song Dynasty wrote in his book *Bird's Words in
the Stone Forest*, "Fujian's books and printings are all over the
world". Thirdly, wide variety of contents printed. The printings
included fashionable classic and historical works and poem collections of a hundred schools, historical abridged editions, poetry
analects, contemporary examination reference books, books of
calligraphy, rhyme, and agricultural, medicinal and miscellaneous folk daily reference books. Fourthly, creative editorial models and varied typefaces. To name a few, there were types of
dark-line, corner-note, text and note-in-one.

Increasingly busy transportation and trade. Because of Fujian's large population and deficient land resource, Fujian had
engaged in overseas trade. The Song Dynasty set up provincial
shipping department in Quanzhou which became the largest commercial port contacting with more than 40 countries all over the
world. According to the textual research by Xie Bizheng who is a
Sino-foreign relationships expert, there had been more than six
lines starting from Quanzhou, such as from Quanzhou to Zhan-
shi, to San Fuqi, to Boni, to India, to the Persian Gulf via the
Strait of Malacca, to the South China Sea, to San Fuqi into the
Persian Gulf, to the Philippines and to Korea and Japan.

VII. The Min Culture in the Yuan Dynasty

In the Yuan Dynasty between the beginning and the 17th Year of Yuan (1280) Fujian was set an administrative province. It was the first time in history that Fujian became a province, although at the same time there existed Quanzhou and Longxing administrative provinces. Later, within Fujian territory eight districts were founded to be controlled by Zhejiang administrative province. It was not until the 16th year of Zheng (1356) of the Yuan Dynasty that Fujian province was established. In the Yuan Dynasty, some cities and towns were preserved perfectly. For instance, Quanzhou Pu Shougeng who held mighty military and political power in Quanzhou abandoned the Song and surrendered to the Yuan. As a result, the port of Quanzhou avoided the disaster of war and was capable of marching for prosperity after the Southern Song came to power. At the beginning of the Yuan Dynasty, heavy military forces entered the boundary, which reduced the population in the rural areas and consequently greatly destroyed the production forces as farms and growing land forsook were. The rulers of the Yuan implemented a policy. that granted titles and territories to imperial clans and relatives in the south of China. In Fujian, there were nine metropolitans, two princesses with their husbands and one thousand royal families. The divided offers and self-supply policy aggravated the people's burden. Nevertheless, with the consolidation of the power over Fujian, the rulers adopted some effective measures to stimulate overall development in Fujian, for instance, to set up learning schools and carry out education, to construct irrigation works, to encourage the growth of agriculture, handicraft industry and trading.

In the Yuan Dynasty, Min study got developed by right of timeliness and favorable geographical position. The Yuan rulers made effort to praise and honor the theory of Zhu Xi, appointing his *Annotations to the Four Books* as court formula of examination models. Since it was necessary to pass the imperial examinations before one could serve as a government official, the theory of Zhu Xi was widely needed, which led to different studies on the theory and attracted many talent scholars to inherit the learning and enrich the theory. For this reason, Fujian became a sacred place for the pilgrims, who were determined to pursue the Confucius idealistic philosophy, and a popular resort for brilliant scholars.

The Yuan Dynasty encouraged overseas foreign trade. Quanzhou Port continued to develop in this period, becoming one of the biggest sea-boat building bases. The overseas trade was unprecedentedly prosperous. The Yuan rulers changed the shipping department organization many times but never disthroned or merged the Quanzhou department, which showed that the rulers paid importance to the port. The countries that had contact with Quanzhou increased in number from the previous 50 in the South Song Dynasty to 100 and towards the end of Yuan and after the Yuan period, Quanzhou became one of the biggest port in the world. The Italian traveler Marco Polo set off from the Quanzhou port in 1291 and described Quanzhou like this, "Chitong(Quanzhou) is one of the biggest port in the world where clouds of merchants converge here and heaps of goods piled up like mountains. " In 1345, a Morocco traveler who had been in Quanzhou also said, "the port of this city is one of the largest in the world, or perhaps is the only largest one. I can see there are about hundred big ships mooring at the port, and there are small boats too many to enumerate. "

Ⅷ. The Min Culture in the Ming and the Qing Periods

In the 1st year of Hong Wu (1368) of the Ming Dynasty, the eight districts were changed separately into eight prefectures of Fuzhou. Jianning, Yanping, Shaowu, Xinghua, Quanzhou, Zhangzhou and Tingzhou. And in the 9th year of Chenghua (1473), the deposed county Funing was resumed and put under direct governing of the political department. They accounted for eight prefectures and one city. During the Ming period, Fujian's shipbuilding, printing industry and ceramics were still leading in the country. Its education came into another prosperous period after a lap of declination in the Yuan Dynasty. Although Wang Yangming's theory made an impact on Zhu Xi's theory, the Min study was not only vigorous but also made creative progresses. In the 14th century that was full of hopes, Fujian should have been the first one to grow up depending on its long-time developed industrial and commercial economic mechanism and proper coastal geographical conditions. Wang Shimao took down in his works *An Annotations to the Min's Society* what he had known about Fujian in the Ming Dynasty, "Everyday across the watershed and through Pucheng narrow pass there are soft silk made in Fuzhou, gauze silk made in Zhangzhou, blue cloth produced in Quanzhou, iron produced in Fuzhou and Yanping, oranges grown in Fuzhou and Zhangzhou, lychee grown in Fuzhou and Xinghua, sugar produced in Quanzhou and Zhangzhou, paper produced in Shunchang were transported to Wu (now Jiangsu) and Yue (Now Zhejiang) like flowing water running towards sea, and there are so many shipped by sea that they may cloth and cover the whole land under the sun". Nevertheless, the Ming rulers were determined to eradicate the existing city economic base along the coast, and troubled by the Japanese's invasions, they brought into effect many times ban on maritime trade along the coast, prohibiting local people to make deal with foreigners without official permission. Those who disobeyed would be convicted death penalty, family members sent to defend border as a solder. Some islanders along the coast were even forced to move to the inland. The ban on maritime trade exercised for 200 years had seriously restrained Fujian from development.

The nongovernmental smuggle trade is one of Fujian's cultural features in the Ming Dynasty. The Yue Port of Longhai in Zhangzhou was the center of smuggler trade. As was endowed with unique geographic conditions, it gradually became the largest smuggler trade port in the southeast part. The folk maritime merchants did business in varied ways involving more and more people each day. Big and small boats were busy shuttling back and forth over the Yue Port, and for a period of time it was regarded as a metropolis of the south of Fujian and owned an honorable name "a small Su-Hang". After the 1st year of Longqing (1567), the ruler had to open up to the foreign countries, and the Yue Port became busier and more prosperous ever since, trading with over 47 countries and nations such as Jiaozhi,

Zhancheng, Luzon, Korea, Japan, Ryukyu, etc. Among the commodities for foreign export, handicrafts and native products had made up a large proportion obtaining surpasses over import. The significance of the Yue Port lied not only in that it became a fourth port after Fuzhou port, Quanzhou port, and Xiamen port, known as Four Big Ports in the past, but also that the Yue Port was born accommodating the commercial economics. It had altered completely the governmental monopoly over maritime trade and fought against feudalistic bondage on free trade with an hiring employment operation of the capitalism. The influence over Fujian's society has been considerably far and wide.

The Qing Dynasty appointed to Fujian a Min-Zhe Governor-General and a Fujian Xunfu (a senior official that holds civil and military administrative right in the Qing Dynasty). At the early Qing, there were eight prefectures, namely, Fuzhou, Xinghua, Quanzhou, Zhangzhou, Yanping, Jianning, Shaowu and Tingzhou under the provincial government. In the 23rd year of Kangxi (1684) Taiwan prefecture was added to Fujian from where Taiwan departed away and became an independent province by the 12th year of Guang Xu (1886). Until the end of the Qing Dynasty, Fujian had derived 9 prefectures, 2 cities, 58 counties, and 6 bureaus. The early Qing royal court prohibited the local commercial ships from carrying goods overseas in order to cut off the relation between the coastal people and Zheng Chenggong; later the court gave order that all the coastal areas move back into inland for 30 li. Busy and prosperous scene were gone like fleeing clouds, and great disaster fell upon the people. Though it was allowed to return to the original bound, the areas took time to recover with the strict shut-up policy. It was not until the Qing government united Taiwan that the commercial merchants were allowed to go overseas to do business. The commercial center therefore transferred to Xiamen with Quanzhou and Zhangzhou on its both sides. Most boats and ships went to the Southeast Asia in winter and returned in summer.

During the Qing Dynasty, Fujian's educational system was quite developed. The style of study was at its height of power and splendor. About 70 percent of the prefectural colleges and most part of county colleges were newly built. According to imperfect statistics, there were 300 colleges in the Qing Dynasty, and provincial colleges in Fujian: Aofeng, Fengchi, Zhengyi and Zhiyong. To the end of the Qing period, there appeared a university run by the government, ship administration college run by the Westernization Party, and mission schools founded by foreign churches.

The rise and prosperity of education promoted the growth of other cultural enterprises. For instance, in the Qing Dynasty, the school of the Confucius idealistic philosophy became so more popular in Fujian that the Emperor Qian Long called Fujian the native place of the Confucius philosophy. Some famous learning institutions such as Aofeng institute successfully taught a large group of talented Confucius scholars. Several dozens of works on Confucius philosophy were in fashion at that time. In the Qian Jia's time, the school of the Min kept on developing with no sign of decline despite the fact that the school of Han was almost solely respected by all simultaneously. There had been many outstanding and successful figures who undertook the research

on the Confucius philology. Meanwhile, there was another remarkable upslurge other than compilation of local historical records. The current local history records, principally provincial
records available are mostly compiled in the Qing period. The
representative ones from the Qing period to the Republic of China (1912—1949) are as following: *Fujian General History* in 64
volumes edited by Zheng Kaiji and others in the 23rd year of Kang
Xi (1684), *Fujian General History* in 78 volumes edited by Xie
Daocheng in the 2nd year of Qian Long (1737). The *Continued
Fujian General History* in 92 volumes edited by Shen Tingfang
in the 33rd year of Qian Long (1768), *Fujian General History*
edited by Chen Shouqi in the years of Dao Guang, *Fujian General History* edited by Chen Yan in the period of Republic of China
etc.

Chapter Two
The Source and Course of the Min Culture

The formation of the Min culture has passed a long and extremely complicated course. From a general point of view, its formation has involved the following aspects.

I . The Influence of the Cultural Heritage of the Old Yue

The Old Yue (Yue is the name for an ancient kingdom) is a name generally referring to the minority nationalities that inhabited in the south of China. The native inhabitants in Fujian might be a branch of the ancient Yue that was called Min Yuers that had immigrated to Fujian with the Han people from the Central Plains. All over Fujian their host status had been replaced gradually, but their long cultural traditions have been passed down and conserved in different degrees. For example, the snake, the token of the Old Yue, is written about in *Talk about Words and Explain Characters* like this, "Min, the Yue living in the southeast is the snake strain of the insects within the household. " Here, "the snake strain" means "snake race", which believes in god of snake. The formation of the Chinese character for Min is a combination of insect that is an equity for the word that stands for snake and the Chinese character for door, which stand for a race that worships the snake at home. The reason that the Min Yue people took snake as their totem is that their ancestors lived in a warm and humid mountainous land that was intercrossed with rivers and valleys where a variety of snakes multiplied. To lives and productive work of the Min Yue inhabitants, the snakes imposed a great threat. *Taipingguang Records* quotes from the *Records of Xuan Shi* that "In the south of Quanzhou there is a mountain with precipitous peaks and rocks. At the foot of the mountain there is a pool so deep that it is impossible to measure the depth. Around it is a dozen acres of land. In the pool there is a flood dragon that would always bring disaster to human beings. If someone should get close to it by mistake or some cows or horses should go over to drink water, it would swallow them — a disaster from which the dwellers have suffered for many years. " As a result, people carved a snake on the rock at the entrance to the mountain and built a temple so as to impetrate the protection from god or spirits and receive good result through prayers. This kind of worship passed down on. Until this day there preserved temples for the king snakes in some of the places in Fujian. The Snake King Palace outside the west city door and the snake totem joss house beside the stream of Pingyuanli in Changting County in the west of Fujian, the king snake temples in Fuqing and Putian, to name a few. Villagers in Sanpingshi of Pinghe County, and across the boundary of Zhangping County have been respected snake as father of bellboys. To worship the snake as god with great honour and even to sleep with snake in the same bed and to live in the same room can be quite a quotidian affair. In Zhanghubang of Nan Ping, the customs of worshipping snake is usually carried out solemnly. At the end of every year, villagers would go out to catch snakes everywhere and in July 7th, long and enormous processions of welcoming snakes would send the caught snakes to the temple setting them free in life.

Min Yue people living around Wuyi Mountains have kept a history of the suspended burial for 3400 years. The suspended coffins do not always contain anatomy in each. The empty ones were prepared for the dead of the same clan, which means that in the consanguineous clan society people from the same clan should be buried in the same place, a tradition still popular in some of the places to this day. For example, in the precipitous Shizi Rock in Huaqiao Village of Songxi County among Wuyi Mountains, there is a Thousand Coffin Grotto 100 meters deep in the cliff cranny. Contained within the grotto are hundreds of coffins of past dynasties that are put on layers of the frame works along the inside edge. The bottom layer of the ancient coffins have already moldered long ago, but some upper layers must have been put inside in the modern time.

Ⅱ. The Introduction of Civilization from the Central Plains

The introduction of the Central Plains culture was realized principally by the immigrants in large quantities. There were four times that the Han nationalities from the Central Plains entered Fujian in a colossal quantity. The first time was at the end the western Jin when the eight clans came into Fujian. Eight

clans were said to be the officials and helmets that had good qualifications. They escaped with family members from the chaos in
Yongjia period. They brought with them offsprings, subordinates and guests that enormously increased the population in Fujian. The second time could be in the Tang Dynasty when Chen
Yuanguang opened up Zhangzhou. In AD 669, the 2nd year of
Zongzhang of the Tang Dynasty, the Henanese Chen Zheng led
3600 soldiers entered Zhangzhou. Only 13 year old Chen Guan-
gyuan came to Zhangzhou with his father. At the age of twenty-
one, he inherited his father's official post and settled down in
Zhangzhou. He started to develop Zhangzhou energetically and
changed the extremely desolate grass-weed overgrown and animal
haunted situation that met the eye everywhere, and thus inspired
the local civilization. In spite of that, experts hold different o-
pinions towards "the entrance of the eight clans" and "the Chen'
s administration in Zhangzhou". These topics have been dis-
cussed particularly in an article and the author will not deal with
them here redundantly. The third time immigration took place
between the end of the Tang Dynasty and the Five Dynasties periods, a time when Wang Shenzhi implemented his administration. Wang Shenzhi, from Gushi of Guangzhou of He'nan Province, led more than 5000 troops into Fujian with his sibling from
the Central Plains. They chose Fuzhou as capital so that he was
enthroned as the King of Min. Wang Shenzhi made a great contribution to the development of Fujian that became a prosperous
state in the south of China in a time when the Central Plains suffered from convulsions. The fourth immigration happened when
the Northern Song Dynasty moved toward the south. Before and

after the southbound immigration of the North Song, in order to
run away from war, people in the north again surged into the
south bringing along dependents young and old in such a degree
that the population in Fujian was tremendously increased. Apart
from these, emigrants before the Yongjia chaotic period and to
the Ming and the Qing periods were mostly running-aways, or
exiles, and later time officers and soldiers, governmental officials who assumed office in Fujian or people who came all the
way to seek refuge with Fujian relatives and friends. During the
Tang and the Five Dynasties, those who came from Gushi of
Henan to seek refuge under Wang Shenzhi were too many to enumerate. Large contingents of emigrants in these four times and
those who arrived in succession had brought with them comparatively advanced civilization in various degrees that eventually ex-
pedited the local development and social advancement of Fujian.
Besides, personages coming to the southern areas and the Minnese traveling to the north had eventually more or less introduced
some cultures from the Central Plains. From the period of De-
zong in the Tang Dynasty when Chang Gun was the Observer of
Fujian to the periods of the Ming and the Qing, large groups of
personages with the admiration for the elegant rivers and
mountains or with the purpose of giving lectures and teaching
students came to Fujian to seek shelter and a place. It seems that
their arrivals gave a breath of flesh air to the implosive Fujian
and activated the academic cultures, although they might have
lived here for only a short period of time without settling down
completely. After the Song moved to the south, it became a
fashion that the northern celebrities surged into the south in

groups and was quite a prevalent genius. Additionally, after the middle of period of the Tang Dynasty, the Min people began to go up north to undertake the royal examinations so as to be selected as a scholar or an official. They took in the culture and were edified by the culture. When they became an official and traveled back home, they brought with them the Central Plains culture to Fujian. So did other Min people who visited scholars and pursued knowledge in the northern cities. For example, Zhou Dunyi, Zhang Zai, Chen Jing, Chen Yi, and Shao Yong, etc., all being the founders of the Righteousness School (a Confucian school of idealist philosophy) in the central China attracted many Min people to seek shelter under their doors and were deeply influenced by their ideas. You Zuo of Jianyang origin, Yang Zhi of Jiangle origin were under the Two Chen's instruction, leaving a legend of 'standing in front of the Chen's door in snow'. After their return to Fujian, they vigorously spread the idea of the Righteousness School that was reformed later by Zhu Xi into the Min School. Tan Qiao of Quanzhou origin was a prominent philosopher in the Tang and the Five Dynasties. He went up to the north "via Mount Zhongnan, staying at Mount Taibai, Mount Taihang, Mount Wangwu, Mount Song, Mount Hua, Mount Tai and Mount Yue, meandering and traveling noted mountains" (recorded in the Second Volume of *Biographies of Extensive Immortals* by Shen Fen of the Southern Tang). Tan Qiao proposed a philosophy with emptiness, morale, and conversion categories as its kernel, a theory that the schools of the Righteousness in the Song Dynasty assimilated and emulated in different aspects and developed into a theoretical linkage between the former and the philosophies in the Tang and the Song Dynasties.

Ⅲ. The Diffusion of Religion Culture

In Fujian, four religions were prevailing and spread with a
rapid speed. The Buddhist religion was first introduced into China in the early East Han Dynasty. In AD 282, the 3rd year of Tai
Kang of Wu Emperor in the West Jin Dynasty, there was a Buddhist temple, Shaoyin Joss House, in Fuzhou that was just at its
beginning of development. In the 9th year of Taikang of the Jin
Dynasty (288), Nan'an, too, had a Prolong Happiness and Lon-
gevit temple. In the Tang Dynasty, a master of the Buddhism
came to Jianyang, an event that could be recognized as the start
of the Zen sect in Fujian. At that time, there were sects of Buddhist religion standing in numbers in China, and the most prevailing sects were the Gradual Realization in the north and the
Sudden Realization in the south. Therefore it was referred to as
South Sudden and North Gradual. To the middle period of the
Tang, the temple economy seriously contradicted the state profit
with each day passed insofar that the emperor gave order that the
Buddhist religion be abolished. About 260 thousand monks and
nuns were secularized across the country at that time. Although
Fujian was affected by it with a lot of temples destroyed as was
in Putian, yet Fujian was so far away from the political center
that the Buddhist religion had been thriving all the while, for the
mountain is high and the Son of Heaven is far away. The fact
that the branch of Sudden Realization had not been handed down
to the Tang Dynasty as a fifth sect had much to do with Fujian.
Many founders of important sects were people of Fujian origin.

For example, Yi Xuan, founder of the Lin Ji sect, was a disciple of Huang Bo Xi Yun of Fuqing origin; Wei San Ling You, the founder of the Wei Yang sect, was of Changxi origin; Cao Shan, the founder of Cao Dong sect was of Putian origin; Wen Yan of Li Yun Men sect and Wen Yi of Li Fa Yan sect both were students of Yi Cun who was of Nan'an origin. Hua Hai of Changle origin reformed the commandments of the Indian Buddhist religion with the patriarchal clan system of Chinese Confucian school and stipulated a set of regulations and commandments characteristic of Chinese Zen, known as Hundreds of Regulations or Ruling Formulations of the Zen Sect. He was consequently considered father of the commandments of the Buddhist temple in the late Chinese Feudalistic society. The works on Buddhist religion written by Fujian scholars enjoyed a high reputation among the Buddhist circle, such as *Scriptures on the Rich Mountains* by Shi Wenju of Putian, *The Edge of Religious Mirror* by Shi Shurui of Xianyou, *On Essential Points of Access to the Sudden Realization of Jianzhou*, *The Predestined Speech Relationship of True Realization* by Shi Yichun of Nan'an. When Wang Shenzhi was in office in Fujian, he faithfully believed in the Buddhist religion and built up 267 temples all over Fujian areas. Unexpectedly, the king of Min issued certificates to as many as 30 thousand monks and nuns that had entered religion just as what the poetry described, "Out of the persons met on the mountain path, the half numbers of them would be monks." Likewise throughout the Qing Dynasty, the Buddhist religion was very popular in Fujian and has never shown signs in of crocking up till now. For instance, at the end of the Song Dynasty and the beginning of the Yuan Dynasty, only within the counties that were presided over by Fuzhou government there were more than 1450 Buddhist religion temples, which was a rarity as far as the whole country was concerned. Fujian famous monks not only frequently received orders to call on royal rulers conferring scriptures or delivering teachings in the capital city but also traveled overseas. For example, Tanjing, monk of the Chaogong Joss House of Quanzhou in the Tang Dynasty once followed Monk Jianzhen traveling east to Japan; Mingji, Chujun, etc. of the Yuan Dynasty once went to Japan to deliver instructions. The famous monk Jue Hai of Zhangzhou in the Ming Dynasty also went to Nagasaki, Japan to pass on doctrines, and he even built a joss house there. The introduction of the Taoist religion into Fujian could be traced back as early as to the primitive society period. In Fujian, traces of the necromancer could be found at that time. Wuyi Mountains was named by the Taoist religion as Profound Heaven of Real Ascending Conversion, ranked the sixteenth scenic spots out of the thirty-six cave paradises and seventy-two blessed spots. Liu Shaogong, a noted Taoist monk in Sheng Hua Yuan Temple was the mountain host of Wuyi Mountains. In the Qing Dynasty, Pan Yu of Chong'an origin and You Sanpeng of Minqing origin both cultivated themselves in Wuyi Mountains and built in the mountain a nunnery called "Zhizhi Hut". In the West Han Dynasty, in the Ziqi Mountain of Pucheng, Jiuxian Mountain of Fuzhou, Yanxian Mountain of Nanping, etc. there were Taoists cultivating themselves. In the Tang Dynasty, there appeared Taoist forums and Taoist joss house and professional Taoists in Fujian. Zhang Lin, Fu Qiyuan and others were famous Taoists in Fuzhou. In the Five Dynasties, Wang Shenzhi reverenced the Taoists and many Taoists held power over major issues. In the Song Dynasty, the Taoist religion developed with a rapid pace for many Taoists were offered largess from the royal court and newly built Taoist temples emerging like bamboo shoots after a spring rain—the outstanding ones were Zhen Qing Temple in Fuzhou, Yuan Miao Temple in Yanping, Yuan Miao Temple in Putian, Chongxi Temple in Min County, Yi Fu Temple in Sha County, Wen Chang Temple in Songxi, etc. The statue of the Old Gentlemen Li carved of a stone on the Qingyun Mountain of Quanzhou, about five or six *zhang* (a Chinese old measure unit and one *zhang* is about 3.3 meters) in height, bears high artistic value. Conclusively, all of these show that the Taoist religion was very prevailing in those years. Between the Song and the Yuan Dynasties, there sprang up in Jiangxi a Taoist party called Jing Ming Zhong Filial Piety emphasizing on Taoist skills such as magic figures and incense, taboo, exorcising, protecting pestilence, and engaged in refining thighbone and fasting ceremony, becoming a celestial being and eking out an existence. In Fujian, there appeared two parties, the refining and cultivating and the magic figures, the representatives of the former party being the Taoist Wu Chongyue of Longxin Temple of Quanzhou, Wang Zhongxing of Changting, Yang Wanda of Chong'an and so on and the representatives of the latter being the Taoist Qiu Yun of Tianqing Temple of Zhangzhou, Xie Hu of Sha County, Liang Ye of Changting, etc. In the Ming Dynasty, the Taoist religion was deprived of the title, the Master of Heaven, and meanwhile Zhengyi Tao and Quanzhen Tao presen-

ted themselves in Fujian. In Qing Dynasty, Emperor Qian Long
declared that Huang Religion be the state religion. The Taoist
religion was regarded as the religion of the Han nationality and
started to wither. But in Fujian, praying and fasting ceremony,
and taking pellet were still in fashion and gradually becoming
folk custom. In the early 7th century, Islam, which was born in
Mekka in Arabia, was introduced to Quanzhou via sea-lane as
early as in the middle Tang period. In the Song and Yuan periods
when Quanzhou sprang to become a big oriental harbor, tens of
thousands of Islamic Arabians converged in Quanzhou in such an
enormous number that it became one of the three earliest Islamism religion regions in China. The Muslim descendents bearing
Chinese surnames such as Jin, Ding, Ma, Tie, Guo, Ge,
Huang, Xia, Pu, not only lived and multiplied there, but also
built mosques, which were full of Islamic religious colors, and
spiritual hills and holy sepulchers to bury Islamic virtual ancestors. Many tomb stones carved with epigraph in Arabian, Persian, and Chinese languages were left over. The were earliest
mosque in China has been preserved in Quanzhou till now. In the
Yuan Dynasty, not a few Islamic followers followed the west region troops to Fuzhou via Shaowu so that there are still many Islam religion followers in Shaowu. Most of the Islamic followers
were subject to the Sunnit, advocating the religious doctrines of
the Hanafit school. The diffusion of the Christianity was fulfilled
principally by missionaries. In the Ming Dynasty, the Italian
missionary Aleni of Jesus society supported by Ye Xianggao who
was the minister of the Ming Dynasty, went to the north of Fujian to teach and spread Christianity and later expanded to Fu'an

and Min Counties, etc. for more than twenty-four years. He built twenty-three churches and was referred to as Confucius from the West and the First Man to Teach Religion in Fujian. At the end of the Ming Dynasty, the Philippines religious province sent eleven missionaries to Xiamen and Fuzhou to open up the Dominican Order teaching area that grew very quickly. Zheng Chenggong used to hire missionary as teacher. In the years of Kangxi of the Qing Dynasty, a group of missionaries went deep into Quanzhou Xinghua, Fu'an etc. to teach religions and set up the third St. Dominican Order in Fujian. After the Opium War, different parties of the Western missionaries competed each other vehemently in diffusing religion and setting up schools, churches, hospitals, relief institutions all over towns and villages in Fujian. Judged either from the construction date of the Christian Churches and the time to start missionary work or from the quantities of the religious parties and followers and doctrine delivery, Fujian racked one of the earliest and most popular regions of Christianity. Except for the influence of the above four religions, the local religions exerted themselves likewise, the most remarkable one being the Trinity, a religion that comprised the Confucius, the Sakyamnuni (the Buddhism) and the Taoism founded by Lin Zhaoeng in Putian during the years of Zhengde, Jiajing and Wanli in the Ming Dynasty. Lin Zhaoeng thought that originally the Confucius, the Sakyamnuni and the Taoism were of one source that the afterworld successors knew nothing about and presumptuously split into three parts that were heading for evil all the more. The essence of the propaganda of the trinity was obviously to combine the ethical code of the Confu

cianism with the cultivation of the Taoism and the Buddha's nir-
vana within one system independent of none of the three. Therefore, he considered the principles of the Confucius as basis, the
Taoism as access, and the Buddhism as extremity. Since the
trinity set food in China, it once had extended to other provinces, even to Taiwan and Singapore in the middle of the Qing
Dynasty. Folk religions were also very active in Fujian. The
most famous were three deities: the heaven goddess, Madam Lin
Shui, God Bao Sheng. The antitypes of the three deities were real persons. Worshipped and evolved, they were endowed with
human like quality yet a superman's power of a deity that could
in turn protect people themselves. Although folk religions were
active within certain regions, they produced influence on Fujian
culture far and wide with their enduring vigor.

Ⅳ. The Impact of the Overseas Culture

　　Bordering on the sea in the east, Fujian possesses many
good harbors dotting all over looking like a chessboard and a
coastline of one fifth out of the whole Chinese coastline. As early
as in the Southern Dynasty, Fujian had certain contact with the
overseas. Foreign culture impacts mainly came by way of international trade, foreign merchants settling down in Fujian, and
the Min men returning to Fujian after being abroad, etc. In the
Five Dynasties when Wang Shenzhi governed Min, Fujian had
extensive commercial trade overseas, starting from Xinluo on the
east via the Southeast Asia archipelagos, westwards to the Arabian countries. In the Northern Song Dynasty, Quanzhou became an international commercial harbor known as ten thousand

country commerce in the sound of rising sea, keeping business contact with 36 island countries. Fujian merchants setting off a-broad from Quanzhou to exchange five color decoratively pat-terned silk and books for necessities abroad would return home in one year's time, or if far away in two years'time. By the South-ern Song and the Yuan Dynasties, Quanzhou had turned into a No. 1 world commercial harbour. In the Ming Dynasty, the ruler strictly enforced ban on maritime trade for 200 years, yet at the Yue Harbour that was located in Longhai there was none the less a forest of masts and convergence of overseas guests and mer-chants—the biggest smuggling harbor in China. The ban on mar-itime trade was lifted over in the 1st year of Longqing of the Ming Dynasty. Every year after the first month of summer, hundreds of merchantmen sailing the whole world from the Yue Harbor. To the Wanli's years in the Ming Dynasty, the Yue habour be-came busy with international trade all the more. Because of the prosperous trade, many merchants settled down in the Min are-as. Especially, between the Song and Yuan Dynasties, countless Indians, Persians, Arabian and Europeans attracted by the world-famous trade Quanzhou harbor made their pitch in the lo-cal area and did not return. They were referred to as "foreign guest" and married with the native women whose descendents were addressed as semi-foreign guest. These foreign guests had brought with them the customs, public feelings and religious be-liefs of their native countries. With time went by, the foreign culture infiltrated into that of the local place in complete harmo-ny. Likewise, many Min men settled down overseas. After the Song and the Yuan periods the number increased gradually and

spread to Japan, Korea, and the entire Southeast Asia. In the
Ming Dynasty, tens of thousands of Fujian people would not return with their elder sons and grand children after going abroad.
(*The History of Ming* —*Records of the Philippines*) The o-
verseas Chinese kept a certain kind of relation with hometown
and when they came back to visit their families once in a while
they brought back with them various sorts of strange foreign culture.

V. Blending with Taiwan Culture

Eighty percent of the Taiwanese are of Fujian origin. Being
connected by the same water and so close to each other geograph-
ically and consanguineously, Fujian and Taiwan have similar customs and languages. That is the reason that Fujian and Taiwan
are usually defined as one district as far as culture is concerned.
But because of the particular historical background, geographical
environment and social and economical conditions, Fujian and
Taiwan differ in some cultural aspects that are typical of Taiwan
culture. So on discussing about the cultural association and in-
specting the influence of Fujian's culture over that of Taiwan
that undoubtedly has produced deep and far effect, which is a
most important part, we can not ignore that Taiwan culture has
affected Fujian culture likewise as we see from the followings.

1. Many Taiwanese Hold a Post in Fujian

It is recorded in detail in *The Manuscripts of General History of Taiwan Province* that Liu Qizhuo, who styled himself
Han Zhang and whose alternative name was Weixuan, comes
from Dong'antang of Taiwan prefecture. In the annual contribu-

tion at the end of Kangxi fifth year of the Qing Dynasty (the 54 th year, 1715) and Yongzheng (10th year, 1732) was elected study instructor of Changtai County whose history depicted him as amicable and clearly cultivated, in Qianlong 9th year (1744) he was promoted to be study instructor of Changting and he retired at old age and was given enough money. *The History and Culture of Taiwan* (by Yang Yanjie, published in 1995 by the Strait Literature Publishing House) says that in the period when the Qing Dynasty was in possession of Taiwan, there had been about 80 people sent to hold a post in Fujian among which one had a title of Jinshi, eighteen had a title of Juren, sixty-one had a title of Gongsheng (Jinshi, Juren and Gongsheng were titles awarded to successful examinees of the highest imperial examinations). Some of them attained reappointments. For example, Jinshi Zhuang Jiujing of Fengshan origin successively served as a professor in Quanzhou and Funing, Juren Li Weixin of Taiwan origin successively served as educator in Min County and instructor in Anxi, Gongsheng (a kind of student that was selected and sent to study in the imperial learning institution). Lin Cuigang came from Taiwan prefecture and served successively as an instructor in Xinghua and Qingliu, Cai Fudan came from Taiwan prefecture and served as educator in Mining, Zhangzhou and Yong'an successively, to name only a few. Those who came from Taiwan to hold posts in Fujian had a wide regional distribution that extended to almost every coastal and mountain area bringing with them Taiwan culture to local people. Some of them even wrote articles introducing the natural conditions and social customs of Taiwan.

2. Importation of the Native Arts of Taiwan to Fujian

The most representative one is the import of Taiwan Ge Zai Opera. Out of 18 Taiwan local operas, Ge Zai opera is the only one that is indigenous to Taiwan. It was first developed in Yilan county of Taiwan originating from the Beautiful Songs of the South of Fujian. Having been processed and improved by Taiwan artists continuously, it finally became a complete opera, and afterwards it was introduced to Fujian and developed into Xiang Opera, which is one of the five Fujian operas. Now Xiang Opera has accumulated about 400 traditional plays that are warmly welcomed in Zhangzhou and Xiamen.

3. Visiting Ancestors and Relatives

When Taiwan people of Fujian origin come back to Fujian to visit relatives they bring with them Taiwan customs and social feelings. Take diet culture as an example. Whenever summer season sets in, there is often someone peddling a kind of food called stone flower in the street corner. The stone flower looks like iced lotus root powder but actually it is made from climbing fig juice tasted cool and comfortable to the mouth that has already become a good diet to satisfy thirst and eliminate heat for people in the South of Fujian. The nature of climbing fig is cool and refreshing, originally growing in Jiayi mountain of Taiwan. It was found and processed by dwellers of Tong'an origin and was introduced to Fujian by the immigrants when they came back to visit relatives.

4. Economic Trade

Taiwan and Fujian had economic trade relations since an early time. Historically, the earliest suburb lines and the southern line was mainly responsible for delivering goods to Fujian. Taiwan merchants not only freighted goods but also delivered their ways of doing business and living customs.

V. Infiltration of the Adjacent Regions

Fujian is connected with Zhejiang on the north, with Guangdong on the south and with Jiangxi on the west. The cultures of these adjacent provinces have infiltrated Fujian, particularly the peripheral areas for a long time.

1. Historical Evolution

Before the Tang Dyansty, Fujian was referred to as seven Mins that enclosed the peripheral areas beside the entire territory. Its activities extended up to Wenzhou of Zhejiang province on the north, down to Chaozhou of Guangdong on the south and to Yugan of Jiangxi on the west. During the Spring and Autumn Period when Yue Kingdom was defeated by Chu Kingdom, people went into the south of Zhejiang and into Fujian territory in succession. In the Qin period, County of Central Min was set up which was the first regional administrative construction in the history of Fujian. It controlled an area reaching three prefectures as Wen, Tai and Chu of Zhejiang on the north, and Qianshan of Jiangxi on the west. In the Han Dynasty, Liubang founded a Min Yue Kingdom governing over the east of Jiangxi, the east of Zhejiang and the east of Guangdong. In the Three Kingdoms period, Shun Quan who had conquered Zhejiang turned Fujian into a base for Wu by setting up related county administration. In the Tang Dynasty, Emperor Xuan Zong picked the first syllables of both Fuzhou and Jianzhou to combine them into a name to define

Jinlueshi (an officer title, who took charge of the border military affairs) as Fujian Jinlueshi. Thereafter, the place got its name. From the historical point of view, not a few places that once were governed by Fujian belong to the adjacent provinces of today. So there have been intimate relationships between Fujian and these areas all the time along.

2. Traffic and Communications

After the Tang Dynasty, contact with the outside became more frequent. Those who went up northwards to take examinations, to do business and to visit scholars increased in number. Zhejiang and Jiangxi were the unavoidable routes to the outside from Fujian. In the Song Dynasty, the famous watershed leading from Jiangxi to Zhejiang and then up to the north was the route which literatus from the adjacent provinces frequently took. In the Ming Dynasty, the communications between Fujian areas and the lower reaches of the Changjiang River and the Hai River were also developed either by the route from Jianyang via Shaowu towards Jiangxi, or by the route from Pucheng into Zhejiang or from Chong'an to Jiangxi and Zhejiang. Convenient communications had brought about the infiltration of culture from peripheral regions.

3. Immigration of Population

Long time ago, the populations from the neighboring provinces had started to move to Fujian reaching its peak in the Ming Dynasty and the Qing Dynasty. For example, a lot of farmers moved to the mountain areas on the north of Fujian from Zhejiang and Jiangxi. They made a great contribution in the development of mountain areas just as what was described in the sixth volume of *History of Fujian and Guangdong* by Zheng Lisheng, "Deep in the mountains on the north of Fujian, there are poor farmers from other provinces. They live in the hut built by themselves, undertaking either cultivating land or growing mushrooms or burning out pine tree oil or baking char or striking iron or making paper or making ceramics. Because of the favorable geographical conditions, they gather close and disperse without regulation. Generally speaking, going up they would reach Shangrao of Jiangxi, Yushan, and Qingyuan of Zhejiang in large quantity. " These people brought neighboring culture with them, and "made the native people imitate better ways of cultivation, involving more and more people year by year and from one mountain to another". (by Daoguang, *History of Jianyang County*, Volume II) So on how to grow economic crops, the native people had learned a lot from the neighboring immigrants.

4. Economic Trade

Fujian had a close economic trade relation with the neighboring provinces. For example, He Qiaoyuan of the Ming Dynasty recorded in the 38th volume of the *Min History*, "The fertile soil in Jianning is extremely favorable for raising fish, growing rice, making paint oil and bamboo pieces for commercial purpose. Adjacent to Jianchang, the local dwellers absorb a lot of common practice and conventions from the neighboring areas. " This description implicated the close relation between Jianning of Fujian and Jianchang of Jiangxi. Besides, some remote counties frequently held economic activities with their neighbors. For example, the Cow Meeting hold every Autumn season in Niukou of Taining County is a large transprovincial cow meeting. Cows

from tens of peripheral counties of Jiangxi, Zhejiang provinces
will come join the well-known fair.

5. Sending Officials Mutually

People in Fujian were keen on taking the highest imperial
examinations. Not a few people were sent to take office in Zhejiang and Jiangxi and vice versa, which greatly promoted the interaction of different culture.

Chapter Three
The Characteristics of the Min Culture

The most distinguish characteristic of the Min Culture is its multiplicity that mainly exhibits in the following aspects.

1. Every Region Has Its Own Characters That Differ Greatly from That of Another

Different theses differentiate the existing the Min culture as below. The first theory thinks that the Min Culture should be divided into five regions: the East Min, the South Min, the West Min, the North Min and Puxian. The culture of the North Min is typical of mountain and forest dispositions; the culture of the South Min is typical of ocean and sea culture; the East Min can be defined as a standard integrate culture; the Kejia culture of the West Min is a kind of immigration culture; the Puxian area is a model district of the higher imperial examinations culture. (Xu Xiaowang, *The Outline of Theories and Cultures in Fujian History*) The second theory divides the Min culture into four greatly diversified regions: the East Min, the South Min, the North Min and the West Min. The East Min seeks stability and fears chaos; in the West Min, forefathers and relatives pursue cohesion; the

South Min sail across the oceans and go abroad; the North Min is content with poverty and happy with doctrines and principles. (Ni Jianzhong *The Humanistic China*) The third theory defines the East Min as river operation culture, the South Min as ocean spreading culture, the North Min as mountain cultivation culture, the West Min as immigration development culture. (Li Rulong *Regional Types of Fujian Dialects and Culture*) The fourth theory maps out the Min culture these six regions, namely Fuzhou culture region, Puxian culture region, the South Min culture region, the West Min culture region, the North culture, and the East Min culture region. The ideological culture of each region has its particular characteristics. For instance, Fuzhouers (Fuzhou people) act economically; Puxianese are canny and prudent and restrained, the South Minnese passionate, unrestrained and straightforward, the West Minnese simple and hospitable, the North Minnese obedient and enduring, the East Minnese diligent and earnest (He Mianshan *Fujian Economy and Culture*). Every region can be further classified to discover more differential characters from each other. For instance, the South Min includes Xiamen, Zhangzhou, and Quanzhou. The culture of these three municipalities is different in many ways just as the culture of the coastal Jinjiang and Shishi is different from that of Yongchun, Anxi and Nanan of Quanzhou municipality.

2. The Characters of the People from Different Regions Vary Greatly

The unrestrained and straightforward Shandongers, the prudent Shanghaiers, the smart Zhejiangers, then what can be said of Minnese? In *City Seasonal Winds* Yang Dongping quotes

from a South Korea magazine that evaluates Minnese like this,
"The Minnese is extremely penny-pinching. When it rains, he
will bring two umbrellas with him, one for himself to protect the
rain and the other for sale. " In fact this does not count a representative. The characters of Minnese differ greatly from each
other. If he is a South Minnese, he will without more ado give
his umbrella to some one so as to make a friend with him whom
he hopes might bring about an opportunity in the future. If he is
a Fuzhouer, he will probably take as many umbrellas as possible
and try to own money as much as possible. There is no cheating
and inveigling. What happiness! Why not? If he is a North Minnese, he will probably take one and that is enough, for he would
think that it was too worldly to send it to another and it was
quite unnecessary for him to do so. In advertising a brand, different people have different attitudes. A Shishi Man of the South
Min will probably think that it is quite necessary to put up adver-
tisement on television program for a long period of time, employing a ferocious beast-wolf as an ad visual image. Only one wolf
is not enough but a seven running and pushing back and fore
wolves, which makes a sense of dancing with wolves — the natural quality of a real hero. This famous "septwolves" advertise-
ment not indicating a proper product may refer to garniture or
cigarette product of Shishi, which forms a large investment that
a Fuzhouer would consider too much to afford and would not
take the risk. A West Minnese simply has no such courage, but
would be willing to try a venture operation, advertising the "septwolves" for his own product such as cigarette, which he might
think a more safe investment. Fuzhou has a common boundary

with Putian, but characters of the these two peoples are rather
different. For instance, Fuzhou women usually like to wear the
pants and remove the husband's objects to her mother's home,
keeping a close eye on her husband, as the saying goes in
Fuzhou, "Wife is playing mahjong games while husband is cooking evening snack." Or "Wife is lying in bed while the husband
has to go to clean the nightstool." There is a joke that might be
well implied the wife's control over the husband: A house has
been stolen by a theft. The wife who is outside makes her husband a call to inquire intently if the money has been stolen. The
husband relied, "I have failed in discovering the money you have
hidden for ten years. How could the thief be more successful
without effort?" According to studies, the Fuzhouers are quite
good at cooking dishes, which might well be said as "bears and
eyebrows" (to indicates a man) would not yield to a woman. But
the Putian women, on the contrary, are very diligent and
thrifty. They maintain their family with whole heart and wisdom, which could be said as to bear the burden without complain
and regret for all of their life time. They do not possess any
more unrealistic desires and never try to control their husband
who would go off the moment they have eaten up the meal and
also never care for those trial womanishly fusses. They think it
goes without saying that a husband be ahead and support his
family. So if a Fuzhou girl wants to marry a Putian boy, both
parents would have a kind of apprehension. A Putian firmly
holds that a married woman must take care of the husband's
family. There is no reason that she takes things to her mother's
home. On the contrary, the Fuzhou girl thinks that mother's

home is her support. She will seek help from her mother's family whenever she meets troubles.

3. Complicated Dialects

Out of the eight Chinese dialects in China, Fujian has three dialects. Counting in the overlapped areas with other provinces, Fujian might as well have seven Chinese dialects spoken within its boundaries, the whole nation's Chinese dialects in epitome. The complication also showed that within the same dialect region, for instance, within the South Minnese dialect region, Xiamen dialect, Longyan dialect, Datian dialect and Youxi dialect are quite different from each other. Amusingly, in some county several dialects are spoken simultaneously. For example, in Datian County, the South Minnese dialect, Datian dialect, Yong'an dialect, and Kejia dialect are popular all the same. In Youxi County, the South Minnese dialect, Youxi dialect, and the East Minnese dialect are spoken. Yet counties such as Liancheng, Qingliu and Datian simply have no general dialect of their own. Just as miraculously that some dialect can not be understood over a mountain or beyond a bridge, a rare phenomenon in the whole country. Because of the numerous and jumbled dialects, it is inconvenient to communicate in Fujian, despite of the manifold culture in various languages. According to records, once there was a Shishi delegation from the South Fujian attending a trade negotiation in the northern part. The delegation made a speech to the meeting and meant to say "Welcome to Shishi to invest in trades". But haunted by the dialect accent, the sentence was pronounced and understood as Welcome to CC to steal chickens and feel out ducks. Nobody could understand but thought that it

was a sense of humor of Shishi. Another example, a leader who
did not know anything about the Putian dialect went on a tour of
inspection in a village in Putian and listened to an introduction
with an Putian accent, "In the past, there was nobody raising
eels and it is difficult in doing spiritual civilization work, but
now there are many people raising eels and the spiritual civilization work is much easier to do." Actually the phrase "raise eel"
was pronounced as "barbarism". Such cases are too many to enumerate. That is just as the saying goes "Neither get afraid of the
Heaven nor of terra, but only of the Fujian people speaking official language."

4. Too Many Jinns or Spirits Worshipped among the People

The magnitude of the created spirits among Fujian people is
so fabulous that the Heaven, the world and the hell are much
congested. Usually in every county, every town or village worships its own particular jinn or spirit as its aegis. To uplift the
aegis to go on a parade is usually limited within abuttals. For example, in the old time, Quanzhou, the city area of which was divided into 36 *pu* and 94 *jing* (*pu and jiing* were sub-area in old
China), worshipped more than 100 jinn and spirits. This is only
because that people in many areas of Fujian would rather believe
than disbelieve and are more practical, for if they worship a spirit
that does not produce effect instantly they will probably turn to
another.

5. Different Folk Customs and Folkways

It is said that there is no similar wind within 5000 square
meters of area just as there is no similar custom within one village, which vividly speaks out the differentia of the folk customs

in Fujian. This does not mean the changes of a folk custom or the changing frequency of a custom within one area in a period of time (On the contrary, a custom within an area of Fujian usually survives generation and keeps from being changed much and comparatively stays stable), but means the different exhibition of the same custom within one area. Take traditional festivals as an example. Different places have different ways of celebrating a festival. Because of varied customs and points of view, many folk proverbs mean just the opposite. For instance, in regard to the age of a marrying couple, the adage popular in Shanghang says, "When the girl is five years older, she surpasses the old mother; when the girl is three years older, the boy enjoys prosperity as if he is holding a gold brick in his arms." A Fuzhou adage says, "When the boy is three years older, he can stand a mast in front of the door; when the girl is three years older, the well will be drawn up dry." A Longhai adage says, "Drink rich tea and marry an older woman" and they believe that it is better to have a wife older than husband. A Wuyi Mountains adage says, "Husband can be five years older than wife but not six years older." A Longyan adage says, "Rather marry an old man than a thin man." A Wuyi Mountains adage says, "A woman of forty is a twig of flower, but a man becomes an expert at the age of fifty." Again take the facial appearance of the marrying couple for example. A Huaan adage says, "Big mouthed boy eats everywhere while a girl with big mouth will eat up her dowry." A Fuding adage says, "A man with big mouth eats Heaven storehouse while a woman with big mouth will support husband." A Luoyuan adage says, "A big mouthed man eats heaven food while a woman with big mouth will eat up her dowry. "

　　6. Varied Arts Difficult to Interrelate but Keeping Distinctive Local Colors

　　There is no one or a few commonly accepted operas in Fujian just like Beijing opera in Beijing, Yue opera in Zhejiang, Huangmei opera in Anhui, Yu opera in He'nan, Chuan opera in Sichuan, Dian opera in Yunnan, Zhuang opera in Tibet and Long opera in Guanshu. In Fujian, as many as twenty-nine operas are showed but none of them can be prevailing across the whole province, not to say there is one that might be a representative of Fujian opera. The most famous Min opera, Putian opera, Liyuan opera, Gaojia opera, Xiang opera are only prevalent in limited areas. If these five operas were to be put up in other places than their particular areas the effect could not be good regardless of the well-refined performing arts. Again, dance is an art of body movements requiring no singing and composing non dialect obstacle. But dance drama such as the most famous "patting chest" dance of South Min is unable to prevail or in the other words to meet boson friends in the North Min because of the differentia in regional culture. The people in the South Min are extraordinarily unrestrained and straightforward. The patting chest dance is way to express and unbosom one's emotions; nevertheless, the North Min is the home of the Righteousness School that especially stresses on self-possession and courtesy. It is impossible to imagine the North Minnese will pat their bare body all along the street. On the other hand, the "picking-tea-lamp dance" is exquisite and strictly regulated. Its uniquely light small dancing steps will not prevail in the South Min. The reason that Fujian folk songs have difficulty in getting themselves popular in province is quite obvious. Yet this is the very reason that the various forms of arts do not interrelate but preserve their particular artistic charm.

The following three factors should be inspected in regard to the formation of the manifolds of the Min culture.

① Geographical Factors

Fujian leaning against mountains and close to seas is both a southeast mountainous kingdom and a vast watery Min for the high mountain swift fountains divide Fujian into several natural regions with each region subdivided by stream tendency and mountain ranges to form smaller occlusive districts that are difficult to reach and communicate with. It seems that the solemn and quiet Wuyi Mountains is out of harmony with the rich and splendid Chitong Harbour, the closed mountain economy develops slowly while the coastal areas lead social vogue and march on in front of the nation.

② Complicated Compositions of the Min Culture

The formation of the Min culture has an intimate relation with the heritage of the Min Yue culture, the introduction of the Central Plains culture, the spreading of the religious culture and the overseas culture with unlike degrees of significance. Further more, every of kind of culture influence would not have concentrated over one region for a very long period of time, the center of which would easily move on to other regions. For example, the Min Yue culture in the Qing Dynasty, Zhangzhou culture in the Tang Dynasty, The Min Kingdom culture in the Five Dynasties, the Jianzhou culture in the Song Dynasty, Quanzhou cul-

ture in the Yuan Dynasty, the Yue Harbor culture in the Ming
Dynasty, the Houguan culture in the late Qing Dynasty. Each
one of the cultures presented itself in the history. None could
have secured a monopolistic position over another, and none
could have taken the place of another.

③Extension of the Central Plains Culture to Fujian Affected
by the Min Culture in Degrees and Formed No Staunch Kernel

Although the Central Plains culture intruded Fujian more
than one time with the long duration of time and the plenitude of
contents that was rare in other province across the nation, yet it
entered by stages and in batches and was isolated by the comparatively occlusion of the Min. Conclusively the intruding culture
has the properties of parasitism and unable to unify the culture in
the Min land.

Chapter Four
Arts

I. Music

Fujian is usually called the home of songs. The folk songs that have been passed down from generation to generation and sung by people nowadays give off a strong flavor of rural soil. Fujian lies at the foot of mountains and faces the sea with rivers and streams stretching southwards and northwards within its boundaries. Its mountain culture, river culture and ocean culture interlace each other featuring the most outstanding folk songs—songs of mountain and songs of fishermen.

Over 95 percent of Fujian territories are mountainous regions and hilly lands. Songs of mountain are the most popular ballads that have been affected by regional dialects and widely different in tones and melodies.

1. The West Fujian Mountain Songs

The West Fujian mountain songs have loud and sonorous melodies, free rhythm, fairly wide diapason, most of which are

Hui melody and not Shang melody. The principle tones are the lowest undertone of the whole song that produces a simple and original effect. Every song is usually divided into musical phrases, and the period is made up of two parallel upper and down phrases. Usually, three and four musical tones constitute one song. Influenced by geographical customs, the folk songs in the south of Fujian can be classified into three kinds.

(1) Folk Songs of Hakkas

This kind of folk songs is popular and circulates in the counties such as Changting, Wuping, Shanghang, Yongding. Its melody is continuous with fewer words and many tones, such as in the song *Selecting Seeds*: Phoenix gives birth to phoenix, dragon(he) gives birth to dragon (hei lou); in the fields (he) selecting seeds(ai), don't relax (he hei you); good seeds can surely gather in more (hei you), and four baskets are heavy than five baskets (hei you).

(2) Folk Songs of Longyan

These songs are popular in Longyan and Zhangping mountainous areas. Most of the songs have seven words to form one phrase and four phrases to form a complete song in a precise structure. The structure of melody of the song is mainly repetition of the first and second phrases. Such as in the song *The Tone is Higher When Sung More*: The tone is higher when singing more (ou), Yue-kin and Kowloon flute (ou); a stanza of mountain song is a piece of fire (ya), singing to burn fire all over the hill (ou).

(3) Folk Songs of Liancheng

Popular in Liancheng and the boundary areas of Shanghang

and Longyan, the songs have swift cadence with more words
other than fewer tones, such as in the song *Gale Blows Breeze
Cold*: The gale blows breeze feels cold (ya), man eats sugar
cane and sister lo eats sugar; man eats frozen ice and sister eats
snow, frozen ice is as cold as lo snow.

2. Folk Songs of North Fujian

Folk songs sung in the North of Fujian have many modes—
Falchion Flowers Songs, *Oil Tea Ballad*, *Lock Songs*, etc. On
singing *Falchion Flower Songs*, the singers strike tea falchions
on bamboo poles to rhyme the melody, from which this kind of
songs got the name. Performance of this song can be both in uni-
son and in antiphony. *Oil Tea Ballad* is sung when gathering in
a bumper harvest. Its melody is full of vigor and rich changing
steps. *The Lock Songs* is sung by one singer asking a question
and answered by another singer, i. e. to lock means to raise a
question by one and to unlock means to answer the question by
another. Questions and answers link tightly and the melody goes
slowly and swiftly alternatively. Besides, the folk songs of the
South of Fujian, the folk songs of the She minority, the folk
songs of Puxian, the folk songs of the Middle Fujian, to name a
only few, have features of their own.

Fringed by lengthy coastline, Fujian possesses many rivers
and streams within its boundary including twelve rivers that have
a 500 square meters lower reaches such as the Min River, the Jiu
Long River, the Ting River, and the Jin River. Fishermen who
live on fishery always sing songs to express their feelings about
life. Fujian fisherman's songs can be classified into two kinds.

1. Fisherman's Song at Sea

Popular chiefly in the counties in the East Fujian and the coastal counties in the Middle Fujian, fishing songs mostly reflect the fisherman's real life at sea, such as sung in a Fuding song *Back from Sea with Boat Full of Fish*: Ai pieces of white sail shining in the sun, back home from sea with boat full of fish; man and woman young and old rejoice together, tomorrow sails will again set off for distance voyage. The long-drawn-out melody and the wide range of tones are full of passions to life and great joy to harvest. Some of the fishing songs are sung directly to accord labor situations, as in a Fuding song *Pull out Sail to Raise Anchor*: The middle sail is pulling up lelesouou, raise anchor and blow snail horn to set off; every fisherman has arrived ou, boats in the fishing ground must strike. Herein, lelesou means the sound of raising the sail, 'strike' means to strike a kind of bamboo canister capable of giving out a sharp sound to shock the fish dead in order to round up it. The rhythm is of strong step and the melody is full of flavor of life.

2. Fisherman's Songs over the River

The songs mostly circulate in the counties that are stretched with rivers and streams crosswise in the Middle Fujian and the South Fujian. Among the fisherman's songs of the Min River popular in Fuzhou area, some songs are passionate, such as in a Fuzhou song named *Song of Fishermen* that goes as: This father has been on the river side since a child, neither afraid of the Heaven nor afraid of the earth; behold green hills and blue rivers endlessly, enjoy fish and shrimp endlessly. Some of the folk songs describe the hard life on the river, such as a Fuzhou Changxia song *A Fisherman's Song on the River*: I am a woman along

the boat, going out to sea with my daughter; it is my good day
when it is fine, I have no way when it rains. I am now pulling
sail with all my strength, a sail that can protect winds from all
directions; the sail is turning to the wind to keep the ship going
fast to a good place ahead. This kind of fisherman's song has
regular rhythm and a symmetry structure. The librettos are
filled up with sundry dialects.

There are other forms of folk songs in Fujian such as work
songs, singing verse, canzonet, dancing song, custom song,
children's song and living tone, etc. The most famous children'
s song is the one that is popular in the South Fujian named *The
Cloudy Sky*: The day is getting black, for it is going to rain. Father is lifting a hoe digging dasheen, digging and digging, digging and digging, dig up a big eel. How interesting. Father
wants to cook it salty and Mom wants to cook it light, they fight
each other and break the pan. Yi Ya Hui Du Dang Qi Dong
Qiang, Ha Ha Ha. The first part of the song says that father
has caught a loach and the whole family is intoxicated with happiness; the second part says that the parents have a quarrel and
break the pan. Each part is composed of two periods and the
melody is based on the first part, developing slowly, and the
range is moving upwards with clear levels. At the end of a period, supporting tone is usually used as if the sound of a breaking
a pan, full of humor and wit leaving a endless aftertaste. The
whole song is always one tone for one word similar to spoken
language that sounds simple and natural; and the tone is humorous and lively; the musical image is plain and pure, unfolding a
picture of countryside life in the South of Fujian.

The narrating and singing arts and music typical of Fujian
local styles are displayed in over twenty forms: South of Fujian
Music, Jin Songs, South Verse, Appraising Talk, Chi Singing,
Jianou Drum Verse, Xiangqiu Singing and Talking, Board Chord
Singing and Talking, Li Songs, Ferula Songs, Lotus Flower
Falling, Ten Tones and Eight Songs, Beiguan Songs, Jiu Lian
Songs, Money Source Trees, Cross-talk Drum, Song Books,
Ancient Prose Talking, Story Telling, etc. among which the
most famous and ancient one is South Music that is typical of rich
regional colours.

The South Music is also called *Nanqu*, or *Nanyue*, or
String and Wind. Judged by the instrument, performing ways
and the names of the tunes upon which musical piece is composed, the South Music has close relation with the music of the
Tang, the Song, the Yuan and the Ming Dynasties. It is a most
complete and rich musical type that has best preserved the Chinese ancient music culture. It is often referred to as "a living music history" or "music fossil". From the South Music, we can
find the influence of the Yan Yue Miscellaneous Musical Piece in
the late Tang Dynasty and the early Song Dynasty; we can also
find the tones of the South Opera of the Song Dynasty, of the
long lost Hai Yan Tune from the opera and drama history, and
of the early-period Yi Yang Tune, the Qingyang Tune, Kun
Shan Tune and Erhuang Tune. So the South Music can live up to
the name of a unique music. The South Music was originated
from Quanzhou gradually prevailing in the south part of Fujian.
It has been used in some of the local operas of the South Fujian
constituting an important part of the tone and the instrumental

music. As to performing format, the music is divided into two kind: upper four winds and lower four winds; the upper four winds part is rather quiet and elegant suitable for chamber performance. When the chief instrument is the hollow xiao (a bamboo flute), the music is called Dongguan; when the main instrument is Pin xiao, the music is called Pinguan. The lower four winds are more brisk and complicated to perform, suitable for the out door or folk cavalcade ceremony. Instruments used to perform the South Music include hollow xiao, erxian, pipa, paibang, suona, sanxian, etc. Percussion instruments include xiangzhang, small gong, wooden fish, four treasures, golden bell, flat drum, etc. Pipa used in the South Music (also called south pipa) is hold horizontally and plucked with fingers when playing unlike the north pipa that is hold upright and plucked with a special pluck. The sound of the south pipa when being played sounds like the deep bell tolling unlike the north pipa whose big strings sound like fast rainfall, which are of entirely different interests. The artistic manner of the South Music can be summarized as "simple and unsophisticated; mild and gentle". Its operas fall into three parts.

1. fingerings, or "fingering set": means that every set of songs comprises librettos, music text and lute playing fingerings to form a complete structure. There are forty-eight sets with each set divided into several sections and every section having an independent music.

2. music score: Every set of songs includes gongchipu (old composition formula) and indicators of playing skills. There is no libretto here. There are sixteen sets all together with each set

contains three to eight nominated tunes (names of tunes on which the music is composed) that mainly describe scenery of the four seasons, flowers and birds and scenes of courser speed coursing.

3. songs : i. e. verses accounting for more than one thousand pieces with short structure, lively librettos. Most of the songs express emotions, depict sceneries and narrate stories. The librettos are mainly taken from Li Yuan drama as well as from Kuen tune, Yiyang tune, Chao tune and folk songs and have developed a unique style. Because of the compact structure and beautiful tunes capable of expressing emotions and feelings, the South Music has become a local music that can be played by themselves in the South of Fujian.

There is a great variety of folk music instruments used all over cities and villages in Fujian. Almost every region has representative musical instruments of its own. We choose a few from them to get a general idea.

1. Fuzhou Shifan

There are different ways about the origin of the appellation 'shifan'— as it recorded in the eleventh volume of *The Records on Paintings on Boats in Yangzhou* written by Li Dou of the Qing Dynasty, ten kinds of instruments including flute, pipe, xiao, strings, violin, yun-gong, tang-gong, wooden fish, hardwood clappers, big drum played by turn in many repetitions were named "shifan"; some people thinks that in Fuzhou dialect "fan" is in homophony with the word "huan", so "fan" is developed from "huan". The music played by shifan in Fuzhou is a well-known performance played by the folk musical instruments. At

first it was applied to the local folk dragon lantern dance involving the instruments of langzhang, Qing-drum, big and small
gongs, big and small cymbals, etc. , and later gradually including some traditional strings and woodwind instrument such as
flute, pipe, sheng, coco-hu. There are more than one hundred
songs composed upon the shifan instruments. The melody and
tune largely come from four parts: (1) songs, the folk music
popular in local areas ; (2) canzonets, that have been played by
instrument ; (3) hua songs, the suona tunes popular in the local
areas ; (4) percussions, pure tunes of gong and drum that are
played by percussion instruments

The most often used five tones are Dongou Poem, West
River Moon, Nanjingong, Beiyundun and Yuezhonggui. There
are two performance styles, chamber performance and outdoor
performance. The outdoor performance is carried out in a parade. The chamber performance is divided into the antechamber
and the back chamber with the former based on jinge (probably
indicates percussion instruments) instruments and the latter
based on strings and woodwinds instruments. In order to play in
the chamber, the flute played the first two periods of music that
serve as an introduction that is followed by the other instruments. The performance sounded loud, vehement and elegant
and expressive with a clear cadence, perspicuous pause and tran-
sition in melody, and up and down emotions. The transfer of
pace is smooth and regular—slow as running water from high
mountains, and swift as thunder and lightening. The whole music eventually ends in an ardent atmosphere.

2. The South Fujian Shiyin

It is generally believed to be introduced from the north and has been strongly provincialized after absorbing much essence of the folk operas, folk songs, folk instrumental music of the South of Fujian on the process of its evolution. Its tunes usually classified into six kinds—still and quiet, elegantly beautiful, active and rejoicing, humorous and cheerful, warm and enthusiastic, high-spirited and fervent. Instruments used are divided for chief music and assistant music; orchestral music is based on Suonan and percussion music is based on board drum that controls the beginning and the ending and degree of force throughout the performance. The basic tunes of a Shiyin music when being performed is usually repeated for three times in respectively slow, medium and fast speed to complete a whole performance. The outdoor performance is played to a parade, which is commonly called caijie, in which the percussion instruments are arranged in front and strings and woodwinds placed at the rear while the chamber performance is commonly called zuozou where the strings and woodwinds instruments are placed in front row and percussion instruments at the back rows.

3. The West Fujian shiban

It is a band of ten players playing ten instruments respectively and thus get this name. It was introduced to the West of Fujian by outgoing traders from the southeast areas of the Jiangxi, Zhejiang or Hankou, later became popular and localized. The names of the songs performed fall into three kinds. (1) Dapai, a special program performed by the instruments of the Shiban, whose music is very classic and beautiful. (2) canzonet, taken from the folk songs that were played to accompany the ship lantern show. (3) cluster of drama music, usually taken from the interlude music of the Han opera and the Chao operas, played by flute, pipe, tao-string, erhu, three-string, yue-kin, pipa and clappers, etc., in seated performance and street performance.

4. The Putian Shiyin

A folk music with singing and playing that is popular in Putian and Xianyou counties. Performed by a group of ten players on ten instruments respectively, it has two forms of playing. (1) Gentle shiyin: instruments including sheng, xiao, pipa, three-string, pillow-violin, yun-gong, ancient-hu, erhu, pat-drum and drum of red leather. The performance of the music is lax in rhythm, mild in melody with fewer librettos and more tones in a classic style. (2) Powerful shiyin: the instruments including one yun-gong, three flutes, one bowl-hu, shi-hu, chi-hu, gong-hu, eight-cornered violin and three-string. Its performance makes an enthusiastic atmosphere by the largely modified tones. Other Fujian folk instrumental music include Jinjiang Shifan, Jingban, Fuding Shijin, Longxi Xibi, the South Fujian Longchui, Changting Gongmachui, Liancheng Guchui, Yongchun Naoting, Jingguchui, Wuyinchui, Zhangzhou Shibayin, etc.

II. Dance

The main character of Fujian folk dance is its plentiful variety and different conformation. Up till now there are more than 700 kinds that have been discovered in various styles and particular charms. Our comments and discussions will cover the following chief varieties.

Lantern Dance: such as *Dragon and Phoenix Lantern* for the Lantern Festival (15th of the first lunar month) popular in the Hakkas inhabited areas in the South of Fujian. For the Haskas, the word "lantern" is a partial tone for "man", and so "go to hang the light" means "to have a baby born to a family". At the night of the Lantern Festival, the villagers will start from the ancestral temple and tour their entire village. The performers will dress up in the roles of sheng, an and chou (characters in Chinese opera, sheng generally stands for a young man, dan for a young woman, chou for clown in a drama) and attach the colorful lanterns of yellow dragon, phoenix, male lion, fierce tiger, white crane, big elephant, deer to their waist with their heads looking forward and tails remained rearwards. Simultaneously the players will hold a drum shaped lantern or dragon head lantern or a flying butterfly lantern in the left hand and hold a horsewhip in the right hand to instigate two strong red bamboo horse lanterns in the front of the parade. The order of the parade is constantly changed in order to form various meaningful models such as *Guangong Patrolling Town*, *Building a Fence*, *Arranging Flowers*, *Making Doors*, *Yellow Dragon Surrounding a Pearl*, *Withdrawing Horses*, *Monkeys Burning Bees*, etc. After the show of one model, a modal of two dragons coming out of water should appear to serve as a connecting link between every two model-pictures to make the order easy to follow. Another active and auspicious lantern dance is Cha Lan Gu that is popular in Liancheng. Every Lantern Festival, young boys and young girls will hold in the palm colorful lanterns called "chalan" and go on a parade along downtown streets. In the Chalan lanterns,

there are red flowers which symbolize to give birth to a female
baby and white flowers which symbolize to give birth to a male
baby for newly-married women or young daughter-in laws who
still have not give birth to a child yet to pick out. At the same
time, a pair of big headed children (used to be called baby's elder brother and younger brother) is sporting among the flower
baskets and colorful lanterns and playing purposefully tricks on
the young women who are contending for flowers. You push and
I pull or you prevent or I block, which makes an interesting
scene. The show is based on the evolution of the parade order
and display of meaningful picture. The most frequently used actions are: single palm holding basket, connected palm holding
basket, swaying basket, comparing flower etc. The flower girl's
actions such as holding case up to the eyebrow, comparing flowers, viewing flowers, selecting flowers are well refined and vivid
to the life. The actions of the big-headed children are on the other hand, very humorous and cheerful. Some lantern parade only
walk and change order in the street but also enter the chamber to
give performance. For example, Tea Lantern popular in Dongx-
iang of Pucheng. The performers hold the tea lantern bright with
candle light inside in the left hand and wave light silk by the
right hand, walking with a round ground steps and dancing varied pictures such as holding lantern, lifting lantern, setting lantern and sawing lantern into the chamber and back yard. After
entering the antechamber, the band performs Plunking Tea tune
and the dancing team go forward to pay a New Year call to the
housemaster. *Dragon Lantern Dance* popular in Fuzhou area is
also representative of the folk dance. To perform the program,

every section of the dragon should have a burning candle light for it held by one man plus a light for the dragon pearl. All together there are ten persons for one dragon. The dragon pearl is held by a person of short stature, while the dragon head is held by a person of high stature, with the rest of the players lining from the short at the head to the tall at the end. Players at different section do different actions. The first section and the second section mainly take 'stride' steps while the eighth section player mainly takes 'sideway horse step run' and 'step run', and the dragon tail mainly takes 'big stride' and the rest take 'dogtrot' steps. The former ones trot and the more latter, the bigger stride will be taken. There are three features about the dancing formula: first, the order is based on the symmetrical 'taiji drawing'; second, a set of fixed movements, for example, the 'dropping of the arm joints' (i. e. each dragon body section dances by dropping from the former player's head top position), 'changing hands and swallowing joints' i. e. the exchange of the left and right arms, the switch to the left side and to the right side, the evolution of the push and withdraw of the upper hands), 'small leaping steps' (i. e. to run by the half sole); third, the art of the dance, such as to follow the former section and to care for the latter section, neither to push ahead nor to pull the latter, to see quickly and to dance smoothly, etc. There are quite a few other lantern dances popular all over Fujian that are representative of Fujian folk dance such as *Horse Boys Lantern* in Guangzhe, *Bamboo Horse* in Yongding, *Barn Lantern Dance* in Liancheng, *Stepping-on-Horse Lantern* in Changting, etc.

Ball Dance, which is mainly popular in Quanzhou area. For

instance, Dance of *Throwing Balls*. The performers usually
walk in front of the parade of welcoming deity and throw balls to
the audience without their consciousness from the crowd. The
colorful balls, 14.5 in diameter are made from splints which are
enwound with colorful band, and is suspended on a cotton string
of 230 cm in length. To the other end of the string, attached a
cluster of fringes. The performers hold the end of the strings in
hand and throw or swing or fling or draw in the balls at such a
large extent that the balls fly up and down and around like flying
stars, and make the audience to shy away. The dance is showed
along with the parade, but sometimes the parade stops to let the
dance be carried out in a paddock. When the colorful balls fly up
and down, left and right, they present a scene of splendor. Colorful Ball Dance is another example. A boy and an old woman
lead a group of girls to dance, the boy tossing the ball up and
down, and left and right and causing the girls to kick ball by foot
and touch it by keen and catch the ball by hand while the old
woman teasing the ball with her head, hand, body and foot in
cheerful and humorous performance. The whole performance is
of a vivid and active picture of interest. There are some other
forms of colorful ball dance programs such as Throwing Ball
Dance, Rolling Ball Dance, and Embroidery Ball Dance.

Military Dance. Originated from a military inspection dance
brigade of an army bale fire battalion quartered at Qingyu of Fuding, and later became a folk activity, the Vine-board Dance is
popular in the east of Fujian. The dance team divide into two
columns. One column dress up in pure red of army, another column dress up in blue navy holing a vine board of tiger head in the

left hand and a broadsword marching along the street in the
rhythm of the percussion music. When arriving at a spacious
place, the parade stops to give a show in a paddock. Flag holder
dances in round steps, which are followed by the appearance of
the army and navy from both sides. Their right hands hold
broadswords to do the attack movements of chopping, killing,
cleaving, puncturing, sweeping and supporting. Their left hands
hold vine boards to do defensive actions such as resisting, keeping off, hindering, supporting, and pushing up. The harmonious
cooperation of two hands, the forceful and brave and valiant
movements, the loud and clear attack of broadswords and the
vine boards create a picture of mighty power and heroic vigour of
male beauty. The evolution of order gives priority to horizontal,
vertical and round shapes. Occasionally, it also serves as a simple fighting shows of the army and the navy. Another similar
dance is *Fighting Regiment* known in Jianning County.

The Nuo Dance. It is a kind of dance dressed in mask and
prevailing in the north of Fujian. The word 'nuo' means 'to e-
liminate'. It is said that in the ancient time people would feel
quite hopeless about the pestilences and would appeal to spirits
for protection. They put on wooden, paper or oil cloth masks to
drive out epidemic diseases as well as evil influence. The Nuo
dance in the north of Fujian is affluent in variety, having *Dancing Monk*, *Eight Dancing Horses*, *Dancing Maitreya*, and *Five
Dancing Spirits*. The Nuo dance is mainly performed collectively in a group with one or two leading dancers. To begin with,
God of Carving out the Way will clear up a ground within which
he dances individually for some while in bowing steps and

strides; to accompany the order evolution, he will take back-ward-kick steps or fox steps. *Eight Dancing Horses* popular in Dafugang Village of Shaowu County is put on show every first day of June in lunar calendar, a date when villagers must go on a tour to offer sacrifices. Eight men dress up in pair in masks of the way-carving god, Maitreya, the black face and the green face. The carving-way god holds a gong and the Maitreya holds a jian (an ancient Chinese weapon), the black face and the green face each hangs a flat drum dance in two groups in single col-umn. When the audience grows larger, the single column begins to change into a ring and into a square mainly in 'backward bow-ing step'or 'turning bowing step', or 'continuous turning step' accompanying the exaggerated and beautified hand actions of striking and hitting in rotation.

The She Minority Dance. The She minority distributes in more than forty counties and municipalities over Fujian province, especially gathering in the east of Fujian area. The She minority good at singing and dancing has created many uniquely styled folk dances. Planting Bamboo popular in Fuding is a dance for a She rabbi when he carries out practice. Bamboo is an auspicious object used by the rabbi to beat and drive out apparitions that will never turn over for aeon. On carrying out the Taoist prac-tice, the rabbi will dance lightly and freely to the east and the west, the north and the south and the center directions. He imi-tates the complete procedures in real life from planting a bam-boo, making paper of bamboo to offering paper money to the Bo-dhisattvas in the upper, middle and down worlds. His move-ments are smooth, elastic, and moderate in flexibility and force, and the cooperation of body and four limbs are in harmony. Further more, when the dancer turns round to the left and to the right swiftly, his skirt will open like an umbrella and appears very beautiful and elegant. *Hunting Dance* popular in Zhangwan of Ningde manifests the hunter in the round up process. Four young men of the She minority hold snail horns in the left hand and hunting swords in the right hand to show actions of "prying about", " rounding up", "getting over blocks", "blowing horns", "killing"and "returning triumphantly", to stress a scene of young people hunting in the deep jungle or forest. Lei Rhymed Formula known in Fuan is a set of actions performed throughout so called "protecting and ridding evils"gestures when a koradji is holding an offering sacrifice ceremony. Only one player performs a series of 46 gesture actions that are further divided into four kinds as Hiding Rhymed Formula, Beating Ghosts Rhymed Formula, Hanging Building Rhymed Formula and Luo House Rhymed Formula. Out of the four parts, the Hiding Rhymed Formula making up of the main actions of whole dance is performed by character gestures of Kwan-Yin, Ne zha, Mother Lady of King Lady, Luban, tiger, tortoise, snake and crane in order to frighten the evil spirits and ghosts. The Lei Rhymed Formula can be called a compilation of koradji gestures. *Falchion Dance* popular in Badu of Ningde, *Greeting Dragon Umbrella* in Lianjiang, *Pray for Happiness* in Xiapu and *The She Wedding Ceremony Dance* are classical dances of the She minority in Fujian.

Religious Dance. In Putian, there are many dancing scenes in the Taoist's ceremony. For example, at the midday in the

third day of March in the lunar calendar, the Taoists would hold
Xiaojiao ceremony called Ying Zhen (means to receive the true
spirit from the heaven). To build a high platform symbolizing
the quarter for the superior and to place an altar there, too. Sev-
en Taoists face the platform upward from the altar and welcome
the descend of the superior. They cut through the yard backwards and forwards in repetition and make a marvelous picture.
When come to "contribute to the stove", i. e. the end of the ceremony, all the unsealed envelops are piled up and hold in both
hands to the stove outside the yard to be burnt for "entering the
heaven", the Taoists surround the stove and dance. Present
Cymbal is a dance that one Taoist performs in the ceremony to
release souls of the dead from purgatory and enable the dead to
get house and silver. More than twenty movements to symbolize
actions such as "to push out", "to look at mirror", "cloudy dragon passing by the sun", "heating teas", will be performed for o-
ver two hours. That is the reason why usually there are two performers to give performance by turn. Expect for some fixed sequence, the dancer can freely select movements and wing it.
Shocking and dangerous movements such as throwing copper
cymbals high into the air and receiving the circling cymbal with
another cymbal or by a finger while posing a series of difficult actions are named as "spinning cymbal", "to send straight upward"
and "to catch the pedicel of cymbal", etc. *Wearing Flowers
Dance* popular in Fuqing is a kind of dance used by both the Buddhism and the Taoism: in the Buddhism religion, this dance is
performed by monks in Pu Du (In Buddhism, it means a ceremony to release people generally from sufferings). General Release

ceremony for the dead to come back and to release souls from
suffering; in the Taoism religion, this dance is used when the
Taoists set an altar to execute paying filial piety religious ceremony to release souls from suffering for the dead parents. To
perform the dance, eight performers carry copper bells in the
right hand and a lantern in the left hand, step into the sight accompanied by folk music. They walk dancing steps circling along
the credence with proper changes of order and moderate pace that
appear so elegant and smooth. Wet Nurse popular in the northeast of Fujian, Bao Zou popular in Sanming and Yong'an, Fairy
Washes Mirror in Yangkou of Shunchang, Fragrant Flowers in
the east of Fuijan, Battle Field Drum in Xiayang of Nanping,
Zhao Li Bai in Putian and Xianyou, etc. are representatives of
Fujian religious dances.

　　Stilts. *Flapping Butterflies in Stilts* is a popular program
in Changting of the west of Fujian. One of the two players dresses up to play the Ugly Father, who is holding a fan in the left
hand and lifting a bamboo slice with a butterfly attached to it,
the other player dresses up as Ugly Mother, who takes the important part of the dance performance. The Ugly Father is teasing the Ugly Mother with the butterfly ugly while the Ugly
Mother is chasing after him left and right, backward and forward, sometimes laughing joyfully, sometimes blinking her eyes
and biting her lip, sometimes looking namby-pamby, sometimes
utterly discomfited. Through the expatiation of scenarios such as
looking at the butterfly, teasing the butterfly, chasing the butterfly and flapping the butterfly. The dance vividly conveys the
plots of the father making fun of the mother and the mother flap-

ping the butterfly in a happy and light scenery. The performance
exercises a lot of skillful actions such as "minute yango step",
"minute wearing step", "single-leg leap", "double-leg leap",
"lowing front waist"and "do the splits".

Let us make a survey as to the many causes as to the variety
of Fujian folk dances. Affected by the inconvenient communications and the sundry dialects, Fujian folk dances are unable to
circulate in the entire territory. None of the dances is able to
cover the whole province. In the communications and economics
developed areas such as the South of Fujian, some kinds dances
have circulated a comparatively wider area after a long time's interaction, blending and spreading. But in some comparatively
close areas, a kind of dance can only spread in one county or a
town or even in a village. For instance, Striking Cart Drum originated in Hushi Village, Huyuan Town of Sha County is a dance
performed in the Ming Dynasty by youngsters in the village to
seek for peace for family members. After many generations' polishing and processing by folk artists, the dance becomes rich in
form and perfect in content, but it only popular in the village.
Walking Battle Array (also called *Falchion Dance*) popular in
Guaodi Village of Ninghua is an ancestor worship dance handed
down from a Chi family of the Guaodi Village for many generations. Although it came into being long before the Southern
Song Dynasty, yet it can only be put on and appreciated in the
same village until now. *Lifting Cats with Hands* known in
Jingxi Guankou Village of Minhou County is a dance vividly de-
picting the story of a hunter who has hunted a tiger and returned
happy with fruitful results. But ever since it was first created, it

has never gong beyond the village, and remained the only dance
of the village. Further more, there is the difference about the
folkways. Just as is said about Fujian that there is no similar
folkways within ten li area, and every village has its own customs. It might not be as hard to imagine that people in the
northwest of Fujian will accept the bear-bodied and along-the-
street *Patting Chests Dance* popular in the south of Fujian as
that the more exquisite dances such as *Plucking Tea Leaves* will
become popular in the South of Fujian.

The origins and formation of Fujian folk dances mainly relate with the following five aspects.

1. Originating from the native life in labor. Fujian folk
dance is an art to express emotions of the people who have lived
in the vast land of Fujian. The dances embody the peoples actual
existence, labour life and fully express people s conviviality and
longing. For instance, *Falchion Flowers in Bamboo Forest* popular in the north of Fujian reflects the people's real life at working site. At first, when people set off for working site they
strike bamboo poles with firewood cutters that they bring with
them at discretion just for diversion; sometimes accompanied
with folk songs, they change striking rhythms to suit dancing
steps for self-enjoyment. Later after constant modification and
polishing, it becomes a dance to express the people's working
sentiments. *Tea Lanterns Dance* popular in the north of Fujian
absorbs various tea plunking movements in realistic working situations. So the origins of Fujian folk dances have close relations
with the particular folk customs of a certain place in Fujian.
Teasing Lanterns which is also called *Snatching Lanterns* origi-

nates from the folk customs: There is a convention called "giving lanterns"in the south of Fujian that says that parents must buy colorful lanterns and send the lanterns to their married daughters who get wedded not up to three years yet by children in the family every Lantern Festival. For the first marriage year, they send their daughter a pair of lanterns—one is a lotus lantern symbolizing the possibility to give birth to a male baby, the other is embroidery ball lantern symbolizing the possibility to give birth to a female baby. For the second year, if the daughter has not given birth to a baby, they will send another pair of lanterns; if she has had, send a peach lantern. For the third year, another pair of drum lanterns will be sent. The dance *Teasing Lanterns* shows: a young girl at the Lantern Festival sends a colorful lantern to her sister's mother-in-law's home by her parents's order; on the halfway, a boy who is playing a bamboo horse will snatch the girl of the lantern. One is snatching and chasing, the other is dodging and avoiding, which presents a picture of children's puerility and vivacity. The folk traditions also contribute to the formation and development of the folk dances in Fujian. For instance, *Battlefield Drum* popular in Xiayang of Nanping tries to describe the soldiers in the battlefield along with the drumbeats in a vigorous atmosphere. It is imparted by a Professor Xue, a veteran in Xiayang who used to be the flagman in the Zheng Chenggong'army. But it is owing to the strong local tradition of practice of martial laws that this dance can be handed down from one generation after generation. In Xiayang, there are many families that practice martial arts and many people who successfully pass the military examinations and become military

Jinshi or appointed officials in the royal court. Fujian folk dances also connect with the desire to express people's passion of love and hatred and amorous feelings. For instance, when to perform *Big Drum and Umbrellas* (also called *Flower-Drum Array*) popular in Zhangzhou and Longhai, the actors with drums over the shoulder beat the drums as they dance and several actresses hold colorful umbrellas shading from the sun for the drum beating actors. Go against history, it is a historical incidence that happened when the people in the south of Fuijan beat drums to celebrate the army of the Qi family returned in triumph. The national hero Qi Jiguang seeing the drum beaters sweating under the burning hot sun (or in the rain) was deeply moved and gave order that soldiers and woman servants hold umbrella for the drum beaters and move on with the parade. So comes the dance scenario into being.

2. Introduction from the other places in the country. The folk dances that have come into Fujian are roughly classified into three. (1) Introduction from the Central Plains. There have been many times in the history when the culture of the Central Plains intruded Fujian that generally led to the assembly of numerous folk dances in Fujian and by the advantaged historical and geographical conditions these introductions have been preserved and accumulated. For instance, *Dragon and Phoenix Lantern* popular in the Haskas areas of the West Fujian is originally a Central Plains dance that has been come down from six or seven hundreds of years ago to this day without any changes. (2) Introduction from Taiwan. *Dancing Drums on the Feng Po* popular in Feng Po Village of Nanan comes from Taiwan. Two hun-

dred years ago, a man went to Taiwan from Feng Po to make a living by sawing straw coating. In Taiwan, he learned how to dance "dancing drum" and it happened that in his hometown there was a ceremony of offering incense to respect the dead when he returned from Taiwan. He performed this dance and from then on this dance would be performed at the folk ceremonies. (3) Introduction from the Southeast of China. For instance, *Playing Regiment Cards* popular in Jianning came from Hunan in the Ming Dynasty. *Nine Interlinks* popular in the west of Fujian, insofar as the performing property is concerned, it may have been the Lianting (also called the overlord's scourge) originated in Jiangsu and Hunan areas. During the convulsion in the Ming Dynasty, common people run away to the west of Fujian. To make a living, folk actors sold singings at the corner of the street in Tingzhou, and the songs they sang was Nine Interlinks that later became a folk dance in the west of Fuijan. The opern and war drum in the *Plunking Tea Lantern* popular in Longyan were introduced from Guangdong by the seventeenth ancestor of the Lin family in Meishan Village of Shuban Town, which happened about 250 years before.

3. Born out of dramas and songs. Being a home of dramas and songs, Fujian has not a few dramas and songs with excellent performing movements and music that possess the property of dancing elements. Therefore many folk dances originated from the dramas and songs. For instance, *Walking in the Rain* popular Putian, Xianyou used to a scenario in the Puxian drama *Ruilan Walks in the Rain* in which the character Ruilan and her daughter hurry their journey in the rain. The dance *Four Men*

Carry a Litter popular in the west of Fujian is also taken from a
drama in which the dramatic movements such as carrying a litter
is depicted so incisively and vividly in the Liyuan opera and Puxian opera that its humorous style and subtle expression is imitated and adopted by dancing e art: four performers wearing a
sharp-topped hats and litter carriers suits mimic the particular
movements of carrying a litter climbing a mountain, going down
a slope, fording a shoal and walking across a bridge accompanied
by a litter song typical of the south of Fujian. *Trays Dance* popular in Chewu Village of Changting adopted and modified from a
certain scenario of a Hunan drama that once was put on in Chewu
Village. *A Source of Money Tree* now popular in the south of
Fuajin used to be a beggar's dance and later is adopted by Guaoja
opera and becomes a dance that will be performed at the Spring
Festival.

　　4. Influence of religions. *Hairpin* Litter now popular in
Fengting of Xianyou is introduced by the Taoism with a strong
religious color. *Nine Lotus Lantern* now popular in Putian uses
lotus lantern as the light of the holy suggests that the light shine
through the layers of dark grounds and people cultivate merits to
turn to the pure heaven so as to guide human spirit to shake off
worldly dust and ascend the Heaven. Between the sections of
dance there interlude the teachings of the doctrines of the religion
in singing.

　　5. Influences of Various Factors. Many dances are affected
by various factors and integrate themselves with foreign compo-
nents as well as local edification. They absorb essence from mul-
tifold fields and become rich in connotation and manifestation.

Patting on the Chest now popular in the south of Fujian is one of the most representational works of Fujian folk dances. Performers are male wearing straw hats and bear-bodied with single-rhymed strike, pat, nip and stamp or squat on the chest, the arms, and the palms and the shoulders as main performing movements. There are different parlances about the source of this dance : First, relating to the sacrifice ceremony dance of the ancient Min Yue nationality whose relic can be found in the external performing format and internal melody. Second, relating to the stamping songs of the ancient central plains. As the mien, dynamic, conformation of the dance bear similarity with those that are displayed in the picture named *Stamping Song* by Mayuan in the Song Dynasty that was brought into Quanzhou with immigrants from Zhongzhou. Third, relating to the bear-foot working habits of the people in the south of Fujian. People in the south of Fujian used to be bear foot at work and when they took a rest they would clap hands and pat on the chest dancing for amusement. Fourth, relating to certain religion. It is said that during the Tang and the Song Dynasties monks and nuns gathered in Quanzhou. Patting on the chest was a kind of dance in the spirit-welcoming ceremony competition. Fifth, relating to dramas. In the Liyuan opera *Li Ya Xian*, Zheng Yuanhe and the beggar dance like that. For a long time, the dance has been influenced by many factors simultaneously and absorbed essence from many factors other than from a single one. Because of its encyclopedically containing ability, this dance unfolds profound contents and provides a high aesthetic value of the folk dances.

Ⅲ. Dramas

Fujian did not start to develop operas and dramas until the Tang Dynasty, but the formation of the opera and the drama began almost at the same period as that of the other places in the country. Xiantong the second year in the Tang Dynasty (861), Rabbi Zong Yi of Fuzhou Xuansha Temple "travelled southward to Putian and the county prepared one hundred dramas to welcome him" (the 18th volume of *Jingde Records* by Daoyuan in the Song Dynasty). To the Song Dynasty, the miscellaneous operas of the Song were introduced into Puxian, Fujian and resulted in Puxian operas that were prevalent at the time and integrated folk ancient music and hundred dramas that sung in Puxian dialect. As Puxian belonged to the Xinghua regiment, the local opera was then called Xinghua opera. Putian poet Liu Kezhuang recorded in detail the pomp of Putian dramas: "Dressing up and in the fine clothes the whole city is busy and half of it is in the theater"(*Three Poems on Present Events*). The miscellaneous operas of the Song Dynasty were very popular in Zhangzhou. In 1197, Chen Chun wrote in his works about the prevalence of operas in Zhangzhou. In the late Song and early Yuan, the South opera started to infiltrate into the Xinghua opera of Putian, Liyuan opera of Quanzhou, Zhuma opera of Zhangzhou, and improved their list of plays, performance and music. Fujian operas germinated in the Tang, formulated in the Song and matured in the Yuan. Reason one, from the late Jin to the Tang and Five Dynasties, the northern people moved southwards to Fujian and brought with them the Central Plains culture as well. Reason two, in the Tang Dynasty, Fujian was comparatively more stable and prosperous. Banquet dances in the mansions were quite frequent, and folk dancing houses appeared. Reason three, in the Tang and the Five Dynasties, the Buddhism religion was quite prevailing with frequent rituals and a lot of temples. Temple fair was a dancing performance site. Reason four, in the Song Dynasty, there were many people passed the imperial examinations and took official positions in the royal court far away from Fujian. When they returned home they usually brought with them servants and dancers for recreations. Reason five, when the Song moved to the south, large quantities of royal family members entered into Fujian. Further more, there were more Fujian people took official positions in Zhejiang than Zhejiang people took official positions in Fujian. When they returned to Fujian, royal families and officials brought back various colorful lists of operas that were popular in Hangzhou and Wenzhou and finally went down into the common people.

The Ming Dynasty was a period when Fujian'operas got developed. Yiyan Tone, Kungshan Tone and Siping Tone began to take roots in Fujian successively and were absorbed by local operas. Many new tone operas came into being and at the same time imposed impacts on the rules, trade, costume and types of facial make-ups of the existing operas. New operas and old operas competed each other and displayed an extraordinary artistic charm. According to related records, from city to countryside, various kinds of operas were frequently put on stage and many dramas were put forward. For instance, *Story of the West Wing-Room*, *Chen San and Lady* Wu were shown in Quanzhou,

Xi Shi Presented by Fang Li Pan Bizheng, *Huo Xiaoyu* were performed in Putian; *Notes on Singing Phoenix*, *Notes on Colorful Brush*, *Plunking Teas*, *Going out to Boundary Fort* were put on in Fuzhou. Further more, Fujian operas were warmly welcome in the Ruykuy Kingdom during the Ming Dynasty.

The causes for the development of the operas in Fujian in the Ming Dynasty can catalogued into the following four:

Cause one: multiple approaches for the introductions of the tunes from the other places in the country. The introduction of Yiyuan high tune, Kun tune, Huizhou tune, and Qingyang tune took place with the entrance of the merchants from Huichi. On the other hand, the return of officials of Fujian origins was another approach to the introduction. For instance, when Chen Yiyuan, who used to be the chief administrator of Jading County, Jiangshu province and was keen on Kun operas, returned to Fuzhou, he brought home a Kun opera *Singing Child* to entertain his guests.

Cause two: multiple routes for the introduction. For instance, the introduction of Shiping tune had taken the routes. The first route is from the east of Jiangxi via the north of Fujian to Zhenghe, Pingnan and Ningde; a second route is from Zhejiang through the coastline to the middle of Fujian such as Fuqing, Changle, and Pingtan; the third route is from the south of Jiangxi via the common boundary area between Fujian and Guangdong to Pinghe, Zhangzhou and Nanjing.

Cause three: a group of playwrights and works emerged. For instance, Continued Peony Booth by Fuzhou Chen Shi, *Notes on Weird Dreams* by Chen Jiefu, *Notes on Green Dragon* by Fuqing Lin Zhang, and *Notes on the West-Wing Room in the North* by He Bi.

Cause four: a group of outstanding critics emerged. For instance, Xie Zhaozhe of Changle, Yao Lu of Putian, Li Zhi of Quanzhou, Chen Di of Lianjiang, and Cao Xue Qiang of Fuzhou.

The Qing Dynasty is a period during which Fujian saw its operas got thriving, the indications of which fall in the following three aspects.

1. Numerous theatrical troupes. According to *Records on Pu Ji* by Putian Chen Hong of the Qing Dynasty, there were twenty-eight theatrical troupes in Putian. Officials often stored up theatrical troupes to perform operas at home. Even Xiamen Coast Defense Bureau set up theatrical troupe to give performance to the government officials and officers.

2. Spreading to foreign countries. During the years 1685 to 1688, Fujian theatrical troupes visited Thailand palace and other big cities to perform comedies and tragedies, etc. From the year 1840 to the year 1843, Gaoja opera troupes visited Singapore, Malaysia, Indonesia and Burma to show *To Anger Zhouyu Feel Three Times* and *Legend of White Snake*.

3. Wider Popularization of performance. Every county's historical records has recorded the pomp of theatrical performance in details as did in the *Pinghe County History* of the Kangxi period in the Qing Dynasty, the tenth volume *Histories of Natural Conditions and Social Customs* : every youngest dresses up to take part in the Shini, *Eight Immortals* and *Bamboo Horse*. The *History of Changtai County* in the Qianlong period of the Qing Dynasty, the tenth volume *On the Mores* records that: a defending noise of drums and gongs, decorating with lanterns and

colored streamers, banners and flags shutting out the sun, one performance after another. *Longyan County History* of the Daoguang (period) of the Qing Dynasty, the seventh volume *On the Mores* says that from the morning till evening of the New Year's Day, the theatrical troupe gives performance from one household to another and gets money as award by beating gongs. *Yongding County History* of the Daoguang (period) of the Qing Dynasty, the sixteenth volume *On the Mores* says that Greeting the spirits to state respect, giving performance to entertain people cannot be stopped in three or five days. *Luoyuan County History* of the Daoguang (period) of the Qing Dynasty, the twenty-seventh volume *On the Mores* says that: actors and actresses from the other places arrive at Luoyuan this month and give performances in the temple under the full moon light. An official of the Qing Dynasty wrote vividly in the book *Watching Operas* about the pomp of theatrical performance in Fuzhou, staying inside the boudoir, hardly able to read and write, yet capable of understanding and reciting the drama *Notes on a Happy Couple*. Not being jealous or suspicious of the incessant streams of fragrant horses and carriages, everyone is engaged in putting up a canopy of one zhang in height as a sign; no body chatted with someone else before his own canopy. But as soon the singing started, the spectators began to be arose in excitement… enjoying the performance so much till late in the evening, just to feel that there in the librettos hold emotional appeals. The prosperity of the Fujian operas in the Qing Dynasty literarily lies in the fusion of the outside operas with the local arts that results in a special regional opera with its unique characteristics. For in-

stance, from the middle period of the Qing to the 30s of twenty
century, a Qiyang theatrical troupe from Hunan via Jiangxi arrived at Longyan, Liancheng and Ninghua, many artists settled
down along the journey and at the same time absorbed the puppet
show of the West Fujian, folk military music drums and Xiqing
opera together to produce an opera later called West Fujian Han
Opera. Thrumming based on wind tune was introduced into
Shouning, Gutian, Pingnan, and Fu'an in the northeast of Fujian through Zhejiang and Jiangxi. After absorbing the local
arts, it became an opera later called North Way Opera. Hui
Troupe came in via Zhejiang and Jiangxi into Meilin of Taining
County in the northwest of Fujian, after taking in the local Taoist music and folk song's canzonet, it became Meilin Opera.
Jiangxi troupe came to Pucheng in the North of Fujian, and later
was known as Guang Opera.

Among the operas, the most prominent operas are Min op-
era, Puxian opera, Liyuan opera, Gaojia opera and Xiang opera.

Min opera conventionally called Fuzhou opera is popular in
the Fuzhou dialect spoken area together with Ningde, Jianyang
and Sanming. Min opera has syncretized the artistic styles of
Rulin opera (that was influenced by Hui opera and Kun opera,
based on singing and teasing tunes) of the late Ming Dynasty,
mixed tunes since the middle of the Qing Dynasty and Pingjiang
opera. Min opera has developed as many as 1500 traditional dramas. The most famous ones are *Twin Jade Cicadas*, *The Body
Carried by Woman*, *Gan Guo Bao*, *Chen Ruo Lin Beheads
Prince*, *Old Wu and Zhou Liang Xian*, *Notes on Red Skirt*,
and the modified Cook Tung Oil with Rice Noodles, *Hairpin*

Phoenix , *Smelted Imprint* , etc. The tones and tunes of Min opera have a strong sense of local character comprising elegantly
graceful and restrained "teasing tune", rough and violent "Jiang-
hu", earthly fluent "Overseas Songs" and flesh and lively "canzonets". Its accompanying musical instruments divides into two
types: one is " soft piece", which is based on traditional stringed
and woodwind instruments such as jing hu, three-strings, flute,
sheng, and suona; the other is "hard piece", which comprises
sheng, drum, gong, cymbal, fish drum, etc. The role professions, at first, comprising sheng, dan and chou (that stand respectively for young male characters, female characters and old
aged characters in the opera), include positive sheng, junior
sheng, senior sheng, intimate sheng, and militant sheng; positive dan, qingyi (middle-aged female characters usually in green
clothes), hua dan, junior dan, militant dan, senior dan and ugly
dan; clown, san hua (the ugly character), militant san hua,
senior hua, secondary hua, militant secondary hua; mo (middle
aged male character), wai (old aged character), zha (multi-roled
character), etc. The performing movements used in the Min opera are literarily violent, rough: "three times of driving and pur-
suing, twisted mouth and face, trembling and shaking of feet and
hands, playing with hair and swinging beard, etc. "are quite often used. But movements used by sheng and dan are partially refined and especially performed by the dan. Min opera is strict
with the body motions emphasizing on the movement "from leg
to arm, from arms to body, and then to the whole body and every joint".

　　Puxian opera is popular in Putian, Xianyou and the neighboring counties that Xinghua dialect is spoken. For in the Song Dynasty, Putian, Xianyou both belonged to Xinghua military region and in the Ming and Qing periods, they belonged to Xinghua government, therefore the opera was also known as Xinghua opera. Puxian opera has a long history. As early as seven hundreds years ago, the famous Putian poet Liu Ke Zhuang depicted the pomp situation of the opera prevalence in his poems. Puxian opera has inherited a rich traditional legacy with over five thousands dramas in eight thousands editions. Liu Nianchi points out in the book *New Evidence for the South Operas* (China Publishing House, 1986) that the play books of the Puxian opera are in such a great number that no opera can parallel it throughout the nation even over the world. Puxian is a most abundant library and museum that has collected the world theatrical works of art. Its distinguish traditional dramas are as following: *Mu Lian*, *Ye Li* (also called *Lady Ye Li*, *Lady Weng Yi*), *Zhang Qia*, *Spring River*, *Shangke Teaches School*, etc. , and the adapted plays like *After Reunion*, *Number One Scholar and Beggar*, *Chun Cao Rushes in the Hall*, *Qing Tao*, *Shong Kuo Shi*, etc. The music of the Puxian opera is of Xinghua tone in Xinghua phylum. Its aria structure is based on the nominated tunes system and there are over one thousand nominated tunes that have musical compositions. Male and female use the alike tones and tunes that go lingering and touching. Accompanying musical instruments include, at first, gongs, drums and flute, later, fife, big hu, erhu, yue-kin, three-strings, wen drum, single leather drum, bell drum and bowl gong, etc. It is said that all kinds of gongs and drums account for five hundreds species and the facial make-ups that can be available now are over two hundreds. The facial make-ups use red, white and black colors. According to the introduction made in *The Traditional Proscenium Arts of the Puxian Opera*, up till now, there have collected three hundreds kinds offacial make-ups. There are seven role professions such as sheng, dan, mo, wai, tie and ugly, with sheng, dan as the most important roles that are daintily portrayed as beautiful and refined and full of dancing attributes, especially the ancient females' stamping pace that are required to 'walk without touching the skirt' by clamping the keens tightly, enclosing the feet and walking scraping the ground by the toes up and down alternatively. When trained to walk this step, the joints of the legs should hold a copper coin in between. The successfully skillful legs are those that are able to walk with a coin in between keens yet without dropping it.

Liyuan opera is popular in Quanzhou and other South Fujian dialect spoken areas. In the first year of the Song Dynasty, the folk dramas and operas absorbed the dramas of the South opera and performing arts that led to the formation of an opera which is based on the South Fujian dialect and the South music as its performing language and tune. Liyuan opera has three artistic genres —Shanglu, Xianan and Xiao Liyuan with latter performed by virgins. Each school has its own particular dramas and aria of nominated tunes. Liyuan opera has more than one hundred dramas. Outstanding dramas that are performed by Shanglu school are as followed: *Wang Shi Peng*, *Wang Kui*, *Liu Wen Liang*, *Zhu Wen Encounters Ghost*, *Zhu Shuo Chang*, most of which are stories about vicissitudes of life between a husband and wife per-

formed in an literarily simple and unsophisticated style. Well-
known dramas that are put on stage by Xianan school are Liu Da
Beng, Lu Meng Zheng, Zheng Yuan He and Shu Qing, most of
which satirize the feudalism and part of which are on legal cases
with rough and vulgar librettos and rather bright and straightforward ways of performance. The famous traditional dramas by Xiao Liyuan school are *Chen San and Lady Wu*, *Guo Hua*, *Dong
Yong*, *Jiang Shi Long and Hang Guo Hua*. These plays mostly
have vigorous structures, elegant librettos, accurate drawings of
the innermost feelings, gentle performing styles with singing and
dancing. The music of Liyuan opera is composed of South music,
Longchui, Shiyin and part of Chao tone. Its aria structure is
based on the nominated tune system. The nominated tunes of
Shanglu school are rather powerful, simple and sorrowful while
the Xianan school is more bright, straightforward and humorous, and Little Liyuan is comparatively more elegant, fine and
lingering. The role professions adopt the old system of the south
opera. Little Liyuan has sheng, dan, jing, the ugly, tie, wai and
mo with both Shanglu and Xinan schools having senior dan and
secondary dan. The performance is executed in a fine and elegant
way with strict rules and precise order demanding proscenium
effects in terms of a period of singing with a set of steps; hands
raising to no higher than the eyebrow, hands stretching from the
bellybutton, and hands cupping to make an obeisance to no higher than the lower part of chin and advance in three steps and
move back in three steps, arrive at the front of the platform in
three steps.

Gaojia opera is popular in the area the South Fujian dialect is

spoken, originated from the folk street dress-up parade in
Quanzhou area in the Ming Dynasty. At first it only performed
the story of Songjiang, a hero in the novel *Biographies in the
Watershed* and so was called "Songjiang opera". In the middle of
the Qing Dynasty, Songjiang and Hexing Theatrical Troupes in
Lindou Village of Nanan interacted and accepted each other
breaking through the original performing framework. At the
same time, it received influence of Yiyang tone, Hui tone, Kun
tone, Shiping tone and later Beijing opera. Throughout a concurrently absorption and accumulation, the Gaojia opera came into
being as we see today. There are about six hundred traditional
dramas that performed by Gaojia opera, most of which come
from the stories in puppetry, hop-pocket shows and classic novels, some from folklores. The noted plays are as the following:
Make a Trouble in Hua Mansion, *Brocade Palindrome*, *Elder
Brother's Wife Zhang lodged a Case to the Emperor*, and the a-
bridged plays such as *Being Promoted Three Ranks in Succession*, *True and False Wang You*, *At the Peach Blossom Ferry*,
Xu Xian Thanks Doctor, *Dreams on Phoenix Coronet*, etc. The
music mostly utilizes the nominated tune system of the South
Music, at the same time, absorbs some of the puppet music and
folk songs. There are all together 200 traditional tunes. The
singing librettos and moving tones mostly sound powerful and
high in spirits, but some graceful and refined. The musical instruments divide into two kinds—gentle music and powerful music with the former including suona (the most important one),
pinxiao, dongxiao, three-strings, two-strings; the latter including bai drum, small drum, tong drum, big and small gongs, big

and small cymbals. The role profession includes sheng, dan, bei, ugly, and zha, and the performance of the female and male ugly are of most characteristic. The male ugly role includes the gentle and the powerful ugly. The gentle ugly includes "long robe ugly" and "short robe ugly"; the powerful ugly includes "master ugly" and "bundled body ugly"; the female ugly includes "madam ugly", "matchmaker ugly", "wife ugly" etc. The performance specializes on elegant body movements, humorous and cheerful and witty facial expressions.

Xiang opera is also referred to as "singer's opera", popular in Zhangzhou and other south of Fujian areas. In the later Ming and early Qing periods, with Taiwan recovered by Zheng Chenggong, folk music such as Jin songs and Chegulong of Zhangzhou area was introduced into Taiwan and infiltrated into the local folk arts and, after absorbing the elements of other local operas, gradually evolved a new opera— singer's opera. In 1928, Taiwan Sanlexuan theatrical troupe visited Zhangzhou and Xiamen and some other places in the South Fujian and was warmly welcomed by local people. So it developed very rapidly in the native South Fujian. Xiang opera possesses four hundred traditional dramas. Most of the plays take stories from folklores, fables, legal cases, legends and historical novels such as *Shanbo and Yingtai*, *Burning Building*, *Anan Looking for Mother*, *Notes on Grocery*, *Li Miao Hui*, and the adopted plays such as *Notes on Demands*, *Three Families' Happiness*, etc. Xiang opera has more singing tones and fewer librettos, the former consists of five tunes: seven-word tune, crying tune, Taiwan mixed tune, inland mixed tune and tunes of folk songs and other operas. The musical instruments are divided for gentle dramas and powerful dramas. Instruments for gentle dramas involve tong drum, vertical plank, plank drum, wooden fish, small and big cymbals, small and big gongs; instruments for powerful dramas used are yue-kin, Taiwan flute, erhu, suona etc. Role professions usually have sheng, dan, ugly, and jing (male character with powerful and mighty quality); sheng comprising old, young, gentle and powerful shengs; dan comprising green clothes, senior dan; jing comprising the gentle and the powerful big-flower-face and secondary flower-face; the ugly comprising the male and the female, the gentle, the powerful and thoughtless ugly. The performing arts stress on exaggeration and humorous and cheerful languages. As to fingerings, young females raise hand no higher than to the eyebrow, young males raise hand no higher to the belly-button; the eye skill essences require fingers to reach out in the direction of the eyes, the eyes look with the movements of the hand and fingers, and expression come from the eyes, spirits come from the finger and hand movements, etc.

Apart from the above five important operas, less popular local operas in Fujian may as well consist of the following:

1. Bamboo Horse opera. Popular in Changtai, Nanjing, Longhai, Zhangzhou, Xiamen, Tongan, Jinmen, and originated in Hua'an and Zhangpu from the folk dance *Bamboo Horse*, called such as the dancer would perform with bamboo horse fixed to the body.

2. Chao opera. Also referred to as vernacular character opera or Chao tone opera, circulating in Zhaoan, Yunxiao, Dongshan, Pinghe, Zhangzhou, Nanjing and Longyan. It came into

being before the middle of the Ming Dynasty in Chaozhou and
Shantou of Guangdong, and Fujian areas in which Chao dialect is
spoken.

　　3. Big Tone opera. Popular in Sanming, Yong'an, Datian
and Youxi. It is so called because it is performed in big high
voice with big drums and gongs.

　　4. Shiping opera of the South Fujian. Popular in Zhangzhou, Pinghe, Zhangpu, Zhaoan, Yunxiao, and Nanjing areas,it
is also called "big opera" or "old opera" because it is performed
in a large platform with strong lighting and loud drum and gong.

　　5. Clear wordage opera. Popular in Fuqing, Pingtan and
Changle. When first introduced from Zhejiang it was sung in official language so as to be understood by the local people, stress-
ing on clear and easily understood wordings and singings.

　　6. Pingjian opera. Popular in Pingnan, Gutian, Ningde,
Fuan, Minhou and Changle. It is performed in the local dialect
and so gets the name.

　　7. The West Fujian Han opera. Popular in Longyan, Sanming and Youxi, its tune belongs to south and north flipping
tones and thus is called 'thrum', and it is also called 'outside
opera', for its tunes came from operas of other places.

　　8. North Route opera. Popular in the north and east of Fujian, its main musical instruments are long film flute. Also called
'vertical xiao opera'.

　　9. Meilin opera. So called for it was originated from Meilin
Village,Zhukou town of Taining County and is popular in Sanming, Taining Mingxi and Jiangle areas.

　　10. Triangle opera. As the opera only have sheng, dan and

ugly characters, it is also known as "three person opera" popular
in Shaowu, Guangze, Taining, Jianning areas.

11. Small tune opera. Introduced from the east of Jiangxi
and is also called Jiangxi opera that is popular in Youxi, Yongan, Datian, and Sha County areas.

12. Across the Town opera. Evolved from the religious ceremony "thrashing across the whole town to release souls from
purgatory", it is also referred to as monk opera or Taoist opera,
popular in Quanzhou, Jinjiang, Nan'an, Longhai, and Zhangzhou areas.

13. Folk song opera. As it is developed from the folk songs
in the West Fujian, it is popular in the areas of the west of Fujian.

The characteristics of Fujian local operas lie in the following
five aspects.

1. Fujian operas have preserved in China the maximum
number of the South opera dramas and ancient Central Plains
dramas that are literally referred to as the remaining sound of the
South opera and living fossil of the ancient Central Plains operas,
especially Puxian opera and Liyuan opera which have embodied
intimate relationships with the South opera in the traditional dramas, music composition names and role professions. Among the
traditional dramas available, over fifty dramas are similar or almost similar with those that are recorded in *Past Records on the
Song and Yuan* of *Continued Records on the South Wordage*.
Puxian opera has preserved a large quantity of ancient and rare
music composition nomination from the South opera and some of
the names of the music composing system, musical tones and

metres are quite similar with those in the great songs and verses
of the Tang and the Song periods. Puxian opera's performance
and dance also keep traces of the great songs of the Tang and
Song. Liyuan opera not only preserves a large number of drams
of the South opera in the Song and the Yuan periods, but preserves the characteristics of the ancient Tong music and its performing style.

2. The complicated formation of the operas and absorption
of rich nourishment. The reason that Fujian operas have a vague
identification from the outer operas and the native operas lies in
the multitude influences it has experienced, and it is the result of
interaction of various arts and opera. Take the Chao opera as an
example. It seems that Chao opera is a pure alien opera originated in the Chao and Shan area of Guangdong. Nevertheless,
Chao opera in the early period was called 'standard tone opera'
which meant that it was performed in the Central Plains's official
language, a branch of the Song and Yuan south opera. Later it
was affected by the Liyuan opera and used the same instruments
as that of the Liyuan opera. Chao opera's traditional drama
Notes on the Litchi Mirror was written in mixed Chao dialect
spoken in Quanzhou. Besides, the Chao opera had been affected
by the She songs and Zhou dances. In many traditional dramas,
contesting songs of the She minority and the Zhou minority's
dances on the boat can be found.

3. Many kinds of rare operas have been preserved. This is
the result of the geographical occlusion of Fujian's territory.
Just as many theatrical historians believe that Shiping Tone has
extinguished as an absolute opera. But in 1981, they found the

remaining sound of the Shiping tones in two remote small villages: Meiyu of Yangzhong Village in Ningde and Longtang of Xilin Village in Pingnan County.

4. Frequent tour performances in the Southeast Asia. According to *Histories on Fujian Operas*, from the Wangli period of the Ming Dynasty to 1948, over thirty theatrical troupes of Fujian province had been to the Southeast Asia to give more than thirty-five performances in Gaojia opera, the West Fujian Han opera, Puxian opera, Liyuan opera, the Min opera and the Xiang opera. It is rare for provincial operas in the whole nation to have such a long history of going overseas to give performances with such frequent times and large numbers of the theatrical troupes and operas and dramas.

5. Various conventions and habitudes. It is rare to find that there numerous and minor customs and habits to go through at the beginning, in the middle and at the end of a show. Take the West Fujian Han opera as an example, before a performance, there shall be an actor to act as "the emperor of the Tang Dynasty" reading aloud: favorable weather and peaceful nation and safe people. The Chao opera shall perform a " reunion" before the play starts. When a new play is to be put on stage or a newly built canopy is to be put into use, there shall be certain conventions to go through. Xiang opera has a habit of washing the platform whenever it starts to play on a new stage and the washing ceremony is extremely complicated. Puxian opera would show a play *Father Tian Steps onto the Platform*. Some operas particularly shun away certain dates or certain plays or the host's redbags (courtesy award to actors for good performance) with regu-

lations. Every opera has its own safeguard god. For instance, Puxian opera worships Marshal Father Tian; the Big and Small Tones both worship three opera gods—Tian Qing Yuan, Dou Qing Qi and Ge Qing Zhuang. Every opera has it own special trade language and a pithy formula. For instance, Liyuan opera would say "a period of singing to suit a set of performing movements", which requires players to choose movements best to express every line. Those who show excessive movements are referred to as "bad actors who have too many movements and bad creatures who have too many circuitries". As soon as the drum is beating, the actor must start to give performance as army's order is not as important as bet order, and the bet order is not as important as the opera's order, etc.

Fujian operas have commanded many praises for their extraordinary performing arts. Although all of the operas are performed in the local dialects in Fujian for presentation shows, yet they successfully win praises from the audience each time and get award. Even though the audience can not understand the actor's line, they can still enjoy the esthetical beauty from the superb performance. Fabrication is one of the points that are typical for Chinese operas. Body shapes and movements are the main methods to convey fabrication. "Though the actor's body shapes and movements, the actor conveys substantial imagoes of the abstract objects to the audience. There is nothing on the platform, but everything is in the actor's mind" (See also *The National Characteristics of Chinese Ancient Operas* by He Mianshan in *A Guide to Chinese Literature*, second edition in Feb, 1990 Beijing University Publishing House).

Every Fujian opera pays attention to the training of basic skills fastidious about the cooperation between steps, and arms and shoulders. But each opera has particular regards. Take the footwork as an example. Puxain opera has a footwork of moving with three paces, dancing step, swaying step, dragging step, picking step, cloud step. The Min opera has straight step, flat step, quick step, slow step, piling up step, lifting step, sparrow step, alternative step, hurrying step, bumping step, cloud step, feeling step, old step, keen step, turning step, backward step, striving step, arrow bow step, leaping step, lowering step, dividing step, exploring step, gliding step, striding step. Xiang opera has adherent step, quick short step, piling up step, grinding step, kicking step, running step, stumbling step, upstairs step, striding step, bumping step, duck like step, bowing step, hook step, kicking step, lowering step. Meilin opera has marking step, stomping step, stumbling step, jumping step, keeling step, cloud step. Different roles have different usage of footwork. For instance, in Puxian opera, the main footwork that the dan takes is called dancing step, requiring two heels and two keens stand closely to each other and by walk with two toes up and down by turn rubbing forwards constantly in order to show the elegant manner of an ancient lady. The principle footwork that the sheng role takes is called three pace movements, requiring the player to lift up toes slightly when to take steps and to bend first and then unbend when to step on in order to show the refined and sober manner of a gentleman. Again in North Route opera, when a young woman shows exulting mood, golden bird pace is normally taken, i. e. to let the toes fall on the ground and leap forward with body and head cooperating closely and act in a natural and legerity way. When a middle-aged woman shows, certainty and firmness heel step is usually taken with heels step on the ground and lightly move her lotus feet backward and then forward, i. e. to take one step forward and take one step backward or one step forward and three steps backward.

As to the fingerings, every opera has strict regulations. The Min opera has orchid hand, chrysanthemum hand, arc hand, holding-fist hand, upper arm hand, back hand, crying hand, keeping out rain hand, cloud hand, shaking hand, turning upside down hand, pulling on hand, holding hand, pointing hand, blocking hand, enclosed fist hand, spreading palm hand, drawing hand, fluctuating up and down hand. In Bamboo Horse opera, the "pointing hand"requires the right hand to draw a curve line in front of the chest the lower abdomen and then point to the right frontage direction with the palm toward outside and fingers upward, hand raising no higher than the nose, at the same time the left hand is placed at the waist. To do "dividing hand", two hands form a crab structure and turn up and down from both sides; to do "pecking hand", the left hand inserts at the waist, and the right hand poses a Guanyin-gesture drawing to the chest and then point out with force. The functions of each fingering and gesture have strict regulations. For instance, in Liyuan opera, "pointing hand"means to indicate a person or object or direction; "pecking hand" is used to mean shyness, peeking, watching and thinking secretly about a faraway object; clapping hand expresses exultation, admiration and celebration of reunion; lifting hand means to express discredit, surprise or rhetorical questioning or bewilderment; enclosed fist hand shows respecting; dividing hand shows "no", asking a question, or bewilderment.

Fujian operas belong to the local opera, limited by the dialects used. Nevertheless, many regional theatrical troupes have transplanted dramas of the Fujian operas. For example, Puxian drama Chun Cao Rushes into the Hall has been transplanted by more than one hundreds troupes; Gaojia drama Promoted Three Grades in Succession has been transplanted by thirty troupes across the nation. One of the most important reason for this is the superb performing arts. The act Yingchun Leading the Dog from the Puxian drama *Notes on Killing the Dog* shows that slave-girl Yingchun by order of the hostess goes to Mother Wang's home to fetch the dog. The act, having no lines and singing, depends on Yingchun's gesture, stage step, body shape and eye expressions to show the existence of the invisible dog. According to the *History on Fujian Operas and Music*, the performing procedures of this act by Yingchun are arranged as following:

1. Yingchun leads dog with a long arm and a short arm, running along in a circle;

2. the dog runs backward and Yingchun drags three times and pulls three times;

3. Yingchun pulls tightly by the dog cable with short and long arms turning three times in succession to face the dog;

4. The dog is running head-on, and Yingchun jumps to avoid it three times smartly;

5. Yingchun falls to the ground pressing on the dog's cable;

6. Yingchun pets the dog on the head to calm it down;

7. Yingchun is teasing the dog and walks in a small ring;

8. Yingchun throws the dog's rope to the dog's head three times to set it round the dog's head;

9. Yingchun catches the dog by the left hand and heats the dog on the head, the dog so sits down on the ground. Yingchun takes out an oil cake to feed it to the dog;

10. The dog eats the cake, and Yingchun leading the dog along walks in sparrow step happily off the stage.

The whole scenario of leading a dog is thus performed in carefully depicted visualization.

The play *Calls on Relatives Riding on an Ass* of Gaoja drama can serve as another example. Mother-in-law is an old smart farmer, who is wigwagging a scourge to drive an ass. The ass jumps forward a step and jumps backward two steps at one scourge. At two scourges, the ass jumps two steps forward and one step backward. At another scourge, the ass suddenly gallops, and after circling two rings, the ass finally calms down. The player uses legs, shoulders, neck, even eyebrow, eye and mouth to perform an existence of an ass that is difficult to rein, an interesting scenario of an impatient people with a patient ass.

Fujian operas even borrow fan and umbrella (various of small and big properties and settings, also generally called Qiemo, a name originated from the Yuan) to the characters and emotions of a part. According to the *History on Fujian Operas and Music*, Out of Puxian drama *Pavilion of One Hundred Flowers*, in the plot of *Present the Sward in One Hundred Flowers*, the sheng and the dan both open fans slowly to the left side to pose a "dark cloud above head" and then both pull apart their position on the stage, opening fans to the left side and to the right side to pose a "double flying fans". Again they close their fans to do a "double lodged fans" with three ups and downs, and then they exchange positions to do "male and female fans" flapping to the left and to the right, and then they go down slowly face to face. Follow that they do "lifting fans three times" and two fans keeping each other at an arm's length flapping like a butterfly dancing lightly to form a fan dancing picture of "flower and fish playing in the river". In the play *Waves of Sun River* of Gaojia opera, the character Wu Shirong, who is a government official childe, reaches out his hand from the curtain and turns and then convolves upside down his fan without showing his appearance, and then covers his face with the fan; he draws the fan to the right side to show half of his face; he draws the fan to the left side to show other half of his face; once more he draws the fan downwards slowly to declare his entire view; then he puts the fan on the shoulder and lolls out his head forward to complete a vivid playboy image. Different opera exercises a different set of fan skills. For example, Xiang opera exercises: to hold fan by one hand, to hold fan in both hands, to dot fan, to turn over fan, to open fan, to hold fan to the cheek, to stare at something with the fan, to cover up embarrassment with the fan, to nip the fan at the back, to place the fan at the waist, to cove fan, to put the fan on the back, to flap butterfly with the fan, to lie fish on the fan, to keep of wind with the fan. etc. Chao opera also pays attention to fan skills requiring every fan work to describe a certain formula. For example, to express excitement or enjoy a landscape, the player uses the right hand fan to hold up the left sleeve and quivers the fan; when to express the discovery of a nearby scenery, the player must use left finger fan in accord with the line; when to show a civility image, the player strikes a pose on the stage with the fan at the back. Now let us take a look at the umbrella work. Liyuan opera has eighteen umbrella branches of skills. For example, in the act Send Winter Clothes in the play Young Woman Meng Jiang, the actions of opening umbrella, supporting the umbrella, propping up the umbrella, applying the umbrella, rising and lowering the umbrella, waving to and fro the umbrella, setting free the umbrella all vividly depict the situation in which the character is struggling in the storm. In the play Gao Wen Ju, the character Wang Yuzheng puts up a sort of frightened and staunch feelings of a lonely traveler by holding umbrella, supporting the umbrella, pausing the umbrella, carrying the umbrella on he shoulder, flapping the umbrella, dragging the umbrella, and discharging the umbrella. In the scenario Asking Chen San to Stay, Chen San angrily wants to go away and the slave-girl Yi Chun tries hard to detain him. Through the scrambling for an umbrella, they show the different psychological states of the two people: Chen San picks up the umbrella and carries it on the shoulder desiring to go away, Yi Chun chases after him and detains the umbrella, each holding one end; Yichun seizes the umbrella and puts it on the ground. Chen San wants to pick it up but Yi Chun puts a foot on the umbrella that then hurts Chen San's hand. Chen San draws back his hand and Yi Chun feels regret. Chen San again picks up and carries the umbrella intending to go but Yi Chun seizes the umbrella. The two hold the umbrella turning round a circle. Finally Chen San seizes back the umbrella, and Yichun steps forwards to grasp the handle of the umbrella and eventually speaks out the reason.

Fujian operas always use body gestures to display void objects so vividly as to lead audience into the real scene. For example, to play a " punting boat" plot, the player shall keep in mind that he is on the boat and the boat is on the river and through his body gestures to show to the audience the invisible boat. (Please also refer to He Mianshan's *Appreciation of the Chinese Operas* in *A Guide to Chinese Readings* published by Chinese Economics Publishing House Feb. 1994) In a Min drama *Fishing Boat and Candlestick*, Yuzheng jumps onto the swaying boat staggering and gingerly. On the boat, Yuzheng's footsteps stagger along and she hits her head on the mat of a boat to show the narrowness and the weakness of the boat in waves. In Bamboo Horse drama *At the Peach Ferry*, the dan player simulates to support the oar with the left hand slightly leaning over the body. When to draw back the oak hands towards the chest, she would put her left foot under the right foot; when the left hand pull the oar, she would put the right foot under the left foot to present the turbulence of the water. To carry the litter, the players shall exercise a series of actions that are remarkably like the true to present the nonexistent litter. In the Liyuan drama *Shang Lu*, Prime minister Wu wants to sit in litter to go to the palace. First of all, the servant lifts up the certain of the litter and the Prime minister lowers two legs as if to sit up in the litter. The servants hoof around swiftly and slowly to simulate the different velocities. The most remarkable episode that is worthy of comments is Asking for Evidence in Puxian drama *Chun Cao Rushes in the Hall*.

The county official lets Chun Cao sit in the litter and he himself goes on foot along with her.   Chun Cao, the county official and the litter carrier adopt respectively mark-time step, double-leap step, double mark-time step, dancing step, striding step, lowering step, take-out step, bumping step to present as vividly as possible the air and movements of characters on climbing a slope, running straight forwards, turning around, paddling water or crossing a channel, etc.   The audience can feel intensively the existence of the litter on the stage.

VI. Paintings

It is principally after the Tang period that records for painters in Fujian are available for research and study.   According to *Records on Paintings and Calligraphies in Fujian* edited and composed by Huang Xifan, who was born in Haiyan of Zhejiang province in the Qing Dynasty, in Fujian there are all together eight hundred and two painters.   Among them, there are four painters in the Tang Dynasty, fifty-two in the Northern Song Dynasty, twenty-four in the Southern Song Dynasty, two in the Jin period, twenty in the Yuan Dynasty, four hundred and eight in the Ming Dynasty, one hundred and eighty-eight in the Qing Dynasty, out of which twenty-four are female, nineteen monks, eighteen Taoists, seven travelers and thirty-five traveling officials.   Huang Xifan had been traveling in Fujian for ten years before he returned to Zhejiang.   He had quoted from three hundred and twenty-seven books and revised his work five times before it was published.   So what it recorded must be reliable.   But the record was finished in the sixth to twelfth year of Jiaqing period

(1801—1807) and therefore painters after that period have not been incorporated. According to related materials, there were about three hundred painters in the Qing Dynasty, a number that almost equals to that of the Ming Dynasty. The distribution of Fujian painters has the following two characters. One is the wide distribution— almost every county was able to produce painters; the other character is that painter colonies only focused in a few counties and cities. The contemporary work *Thesaurus of Chinese Painters* published by China National Lights Publishing House in 1934 has incorporated three hundred and fifty-five Fujian painters. According to its records, the most large painter group is in Putian, almost fifty of them; the second large group of nearly forty persons is in Fuzhou; the third group of about twenty persons is in Jinjiang; smaller groups of around fifteen persons scatter in Jianyang, Shaowu, Zhaoan and Sha County.

The most distinguishing feature of Fujian painters is the amalgamation of the strong points of different schools to break through the old legality and to create something new, which is an outstanding point that is unique in Chinese painters of the past dynasties.

The painters in the Song Dynasty though few in number had brilliant characters. Hui Chong, born in Jianyang is accomplished in flower, bird and landscape. His paintings, known as Hui Chong Small Landscapes, are full of the pastoral sentiments typical in the south parts of the Changjiang River, which forms a painting style that is originated from the southern landscape school but has different interests. It is said that the painter portrays what he has mythically encountered and subtly realized in studies of the Buddhism into the small landscapes that appear especially intelligent, desolate and dreary. In the picture *Stream and Mountain* in a Spring Morning, against the obscure chains of mountains and limpid water flows, a fishing boat is just setting off and flying birds are singing, which brings forth a beautiful scene of a spring morning of the countryside in the south part of the Changjiang River. The composition of the picture employs plane-even method that can best describe mountains and forest stretching unevenly and stream and land link together. Chen Rong, born in Futang, is good at (today's Fuqing) drawing dragons in whole or in part, a head or a claw, in such a vague manner that they are indescribable. In his *Cloudy Dragon*, the huge dragon circles from the top to bottom and settles in the middle of the picture with its head holding high, two eyes staring in shock and sharp claws raising to snatch. Surrounding it are rolling clouds in a vast obscured background that visualizes a dragon which seems to be able to gulp the world and shake the earth. At right lower corner of the picture, he inscribes a four-line poem. So drawing, poetry and inscription, the three can be ranked as the masterpiece of perfection. The three-in-one-work technique was started by the literati of the Southern Song Dynasty in their pictures but very few in number. Che Rong must have been the pioneer of the Yuan Dynasty and later generations.

The most famous painter in the Yuan Dynasty in Fujian is Zheng Shixiao, who was born in Lianjiang but came to the Yuan with the Southern Song. After that, he retired at home without doing official work. His work *Black Orchid* presented sparse and dreary flowers and left without soil implicating that his homeland

was invaded and trampled by the outsiders and that the orchid
was not willing to live on the land. The shot-stem and small-pis-
til orchid in strong ink stretches bravely and firmly to show its
vigor and elegance. This kind of rootless orchid which did not
grow from the ground and has no root was a creation and later
becomes a painting genre popular in Fujian till the end of the
Qing Dynasty.

In the Ming Dynasty, many Fujian painters enrich Chinese
painting treasury with their innovations. Bian Jingzhao from Sha
County was skillful at drawing birds and flowers and fruits. He
followed teachers of the Southern Song who integrated drawing
skills with strong colors and had his own innovation. He paid attention to the characteristics of the appearance and spirit of the
image. His *Bamboo and Crane* presents that beside the stream
and under the jade green bamboo forest two white red-crowned
cranes stayed together leisurely. Their appearance and bearing
looked so lifelike and free. Again in his *Three Friends and Hundred Birds Picture*, he drew that in winter season hundreds of
birds dwelling in the plum, pine and bamboo trees, were flying
and dinging, or sporting or resting, echoing and looking at each
other, all displaying a state of their own. The picture so full of
birds and trees was complicated yet quite in order under the pen-
cil of the painter. This is rarely seen in the Southern Song painting school system. Putian Man Li Zhai assimilates the strong
points of different schools and further innovates his paintings.
His fine and glossy drawings were comparable with that of Guo
Xi; his bold and unconstrained drawings parallel those of Ma
Yuan and Xa Gui. He inherited the Northern and Southern

Songs's academic painting systems and learns from the Yuan's literati and he also devoted his attention to the studies of the techniques of Dai Jin and Wu Wei. He formed his own style finally. His painting Qing Gao Rides on the Carp describes a myth which says that Qing Gao, a Zhao Kingdom Man in the Zhou Dynasty on returning to the water world, says good-bye to his student. Both characters and natural background are carefully and beautifully depicted. Against the surroundings of writhing river, wild tearing winds, trembling mountain and shaking earth, Qinggao was riding on the carp away to become a celestial being. So this is also a beautiful landscape painting. Li Zhai together with Ma Shi and Xa Zi, painters in the early Ming Dynasty painted a *Return and Come* based on Cao Yun Ming's work, of the Eastern Jin period. His other paintings such as *Consoling Solitary Pine Tree and Lingering Beside* It and *Inditing Poems at the River Side* set out an ample and unconventional spiritual ambit that is unique in the early Ming's academic painting systems. Wu Ping, born in Putian, was good at drawing personalities and accomplished in figures of Buddha with various monstrous appearances which was quite different from the precedents, forming a style of his own. Professor James Chahill of Harvard University of the U. S. A. made a comparision of Wu Ping's works with some engravings that were introduced from the west in the early seventeen century and believes that Wu Ping's paintings have been influenced by the western styles—an opinion has some insight. (Please refer to *The Compelling Image* printed by Harverd University in 1982.) The landscape paintings made by Wu Ping reveal an imagined subjective world, a combination of dream and illusion. The natural world is exaggerated and altered in appearance under his pen. In his picture *Celestial's Hill and Eminent Scholars*, there are queer peaks sticking up, clouds and fogs rising, huge rocks surrounding, all of which construct an unreal world that is about to fly up into the sky. The style of his *Almond Trees and Double Birds* is astonishingly tricky for he puts the mandarin ducks that are used to staying in the water onto the trees and the almond trees look odd and primitively simple. He then put signet between a branch of withered leaves, an personal habit that is entirely different from that of the literati of the end of the Ming Dynasty. Zeng Jing, of Jinjiang origin, contributes to the portraiture in a unique way. He breaks through the old standards and invents new ways of manifestation. It is said in *Records on Paintings of the Nation* that, "There are two groups of figure paintings. One group pays attention to ink bones. Once the ink structure is done, the colors are applied to. The spirit has already been sent into the ink bones. This is a learning that the Fujian painter Zeng Bochen (Zeng Jing) practices; the other group will ink out the facial features faintly and then use bright colors to strengthen. This is the traditional method that painters in the south part of the Changjiang River employ and Zeng is good at it." The former group is created by Zeng and the latter is the traditional method of portraying. According to *The Poetic History of the Soundless*, whenever Zeng Jing "draws a portrait, he will apply colors to it several times until it is soaked with craftsmanship. It is not by accident that his fame in the artistic circle reaches far and near. This innovation gives portrait a third dimension that is known as concave and protruding method".

There appeared a group of prominent painters in Fujian in the Qing Dynasty. Shangguang Zhou, of Changting origin is an ancient people worthy of remarks. He produced one hundred and twenty figure outline drawings with refined skills. He pioneered another path away from Tang Yin and Chou Ying. In his work *Portrait of Wang Zi'an*, Wang Bo (a famous poet of the Tang Dynast) appeared with elegant features and plump cheeks wearing a long robe with wide sleeves, standing on a piece of large banana leaf, his left hand holding a big fan and his right hand holding a big goblet, two eyes slightly open. It seems that the poet was drunken yet insisted in drinking more. The painter tackles the poet's conceit and addiction to wine and brought forth implicitly a poet who was self-indulgent and self-conceited because of failure in achieving his ambition, and who was still unwilling to be strained unsuccessful career. Hua Yan, born in Shanghang, never drew "a picture that will not mark something new and strange, to show the nature and human interests are in harmony"(Qing Zuyong in *Paintings under Tung Trees*). His "tour de force" has developed a school of his own in the painting forum. In his landscapes, he poured into them an unconventional spirit that makes the pictures look lustrous and clear and bright, and set up an artistic conception that is within sight but unattainable, so pretty but undesirable. His flower and bird paintings unprecedentedly possess an indention without sentiment, reaching an ambit that can "parallel Nantian and surpass the contemporaries"(Qin Zuyong in Paintings under the Tong Trees). He pioneered a new way of producing flower and bird paintings which was initiated by Yun Nantian and later mainly based on Mo Gu method (Bone Structure submerging method) of Xu Chongsi of the Northern Song. In this way he makes a great contribution to the development of the flower and bird painting in the middle of the Qing Dynasty. On his *Picture of Landscape*, there stand protruding rocks on the left, above them there are scant trees and forest; on the right, there lies a long steep slope below which there are piles of stones and stretches of sand; between the slope and the rocks there a winding river running from the distant mountain ranges. Within the limited space, towering severity and smooth stretches, dander and safety integrate so naturally and in such a harmony that no trace of artificial strokes can be seen. His *Snow-Covered Tian Mountain* conceives a scene of a traveler walking with his camel in the snowy mountain path. A lonely wild goose is flying across giving off crows that make the traveler and his camel look up. Large portion of the picture lay domineering snowy mountains and obscure worrying clouds, but the snow and high mountain under the feet of the traveler and the camel do not seem so awe-striking. His *Double Ducks in the Spring Water* conveys a scene in which two ducks sport in the clear spring river. One of the ducks is plunging into the water to seek food with two eyes wide open, the other duck is floating over the water staring peacefully with its head contracted. Two ducks look so lively and vivid in dynamic and stable states. His *Thrush in the Red Leaves*, he draws with dedicate and slender strokes a thrush tweedling in the branches. Clearly the painter is imitating the techniques of dedicate-stroke and true-life ploy from Huang Quan, who was a royal court painter in the Five Dynasties. But Hua Yan had his own emotional appeals of a sort of unconventional ease, fallowness and indifference, and was able to use an unearthly dexterous yet refreshing tact of his own. His *A Bird Dings in the Autumn Trees* conceives that a thrush stays on a branch of autumn tree dinging in a high tone and shows its indifference to the autumn frost. The hard rocks and firm bamboo trees strengthen this heroic ambience. The little bird and the autumn trees are drawn by Mo Gu method giving off a tender, easy and comfortable charm. Huang Shen, born in Ninghua was at his best when drawing figures. At the early ages he drew by gongbi (traditional Chinese realistic painting characterized by fine brushwork and close attention to detail), since middle ages he used wild cursive hand to paint. So he actually combined calligraphy and brushwork and painted and wrote with a thick brush to simplify the complicate and established a rough yet chastening artistic style unique in the painting forum. His *Poetic Thoughts on the Camel's Back* is a Minimal Strokes work, in which he used a dried up brush and ink with charcoal drawing method portrayed a vivid and brief figure of an old poet riding on the camel's back deep in thought, his left hand touching his beard. His *Drunken and Sleepy* piles up figure, calabash, package and iron stick together to form a triangle. The big calabash is drawn with few lines that weakens the solid object; the forehead of the figure is protruding, hair and eyebrow pasted up and dotted with a few brushes look extremely natural and real; the lowered eyelids and big bottle nose are thoroughly typical of the image of the Ironstick Li. His *Su Wu Shepherds Sheep* is done by semi brushwork and semi life-true style of drawing. The old tree with scars all over yet still having a strong life, a world of ice and snow in such a terrible weather serve as a foil for the white-beard and white-eyebrow Su Wu. The layout of the painting is extremely true to life. In his *Old Fisherman*, an old fisherman with a slightly bending back is carrying some alive fish in one hand, and fishing rod in another. The old man seems to request someone to buy his fish. The author's brushwork possessed cursive hand style for his strokes go wild and rough, look natural and unstrained. Details like the figure's clothes plaits tell secretly the painter's sentiments and interests.

The fact that Fujian painters had the courage to innovate new ways of painting can be attributed mainly to three causes.

1. Painters of Fujian origin, mostly had experiences out of hometown. They had a wide horizon and open minds, and therefore were capable of accepting the strong points of all kinds of schools and establishing their own thoughts. As to the outgoing, the painters would take one of the following approaches.

(1) To take part in the imperial selection. For example, when the Ming Dynasty selected painters all over the world to take official positions in the capital, many Fujian painters answered the selection successfully. Bian Jin Zhao from Sha County was elected to serve in the Wu Ying Palace as a painter for the royal court, and got the chance to learn from The South Song academic painting systems and eventually became a master of flower and bird paintings in the early Ming Dynasty. Li Zhai from Putian, was selected for the capital with Dai Jing, Xie Huang, Shi Lui and Zhou Weijing to serve in Tongzhi Renzhi Palace. They learnt from each other's strong points to offset their own

weaknesses. They even had the opportunity to exchange ideas about painting techniques with Xue Zhou, a Japanese monk painter. Zhou Weijing took the test in the court to draw a picture entitled Withered Tree and Jackdaw and received first prize. So he was elected to official positions for Hong Lu Xu Class several times. Zheng Zhaofu from Min County, Shang Guang boda from Shaowu, Zhan Linneng from Pucheng, to name only a few, all were selected to paint in the court.

(2) To travel and tour. The natives of Fujian born to the picturesque scenery south land, on browsing at strange lands, always had special discoveries of their own and manifest the sceneries with a unique point of view. For example, Xu Jingzeng, born in Ouning (today's Jianou) of the Northern Song Dynasty, traveled all over the famed mountains and rivers; Ge Changgeng, born in Minqing, a Taoist monk in the Southern Song period, started to travel all over the famed mountains and rivers at the age of fifteen; Shang Guangzhou once traveled to the east of Guangzhou at his late years.

(3) To assume official positions. To assume governmental official positions outside of hometown enriched the painters' lives and broadened their views. The fact that official career had no regulations to follow deepened their understanding of the matters in life. For example, Chen Rong used to be the director of Guo Zijian (the Imperial College, the highest educational administration in feudal China) and assumed position in Putian; Wuping used to be the director of the work department and later was put into the jail; Zhang Ruitu from Jinjiang in the Ming Dynasty, used to the bachelor of Zhuo Wu Ying Palace and later dismissed

from the office. Their paintings revealed the impressions of that part of lives.

(4) To reside away from hometown. Especially after the Ming Dynasty, many Fujian painters resided at other places, which provided them chances to take in various alimentations. For example, Song Yu of Putian origin in the Ming Dynasty, and Zeng Jing both resided in Jin Lin for a period of time; Hua Yan once lived in Hangzhou and Yangzhou and sold paintings to make a living; Huang Shen also lived in Jin Lin and Yangzhou for some time. Both of them were known as "Two Weirdies" out of the "Eight Weirdies of Yangzhou".

2. It very often happened that a student followed the patterns of the family, his countrymen, teachers and classmates and eventually surpassed his teachers and invented a new style or a school. Among the Fujian painters, many are father and son painters or brother painters. For example, Father and son Lin Xiyi and Lin Yong of Putian origin in the Song Dynasty; brothers Xu Jing and Xu Dezheng of Ouning origin (today's Jianou); Shu Kun and his son Shu Zheng of Jianan origin in the Ming Dynasty; Chen Yuan Zao and his younger brother Chen Yuangun of Putian origin; Zheng Shimin and his son Zheng Wenying of Jiangle origin; Zheng Lin and his son Zheng Huang of Fuqing origin; Zhou Wenjin and his son Zhou Ding of Min County origin, etc. The formation of various genres was from the interchanges and mutual promotions between teachers and students, countrymen. For example, Bian Jinzhao, born in Sha County was the forefather of the flower and bird paintings of the Ming Dynasty. His son Chu Xiang, his son-in-law Zhang Kexing, nephew Yu Chun-

sheng, countryman Deng Wenming, Luo Zhi, Liu Qi and Lu
Chaoyang all learnt from his style and produced an influential
"Sha County Painting Style". Zeng jing (character name Bo Chen
)'s figure paintings were unique in the art circles. He accepted
many apprentices. His disciple Xie Shang, Jin Gusheng, Xu Yi,
Guo Gong, Shen Zhao, Liao Ruoke, Liu Xiangsheng, Zhang Qi,
Zhang Yuan, Sheng Ji, Xu Zhang, to name a few, had inherited
his painting techniques and established a fashionable Bo Chen
School. In Kangxi and Qianlong periods, figure paintings of Bo
Chen Style almost occupied the whole painting forum. In the early Ming Dynasty, Shang Guangzhou, of Changting origin
stressed on the lifelikeness of the figure painting and opened up a
Fujian school painting style. His disciple Huang Shen, not being
strained by his teacher's techniques believed that "It is difficult
to contend with my master's tour de force and his population.
But I am determined to establish a fame of my own. How could I
rank behind the others ?" Shang Guangzhou spoke highly of his
ambition. Between Dao Guang and Xian Feng periods of the Qing
Dynasty, Xie Yingsu and Shen Yiaochi inherited the brushwork
from Shang Guangzhou and other Fujian painters and formulated
a style of Xie Yi painting (freehand brushwork in traditional Chinese painting characterized by vivid expression and bold outline)
which was based on Gong Bi painting (realistic and detailed
brushwork) and featured coldness and simplicity and elegance.
They influenced a dozen of painters in the Fujian painting circles
and were referred to as Zhaoan Painting School or Min School.
Up till now, Lin Shu from Fuzhou, Li Geng from Xianyou, Ma
Zhaolin and Lin Jia from Zhaoan are also influenced by this

school to a great extent.

    3. The circulation of various critics on painting theories. Traditionally various literary and art critical theories had been flourishing in Fujian and the criticism on painting theories had not been in the shade. Fujian painting critical theories involved a wide range of subjects. First, Parts of the criticism are comments on Fujian painters. For example, *Records on Fujian Paintings* edited in the Ming Dynasty and later in the Qing Dynasty by Lin Jiaqin and Lin Fengyi, has commented on many Fujian painters' works exactly and briefly; second, many critics wrote biographies for Fujian painters. For example, in *Records on the Paintings and Calligraphies* edited by Huang Xifan of the Qing Dynasty; third, criticisms on painting science. For example, in *Postcript on Metal and Stone Paintings and Calligraphies in the Retreat Hut* edited by Liang Zhangju, there are precise comments on the painting sceneries; fourth, commentary remarks on both poems and paintings such as in *The Burnt Books—Poetry and Paintings* by Li Zhi who corroborated the poems with the paintings; fifth, comments on the paintings in various corpuses. Many literati had original opinions about paintings. Their view points were collected in their corpuses. Only about the painters in the Song Dynasty, there are collected works by Fujian writers such as *Liang Xi Corpora* by Li Gang, *Return from Lu Chuang* by Zhang Yuangan, *Collected Works of Revered Zhu* by Zhu Xi, *Complete Collection of Mr. Hou Chun* by Liu Ke Zhuang, *Continued Collection of Bamboo Stream Room* by Lin Xiyi, *Collection of Anya Hall* by Chen Lu, *Collection of Autumn Sounds* by Huang Zhencheng.

Chapter Five
Arts and Crafts

I. New Year Pictures

Apart from the Chinese paintings that are mounted in scrolls and volumes, there is a kind of New Year painting that is made by another form of craftwork. The New Year paintings are mainly used at the Spring Festival for marriage ceremony or sometimes for Taoist activities. People put up the paintings directly on the earthen walls or wooden windows, doors or closets. Quanzhou, Zhangzhou, Fuan, Fuding are the important places that can produce New Year paintings made by a xylograph. First of all, soak into the water woods of pear, megranate, etc. for one month before being carved. And then dry up and cut them into pieces of slabs, on which sheets of manuscript papers are pasted to dry up. When they are dry thoroughly, use some straws to abrade the papers to be thinner until the lines of the picture can be seen clearly from the back face, and then carve the lines on the paper with a knife. The subject matters presented by

the New Year paintings in Fujian can be numerous almost involving all aspects of daily life like pictures of some divinity to be
put on the doors, of historical dramas, of persuading goodness
and satirizing the world, on man ploughing up the field and
woman weaving the cloth, about celebrating birth of a baby or
collecting property into the household, etc.

Paintings made in Zhangzhou are the most popular ones for
their unusual qualities of the roughness of the northern New
Year paintings and the elegance of the paintings made in Jiangsu.
The pictures look simple and vigorous in concisely contrasting
colors. As to the lines, thin and thick lines are used according to
the contents and color effect; Dou Ban Printing Method (the old
name for the woodcut watercolor block printing method; because
of composing of several blocks looking like Dou Ding, a kind of
food) is used to print colors first and to print outlines later. And
according to the seasonal demands, red colored and dark colored
pictures are produced to meet the happy events or bereavements.
Zhangzhou's New Year picture production pays attention to the
main features of the figure's identity and is capable of producing
single picture or multiple pictures of stories about a person or a
folktale. For example, eight-sheet New Year's pictures on *Former Part Story of the Meng Jiangnu*, present the stories of
Meng's marriage with her husband, her husband being caught
and her looking for her husband through a great deal of hardship
in passionate and diversifying tableaus. In the picture which the
husband is captured away, five figures show different expressions: Meng Jiangnu is running after him from home with both
arms reaching out as if she would drag back the fastened hus-

band, looking worried and miserable. Her husband looking backwards, two hand in wooden bondage expressing profound reluctance to leave. One of the servant soldier is pulling the wooden bondage by one hand and holding a club in the other looking back at Meng as if he were frightened by Meng's crying. The county official is holding up an order banner to defend any kind of disobedience. The other servant soldier is leading the horse in the distance looking at Meng too as if he were moved by the woman's cry. Zhangzhou is good at getting rid of the stale and bringing forth the fresh in the development of traditional subject matters. For example, *Mouse Having a Wife* is a familiar theme in Chinese New Year's pictures, but Zhangzhou's *Mouse Having a Wife* displays another flavor. In the picture, there are mice holding fish, holding chicken, or blowing trumpet, playing flute, beating drums with legs, or carrying litter, or showing the way with a ceremonial stick. Every mouse looks sharp-cheeked and thin-legged in such a naive way that nobody is able to hold back laughter. To be more amusing, the bridegroom is not riding on a horse. Instead, he is going on foot, wearing an official hat of the Qing Dynasty and holding a fan in hand. He is too anxious to wait to look back at the bride frequently. The bride is sitting in the litter and peeping in the bridegroom's direction, appearing very lovely.

Quanzhou's New Year's pictures always relate to country folk-customs. For example, Cumulating Capitals printed in Li Fu Ji Hall, is overprinted in black, green, yellow and red colors. In the middle of the picture, there is a big ancient coin upon which four Chinese characters meaning ' cumulating capitals'are carved. The big coin is held by two boys known as Two Saints of Peace and Union . One is wearing cloud-lined yellow clothes and the other is in green flower brocade. Whoever worships them will be able to return home even if he is thousand miles away from home. As Quanzhou people mostly sail across overseas, they like this kind of picture the best. Again, *Longevity God of Blessing and Fortune* printed in Li Fu Ji Hall, has bright red background and is overprinted in purple, yellow, green, pink colors. In the middle of the picture, a Heaven God holds a ruyi (S-shaped ornamental object, usu. made of jade, formerly a symbol of good luck) in one hand. On his left side, there is the fortune star who is holding a baby in the arms. Two fairies each hold a blocking fan standing on both sides of them. On the right part of the picture, is the Longevity God who holds a peach. In front, there is the boy uplifting an embroidery ball and wearing a purple crown on his head. The whole picture brings forth an auspicious and harmonious and pleasurable impression, therefore is quite popular among the overseas chinese in the Southeast Asia. Fuding's New Year's pictures also have a unique style. For example, *Eight Hammers Make a Loud Noise in Zhuxain Town* is adopted from *Biography of Yue Fei*. In the picture, Yue Yun, He Yuanqing, Di Lei and Yan Zhengfang each have a double-hammer to fight Lu Wenlong who is holding two guns in both hands, and Jin Wushu wears a summer hat at the rear watching the battle. In clearance, Wang Zuo shows up a half of his face. On the outer edge of the entire picture there prints a beauty, wearing flower on head reclines over a musical instrument table. Behind her there is some green bonsai in flourishing. Beauty and fighters in the same picture are rarely seen in other New Year's pictures. Fuding's New Year's picture Visit Grave is adopted from the folklore that tells that Liu Lujing succeeded in the imperial examination and did not return to hometown, so his wife thought he was dead and went to visit his grave to cherish the memory of him. After Liu assumed a county administrator and on his way back home, he found a woman in mourning dress crying at a grave. At inquiry, he found that the woman was his wife. In the picture, Liu Lujing is wearing official robe and hat but his wife is wearing a loose-front dark-colored clothes and a plain piece of cloth over forehead, holding a candle line and plate in both hands for memorial ceremony. Behind them, there are two governmental servants. The picture beautifully made, must be the only excellent copy extant of the New Year's pictures.

Ⅱ. Stone Carving

The most famous stone carvings in Fujian are Huian stone carving and Shoushan stone carving. Huian stone carving includes architectural ornaments, figures, animals and appliances. The skillful works by Huian stone carving craftsmen can be seen in many places at home and abroad: the ornamental columns of the Nanjing Sun Yat-sen Mausoleum, the eight pairs of dragon columns in Taiwan Longshan Temple, the ornamental stone carvings in Southern Putuo of Xiamen, the figure carvings in Chen Jageng cemetery in Jimei, the stylobates in the People's Great Hall of Beijing, the temple of Ying Lin mountain of Taiwan and the five hundred arhats, the grave garden of the Japanese monk Jiangzhen, the large fresco of Bai Lake, the Obliga-

tion Repaying Tower in Xi Chan Temple of Fuzhou, the highest
tower of this kind in China, to name only a few. Huian stone
carvings can be divided into four kinds. 1. Round carvings. To
make a round carving is to empty the stone from the upper and
the bottom, from left and right sides, and the leftovers of the
stone are carved into accessory ornaments such as the rolling
stone pearl kept in the so called South Lion's mouth, and the
hundreds of Japanese stone lanterns in various size and shapes.
Among the round carvings, there are many works that might ac-
claim as the peak of perfection. For example, the stone carving
Wrestle between Eagle and Snake displays that the eagle's sharp
claws vice the waist of the snake, and the leg of the eagle is en-
twined by the lower part of the snake, two heads confronting
each other. It seems that the sharp claws have the strength of
lifting up iron and the tongue is disgorging fire in a cloud floating
high up in the sky. 2. Relievos. To make a relievo is to carve the
surface of stone slate with special care to make the design pro-
trude with three dimensions. Relievos are mostly used as ornaments in constructions like doors, windows, poles and metope of
towers. The construction carvings in Jimei Ao Garden in Xiamen
are all relievo skill works: all kinds of flowers, trees, flying
birds, insects, fish, animals, landscapes and historical figures,
etc. displaying in their own stances and looking true to life. The
famous work *Sword Dance* depicts an ancient girl dancing lightly
with a sword. The sharp sword thrusting from the air is about
half of *Chi* (a Chinese unit of length, one chi is equal to 1. 0936
ft.) in length and a half of a centimeter, and attached to the
stem of the sword is a tassel with two bowknots flying in the air.

3. Sunken carvings. To make a sunken carving is to carve the design out of a slate and the picture is sunken in the slate with clear outlines. The works are mostly letters, flower patterns that are used as steles, partial decorations in architecture. The famous "small door screens of four seasons" are carved on four bluestones which are connected together with patterns of flowers in blossom in different seasons and letters, looking small and exquisite. 4. Image carvings. That is to cut the blue stone into slates of one centimeter in thickness and polish the slates. Put a film of ash on the polished slates to turn them into black color. And then carve the slates with different sizes of sharp steel needles carefully. The picture is reflected out by the points of the needles of different density and depth. The needled pictures can reproduce the true to life effect of photography and the proper shades of ink stroke characterized by Chinese painting. They can also present very well the artistic conception of the original work. For example, works like the grand Great Wall, the unsophisticated Quanzhou East and West Towers, the rushing horses by Xu Beihong, prawns of Qi Baishi appear lifelike and attractive. Shoushan stone carving is named after Shou Mountain in the suburb of Fuzhou city from which the stone carving materials are taken. The stone nature of Shou Mountain is grease and smooth in multitude colors of bright red, purple, green, yellow, black, and white. There are some stones contain all the colors. Shoushan stone carvings started long before one thousand five hundred years ago. *The Lying Pig* of Shoushan stone carving unearthed in a Southern Dynasty tomb looks vivid to life by simple and plain carving skills. People in the Tang Dynasty had used

stone carved figures of Buddha, incense burners, pray beads as
religious articles. In the Song Dynasty, the government organized workshops to produce various tomb figures from the Shoushan stone in order to provide the aristocrats with burial articles.
Between the Yuan and the Ming Dynasty, handicrafts men of the
stone carvings created a unique signet carving technique. To the
Qing Dynasty, Shoushan carving was in full flourish with all
kinds of artistic schools competing for uniqueness and gorgeous-
ness. Some works make a feature of purity and simplicity, and
others of refinement and exquisiteness. The most exquisite
works ere collected by the royal court. In the museum of the
Summer Palace of Beijing, the famous *Nine Dragon Signet* is
carved with many old fashioned patterns and nine dragons of different bearings and varieties on the upper part of the signet—Li
dragon, Yellow dragon, Hang dragon, Zhu dragon, Pan drag-
on, Shrimp dragon, Pincers dragon, Kui dragon. Shoushan
stone carvings fall into five kinds: round carving, relievo carv-
ing, engraving carving, filmy carving, and signet button carv-
ing. The carving techniques can be used to make thousands of
exhibits like flower and fruit, figure and animal, ancient beast,
landscape, and articles for daily usage like seal, stationery,
smoking set and jardinière. Among them, the most famous carving decorations based on themes that are typical of South of Fujian province are lichi, snow-white lotus root, Buddha's hand,
crab basket, grape. The artistic value of Shoushan stone carving
is characterized by its stone theory which pursues so-called
"sculpture in accordance to the potential of the stone" or "ten
percent of watching the stone is more important than ninety per-

cent of labor at the stone", i. e. to decide a proper carving theme according to the actual quality, veins, shape and color of the stone. *The Chicken Paying Court to His Mate* displayed in the Fujian Hall of the People's Great Hall in Beijing is an example of making use of the red colored part of the stone to carve out a cock which is standing high up on the bamboo cage with its two wings drooping and paying court to the hen which is uneasy in the cage with young chickens looking for foods around her. The work looks remarkably like the true and overflows strong artistic appeal and interest.

Ⅲ. Woodcarving

Fujian teems with forest and woods. Folk woodcarving is very popular. It first originated from architectural decoration, the figure of god and furniture ornament. The unusual woodcarving curiosa *Happy Dancers Flying to the Sky* is a series of twenty-four figure carvings attached to the surface of arch in Kai Yuan Temple in Quanzhou. Many dwelling houses have exquisite carving ornaments of some story patterns decorated on the outer girders, brackets, rafters, door and windows, partition boards. Some appliance is entirely an installation of carving pieces such as the imperial litter made in Yongchun. The litter is an assembly of carvings of figures, animals etc. , dexterously combined and connected together by relievos as surface with proper spacing and density in accordance to the actual conditions. The carvings decorated on beds popular in the East Fujian are usually based on the drama stories. On each of the arks installed above a bed there engraved a picture. Some ancient beds have as many as thirty

pieces of woodcarvings about a drama or a story in succession.
The woodcarving in Fujian gradually develops into an independent woodcarving craftwork using specific woods like longan
wood. Longan wood is one of the principal wood materials for its
comparatively fragile quality, fine and dense texture that are
suitable for carving. The longan wood carvings will be washed in
soap and alum water to be deprived of resin. After dried up,
they are dyed in colors of orange yellow, bronze, longan kernel
or lichi kernel. And then covered with a lay of paint, they will
never fade. Besides, camphor wood, Nan wood, rosewood, fir
are also can be used as carving materials. Towards the end of the
Ming Dynasty and early Qing Dynasty, a Changle Man surnamed
Kong utilized old aged, stream water soaked and weather eroded
tree roots of all kinds of weird shapes to create natural root carving art works. Since then, root carving techniques developed
gradually. Handicraft men create from the tree roots various
conceptive themes depending upon the natural scars, lines, con-
caves and protrusions, bends and veins. Artistically they would
pursue a harmony of nature and human work with skillful cuts
and charming carves. And paint over the works an original paint
so as to present an ancient, simple, modest verve. In the Qing
Dynasty, there were mainly three schools of woodcarving in
Fuzhou: The first school is Da Ban Village school represented by
the handicrafts man Chen Tianci in Da Ban Village and consisted
of other thirty persons mostly engaged in carvings of Maitreya
figures, the eighteen arhats, the Eight Immortals, Kwan-yin,
official women, animals etc. The second school is Yanta school
represented by Wang Qingqing from Yanta Village, mainly un-

dertaking the carvings of flower patterns and relievos designs used on the lacquer works. The third school is Xiang Yuan Village school represented by Ke Qingyuan who was accomplished in inventing insects and flowers or compotes etc. The grand old handicrafts man Ke Shiren was accomplished in Buddha figures and was skillful at employing important traditional techniques to invent works from box wood, rosewood. Chen Wangdao had made progress in the carvings of figure's eyebrow, eyes, noses, hands and legs and trappings.

IV. Puppetry

The essence of the puppetry in Fujian is the heads of puppets which serve as the properties of the stage and are exquisite folk craftworks that can be displayed on the desk. The puppet heads made in Fujian mainly are cataloged into three types: the heads that are adopted from the facial make-ups of the Liyuan opera of Quanzhou; the Shima puppet heads that are adopted from the facial make-ups of the Beijing opera; the Zhangzhou puppet heads that are adopted from the Hakka Tone's facial make-ups. Out of the three, the Quanzhou puppet heads are the most distinguished ones. The processing arts and crafts of the Quanzhou puppet heads are very complicated. First, cut the camphor wood into wooden block in the size of a puppet head. And draw a line in the middle of the block in order to carve out the cheeks of the head and decide the positions of the five facial features. Then back up a sheet of cotton paper over the white figure head, polish it, paint colors on the features and cover a lay of wax. The final step is to fix on the puppet head hair and beard. The early well-known puppets were made by a technician who named his products as Xi Lai Yi and by Huang Liang Shi and Huang Cai Shi who named their products as Zhou Mian Hao. Their puppets looked true to life and had strong characters typical of the nation's facial composition and make-ups. The contemporary famous puppet maker Jiang Jiazou lives in Beimeng Huayuantou of Quanzhou city, whose puppets are referred to as Hua Yuan Tou puppets. Jiang Jazou has made more than ten thousand puppets and invented more than two hundred kinds of puppets in different characters. His works contain the presentation skills of the folk wooden god figure making and the theatrical facial make-ups and adsorb the strong points of both Xi Lai Yi and Zhou Mian Hao and subtly integrate the techniques of carvings with techniques of painting. He often exaggerates and deforms the figures with skills of painting to serve a foil to the representation of the figure's characters. For example, the head of the No. One harlequin, his forehead occupies the thrice of the lower part of its face. The upper part of the forehead is painted with vermeil and on the lower part of the forehead there drawn two upward-flying rolling round black eyeballs to contrast the white and eyebrows and thick beard, an image of a devil. Jiang Jazou is good at inventing personae with thumbprints. He believes that the smile of the matchmaker is a forced one for her heart is full of misery. So the mouth of the matchmaker can be opened and closed, and on the corner of the mouth there is a long hair beauty spot. And above the thin face, there are a few wrinkles around the eyes and two faint pastes over the temples. This matchmaker is a character that is known as being adept in scheming and playing to the scores all day long and is apt to induce both criticism and sympathy. The White-Wide Forehead created by Jiang Jazou has on the forehead four wrinkles which are so thick and so long that they reach the lips, otherwise they might not have conveyed the spirits of the image of a benevolent and wise gentleman who has thin eyes, big nose, silver-white and long eyebrows flowing over the face. Most of harlequins are given slanting eyes, black foreheads and sometimes no mouth and are recognized as foxy or dumpish roles at first sight. As required by the plot of a puppet show, he makes all sorts of characters no matter they are faithful or wicked, and even puppets that can move their eyeballs up and down, left and right, either can their mouths, noses and tongues.

V. Paper-Cut

Paper-cut in Fujian is very popular as every place has the habitude of paper cutting, a folk art that is fond of by rural women. Paper-cut has its wide usages: as window decorations, wall decorations, and front door decorations during festivals and happy decorations put on the dowries, sacrifice decorations at a festival for memory and worship of the ancestors and the gods, birthday decorations to show respect to the eldership, etc. The techniques are manifold: flat-lien, symmetry, multi-folded and network patterns of cutting are mostly utilized. In Fuijan, Quanzhou, Zhangpu, Zherong and Pucheng are places that paper-cut are relatively prevalent.

Quanzhou's paper-cut, as it is said, began in the Tang Dynasty and flourished in the Song Dynasty. During the Spring

Festival, cutting of "red letters" like blessing symbols and
Changjin. The blessing symbols are composed of five pieces in a
set putting on the lintels of a hall, each piece being four inches
wide and six to seven inches long drawn with kylins, carps jumping to the dragon's gateway or simply a Chinese charater Happiness or Longevity, and further around drawn with age-old coin
designs around the patterns; The Changjin paper-cuts are usually
put on the upper lintels of a living room, each piece two inches
wide and six inches long drawn with pied magpies on the plum
branches or abundant five kinds of corns; some paper-cuts are
used as common lamp decorations. Zhangzhou's paper-cuts came
down to the folk as early as in the Northern Song Dynasty.
There are historical records that say, "The lamps are lighted on
the New Year's Eve and people cut paper into decorations with
all kinds of skills. " Zhangzhou's paper-cuts are known as scissor
flowers. Patterns like Mandarin ducks, peony, fish and flowers,
bats and deer etc. to make up an auspicious decoration that is to
be put on shoes, on the vest and on cloth wearing over the pigs.
There are paper-cuts of other themes that are based on folklore,
drama, and historical personae and are very popular on the people for they are full of strong sense of life and countryside sentiments. The most outstanding features of these paper-cuts are of
nicety and elegance in style. To present tiny objects like peacock's feathers, leaves of peony, needles of the pine tree or
scares of dragon, and hairs of animals, arranging cutting skill is
utilized. Zherong's paper cutting integrates several kinds of cutting skills and usually exaggerates the objects like a shrimp, a
piece of fish, a flower and a leaf in a rather rough and abstract

and free style. For example, the face-to-face folding and then the multi-folding skills are used in order to make a "hoof enclosing flowers": first to cut a pig-hoof shape outline and cut the inside into a several flower patterns. Paper-cuts inwrought with embroidery for hat and shoe decorations are the most commonly seen. Pucheng's paper-cuts also have many years of history. Liang Zhangju of the Qing Dynasty, once was a lecturer giving lectures in Nanpu College of Pucheng. He described in his book *Trivialities after Returning to Farmland* about the paper-cutting in Pucheng, "I often find on the presents of fruits people sent to each other, no matter the box is big or small, there are a piece of red paper in round shape or square shape that is cut out with four characters something like longevity and prosperity, things-go-as-one-wishes". At the houses that have a wedding ceremony, the red paper cuts are used frequently. Pucheng's paper-cuts have a large variety of sizes and shapes, either big or small, either long or diamond shape. Paper-cuts often uniquely contain patterns and the patterns contain characters.

VI. Pottery and Porcelain

Fujian has a long history of making pottery. Ever since the Shang and Zhou Dynasties, the ancestors of Fujian began to burn primitive celadon. From the primitive celadon unearthed from the Han city in Chongan we find that from the Warring Times to the Qin Dynasty, the ancient Fujian Min Yue kingdom had certain ability to burn pottery. The rather exquisite porcelain discovered in the tombs of aristocrats before the Song Dynasty within Fujian boundary also reflect the high level of pottery mak-

ing skills from the Wei, the Jin, the Southern and Northern Dynasties to the Sui, the Tang and the Five Dynasties periods. In
the Song, Yuan, Ming and Qing periods, Fujian porcelains were
well known across the nation as well as over the world, and became the curiosities of the collectors. Fujian ceramic industry developed from the native land, so no matter what kind of pottery
it is —primitive pottery, celadon, green and whit porcelain,
black and white porcelain, pure white porcelain or green patterned porcelain, it possesses the local characters of Fujian. During the long course of development with the influence of manufacturing techniques of other provinces, Fujian ceramic industry
became increasingly mature. Underground ancient kilns scattered
all over the province, and the quantity of the kiln may rank the
first place in the nation.

The most representative of Fujian pottery may be the black
ceramic glazed porcelains made in Jianyang Shuiji Kiln of the
Song Dynasty, the white ceramic glazed porcelains made in Dehua kiln in the Ming and the Qing periods, the green patterned
ceramic wares made in Dehua kiln, Anxi kiln and Pinghe kilns in
the Ming and the Qing Dynasties.

The black ceramic glazed porcelains made in Jianyang Shuiji
kiln in the Song Dynasty had wonderfully beautiful colors. The
ceramic colors display in six kinds ranging from pure black ceramic glaze to rabbit hair ceramic glaze, partridge feather spot
glaze, oil dropping glaze, shining glaze and the mixed colored
glaze, the disposition of which gave out a feel of mild and smooth
and glittering nature. The primary black glaze porcelain is a
small bowl with larger mouth and smaller bottom, looking like a

filler, commonly called Jian Calix. There are two types of this calyx, one with open mouth, the other with narrow mouth, the former one produced in the majority. Its clean and smooth black glaze emitting tiny flashes silvery color like the hare hairs resulting in the name Hare Hair Calix. The other quality of Jian Calix is characterized by the hairy veins under the glaze which is made from the acid ceramic glazing material as a decoration. As the Jian kiln burns all of the pottery wares upside down in the kiln, the glaze water drops so as to form a slighter color around the mouth of the wares. If slanting pitch is different, the velocity of dropping of glaze water is different. The fast dropping makes the tenuous hairy veins while the slow dropping makes thicker veins. Jian calix's mouth edge is comparatively thin, and its body is comparatively thick and heavy. From its belly to the bottom, the thickest part can be as thick as one centimeter. Some have characters like "presented calyx" or "imperial offerings", etc. on the bottoms. Jian calyxes once were brought to Japan as treasure. At present, the shining glazed ceramic bowl that is collected in a Tokyo Jing Tang Library as Japan's national treasure, is of 6.8 cm in height and 12 cm in caliber with a thick and heavy structure, and a black and shining glazed appearance. Inside the bowl, on the black bottom, there are many big and small oil-drop spots surrounding which look like moving clouds or dispersing blue crystals. The whole bowl is shining faintly like the stars twinkling in the dark shy. Some spots radiate faint radiant rays.

During the Yuan and the Ming periods, white glazed porcelains produced in Dehua kiln and known as Jian White, look moistening bright and feel smoothly solid, so purely white that there appears a faint yellow color, so purely white and flawless that they feel like silk. The embryo and the glaze integrate into one mass that is as bright as crystal, meaningfully elegant and full of aftertaste, needless of any colors or decorations. Under the lights, the semi-transparent porcelain emitting a milk yellow or tooth-like red is called "butter white", "ivory white" or "Chinese white", which are representative works of Chinese white porcelains. The most remarkable products from this porcelain are religious statues such as Kwan-yin, Sakyamuni, Maitreya, etc. Their facial depiction is usually elaborate, the lines of their clothes are deep and clear-cut, which can very well present the characters of the religious figures. There are other products like plum blossom cup, the Eight Immortals cup, incense burner that imitating ancient bronze, vase and stationery, etc. The ivory white Kwan-yin made from low aluminium and high silicon has a special aesthetic appeal of tranquility and civility. The Kwan-yin statue that is made by He Chaozong of the Ming Dynasty and is now collected in Guangdong Museum is 22.5 cm high. She holds a book in the left hand and leans over a rock optionally with two eyes slightly closed and head appreciably bowing over, looking extremely kind. Her hair is done highly upon the head, and her plain long robe and sleeves are flowing over the left set leg. Her right leg is erectly set, and her hands are placing on the right keen. The lines of her clothes scatter all over so fluently and naturally. *Kwan-yin Across the Ocean* now collected in Haijiao Museum of Quanzhou is also made by He Chaozong. The statue is 46 cm high, wearing a hair kink over head, and a shawl over shoulders with clothing in dark color and ribbon in knot. Her two arms hold up in the sleeves, one bear foot stepping on lotus flower, the other foot covered up by splashing water, eye's lips drooping, mouth closed tightly with a faint smile at the corner of the mouth. *One Hundred Pictures of Ancient Chinese Statues* published by People's Arts Publishing House in 1980 collects a picture of a statue of Kwan-yin Sitting on a Rock, which is now collected by a foreign collector. The statue was made in Dehua in the Ming Dynasty. Kwan-yin wears a white robe sitting on a rock, her left elbow supports her body on the rock, two arms holding each other, her head bowing slightly forwards, two closed eyes engaged in deep thought. Her plumy and beautiful face and closed eyes look so civil, quiet and dignified. The author conveys successfully the tender and virtuous personalities of Kwan-yin.

During the Ming and Qing Dynasties, Fujian's green pattern pottery were mainly produced in Dehua and Anxi kilns. Dehua kiln produced bowls, plates, cups, dishes, burners and jars with the green patterned porcelain whose embryo structure is solidly white and fine, green patterns containing dark blue striae with quietly elegant or strongly bright glaze. There are many themes for creation: landscape, persona, flower, bird, and fish, etc. The depictions of line decorations go gracefully, freely with preferable force. The composition of pictures is concise and terse. The painting style is simple and plain, with the patterns vivid and brisk, full of strong and honest life tang. Fujian Museum collects a piece of landscape porcelain vase made in Dehua kiln in the Qing Dynasty. On the vase, there are very tall ancient trees and a small building subsiding in a corner of the mountains, and more mountain ranges and peaks stretch into the far background beyond. The personality themes are also dealt with quite elaborately and vividly. Fujian Museum has collected a green pattern porcelain plate of landscape and figure made in Dehua kiln in the Qing Dynasty. The young lady's right arm and palm supports under her jaw deep in thought, eyes looking forward as if she were expecting something. A close slave girl holds a musical instrument with both hands turning around and looking at her. The poplars and willows stand along the lakeshore leaning together in the wind. In the middle of the lake, on the peninsula, stands an exquisite pagoda. Beyond there are mountains and peaks stand erecting in the drifts of clouds. Anxi kiln usually produces green patterned bowls, boxes, plates, and dishes. The structure of the bowls is modeled into chrysanthemum petals or imprinted with petals patterns; inside the bowl printed with twined twigs and flowers. The structure of the box is of various sizes and shapes that are imprinted with patterns outside or under the bottom side. The veins of the modeled patterns are thicker than that of the like products made in Dehua, but the colors of the green porcelains are usually darker so as to appear black under the glaze. The hackneyed patterns are vegetation like morning glory, chrysanthemum, orchid, bamboo, plum and pine, etc. Landscapes are about streams and hills, boats and oars, trees and stones with a few Chinese characters like Happiness, Fortune, Longevity.

The prosperity of Fujian ceramics industry connected with the following aspects apart from the demand of daily life. 1. Advantaged resources. Fujian is rich in mineral resources. The exuberant forests, sufficient fuels and interleaving rivers and streams are convenient for utilization of waterpower, exploration of porcelain clay and transportation. 2. Influence of folk customs. For example, the world-famous 'rabbit hair calyx'made in Jianyang is related with the recreation custom of 'contest of tea' popular among the scholar—bureaucrats of the Song Dynasty when they indited poems while drinking tea. According to *The Records on Tea* by Cai Xiang of the North Song Dynasty, "The color of tea is white, which ought to be hold by the black calyx. The most suitable holder is the calyx that is made in Jianyang. It is black in color with hairy veins, thick of the embryo, long before getting cool when heated. The like products that are made in other places are all inferior because of the improper color and thickness. Other green or white calyxes are naturally not used in contest of tea. " It is obvious that the contestants think a lot of "rabbit hair calyx" made in Jian kiln. 3. Influence of religions. For example, Quanzhou was known as "the Buddha's South Quan Kingdom", therefore Dehua kiln and Anxi kiln produced a great quantity of the porcelain figures of Buddhism religion. Figure porcelain of Kwan-yin, Buddha, arhat etc. are representatives of traditional products. Only in Dehua kiln, Kwan-yin statue had been produced in 72 kinds of postures with more than 200 different sizes. It may be well said that there were no postures or sizes with their particular traits that could not be available. 4. Needs for foreign trade. Quanzhou was an important commercial harbor of Fujian during the Song and Yuan Dynasties and towards the Wanli period of the Ming Dynasty, Quanzhou was at its floruit as an international trade center in the south of Fujian. At present, many countries of the East Asia and the Southeast Asia have discovered a great deal of Fujian porcelains. Exportation of porcelain in quantity was an important financial source for the people of the ceramic industry, and it had not only met the demand of the foreign markets but also promoted the development of the production of pottery.

Chapter Six
Nationalities

Fujian is a province of multi nationalities with the Han nationality as its principal part. The population of 53 minorities is over 500 thousand accounting for 1.54 percent of the provincial population, which is the highest proportion of the minority population in the East of China. Minorities that have lived in Fujian for generations are She, Hui, Gaoshan, Man and Mongolia. In Fujian, there are fourteen counties which have a minority population of over ten thousand respectively; there are 85 towns which have one thousand minority people respectively; there are 17 nationality villages and 444 minority dwelling administrational villages.

The She minority is a principal component of the Fujian minority people with a total population of 380 thousand which tops number one in the country and accounts for 57 percent of the entire She population in the country. Out of the 17 minority towns in Fujian, 16 are She minority towns. The She minority scatter all over Fujian with few concentrated dwelling places: i. e. the West of Fujian community includes the present-day Longyan and the southern part of Sanming She communities with the latter one being the most ancient She gathering place and the South of Fujian community which mostly indicates the Zhangzhou She minority community, which is the most early dwelling place of the She minority and most actively lived area. The Northeast Fujian community consists of the present-day Ningde municipality and the northern part of Fuzhou area, which is the most important She minority dwelling place in Fujian. Only in Ningde municipality, there lives a She population accounting for 60 percent of the total She population in Fujian that has best preserved the cultural customs of the She minority. The Central part of Fujian community indicates Putian municipality and the southern part of Fuzhou, a She minority migrating transfer station.

The She minority nationality is a very ancient people in Fujian that has evolved for more than one thousand years. The activities of the She are mainly based on the ancestry relationship and family relationship just as a She adage says, "San Ha, San Ha, if not of the same clan, then he must be an uncle". Here, "San Ha" refers to a She people. Generally, people of the close consanguinity and the same surname live together in a village. There is no marriage between the same surname but only within four surnames: Pan, Lan, Lei and Zhong. The She has no literary characters of its own but uses the literature of the Han minority. Among the She folk, there circulates A Legend about Pan Hu that describes Pan Hu as a mythical and brave hero and respected as the King of Loyalty and Bravery. He is held in esteem as the primogenitor of the She minority. The legend is drawn into a 40 interlink pictures and will be hung on the wall for worship at the ancestor worship ceremony.

The raiment of the She minority bears strong national characteristics. Women wear Phoenix Dress: red strings to bind up the hair on the top of the head symbolizing a phoenix; clothes and aprons are stitched with various colored chiffon and spun gold and silvery threads resemble the neck and waist and beautiful feathers of the phoenix; on the back of the waist, there is a flying golden belt symbolizing the tail of the phoenix. Many handicrafts made by the She people also feature the minority.

Fujian She minority is very rich in folklores. Many famous folktales go round the people like Tales about the She Ancestors, Gaoxin and the King of Dragon, The Pheonix Crown of the Third Princess, etc. The folktales talk about the ancestors' establishment of the families and the living style, about how they rebelled the invaders, simple and beautiful. The She minority is good at singing and dancing. The folk song is a musical form the She people like best. In She community in the East Fujian , people often hold poem-singing meetings and men and women in their best clothing will attend the meetings to pass the holidays or to celebrate festivals or entertain guests. When She people sing songs they do not have musical accompany. The best performance is versus songs between male and female. Both parties can sing one song or more. The singing activities are often carried out in the courtyards, in the open fields, in the entrance of a village, inside a big hall or the ancestral hall. Versus songs between host and guest, or a passersby, between competitors, between cousins and relatives by marriage, or ceremonial versus singings are the popular performances. The She people are good

at duet singing that is known as "double sound". This kind of
singing method was first discovered and named "a rare pearl" a-
mong the folk songs in China by the well-known Chinese musici-
an Zheng Xiaoying in 1958 when she was in the East Fujian She
community. The traditional dances of the She minority relate
closely to festival celebrations, sacrifice ceremonies, weddings
and funerals as well as production activities.

Particular festivals of the She are ancestral remembering day
on third of March with black color-dyed rice, Dragon Day on the
Chen Day after every lunar Summer Solstice, etc. Some community has its particular festivals like "meeting with relatives day"
on every second day of February when the East Fujian She people
go to Shaunghua Village in Fuding or to Gulou Hill of Houmen-
ping in Fuan to attend the festival.

There are about ten thousand Hui minority people in Fujian. In Huian, Baiqi town is a Hui minority inhabited town.
The origination of the Hui minority is very diversified, but there
are four communities that the Hui people would like to gather
in: Quanzhou community in the South of Fujian including
Quanzhou, Chenli of Jinjian, Baiqi of Hui'an. The ancestors of
these regions are said to come from Silk Road over the Sea, thus
often referred to as Hui Sea so as to make a difference from the
other Hui minority people. This is the cradle place of the Hui
minority in China; Xiamen community in the South of Fujian is
inhabited by the offspring of Hui people who undertook commercial business in the Ming and The Qing Dynasties and had immigrated to this region and settled down ever since; Shaowu community in the North of Fujian, mainly composing of officials and

officers of Hui origin who came to Shouwu to assume official positions and brought Hui soldiers and relatives and slaves with them; Fuzhou community includes Hui people who had come to Fuzhou from all places of China to get employed or to seek for relatives or take official positions, etc. Hui people distribute widely over Fujian and live separately. The reason for this is that the frequent immigrations caused by avoiding natural disasters, agricultural cultivation or commercial business had greatly reduced the centralization of assembly.

The Party Central Committee and leadership of all levels have attached great importance to the carrying out of the minority nationality policies. Since the Third Plenary Meeting of the Eleventh Session, leaders like Ye Fei, Zeng Zhi, Li Lanqing, Wen Jiabao; Ma Shiyi Ai Mai Ti, Bu He, to name only a few, have come to survey the situations of the minority communities. The provincial Party Committee and government of Fujian always attach great importance to minority work, and have held specialized meetings several times to discuss Fujian minority problems and have therefore greatly promoted the development and progress in overall administrational work in Fujian minority regions. The key point to the development of the minority regions is to raise the qualifications of the laborers, and to possess personals that are badly needed for the construction. It is of vital importance that "the education go ahead". Fujian Provincial Educational Committee has constituted a series of policies and measures to ensure the development of minority educational course and governments of all levels have appropriated special funds to support minority education. These are the effective ways to keep the growth of minority education to a degree that has never been reached before. Throughout the province there are 12 minority middle schools and 800 minority primary schools. The admission rate of the school aged children is up to 97 %, and the popularization rate, stable rate and promotion rate are almost equal to those of the contemporary Han minority regions. The vocational educations of the minority regions have come into being and are training a large quantity of personals that are needed in economic construction. Minority middle schools in Ningde prefecture have a history of 40 years, and at present they have become the key middle schools that have the right to recommend students for admission to higher education directly. For recent years, there are about 150 graduates from the middle schools who are enrolled by colleges and universities, the admission rate of which is 80 percent of the whole year's graduates. Almost every key university of China has minority middle school graduates. From the Ningde prefecture committee and government to the lower level of the administrative organizations, about 90% minority cadres are from the regional minority schools. They have become the backbone force in all walks of life.

Since the opening up to the outside world, medical treatment and sanitary conditions have greatly improved. Seventeen minority towns have built up hospitals and some minority villages set up clinics of their own, and 350 of medical stuff work in the minority regions. Fujian government has held meetings on minority medical work and appropriated funds to support the building of village clinics insomuch that these measures have pushed the improvement and construction of infrastructure of the town hospitals. The National Committee of Fujian government and the Department of United Front of Fujian Party Committee have organized and sent medical experts with democratic party membership of the province to the minority regions in Fuan and Ningde to provide free-charge medical diagnosis and treatment, and more than 4000 person-time joined in the charity activity. Minority regions pay attention to dredge up traditional medications. The She minority in the East of Fujian has summarized up a set of treatment typical of the minority who is good at using "pinch", "snap", "eject", "scratch" and acupuncture treatment to heal with acute diseases, and using herbal medicine of secret recipe to treat sterility, and correctitude of bone to treat injury and dietotherapy, etc. Recent years there are about 300 single proved recipes that have been selected out to sever actively the people of the She minority.

Cultural lives of the Fujian minority people are very rich and colorful. The provincial minority literature presentational performances have taken place many times. The representative teams of all minorities have put on their programs and shown their artistic skills insomuch they greatly feasted the eyes of the audience. There held in the East of Fujian many times of She song meeting or She art festival to make friends through singing and dancing. The East Fujian She minority song and dance troupe has been up north and down south and won reputations in Beijing, Guangdong, Macao and Singapore. For many years literature workers have been dredging up and creating over one hundred musical dancing programs of the She minority. Among them, *Happy Harvest*, *Joyful Duck Girl*, *Morning Song*,

Weaving Skirt Strips, *Going to Get Married*, *Shan Ha Belt*, etc. have been put on the national, provincial and regional stages and won prizes. Culture stations of the minority areas also hold various recreational activities to contribute to the spiritual culture construction of the minority regions. Through years of dredging up and compiling, collections of the She songs and ballads, stories, adages have been published. Some counties and towns have started to compile history books. Works that are distinguished with strong local characters won the provincial excellent-fruit prizes of Social Science. The periodical Fujian Nationalities established by Fujian Nationality Committee has published up till now 46 issues. Many articles with original thoughts have been fond of by readers far and near insofar as they encouraged the minority work in Fujian.

In order to push forward the physical culture in the minority regions, Fujian sets up an minority physical culture association sponsored by Fujian Nationality Committee. Recent years, there have held several provincial minority athletic meetings. In November 1995, Fujian sent out an athletic team of 114 members of the She, Gaoshan, Hui and Man minorities to Kunming attending to the national fifth minority sports meet. In five competing items such as dragon boating and the six performing items such as She minority's shooting, Gaoshan minority's pole ball, the team got prizes of the best-achievement in the East of China. The folk sports are also very active in the minority areas. The Beating Size (to strike the bamboo strips with crabstick) popular She sport item in the East of Fujian has been fond of by people; the stick arts of *Pan Brushwood Pestle* popular in Panxi village, the Well Boxing popular among the She people in Bajing Village of Luoyuan County, Fuding, She Boxing popular in Jindouyang of Fuan County, having been dredged up further and recomposed. They now become unique flower in the garden of Chinese martial arts.

To sever the minority economic development, to train up minority cadres is the most crucial. As far as the training and selection of minority cadres are concerned, Fujian has held special discussions many times. In 1995, Organizational Department, United Front Department and Nationality Committee of Fujian province coordinately set down Fujian Working Plan of Training and Selecting Minority Cadres between Years 1995—2000, which brings forward the specifications and requirements. A series of training and selecting measures reinforce the work and build up a healthy environment for minority cadres. Governments of lower levels select minority cadres to work or take up positions or exchange positions in the related upper or lower administrative organizations in the province or in Beijing. Therefore, the utilization of the minority cadres besides training and selecting is fulfilled in this way. The seventeen minority towns are equipped basically with minority cadres; twenty key minority counties are equipped with cadres into the county-level administrative leadership. Up till now, the whole province has nearly 8000 minority cadres accounting for 0.96 % of the total number; there are 48 comrades who are elected as provincial representatives of people's congress or members of the political consultation, accounting for 5.01% and 3% of the either total numbers.

"Developing is a rigid truth." said the former leader Deng

Xiaoping. In order to promote the economic development in the
minority regions, Fujian provincial Party Committee and Government put forward in April 1994 Some Suggestions on Rein-
forcement of Minority Work, requiring leaderships of every level
realize the importance and impendence of developing minority e-
conomy from a strategic viewpoint of politics, economics and social stability. Fujian Party Committee and Fujian Government establish a coordinating committee of minority work, whose members are leaders from the related departments and bureaus. Various administrative organizations place the development of minority regions in an important position in the local development strategic plans with gradually increased investments and the minority
regions enjoy, on a principle base, " priority on equal conditions"on special funds appropriation that were intended for the
minority regions.

Ever since the reforms and opening up, great changes have
taken place fundamentally in the overall economic construction in
Fujian minority towns. For example, in 1997, the seventeen minority towns reached a gross production value of 390 million yuan
and farmer's per capita income 1596 yuan. Fujian minority economic structure has initially diversified into three modals: a industrial development modal, agricultural developing modal and
integration of industry and agriculture modal. The industrial development modal is practiced by Baiqi Town in Huian. Baiqi
Town orients the development of shoe manufacturing and concurrently produces rubber and plastic goods, machines, chemical
goods, matrix procession, paper goods as well as traffic and carrying trade. Now there are 135 enterprises, and 15 enterprises

are capable of getting an annual production value of 10,000 thousand yuan. Per capita production value tops number one in Huian County. Banzong She Village of Fuan set up an industrial mini area centralized in electrical machines and electronic appliances by 237 factories, reaching a production value of 300 million yuan in 1996. Jinhan She Village of Ningde municipality makes a breakthrough in industry greatly developing collective, individual and stock-share cooperated ventures to process building materials as principal part together with other manufactures. The production value of the township enterprises was 216 million yuans in 1996. Huxi She Town of Zhangpu County opened up a Jinli industrial area and introduced 7 foreign invested enterprises. Until now, foreign invested enterprises have started a multiple production development of food processing, farm products, stone material processing and mine exploitation. Another modal is to base on agricultural integrative exploitation as a mainline of economic development, and lay store on multiple management so as to change the traditional inner structure which is based on planting. Qingshui She minority village of Yongan can serve as an example. The village utilizes the mountainous environment to foster reverse—season vegetables, and at the same time tries best to keep the outcome of the grain production together with other cropper and courtyard-economics. Chiling She minority town of Zhangpu County runs creatively a high-quantity farming development area, planting large acres of famous fruit trees such as li-chi, longan etc. and step by step a high-quantity fruit base came into being. Up till now, the goal of per capita 2 mu (a unit of area, one mu equal to 0. 1647 ac) of planting areas has been fulfilled and the base is able to turn out 15 thousand tons of fruits.

Under the impact of economic spring tide, some minority regions build up minority economic development areas. Muyang minority economic development area in the west of Fuan brings national characteristics into full play and develops a commercial street featuring national colors, and a tea trade center, wood and timber trade center that is the biggest one in the east of Fujian, forming a tea, food and drink, garments and commodity trade market. The newly-run stock-share cooperated enterprises help the poor to shake off poverty in the whole area up to 98. 7%. Fuan County sets up a Tie-Fu economic development area in Tiefu Minority Village, Chengyang town of Fuan County. They have introduced an overall automobile and motel service including automobile fittings, truck repairing, accommodation, food and drink and gas refilling. The program has brought alone the economic development of the whole area. Chendai Sijing Hui minority village of Jinjian is a well-known a hundred-million-village in Fujian, which is also a famous shoe-making town. Within the commercial center of the town, there are two streets of hundreds of shoe-making material sellers and shops. More and more minority people from the villages start to do business transactions. They walk out of the deep mountains to do business all over the nation. From the closed minority community, walk out a great number of merchants with modern managerial concepts.

The minority communities make effort to utilize the resources of human culture to develop tourism and the tourist business in turn become a new economic growth point. In November of 1995, in the East of Fujian, there held a She minority tourist festival with She's local conditions and customs. It led to further concern of the minority regions in tourism. In Longjiao She Village of Longhai County, there are natural scenery like an old crater that was alive before 1920, a so-called number one peak of Fujian mountains, and a well-preserved Ming Dynasty's old town, etc. With 1500 thousand yuans of investment, the villagers opened up Number One Holiday Village under the Sun, Ancient Crater Paradise, Zhenhai Ancient Town Beauty Spot and Southern Taiwu Beauty Spot. They also set up administrative offices and entities taking charge of tourism development and business. The newly set up 100 tourism services and related businesses produce annually 12 million yuans of production value. Therefore, tourism has become the backbone industry in the town.

Some minority communities are also accomplished in development of tourism resources. Jinhan She town of Ningde built a Chinese She Palace; Xiaochang Village of Lianjiang County possesses simple but beautiful mountain and lake sceneries; in Baiqi of Huian, there is a street full of Islamic architectures; in Huxi She village of Zhangpu County, there are residence building clusters like Zhaoja Fortress, Lan Ding Yuan and Lan Ting Zhen building colony; Shanghang brings forth red soil culture, etc.

Science and technology are important keys to the well-off state of life. Leaders of all levels think highly of the application of science and technology in the minority regions and try to guide the investment in science and technology. A great number of training programs to popularize practical techniques are carried out in almost every minority village. Under the vigorous support

of Fujian Committee of Science and Technology, the province
called forth minority science and technology demonstration
town, and there are eight minority villages meeting standards are
listed by the Committee of Science and Technology as demonstration villages in order to advocate the minority regions to shake of
poverty. To back up the economic development stamina, the administrative departments of every level try best to invest funds to
strengthen the infrastructure construction and improve the supply of water, electricity and road. Now 78. 5 percent of the minority villages have roads, and 100 percent have electricity.
Clean running water is available to 200 thousand minority people, and program controlled telephone to half of the minority villages. Some advanced villages are now able to invest in infrastructure construction by themselves. Baiqi Hui minority town of
Huian County invested 1. 8 million yuan to build a waterworks in
1997, and 2 million yuan in rebuilding a village road. Zhangpu's
Huxi She Village has invested in succession 5. 6 million yuan in
paving a village cement-blacktop road, and 2. 7 million yuan in
500 program controlled telephones and 750 thousand yuan in
building transformer substation of 35 thousand voltages. Better
infrastructure condition greatly improves the investment environment that in turn enables the further construction of the minority
towns and villages.

In order to solve the problem in dressing warmly and eating
one's fill in some of the minority regions and shaking off poverty
completely, Fujian Provincial Party Committee launched a Benefit Engineering which permitted people to develop and make rich
in other places than at home. In 1994, Fujian Provincial Party

Committee and Government issued Suggestions on Strengthening
the Work on Minority clearly requiring related prefectures, municipalities and counties make out plans and actively organize villagers who live in the remote mountain areas with poor living
conditions to move out collectively to a region with better geographical conditions and improve productive and living conditions. This move has opened up a new stage for the minority
towns to develop their economy and society. Besides the Suggestions also put forwards a series preferential policies and measures
to carry out Benefit Engineering. In 1997, Fujian Party Committee and Government included the housing problem of the She minority into the list of 'the fifteen practical things to be done for
people' and invested, within the year, 7. 22 million yuan and
helped 719 households with 2,859 people complete the rebuilding
engineering of their huts, which ended the history of the hut in
which the She minority had lived for generations in Fujian.

Chapter Seven
Religions

Buddhism, Taoism, Catholicism, Christianity and Islam are the five religions that have had a long history in Fujian and had a great influence over people far and wide. At present, statistics show that followers of religions amount to one million, and religious stages nearly seven thousand.

For the time being in Fujian, there are over four thousand three hundred Buddhist temples, twelve thousand monks and nuns and about thirteen thousand lay Buddhists. Both the amounts of temple and the monks and nuns top those of the Han regions in China Mainland, among which fourteen temples are sanctified as national key temples in Han nationality regions by the State Department, accounting for ten percent of the like temples. These temples are named as following: in Fuzhou, Yong Quan Temple of Gu Mountain, Xichan Temple of Yishan, Dizhang Temple of Jinjishan; Linyang Temple of Rifeng, Chongsheng Temple in Xuefeng Mountain of Minhou, Huangbo Temple of Fuqing, Nanputuo Temple of Xiamen, Huayan Temple in Zhiti Mountain of Ningde; in Putian, Guanghua Temple on Nan-

shan, Guangxiao Temple in Meifeng, Cishou Temple on Nangs-
han; Kaiyuan Temple of Quanzhou, Longshan Temple of Jinjiang, Nanshan Temple of Zhangzhou.

The Buddhism religion was first introduced to Fujian during
the Three Kingdoms period, having a history of more than one
thousand seven hundred years by now. In the history of Fujian,
there have been dignitaries coming forth in great number. The
well-known dignitaries who came from other places to pass Buddhism in Fujian or who were of Fujian origin are named as following: Taoyi, came from Sichuan in Tang Dynasty to Jianyang
to build Jian Temple; Huaihai, born in Changle, Fujian in Tang
Dynasty, stipulated "Baizhang Monastic Rules for Buddhists";
Linyou, born in Xiapu, Fujian, in the Five Dynasties period, established with his disciples a sect called Weiyangzong; Yichun,
born in Nanan, Fujian, in the Five Dynasties period, built up
Xuefeng Temple; Shenyan, born in Bohai, in Five Dynasties period, the founder of Yongquan Temple of Gu Mountain; Yuanx-
ian, born in Jianyang, presided Yongquan Temple for twenty-
three years, who was also the most influential Buddhist monk of
Caodong Sect in the end of the Ming Dynasty; Hongyi, born in
Zhejiang province, a contemporary man who has been passing
Buddhism in the South of Fujian for fourteen years; Taixu, born
in Zhejiang province, used to be the abbot of Nanputuo Temple
of Xiamen and the president of College of Buddhism of South of
Fujian; Yuanying, born in Gutian, Fujian, the first to be appointed the Chairman of Chinese Buddhism Association; Fujian's
Buddhism has a close and long standing relationship with Taiwan
area, Japan and the Southeast Asia. At the end of the Ming and

early Qing, Gushan Yongquan Temple of Fuzhou, Yishan
Xichan Temple, Huangbo Temple of Fuqing had frequent exchanges with Taiwan monks and spread burning incense far to
Taiwan. In the Tang Dynasty, Konghai, the Japanese monk,
the founder of Zhenyan Sect landed on Chian of Xiapu, via
Fuzhou and lived in Kaiyuan Temple, and upward north to
Changan to seek Buddhism. Early in the Qing Dynasty, dignitary Yinyuan from Huangbo Temple of Fuqing led twenty persons
eastbound across the sea to Japan and started Huangbo sect of
Buddhism in Japan. Many Fujian temples possessed sub-temples
in Philippines, Singapore, Indonesia and Malaysia. Until now,
many leaders of the Buddhism religion of these countries are
monks of Fujian origin, who keep a close contact with Fujian
Buddhism religious circles.

All through their histories, temples and fanes in Fujian undertook the work of engraving Buddhist scriptures. In the Song
Dynasty, The Scripture of Chongning engraved by Dongchan
Temple of Fuzhou, and The Scripture of Bilu engraved by
Kaiyuan Temple are the earliest two temple-engraved large Buddhist classics in the Chinese history. Yongquan Temple in the Gu
Mountain of Fuzhou used to be the center of engraving Buddhist
scriptures. Until the Culture Revolution, there were still kept
11,375 pieces of various Buddhist scripture plates engraved from
the Ming and the Qing Dynasties to the contemporary time. The
Great Master Hongyi once said that those plates were "Treasure
hole of the Buddhist Scriptures of old edition". Other famous
temples also treasured up various Buddhist classics. Quanzhou
Kaiyuan Temple stored twelve volumes of Buddhist classics edi-

ted in the Song and Yuan Dynasties. In the history, as Fujian had numerous temples and was far away from chaos by wars, some classics have been preserved in perfect state. Stone inscription on the cliffs, epitaphs and engraved buildings, rare figures of Buddha and various kinds of Buddhist towers are representative pieces of Buddhist classics.

There are six hundred of Taoist palaces and 2600 Taoist monks in Fujian. The origination of the Taoism bore relationship with the fame of the mountain. The Wuyi Mountains go by the name of the Sixth Cavity Heaven out of the Thirty-six Small Cavity Heavens in the Taoist religion; the Huotong Mountain is referred to as the Number One Cavity Heaven of the Thirty-six Small Cavity Heavens in the Taoist religion; the Taimu Mountain in the East of Fujian, the Qingyuan Mountain in the South of Fujian, the Yu Mountain in Fuzhou all have intimate relations with the Taoism. The present famous Taoist palaces in Fujian are named as the following: Jiuxian Palace, Peixian Palace in Fuzhou, Shizhu Mountain Taoist Palace in Fuqing, Yuanmao Palace in Quanzhou, Taoyuan Cave Taoist Palace in the Wuyi Mountains, and Dongyue Palace in Putian, etc.

The Taoism religion was first introduced to Fujian in the Eastern Han period. To the Song Dynasty, there appeared Refinement and Cultivation party and Symbol party. In the Ming and the Qing Dynasties, there were Quan Zhen Tao and Zheng Yi Tao. Quan Zhen Tao claimed that, "To become a monk or nun, it is important to refine aspiration and repose the spirits." The religion started to decline after the modern time. Zheng Yi Tao, referred to as Father of Teachers, drew symbols to capture

bewitches, prayed for happiness, tried to avoid disasters and released souls from purgatory for people. Taoism in Fujian usually
engaged in complicated Taoist activities with numerous names
and complete set of ceremonial presentations. Some movements
and gestures used to drive off the bewitching and capture demons
were full of artistic and aesthetic values and were often borrowed
by dances.

Fujian Taoism religion was of the same origin and the same
flow with that of Taiwan. When people emigrated from the
South of Fujian to Taiwan, they brought the palace and burning
incense with them to Taiwan. The two places worshipped the
same deities. The ancestors of Fujianese living in the Southeast
Asia were especially religious to the deities of their hometown
and would regard them as aegis of their life and work overseas.
Whenever they built a temple, they would name the temple after
their home-town or the temple of their hometowns, and they
would return home to offer incense to the temples.

For the time being, there are about three hundred Catholic
churches, 130 priests and nearly 300 thousand followers in Fujian. Famous churches are named as following: Fanchuanpu
Church of Fuzhou, Chengguan Church of Changle, Gulang Island Church of Xiamen, Dongbanhou Church of Zhangpu, Lin-
dong Church of Longhai, Chengguan Church of Fuan, Muyang
Church of Fuan, Sanduao Church, Chengguan Church, Lankou
Church of Ningde, Dongmen Church of Shaowu, Lazhiping
Church of Jianou, Chengguan Church of Shanghang.

As early as in the Yuan Dynasty, the Catholicism was introduced to Quanzhou. So Fujian is one of the earliest provinces in

which Catholicism was spread. In 1313, Quanzhou set up Chitong Parish and thus became one of the two parishes that took charge of the affairs of the Southeast areas including treaty ports like Hangzhou, Yangzhou, etc. In Quanzhou Haijiao Museum, five crucifix gravestones out of the ten of the Yuan Dynasty were burial relics that the Quanzhou Church offered to priests of other churches. In the Ming Dynasty, Alio of the Italian Jesus Community came to Fujian to pass on mission. He was quite familiar with Chinese traditional culture and good at combining the Chinese traditional customs with his teachings. He therefore was quite successful in China. At the end of the Ming, traditional literati and monks opposed the teachings in a union and wrote articles one after another to "keep away the evil". The articles were compiled into a collection entitled A Collection of Breaking through the Evils by a Zhangzhou Man named Huang Zheng. At the early Qing, Luo Wenzao, born in Fuan, became the first Chinese missionary in a time when the government ordained that no foreign missionaries should pass on teachings. Luo Wenzao was the only clergy of the Catholicism who could openly pass on his mission. In 1696, in Fujian, Catholic Parish of Fujian was established in due form.

The spread of the Catholicism in Fujian turned Fujian into one of the earliest places that the western culture and the Chinese culture conflicted.

Fujian has 1700 Christianity churches, 1200 pastors and 470 thousand followers besides 140 thousand Christianity admirers at present. Influential churches are named as the following: Huaxiang Church, Puqiang Church, Tianan Church, Changxia Church of Fuzhou; Chenguan Church of Fuqing; Chenguan Church of Putian; Meishan Church of Nanping; Jinsheng Church of Jinjiang; Nanjie Church of Quanzhou; Thrinity Church, Xinqu Church, Xinjie Church of Xiamen.

It was about the year 1840 that the Christianity was introduced to Fujian. In 18408, the first church Xinjie Church was established in Xiamen, which was called "Number One Church in China" before liberation by the National General Council of China Christianity Council. Christianity then started to radiate from Xiamen, Fuzhou to the whole country. The Christianity built hospitals, schools and published newspapers, periodicals and books in Fujian, and thus impelled the birth of colloquial South of Fujian dialect.

By now, there are five mosques that can serve as representatives of the Islamic mosques in Fujian, the most famous one being Quanzhou Qingjing Mosque that was built in the years of the North Song Dynasty. It is also referred to as Shengyou Temple. It is the most ancient mosque that has been preserved in China with an Islamic architectural style of the middle age as well as Chinese traditional architectural skills and crafts in many parts of the construction. Other four mosques are Xiamen Mosque, Fuzhou Mosque, Shaowu Mosque, Chenli Mosque in Jinjiang. There are about three thousand followers across the province.

As early as in the Tang Dynasty, Islamism was introduced into Quanzhou by Arabians and Persia Muslim merchantmen who came to Quanzhou and have settled down and lived there one generation after another till now. The Muslins started to build mosque in order to meet the need of their religious life.

To the Yuan Dynasty, with the growth of Quanzhou into a world commercial trade port, the Moslems spread rapidly and they built more mosques, unfortunately noun of which exists by now; to the Ming Dynasty, the Muslims spread to Shaowu; in the Qing Dynasty, the Quanzhou Port began to decline and the Muslims no longer came from overseas. With the enclosure of the mountainous Fujian in the Southeast of China, little connection was built with the inner land Muslims. Thus Fujian Islamism was not as flourishing as in the Song Dynasty and the Yuan Dynasty.

Muslims in Fujian have different origins. Many of them were merchantmen who had come from the Silk Road on the Sea in the Song and Yuan Dynasties apart from those who had come down south from the north to take official position or to be employed as an imam, or seek relatives in Fujian. Because of many times of immigration, Muslims in Fujian mostly scatter far apart and live dispersedly with very few of them in convergence.

Among the many deities that are worshipped by the folk in Fujian, the most famous deities are the Goddess Mazu, Lady Linshui of Chen Jinggu, the Great Baosheng Emperor Wutao. The old name of Mazu is called Linmo, born in Putain in the Song Dynasty. It is said that she had often shown her presence and protected ships coming and going and rescued the shipwrecks and has been regarded as Protective Goddess of seafaring by fishermen. Chen Jinggu was born in Fuzhou in the Tang Dynasty, married to a Gutian Man called Liuqi at the age of eighteen. The legacy goes that Fuzhou was suffering from a serious drought. Chen Jinggu induced an abortion to pray God for rain so hard that she was dying. When her clock stroke, she pledged that she would help the fetus and rescue dystocia (and she became goddess of rescuing dystocia). Wutao was born in the Song Dynasty in Baijiao of Tong'an. He was a folk doctor knowing herd medicine and believed in Taoism. He was well known in the South of Fujian for his superior medical skills and noble morals of a physician. Unfortunately he fell into a deep abysm when he was collecting herbs in the mountain. To commemorate him, the folk worship him as a god. There are other local deities such as Guangze Honorable King, Qingshui Founder, Xiao Taifu, etc. When people from Fujian go to make a living in Taiwan and other places in the Southeast of Asia, these local gods and goddesses are become the deities that are worshipped by the Chinese there.

Manichean is a religion established by a Persian named Manich in the middle of the third century AD In Wusong Huichang period of the Tang Dynasty, Rabbi Hulu introduced the religion into Quanzhou and became flourishing in Quanzhou during the Yuan Dynasty. After the Ming Dynasty, it gradually inosculated with other religions. The Jinjiang Manichean Nunnery built in the Yuan Dynasty in Jinjiang is the only relic of the Manichean in China. The First World Manichean Symposium used the Manichean figure in Jinjiang Nunnery as the badge design. Sanyi (meaning three in one in Chinese) religion was foundered by Lin Zhaoen, in the Ming Dynasty in Putian, which claimed that the Buddhism, Taoism and the Confucian should combine in one. The religion stressed on the digestion of the essence of the three teachings. After it was prohibited by the royal court, it declined.

With the reforms and opening up to the outside world, Fujian provincial leaderships of all levels lay store on the putting into effect of the policies stipulated by the Party and Government about the freedom of religious beliefs. The Provincial Party Committee, Provincial Consultant Council, the People's Congress, Provincial Government, the Provincial Political Consultation and Fuzhou Military Region coalesced to form a check-up delegation to carry out the religious policies. The prefectures too organized the corresponding check-up teams to go deep into basic units to inspect the whole province extensively and completely. Xiangnan and some other leaders took the lead to check up in person the fulfillment of the religious policies in Yongquan Temple of Fuzhou and Kaiyuan Temple of Quanzhou, Nanshan Temple of Zhangzhou and some other temples. Comrade Xiangnan attached a great importance the opinions of the overseas scholars and friends on religious policies of Fujian and made reposes with instructions by himself many times. The examples set by the leaders energetically pushed forward the fulfillment of the freedom of religious belief policies.

The leaders of the religious circle of China are also interested in Fujian's religious work. The Vice President of the National Political Consultation and President of China Buddhism Association, Zhao Puchu had come to Fujian many times to inspect and guide the work insomuch that he greatly encouraged further the smooth development of the religious work in Fujian. And so had other celebrities of Chinese religious circle such as Din Guangxun, Vice Chairman of the National Political Consultation and Director of China Committee of Three-Self Patriotic Movement of China Christianity; Bishop Zong Huaide, Bishop Jin Luxian of China Catholic Delegation; Xie Zongxin, the former President of China Taoist Association; Ma Xian, the Vice President of China Islamic Association.

Leaders of all levels are concerned about religious figures politically. Every wrong and injustice case in the religious field has been justified. There are about 211 religious societies of all levels. About 405 persons from the religious circle are assuming offices in the People's Congress or are committee members of Political Consultation of all levels. Vast religious people firmly believe without exception that the past twenty years have been the golden period in history that policy of freedom of religious belief has been enforced and put into effect. They feel happy and easy in developing religious activities and at the same time devote themselves to the progress of the society. Leaderships of all levels resolutely handled the problem of real estate and inspected thoroughly the fulfillment of religious real estate policy in the whole province. Some of the "hard problem" had been eventually solved. Till the end of the eighties of the 20th century, about 95% of the house properties had been returned to religious societies. Vast mass of religious believers and overseas Chinese moved by the sincerity and determination of the Party and government generously opened their purse to donate money or substances. For example, the rich donations from the overseas Chinese have helped the reconstruction of Chengtian Temple of Quanzhou, Xichan Temple of Fuzhou.

To respect and protect the freedom of religious beliefs is a lasting and basic policy of the nation's government when dealing with religious problems. Leaderships of all levels eliminate various interferences and try best to put into practice of the freedom of religious belief policy. Today, in a time of open-minded political administration with peace-loving people, every religious society and immense mass of religion followers happily undertake all kinds of activities in accordance to ceremonial regulations of every religion.

Every religious society holds missionary activities and develops educational publishing enterprises according to the guideline of running the church by self-management, self-mission and self-support. Fujian Buddhist Association and Fujian Taoist Association established separately their periodicals "Fujian Buddhism" and "Fujian Taoism". To meet the need of vast followers and friends, Fujian Buddhist Association appointed Putian Guanghua Temple as the station of the classics circulation, which connected the provincial Buddhist association and some key temples by network. Putian Guanghua Temple publishes a great amount of Buddhist classic books and Fujian Buddhist Association published many works on Buddhism. Fujian Christianity Three-Self Patriotic Movement Committee edits and publishes many books that illustrate the essence of Christianity. All of these publications have found favor with the followers.

Related departments furnish every means of convenience for the fulfillment of religious policy. In the early 1985 when Chengtian Temple of Quanzhou was being built, the Quanzhou Government supplied a loan of 1500 thousand yuan in purchasing wood materials in order to keep the schedule of the construction.

As to the problem of removing a factory site, the Party Secretary and Chief Executive of Quanzhou led the five sets of leaderships of the municipality to solve the problem on the working site. In 1995, Fuzhou Catholic Parish bought a piece of land in Longtian Village, Guhui Town of Changle and built on the land a series of religious architectures named Rose Village capable of providing accommodation and facilities of religious pilgrimage, touring and cultural exchanges. Related departments from the provincial level to the prefecture level not only offered means of convenience for the construction's procedure examination and approval, but also particularly remitted 400 thousand yuans of various taxes in a manner of special affair dealt with in special way. Bishop Zheng Changcheng of Fuzhou Parish once said to a visiting American Consul General to Guangzhou, "Today Chinese citizens enjoy the right of freedom of religious belief no less than the Americans, perhaps a better right than that of the Americans in regard to the religious tax exemption when the religious circle is in difficulty. "

It is of crucial significance that all sorts of religious colleges and universities shoulder up the responsibility of training and fostering young generations of professional personnel with patriotism designedly in order to follow out and put into effect the religious policy stipulated by the Party and Government. It has been regarded as a basic construction work of lasting importance and urgent affair as well. Since 1983, Fujian religious circles set up or reopened Jianfu College, Southeast Buddhist College, Fujian Divinity School, Fujian Catholic College together with various training classes. Around 1500 young religious personnel have graduated with senior qualifications, which will realize step by step the goal of training out enough young teachers and workers for the religious fields.

Fujian Buddhism College is divided into two departments: the male student department that is residing in Putian Guanghua Temple, and the female department residing in Fuzhou Chongfu Temple. In 1983, Fujian Buddhism College was set up, the earliest provincial college of this kind in the country. The male student department has to this day graduated five grades of training classes, seven grades preparatory classes and three sessions of graduates, all together 600 hundred graduates or students who have completed the required course. Now in college there are 150 male students studying 60% of Buddhist subjects and 10% of political subjects. The school's educational ideology is to foster successors of intellects who love the country and the Buddhist religion as well as the socialism. The college periodically appraises excellent students through comparison to encourage students to study hard. The college at the same time introduced a lot new teaching facilities. The female department opens preparatory classes and additional half-time training classes whose students are coming from nearly twenty provinces and cities of the country. Students of male and female in this college have a reputation of strict Taoist spirits all over the country, which is praised by the President Zhao Puchu as a national exemplar, and he wrote a poem for the male students in the Guanghua Temple that does as the following: Once step into the mountain door in the heart of the Taoism, you take over the traditional spirits of the Nanshan. You bear impressive manner and order in the Taoist fast hall, thinking over the benevolence of the masses contained in every drop of rice.

Buddhist College of South of Fujian was set up in 1925, reopened in 1985, and after then the college stressed on study and reconstruction are of the same importance. Study and application should go together. The college is composed of two departments: the male department is located in the temple of Xiamen Nanputuo Temple; the female department is situated in Xiamen Purple Bamboo Forest. The Chairman of the Nanputou Temple, Rabbi Shenghui, who is also the Vice President of China Buddhism Association, President of Buddhist College of South of Fujian, once said, "Students of Buddhist College of South of Fujian come from all provinces and cities of China, accounting for the magnitude part of students in college of this kind. The college has a powerful backing as the temple residence is also the quarter of the college. Problems in the Buddhist education should be dealt with through better management that has to follow up yet. Running an institute has deep inner relation with management. Under the leadership of Xiamen Party Committee, we have achieved great results. The three things that we need to do as to the improvement of the teaching quality are: firstly to construct a teaching stuff; secondly to cultivate religious sentiments of the students; thirdly to raise the level of a student's knowledge about Buddhism and his overall scope of education. " The administrational office, Taixiu Library and the teaching buildings are well equipped. Excellent students will be sent to higher institutes for further study. Rabbi Zhanru, now a post doctor in the Oriental Department of Beijing University, came from Buddhist College of South of Fujian. The female department resides at the quiet and beautiful Purple Bamboo Forest with teaching facilities and conditions topping the best in the country. Apart from Buddhist colleges, some temples put forth different types of training classes to raise the standards of the knowledge and cultural levels of the personnel in the religious circles.

Fujian Divinity School was foundered in 1983, and excellent graduates from this school are sent to Jinlin Theoretical College for further education. College students study very hard. Every week they will receive some kinds of patriotic education and hold recreational activities. Fujian Catholic College for the recent ten years has brought up 58 friars and nuns, and there are about 67 brothers have been sent to Shanghai Sheshan Monastery and other theoretical or philosophical colleges in the country for further study. Five priests go out abroad for further education. Every parish pays attention to foster better priests. Since 1983, the Southeast Parish has fostered and selected dozens of priests to study in China Theoretic and Philosophical College, and seven of them have returned after graduation and two are still studying abroad.

Various religious colleges and schools have cultivated a large batch of young religious teachers and stuffs and most of them become the backbone elements of different religious societies and activities, which greatly relaxed the lack of personnel and the aging problems resulted from the "Revolution" and gradually overcome the vicissitude process of the old and the young. Parts of the teachers and stuffs are employed to work in the United States, the Philippines or other countries in the Southeast Asia or Hongkong.

To carry out the management of the religious sites in terms of legal, the provincial and municipal leaderships go deep into the theaters. In 1998, Fujian Religion Bureau arranged the inspection of the religious theaters in whole province, appointing Fuzhou Kaiyuan Temple as an experimental unit and applying a series of effective reforming measures like sending excellent young monks to enrich the administrative level and hence changed the visage of the temple. Reforms were welcome by monks in the temple and by followers as well. Besides, various religious societies also attach importance to the regulations on the theaters. Ningde Huayan Temple on Zhiti Mountain stipulates Temporary Controlling Measures on Huayan Temple of Zhiti Mountain in accordance with related rules set out by China Buddhist Association and the practical situations in the temple. Gradually the management of the temple affairs stepped into standardization and system. Quanzhou Taoist Association together with Yuanmiao Temple stipulated several bylaws in accordance with the rules set out by China Buddhist Association and perfected the temple managerial leadership as to straight out the working order.

Ever since the Third Plenary Meeting of the Eleventh Session of the Communist Party of China, the religious circles have stepped out magnificent strides and have been accomplished in the adaptation to the socialism. In order to find out and study on issues existing in the religious circles, in November of 1993, cadres from the provincial religious administrative departments, representatives from the various religious societies and researchers on the religions organized Fujian Religion Seminar and held sundry seminars and activities including publishing Fujian Religions and editing three collections of thesis. Fujian Provincial Religion Bureau often holds meetings and conferences to praise the excellent work and discuss problems or seminars to exchange opinions in an effort to adapt the religions to the socialism.

Under the support of the government departments, Fujian religious circles insist in the guideline of self-supply and self-sufficiency. The main living source of the Taoists of Taoyuan Cavity in Wuyi Mountains is to plant Rock tea and make tourist souvenirs. Fuan Wanshou Temple relies on producing various burning incenses with an annual output value of 600 thousand yuan. The retired can enjoy 80 yuans of subsidies every month. Their incenses even sold abroad. Huayan Temple of Ningde in Zhiti Mountain bases on farming to satisfy the necessities. And do many other temples like Xinghai Temple in Zhonghua Mountain of Liancheng, Chong Sheng Temple in Xuefeng Mountain of Minhou, Guanghua Temple of Putian and Linyang Temple of Fuzhou. Some temples provide special services. Xiamen Nanputuo Temple, Fuzhou Xichan Temple and Yuanquan Temple provide vegetable dishes that are fond of by customers. The religious circles actively offer services for the society free of charge. For example, the Three-Self Patriotic Committee of the Catholicism establishes hospitals, medical clinics and old-aged house.

Fujian religious circles have advocated the exchange between Taiwan. According to the information provided by Taiwan Committee of The Mainland Affairs of the Administrational Department, religious exchanges between the both sides of the focused in Fujian province recently. As early as the end of the 1980s, rabbis from Taiwan Bei Lin Ji Temple, Daxian Temple of Tainan, Honghua Temple of Gaoxong or visiting delegations started to come to Fujian frequently. Towards the 1990s, Taiwan rabbis gave lectures in Fujian. At the end of 1990s, the Buddhist circles of Taiwan and Fujian come and go between themselves more frequently. Former Chairman of Fujian Buddhist Association, Rabbi Jiequan once visited Taiwan Zhonghua Buddhist Institute; Present Chairman of Fujian Buddhist Association, Rabbi Xuecheng attend the Buddhist Education Seminar between Both sides in Taiwan in July, 1998, and he was invited to give a speech in Taiwan Normal University. In 1994, Fujian Buddhist circle went to Taiwan to exhibit pictures and paintings by Rabbi Hongyi. All of these exchanges have been attracting the attention and interests of Taiwan people. Every year, Fujian Taoist palaces will receive near 1000 holy delegations to present incense from all over Taiwan, amounting to 200 thousand persons and times. In March 1997, Quanzhou Taoist delegation headed by Lin Zhou went to Taiwan for an exchanging visit and talked with more than 40 Taoist societies and palaces. President Lin Zhou found that people in Taiwan identified their consanguinity and divinity relationship with those of the Mainland, and he said, "Chinese Taoism has relation with us and we have also invited many Taoist palaces to pay visits to Taiwan. But in the Mainland, Taiwan only invites China Taoist Association and Fujian Taoist Association. To be in Fujian, they feel as if they returned home because they speak the same language. Taoist religion in Taiwan is in favor of the reunion." The Committee of Three-Self Patriotic Movement of Fujian Christianity organized the first delegation in the Mainland to visit Taiwan and increased the mutual under-standing.

Fujian religious circles keep frequent contacts with the over-seas through mutual visits and increasing friendship. As early as 1979, an eighteen-person visiting delegation of Huangbo Sect of Japanese Buddhism arrived at Huangbo Mountain of Fuqing to make a courtesy call to the tower and pay their respect to the founder and then the visitors, coming to Fuzhou to hold a royal Buddhist scripture recitation in Han dialect with Fujian monks in Gushan Yongquan Temple. Buddhist circles of Japan and the South Korea and some other countries have sent many visiting delegations to come to Fujian for exchanges. Some very famous leaders in Buddhist religion in the Southeast Asia have visited Fujian many times. For example, Rabbi Hongchuang, President of Singapore Buddhist Association in General has visited Fujian five times; Rabbi Ruijin, President of the Philippines Buddhist Association and Rabbi Jihuang, President of Malaysia Buddhist Association have also visited Fujian many a time. Fujian Bud-dhist circles often go out to pay visit to the countries of the Southeast Asia. Fujian Islamic religion vigorously holds activi-ties with foreign countries. The President of Fujian Provincial Islamic Association has been out many times to foreign countries for a friendly visit, increasing the friendship between China and the countries of the Islamic world. The world famous Quanzhou Ancient Mosque has received visitors coming from 130 countries and regions in recent years including visitors from 37 Islamic reli-gion countries. They wrote words on the leave-word books to praise the friendship they met in China. Iran, Pakistan, Iraq, O-

man, Saudi Arabia and some other countries compliment away
the exquisite Koran to the mosques. The Committee of Three-
Self Patriotic Movement of Fujian Christianity and Fujian Catholicism have received oversea guests many times. Priest Zheng Jin-
can from Putian Christianity said, "Our churches have a close relation with the Southeast Asia. Many overseas Chinese in the
Southeast of Asia are Christian followers. They hope to have
chance to meet in Putian Grand Church. We will help them with
their investment in Fujian and live and work here smoothly and
successfully. The church is a window to the outside opening. "

In the construction of the Two Socialist Civilizations, Fujian
religious circles well up many advanced units and individuals. In
November 1997, Fujian Religion Bureau held a Conference on
Honoring Typically Advanced for the Four-Modernizations from
Fujian Religious Circles to praise and commend on advanced units
and individuals that had contributed remarkably to the construction of the Four Modernizations. Some of the twenty-two praised
units are as following: Shizhushan Taoist Temple, which had
tried best to upgrade Shizhu Mountain as one of the ten beauty
spots of the provincial grade; Quanzhou Mosque that had built
up a friendly bridge between China and Saudi Arabia; Putian
Guanghua Temple, which had turned the temple into a modal in
the jungle; Ningde Huayan Temple in Zhiti Mountain, which
had been concentrating in both Buddhism and agriculture; Shaowu Municipal Christian Association that had been devoted to
social beneficial courses. On the conference there were seventeen
advanced individuals who were praised and commended, and a-
mong them was Liao Guohua, who was a Catholic, former Direc-

tor of Changle Museum. He contributed his life in the fight with
a ganster in order to protect the cultural relics belonged to the
country.

The course through which Fujian religious circles have come
across for the recent twenty years has manifested itself that religions are capable of adapting themselves to the socialist cause.
Fujian religions have grown up into an important force in the
construction of two socialist civilizations as well as in maintaining
social stability.

Chapter Eight
Folk Customs and Habits

"There is no similar winds within one hundred square miles, and there is no similar customs within one thousand square miles." This is an old saying that is often quoted to describe the richness and colorfulness of the Chinese folk customs; but as to the customs prevalent in Fujian, people would say "there is no similar winds within one hundred square miles, and every village has one custom of its own". Fujian gathers together the essence of Chinese folk customs, so it can be addressed as exhibition hall of Chinese folk customs: customs of other places also can be found in Fujian; customs that do not exist in other places are practiced in Fujian; customs that only existed in other places in the ancient days and now have disappeared still can be found in Fujian; and some customs that have evolved without any traces of the original appearance, however, still keep their former visages. The reasons why the customs in Fujian can keep their richness and colorfulness lie in the following aspects:

1. Manifold cultures concurrently tolerating and accepting each other. The relique of the Ancient Yue culture, the massive

introductions of the Central Plains culture time after time, the wide spread of primitive and contemporary religions, the constant impacts of overseas cultures and long-term infiltration of the neighboring cultures, all of these influences have multicolored the culture of Fujian.

2. Located in a remote natural environment. The inheriting of a folk customs has strong tendency of selecting the natural environment. Fujian, a so-called Southeast Mountain Kingdom, stands in the remote southeast corner of China, and is far away from the political and cultural center. Because of the inconvenient traffic and transportation, numerous natural villages never communicate each other, and thus are not affected by outer situations and affairs. This unique environment helps the deposition of various folk cultures.

3. The extreme strong notion of family. The inheritance of a custom depends upon people's oral tales and behaviors from one generation to the next, which is also conceived as a long lasting and collective form of cultural transfer. Villagers, having long dwelt in the same place, will develop a village collective concept that will try best to ensure that things passed down from forefathers should not be deserted. This enables the prolong life of the old folk customs.

I. Festival and Holiday

Yearly festival custom is a very complicated social cultural phenomenon. Festival customs and habits in Fujian reveal in one way, the experiences of the local people's life and production, on the other hand, they indicate the intimate relationship between people and the unique natural environment of Fujian.

The New Year's Eve is the last day of the year in lunar calendar, and it is also the busiest day of the year. As a Fuzhou saying says that at the New Year's Eve, footless lanterns can run. Fuzhou people will steam well the white rice and put the rice in a rice bowl and place the bowl on the desk as an offering, which is commonly called "food over the year". In the evening, bamboo poles or pine tree woods should be burnt, with some salt scattering over the fire to make cracking sound so that unlucky atmosphere will be driven out of the house. The New Year's Eve is also referred to as a day of "cleaning up unluckiness". People will slip some foil paper of golden or silvery color between the slots on the door to indicate that the fortune of the house is so surplus that it overflows out of the door, which is a symbol of the coming year's prosperity. In the South of Fujian, people will burn up the old broom that has been used through the year at the New Year's Eve, and the whole family, young and old will say together Happy New Year while jumping over a heap of fire one by one. So the coming new year will be happy and auspicious. Zhangzhou people will circle round a stove to spend the New Year's Eve. Dishes of the evening banquet have symbolic meanings. Fish symbolizes rich life; chicken means the flourishing of family's fortune; bean curd means enrichment; leek represents long happiness, etc. Zhangzhou people are especially keen on the blood clam without which the New Year's Eve banquet will not go. In the ancient time, seashells stood for fortune, splendor and value. Zhangzhou people regard the shells of the clam as gold and silver and will not throw them away, yet they will be solemnly placed behind the doors or under the bad as a sign of the coming year's fortune. Moreover, Zhangzhou people must erect behind their doors two pieces of sugarcane with roots and leaves still attached, which is called "lean against the hard wall" meaning that the family's fortune lies on the solid foundation. In the West of Fujian, people will set a big square table in the middle of the hall, and upon the table, place a big dou of rice (a big box shaped unit measure for grain, one dou equivalent to 1 decalitre) together with leaves of evergreen tree, silver coins, silver bracelets that will be attached to the branches of evergreen tree and red eggs on the rice that is called "upgrading year rice".

Spring Festival is the most important feast day in Fujian customs. Fuzhou people commonly refer to it as "to make the year" concentrating on the following five activities:

1. Drink 'tu su'. In the early morning of the first lunar day, people go to fetch water from the well and concoct it with yellow wine, and every member of the family from the eldest to the youngest drink a cup of the wine to avoid pestilence.

2. Make an orderly courtesy call. First make a kaotao to the Heaven and then to the earth, and then on make a courtesy obeisance to the elders in the family according to the generation to congratulate on their birthdays.

3. Turn away from meat and fish. In the first lunar day, people eat " peace and tranquility noodle" that likes today's thread noodle with duck egg.

4. Go to the graves. People clean up and offer sacrifice to the graves of the forefathers of the family.

5. Be enrolled to school. In the fifth day of the first month

in the lunar calendar, parents should send children to school to make an obeisance to their teachers.

People in the South of Fujian strictly arranged the agenda of the Spring Festival just as sung in a ballad to the effect that the first lunar day determines the good and ill luck, disaster and blessing of the year. So there should be a thorough cleaning, and some coins should be put in the chests and cabinets. On the second day, there is no work to do. Women go back to their mothers'homes to congratulate the new year and give out candies to every child they meat. Women stay at their mothers' homes and will not return until the third lunar day. On the fourth day, people should take a bath before they can burn incenses and place dry fruits in front of the god to welcome the descend of god into this family. For the fifth, the feast stops for a period of time and everyone returns to his walk of life. On the sixth day, parents may beat the bottom of a mischief child (for from the first day to the fifth day, parents can not criticize children in order to complete a perfect happy feast day). On the seventh day, cook the remaining dishes and foods, called "seven precious soup" that is said to be good for all kinds of illnesses. On the eighth day, the family gets reunion to enjoy the happiness of a family relationship. If the wife has not yet returned, family members should send a punitive expedition against the relatives of the woman's side. The ninth and tenth days are the birthdays of the Father Earth and Father Heaven. So nine kinds of animal sacrifices, five kinds of fruits and six kinds of foods should be lain out, and there should be opera shows and Taoist monks invited to the houses to recite scriptures. On the eleventh day, son-in-law arrives and is entertained by father and mother-in-law meticulously. But the son-in-law should bring with him red bags to give out to the children in father-in-law's family. On the twelfth day, all the guests return to their own homes. On the thirteenth day, people begin to eat ordinary meals. On the fourteenth day, people build and tie high lamp shed. On the fifteenth day, people celebrate the Lantern Festival.

The Min customs pay special attention to the Lantern Festival. It will last for more than twenty days. In the areas of the South of Fujian, big avenues and streets and small lanes and alleys are decorated with lanterns and streamers. Performances on street like dragon dancing, lion dancing and stepping on stilts will last deep into the night full of jollification. At home, except that people will cook a kind of delicate cake dish called "Nen Bing Cai" to lay offerings to the dead forefathers of the family, there are a few things that ought to be done without fail: for the newly-wedded daughter of the same year, her mother's family must buy one pair of embroidery ball lanterns and one pair of lotus follower lanterns before the Lantern Festival and send the lanterns to the son-in-law's house by a boy to wish for early birth of a baby. Those daughters who have got married must prepare presents like thread noodles and eggs to be sent to Mom and Daddy after the Lantern Festival. In some places, unmarried girls must do"welcoming girls"(also called "welcoming lavatory girls"). Girls eat a bowl of "delicate cake dish" and then go to the toilet of the village in a group of three or five girls and say prayer beside the toilet. Lads of the village will go there in group to overhear the prayer.

Fujian has many uniquely celebrated feast days. Every twenty-ninth of the first month in the lunar calendar is Fuzhou's "Ao Jiu Day" (also called Hou Jiu Day, Mourning Nine's Day or Sending off Poverty's Day). In the early morning of this day, every family will cook a kind of sticky rice porridge with brown sugar, peanuts, Chinese dates, longan, chufa, red bean, walnut, sesame, etc. This Ao Jiu Porridge is then presented to the dead ancestors of the family and sent to the relatives and neighbors as a gift. Married daughters must send a bowl of Ao Jiu Porridge to her parents as a present. As a Fuzhou saying says that, "Whenever number nine arrives, poverty will follow", which means that if a people's age contains the numeral nine or a multiple of numeral nine, the people will most probably meet poor fortune. Therefore he should manage to send off poverty. The fifth day after the Summer Solstice in lunar calendar is "Feng Long Day" of the East of Fujian. In the day, people could not touch ironware or take dung barrel out of the door. They must pray the King of Dragon not to flood their land. The She minority people usually knock off for the day or carry mountain products to Funing for trade, or just talk exchanging production techniques and life experiences. Youngsters would seek for life partners through cross singing of songs.

II. Marriage and Child Bearing

Human being must continue and family must develop. These are closely related to marriage and child bearing and therefore all through the ages in various civilizations, individuals, families and societies have set store on the linkage. From the viewpoint of the evolution of folk customs and habits, human marriage and child bearing possess the richest forms and inherits the longest history, so does Fujian traditional marriage and child bearing.

The procedures of the traditional marriage and wedding in Fuzhou are very complicated:

1. Asking for character. The male family employs someone to persuade the female family about the marriage;

2. Suiting the marriage. To exchange the birthdays of the two sides and see if their birthdays conflict by fortune teller;

3. Sending invitation card. Select a good day to decide the marriage;

4. First part of presents. The male family sends an engagement card of a dragon and phoenix in a red box together with chicken, duck, wine and cake to the female family; The female family send clothing material for garment and trousers in a red box to the male family in return;

5. Second part of presents. One month before the marriage, the male side sends presents of wine and meat and money to the female family, and the female family in return sends clothes and cap, stationery and cakes as gifts;

6. Preparing Marriage. When the female family receives the engagement money, they should prepare trousseaux and, one day before the wedding, send the trousseaux to the male family in accompany of a band.

7. Dressing up in trial. One day ahead of wedding, the bride will wash herself and dress up with the help of a matron of honor;

8. Meeting the Bride. On the wedding day, the bridegroom under the guide of the matchmaker, meets the bride in her house and brings her back home with a flower decorated litter;

9. Sitting on the bad. When the litter with the bride arrives at the female's house, the bride is guided by the matron of honor to bridal chamber and sits with the bridegroom on the edge of the bad. At this time, the bride should slip the garment of the bridegroom under her bottom silently;

10. Meeting gift. After the courtesy wedding obeisance in the hall, the bride should meet all the relatives according to seniority in the family, and the seniors should give red bag to the bride;

11. Drinking together. The bride and bridegroom drink "happy together wine"in the bridal chamber;

12. Making a fun in the chamber. After the wedding banquet, relatives and friends will make fun in the bridal chamber asking the new couple to give performances;

13. Visiting temple. The following day, the new couple pays a visit to the family temple and meets everyone of the family clan in the house;

14. Trial of kitchen. In the evening, the bride goes to the kitchen in person and tries out her cooking skills;

15. "Nuan Niu". On the third day, the bride's parents come to offer foods;

16. Invitatied to return home. The bride's parents family sends "mother's brothers —relatives by marriage" (usually the bride's brothers; if she has no brother, her parents must borrow a boy as a substitute) to invite the new couple to return to the

home of the bride's parents.

17. "Cuo Shi". The female's side junkets relatives and friends at home. Relatives of the bride's side will ask the bridegroom to open his wallet and entertain guests, to set out a banquet or to invite an opera show.

With regard to marriage and wedding, different places have different operations. For example, when Fuqing people "meet bride", there is a custom of "blocking the litter": people can lay a bench in the way to block the litter when the bridegroom carries the bride home. Only after the blockers are satisfied, they will let the bride and the bridegroom pass. The bride and the bridegroom must not get angry. There are more the blockers on the way, the more popular is the bride for her talent and her appearance, and the more proud the bridegroom will feel. Some place has a habit called "to avoid conflict". When the bride arrives at the gate of the bridegroom's home, the male side should greet her with lightened firecracker, and the bride should be escorted by the relatives of her bridegroom or a senior neighbor woman who is esteemed as rich and fortunate and a matron of honor into the household. At this moment, other woman dependents in the house should temporarily shy away, and extinguish the burning fires in stove in the hall. In the hall, the bride can then show her face. Another habit is "to close the bridal chamber": the male family chooses a bright boy to receive the new dowry closestool. As soon as the boy takes the closestool, he will hide it into the bridal chamber and locks the door from the inside with other boys and girls who have hidden in the chamber beforehand. The bride and bridegroom knock at the

door and bargain with boys and girls inside the door over the o-
pening. The longer the bargain, the more patient are the new
couple, and longer will be their days of conjugal love.

The South of Fujian's marriage and wedding contains "six
courtesies" as following:

1. Ask for the name. The matchmaker goes to the both
sides asking about the birthday.

2. Make an engagement. Both sides decide on the marriage.

3. Purchase and present. Both sides present gifts to each
other.

4. Accept money. Send money as betrothal gift to each other.

5. Invitation Date. Both sides present red cards.

6. Meet the bride. The bridegroom meets the bride at her
home.

Different places in the South of Fujian have different modus
operandi about "the six courtesies". For example, with regard to
the procedure of asking for the names and birthdays, some place
will write the names and birthdays of the boy and girl on a piece
of red paper which will be sent by the matchmaker to the parents
of both sides. Then the red papers will be slipped into the incense burner placed in front of the divinity. If someone in the
house breaks porcelain wares or stumbles over a stone within
three days, this marriage will be relinquished. As to the engagement, the boy goes to the girl's home under the escort of the
matchmaker. The girl serves tea for three times. After that, the
male should give a red bag to the female put under the teapot. If
the money in the red bag is even numbers, it means that the male

agrees to the engagement; if the money is in odd numbers, it means that the male does not agree with the engagement. In some places where Hakka dialect is spoken, the male comes to see for himself whether he likes the girl or the girl likes him or not; and if the female treats him with rice noodles and red egg and gives him stirring-fried rice as a gift, she means that she likes him and agrees to the marriage. If she does not cook rice noodles with red and stirring-fried rice, she indicates that he is not her liking.

"Meeting the bride" in the West Fujian displays many unique features. In the day to meet the bride, the bridegroom must sit inside a litter and holds a white fan in the hand to avoid the evil no matter how cold or hot the weather is. After him there are two other litters seated with the bridegroom's friends that are commonly called "Pao Jia". On arriving at the house of the female, the bridegroom will not get off the litter. The female family receives "Pao Jia", and they offer tea in the neighborhood. Pao Jia can take opportunity to steal two cups back and then put them under the bridegroom's bed as it is said to enables a rapid birth of a boy baby. The female family prepares thread noodles and eggs for the bridegroom who is still in the litter, and the male side presents prepared pig feet and rice dumpling for the female's parents so as to repay their sufferings of bringing up the bride. In some places, when the bride leaves her parents' house, there should be a pair of chickens to lead the way and two poles of sugar canes with roots still attaching. This means that the matron of honor ought to take a hen that is about to lay eggs and a cock that is just about to crow as way leading chicken to

lead the way to the male's house. When the bride gets into the
bridal chamber, people will hide the way leading chickens under
her bed and scatter some rice on the floor. If the cock comes out
first, it means that the first birth will be a boy baby. If the hen
comes out first, it indicates that the first birth will be given to a
girl and then to a boy brother. Three days after the wedding,
when the bride returns from her parents' home, she should bring
two strong poles of sugar canes with roots still attaching and
leaves green and fresh. She places the canes behind the door of
the bridal chamber implying the new couple's life will be as
sweet as the sugar canes and their conjugal love long and lasting.

Some minority's marriage procedures relate to the customs
and habits of the minority nationality. The She Minority people
of the East of Fujian are keen on folk songs, so their marriage
and wedding also incorporate singing of songs. For example,
"To be cousin": Before the wedding, the lassie's aunt shall invite the lassie and her mother to be the guests in the house, regardless of times, and the lassie should wear the best clothes to
her mother's brother's village. There the youngsters will sing
songs with her. If she sings well, the lassie will be appreciated
by listeners, otherwise she will be jeered. "To be uncle of the
marriage": two days before the wedding, the male side invites a
good singer as a full-fledged representative who is commonly
called "uncle of the marriage". The uncle will send gifts to the
female's family together with the matchmaker, and sings songs
for two nights after lunch. If he sings well, the male side will
win dignity from the female side and treatment of courtesy; otherwise, women will laugh at him and make him repair the plough

and do labor as a cow. If so, the male side will loss face. In the areas around Quanzhou, there is a very ancient custom of the Hui Minority named Scattering golden beans. The forefathers of the Hui Minority had been Arabian or Persia merchants. They spent the matrimony day in the female's home and read scripture of Nikaha by an Imam. After that, people would scatter gold beans over the bride and bridegroom to celebrate the happy day and benefit the poor. Poor Muslims could collect the beans. Later, the custom evolved, and the folk now scatter walnut, date, peanut and gingko instead and let the beleaguering children pick them up and eat so as to thank Allah for the predestined relationship and pray Allah to oblige a birth of a baby.

Some marriage customs seem very peculiar. For example, in the South of Fujian Huidong women should stay at the mother's home three days after the wedding except that on holidays or busy farming days they could come to the husband's home and stay for a few days. All year long, they have only six or seven days to live with their husbands. Besides, during these six or seven days the women could come at nightfall with her face covered with a piece of black cloth. Only after the lights are extinguished could they take off the black cover. That is the reason that some couples do not know each other even they have got married many years. Huidong women have to stay at their mothers'home until they get pregnant and are about to give birth to baby. After that they may settle down in their husbands'homes. Some of them stay at their mothers'home for two or three years, and some stay for more that ten or twenty years. Those who have to stay long in their mothers'homes are called "not owing debt"; those who live in their husbands'homes are called "owing debt".

Customs and habits about the birth and bearing vary greatly in different places in Fujian as people attach great importance to them. In Fuzhou, a child is addressed with different "happiness" ever since he is in his mother's womb until he is one year old : "Happiness in a family way" in dicating a woman is in pregnancy; "Happiness in lying-in" indicating that a woman gives out a bowl of peace and tranquility noodle to neighbors and close relatives to report a safe delivery of a baby; the receivers must give her some eggs and thread noodles in return; "Happiness in soup and cake", meaning three days after the birth of the baby, the family should set out a "three days" banquet to feast relatives and friends. The female's family should prepare and send the male's family necessity for the baby and foods for the maternity; "Happiness in a full month" means that when the bay is one month old, his parents should set out a banquet to feast relatives and friends who should send some gifts to the baby as well as red bags; "Happiness in sitting" is to set out a banquet when the baby is four months old and is able to sit in the baby chair; "Happiness in doing Zui", when the baby is one full year of life, his parents should prepare a banquet of the largest scale to feast and dine relatives and friends. Guests can send child clothes or toys as gifts as well as red bags.

In the South of Fujian, the bearing customs of every phrase are quite the same as those popular in Fuzhou, but with different names and modus operandi. The day the child is born is called "Luo Tu", inviting close relatives and friends to eat " happy meal". The third day after the birth is called "San Duan", the parents must send oily rice to every relative and close friend and neighbor and send chicken and duck eggs and fragrant cakes and oily rice to mother's brother's home. When the child is one month old, there is a "soup and cake meeting", the parents must prepare oil rice, meat, noodle and wine to offer as sacrifice to the dead ancestors, and then give out these offerings to relatives and friends as gifts. There is also a banquet for relatives and friends. The parents should invite a senior who is esteemed as possessing happiness an good fortune to feel the baby on the head saying some auspicious words and congratulations, and then he would carry the baby on his back and take a walk on the road which is known as "parade the street". He carries the baby to look into the well intending for the smooth growth of the baby. When the baby is four month old, people would call it "Mian Tao". When the baby is one full year old, it is called "pillow bag", and parents treat relatives and friends with oil rice, red-dyed chicken eggs, pork in return to the guests who have come for congratulation.

It seems common to regard man superior than woman in China and it seems to be a more serious phenomena in Fujian. In the history, there was a bad habit of drowning a girl baby. The customs towards a boy baby and a girl baby are quite different from each other. In the north part of Huian of the South of Fujian, the banquet for a boy baby of one month old is far more grand that that for a girl baby. Besides, the male family should make a lot of round breads that are imprinted with bright red characters of double happiness and send the breads to all the vil-

lagers. Further more, two large baskets of breads should be carried with a bamboo pole to the mother-in-law's family, for
whom to give out to the neighbors. Soak another dozen of red
cooked eggs in the basin for the baby to feel and eat. In some
places in the West of Fujian, when a boy baby is born, his name
will be given by the most senior figure in the family several days
later. And the name will be written vertically on a piece of quad-
rate red paper as follows: a new baby named Jack or Tom who
was born on what date in what month of what year, which is
commonly known as "to write the population post". One copy of
the post is put up in the ancestral temple, the other copy is put
on some conspicuous wall in the hall of the house to let people
know that this family has new boy baby born to it. If the baby is
a girl, people take no trouble to write the post, or to give her a
name.

Ⅲ. Birthday and Funeral

Fujian takes the congratulation on the birthday of a senior
generation very seriously. In Fuzhou tradition, "man celebrates
nine and woman celebrates ten". For example, when a man is a-
bout sixty, he celebrates his sixty birthday at the birthday of fif-
ty-nine, one year ahead of the due time. Because the numeral
"nine" is a partial tone of "long" in Chinese pronunciation, a
symbol of long life. Moreover, One day before the real birthday,
there is a "rang birthday" to celebrate first. That is one day before the birthday, younger generations send candles and noodles.
The candles are burning in front of the spirits of the ancestors;
the noodles in three bowls decorated with paper flowers in each.

The younger generations congratulate the birthday person with courtesy obeisance and then sit down to drink and music. If younger generations have money, they could invite a Taoist or a Buddhism to read scriptures and pray for the birthday person a good fortune and longevity from the Big Dipper, which is called "make a obeisance to the Big Dipper". If still more rich, the younger generations can invite a band to play music in the court-yard, which is called "Jia Guan". As to the real birthday celebra-tion, all colorful lights are on with the hall filled with friends and relatives who can send red bags or candles as gifts. Families of high repute usually issue "birthday note" by offspring to ask for "birthday sequence" and "birthday poetry" from all acquaint-ances as a souvenir.

In the South of Fujian, people usually start to celebrate their birthday at the age of fifty-one (nominal age, reckoned by the traditional method, i. e. considering a person one year old at birth and adding a year each lunar new year), which is called "the first birthday". After the first birthday, the celebration be-comes more grand each birthday which is called "great birth-day". Every morning of the birthday, the whole family eats sweet birthday noodles, which implies that only under the bless-ing of the senior generation is the younger generation able to live long. After that, offspring begin to congratulate birthday to the person. Daughters, sons-in-law and nephews, etc. must come to say congratulations with gifts. The birthday gifts are usually noodles, peaches and tortoises made from wheat powder, but in even numbers to mean that good thing is always in double. For the first birthday ceremony (at the age of fifty-one), birthday peach is a must gift taking the meaning of "flat peach for birth-day"(in Chinese mythology, peach is symbol of immortality). All the gifts should be affixed with red paper or dyed red mean-ing that "it is auspicious to see red color". The host should ac-cept parts of the gifts and return the rest to the givers with an implication of mutual congratulation.

Certain places of Fujian have their own modus operandi a-bout birthday celebration. Every third day of the first lunar month is "the birthday congratulation day" for all Xianyou peo-ple. On this day, foot passengers will take in the hand or on shoulder gifts in red bags or red baskets heading for the home of the birthday person who will set out a banquet for the comers. The origin of this custom is said to have derived from the fact that during the Spring Festival every family has stored sufficient purchases and people are less busy and quite at leisure than usu-al. So it is more convenient to celebrate birthdays during the jol-lification period. A kind of "son-in-law birthday celebration" prevail in some places, i. e. a father-in-law and mother-in-law prepare a celebration ceremony for their son-in-law who is at the age of thirty. On this day, the father-in-law and mother-in-law would take birthday gifts to son-in-law's home for the celebra-tion: fish, for its meaning of more than sufficient; rice wine, for its meaning of enough rice; noodle, for its meaning of longevity; clothes, for its meaning of having a support; date, for its mean-ing of giving a rapid birth to a precious baby; orange, for tits meaning of auspiciousness, etc. On receiving the gifts, the son-in-law shall give as good as he gets some noodles, fruits and cakes to father and mother-in-laws and wishes for their long life.

This kind of celebration does not set out in the hall, but treats guests with birthday wine instead.

Funeral is a special ceremony. Ordinary folk think that death is a sorrow for the live but a release for the dead from the world. The folk usually refer to marriage and funeral as "red and white happy event". The funeral is managed as joyfully as with the marriage. As an inheritance of the culture, funeral customs in fact are the results of the spiritual creations that possess their special procedures in the long course of development.

The funeral customs in Fuzhou seem to be practically trivial and costly. When a person is on the edge of dying, his relatives must disassemble his mosquito net from his bad as it is said that it is easy for the soul to leave; when the person is dead, his relatives should employ some worker who is called "wearing clothes" to change clothes for the dead. (Relatives may change clothes for him.) A note of the death, called "Tiebai" written about someone of some house passed away, whose characters should be in even numbers, should be put on the outer door with firecracker being fired. And then send out reporters in all directions to report the death. At the same time, prepare a big wooden barrel filled fully with sand and insert white burning candles in the sand of the barrel, and place the barrel before the bad of the dead (or light on a dozen oil lamps supported by a turning framework of a few layers) so as to lighten the road to Acheron for the dead. The face of the dead should be covered with a white paper, which means that yin and yang (the live and the dead) should distinguish from each other. A Taoist or Buddhist monk is invited to read aloud scriptures or execrations in the hall of the house while mourning sons and grandchildren wailing around the death bad or under the seven layer of light framework, a situation that is so called "Ba Rang Tai" or "Ban Yao Ti".

To "do the seven" is very important in funeral ceremony in Fuzhou. In Fuzhou dialect, "seven" is a homophony of the word "paint". So wealthy Fuzhou folk paint coffin with seven layers of paint. Every seven days till the forty-ninth day of the death, there should be a memorial ceremony for the dead, which is called "to do the passed sevens". All together, there are seven times of ceremonies. The seventh day after the person is dead, there is a ceremony called "the first seven" or "son of filial piety seven". Sponsored by the son of the family, a Taoist is invited to read scripture on a platform, beating a drum and gang and ringing the bell to report the death to the god of town. The second seven ceremony is "close relatives seven", i. e. the kin and dependents of the dead sponsor the ceremony to invite Taoism scripture reading. The third seven is again a "son of filial piety seven". The forth seven is "relative and friend seven", i. e. relatives and friends sponsor the Taoism scripture reading. The sixth seven is "daughter of filial piety seven" that is sponsored by married daughters. They invite nuns to read scriptures in the hall. The fifth and seventh seven are the biggest activities. On the occasion, obituary notice is sent out to all of the relatives and friends inviting them to take part in the condolence. Condolatory people make a courtesy call to the dead soul in accompany of the sons and daughters beside. After the banquet, the funeral procession starts. Right after the coffin, is a procession of mourning sons and daughters with "crying sticks" in their hands followed by woman dependants and other people crying all along the way. When the burial is finished, the crying sticks are planted in front if the grave. The procession back from the funeral is called "returning carriage". The picture of the dead is then installed in the mourning hall of the house and all the mourners say good-bye to the spirit of the dead one by one under the accompany of the sons and daughters who are expressing their grief by the side. After that, the family members do not stop providing oblations to the passed away in the morning and in the evening until the hundredth day.

The funeral customs practiced in the South of Fujian are also very trivial and complicated. There are mainly: Remove bed, i. e. when the person is dying, move the bed to the left of the hall. Read scripture, i. e. after the person is dead, his sons and daughters must read past life maledictions before the bed. Cry on the road, i. e. married daughters of the passed away on hearing the news of death, hurry back and cry along the way in the lane or street. Receive Zhu, i. e. if the passed away is a married woman, her brothers and brothers' wives are addressed as "Zhu". The family of the dead person should meet "Zhu" to find out or examine if the dead person is murdered. Put on coffin clothes, i. e. the mourning sons and daughters wear mourning clothes whose lower parts are not sewn, and their crying handkerchiefs are not to be cut by scissors but torn apart into pieces. Before the mourning son put on clothes for the dead, he himself must put on a bamboo hat and stand on a bamboo stool. Invite water, i. e. the mourning son holds a water inviting earthen bowl coming to the stream or a well. He puts a piece of white cloth and twelve pieces of copper coins into the bowl and throws some coins into the water and then fetches some water home for the dead to wash with. Coffining ceremony, i. e. before coffining, the family of the dead should prepare twelve dishes which will be presented to the dead by a Taoist monk for the dead to take leave from the life. Usually three days after that, the coffin is buried or cremated. Knock the coffin, i. e. if the parents of the passed away are still living and in good health, they must knock the coffin with a wooden pole on the ceremony, which means a condemnation of the dead who has not fulfilled his filial piety of providing and sending off his parents. Start up the spirit, i. e. let a paper "god of carving out the way" with a mighty and ferocious appearance lead the procession and a straw dragon bring up the rear. Jump over the coffin, i. e. if the dead is a woman and her husband wants to marry again, he should carry a parcel on the back and hold an umbrella in the hand and jump over the coffin. Skive the lot, a rite to disengage the relationship with the dead practiced in some places in the South of Fujian. Before the coffining ceremony, one end of a long hemp thread is fixed to the dead and the other end of the thread is held by close family members. A Taoist monk who is reading auspicious scriptures cuts the thread one section after another. The cut threads then are wrapped in silvery paper and burnt in fire so as to mean that the relation with the dead is disengaged and the dead would not come to disturb any more.

There are many funeral customs that have been inherited for a very long time. The customs of the She minority's funeral have many specialties. For example, Pick the remains: every midwinter, the She folk whose relatives have passed away and buried into earth for three years shall go to the grave and open the coffin and pick out the remains which will be put into an earthen urn. The urn is then placed in somewhere kept away from the wind before it is to be buried in some other auspicious day. In Shouning in the East of Fujian, there is a funeral custom called "position of golden bottle", i. e. to burn the coffin and pick out the ash of bone and put it into a bottle for future burial. It is always the backyard of the house that ash bottles of the family are placed. If there is extra position, it can be sold out. The Hakka's funeral is also very special in that there is a custom called "Dao Shou" (an inverse longevity): usually the age of sixty is considered as longevity, but if an elderly person passes away at the age of sixty, he is referred to as "Dao Shou". The word "longevity" is a partial tone of the word "tree", therefore, the folk would cut a big tree from the back of the residence of the dead or from the mountain for fuel of the funeral.

IV. Beliefs and Taboos

Customs of beliefs originate from the worship of all things on earth in nature. The idea of all things having spirits that has been handed down from the remote ancient period has deeply influenced the beliefs of the later generations. Beliefs distinguish themselves with regional characters. Their originality closely relate to the inhabitancy surroundings, production way and life way. In different places of Fujian, there are different forms worship. The worship of snake is very outstanding. It is said that the Minyue clan worship snake, starting from the prehistoric rock pictures in Hua'an. The pictures all have something to do with the snake. For example, in the rock picture of Caozai Mountain in Hua'an, there are two curves that do not intersect or conjoint each other, and between them, there is an irregular half oval. The drawing, facing a small stream, resembles snake as the long curve stands for a female snake, the short one and the oval stand for a young snake and snake egg. There are snake patterns in the stone carvings on the granite rocks of Jiaolin of Hua'an: the patterns look like two intersecting snakes with a snake egg and a young snake that has just broken through the shell of the egg, or like a small snake that is winding in a ring, or like two snakes that are entangling each other, or like a snake whose head and tail meet, or like a group snakes that are wandering around. The tiles of the West Han period unearthed in the Han Town site in Wuyi municipality embodied patterns of snakes. The Minyue clan took snake as their totem is because their ancestors lived in a warm and humid hilly area with inter-crossing streams and valleys—an area teeming with snakes that threaten the life of the Minyue people. The earlier dwellers in Hua'an to the south of Quanzhou carved pictures to imprecate divinity's protection because of the flood and flood dragon. From being afraid, frightened to imprecating and worshipping in the temple, people wish for the best result through prayers.

The custom of worshipping snake popular in Zhanghuban of Nanping has been strictly followed till this day. Starting from the second half of June every year, villagers will go out everywhere to catch snakes. The caught snakes will be handed in to the wizard of the snake king temple, who will then keep the snakes in a narrow mouthed pottery or wooden barrel, and give a certificate to the catcher. Till the seventh day in the lunar calendar, the villagers adopt a snake by the certificate and take part in the snake greeting activity. Procession of greeting the snake appears so enormous and mighty: flags and banners flying in the wind, music band clearing the way, followed by the grand carriages of the king of snake and Bodhisattva, behind them being a contingent of hundreds of people. Everyone holds a snake, either hanging the snake around the neck or carrying on the shoulder or grasping in the hand—an exhibition of indefinite variety of postures and attitudes, a feast to the eyes. Finally the procession arrives at the side of the Min River, in front of the Snake King Temple. All the snakes are released alive to the river.

Some Fujian folks believe in other animals. For example, The Hakka people living in the south part of the West of Fujian believe in tortoise and roe. Most Hakka villages locate along the rivers and streams teemed with tortoises. The Hakka folk regard tortoise as a holy thing that will bring happiness, so they feed the tortoise with good foods like pork and snail as to imprecate riches and honor. They refer to the people over a hundred years as having a "tortoise age". Sticky rice breads that are used in birthday ceremony are impressed with "tortoise mark". The Hakka folk consider roe as a holy being that is kind to common folk and capable of eliminating disaster and curing illness. The She Minority has been worshipping dog as its totem till this day. They neither beat, curse nor kill a dog for food. Instead they prostrate themselves before the dog. When a dog is dead, it will be flown away in the river, its neck fixed with 'silvery currents'. Fujian is a place prosperous with monkeys, having a habitude of worshipping the monkey early in the history. There have been a lot of monkey temples in some places in the South of Fujian. Today, in Nanjing, Pinghe and Yongtai, there are still monkey king temples for the folk to express worship. It is not rare for some Fujian folks to worship forests and trees or mountains and stones. Those rather ancient forests and trees are regarded as divining wood with spirits such as god of maple, god of banyan, king of camphor or father of pine tree. Among them, the banyan tree is treated as incarnation of an auspicious god. No matter in towns or countryside, people will place a shrine under the heavy shade of an ancient famous big banyan for the folk to offer incenses and imprecate peace. Some natural stones inside a village or behind it is respected and worshipped as the divining position of the Father of the Land, super natural spirit that is protected and preserved very well.

There are not few local gods that are believed and worshipped in the folk of Fujian, but the Goddess of the Heaven, Lady Lishui and Emperor Baosheng are the most well known three gods. The antitypes of these three gods are actually three ordinary persons. They were gradually evolved according to the desire of the folk and then endowed with super power that was capable of protecting people themselves.

Goddess of the Heaven is also referred to as Mazu Sea Goddess, originally named Lin Mo, who was the sixth daughter of Lin Yuan, a roving official to Min capital during the Five Dynasties period. She was born in March 23 of Jianlong first year of Song Tai zhong (960), and was raised to the skies in September 9

in lunar calendar on Meizhou Island of Putian, i. e. in Yongxi
fourth year of Song Tai Zu (987). It is said that after she passed
away, she often showed her presence and power to protect ships
passing by and minister shipwrecks. Hence, fishermen consider
her a safeguard goddess of ocean going. The folk address her re-
spectfully as Mazu or Lady Mother. Since the Song Dynasty to
the Ming and Qing Dynasties, the rulers had honored and promoted her many times as from madam, imperial concubine, the
queen of heaven to Goddess of Heaven. Mazu has been thus believed and worshipped as a god by the folks. Every lunar March,
23rd is Mazu's birthday. Numerous people come on to Meizhou
Island to offer sacrifice and pay memorial call to the Sea Goddess
Mazu. Smoke of incense wreaths over the island and it is too
cloudy for the passengers to move around on the island. Besides,
there will be no fishery or whiffing several days before and after
every March 23rd in lunar calendar so as to monumentalize Mazu. Around Putian, there are a lot of customs about Mazu: As it
is said that Mazu wore cinnabar-colored clothing, women on the
Meizhou Island often wear red trousers to keep fit. It is said that
before her death, Mazu wore a ship shape hairstyle, so women of
Meizhou Island follow suit so as to seek aegis. It is said that calamus is obliged by Mazu, so calamus and argy wormwood are
seen hung on the doors in the areas about Putian at the Dragon
Boat Festival. As Mazu passed away on the 9th of September in
lunar calendar, therefore, Putian folks will steam "nine layers of
rice cake" every 9th of September. Furthermore, every ship that
is about to sail off must hang out on the ship a triangle flag em-
broidered with four characters, Goddess of the Heaven so as to

prevent evil.

The original name of Lady Linshui was Chen Jinggu who had been commonly considered the daughter of a Chen family that had lived in Nantai Xiadu of Fuzhou. She was born on 15 January in lunar calendar, in Dali first year of the Tang Dynasty (766) and died on 28 July of Zhengyuan sixth year of Tang Dynasty (790). As the legend goes that she died of dystocia and had pledged, "After I die, I pledge to prevent people from dystocia. Otherwise, there shall be no god. " Her soul betook herself to King of Hell and begged for the magic salvation arts to ensure safe delivery and healthy bearing for women. Thus she is believed to possess a divining power of protecting fetus and infant. When a woman is brought to bed, people will consecrate to the picture of Lady Linshui in the house and three days after the birth of the child, the family shall cook sticky rice and offer the rice before the picture. The more people worship Chen Jinggu, the more divinely powerful she becomes. Even a sterile woman can beg her for a child. A married woman who suffers from the sterility for several years comes to the temple and prostrates herself in front of the picture of Lady Lin Shui and then keels down and holds up the lower part of her clothes. An old woman will take a flower and put it into her clothes saying, "When the child is born to the world, the child must come to recognize Lady Linshui as nominal mother". On so saying, she sticks the flower in the hair of the worshipper. If the flower is red, the child is female. If the flower happens to be white, it means that the child to be born will be a male. Every year, when it is the birthday of Lady Linshui, the temple will invite several longevous and fortunate elder women to change clothes for the goddess in the temple. Women provide incenses and offer worships. In the evening, people raise the statue of the goddess on shoulder and make a parade on the street. But every memorial day, "a boy" is placed in a "bright dou"(most probably a bright box that is big enough to hold 1 decaliter grain) as a substitute of a real child, and the bright box will be placed on an infant bed while the master is blowing a cow horn. Lady Linshui died at the age of twenty-four, so the female avoid to get married at the age of twenty-four.

Emperor of Baosheng has been also known as God of Health whose original name was Wu Tao. He was also commonly called Wu Zhenren, born in the fourth year of Taiping Xinguo (AD 979) in Baijiao of Tongan County of Quanzhou in the Song Dynasty, died in the third year of Jingyou (AD1036). Wu Tao was a folk doctor who believed in Taoism and was proficient in herb medicine and leechcraft. No illness and patient could he not cure of. With a heart to help the world, he treated every one of his patients, no matter he was poor or rich. So he was very famous in the South of Fujian for his super leechcraft and noble morals of a doctor. The folks respect him and worship him. He fell into an abyss and died when he was trying to collect herbs for his patients. People built Immortal Temple (Benevolent Palace) in his birthplace and in the place he used to refine pills and prescribe medicines. The past dynasties had subsequently conferred him imperial titles for nine times such as the title Indefinite Longevity Emperor of Life Defender conferred in the Ming Dynasty. As the leechcraft and the virtues of Wu Tao answer for the im-

mediate interests of common people, worship for him has prevailed for a very long time. Whenever people come down with an
illness, they will go to seek for blessing from Wu Tai. In the
greeting deity competition held in the first month in lunar calendar, Wu Tao, as one of the parade gods, will sit in a litter carried by eight persons. Every March 15 is Wu Tao's birthday.
The folk will march in a procession holding up flags and banners, beating drums and gongs with pavilion and colorful booth
leading the way to Benevolent Palace to present incenses.

Taboo is a special religious custom of negatively defensive
resort or idea containing two meanings: do not use the respected
holy things; do not touch the condemned, unclear, dangerous
things. Do not violate things under taboo, otherwise there will
be sanction and punishment sooner or later. There are various
kinds of strange taboos in Fujian too numerous to be enumera-
ted. Some of the taboos contradict each other and seem very
complicated and confusing. The universality and complexity of
taboos have long infiltrated in the lives and production of people
and will always influence them for the rest of their time.

It may well be termed that taboo is immanent in Fuzhou
people's daily life. A host will fill the bowl with rice as high as a
mount. A guest may say that he is not able to finish so much and
remove some of the rice to the host bowl. To do that he must not
hesitate, and most of all, he must not insert his chopsticks in the
rice, for it is infelicitous, because there usually would be a bowl
of mourning food filled fully to the edge of the bowl with two
chopsticks sticking upright offered as a sacrifice beside one end of
the coffin in the mourning hall in Fuzhou. After the New Year's

Eve dinner, Fuzhou people will wipe the mouth of a child with toilet paper to indicate that if the child happens to talk about death or evil things or words, they do not count. In a wedding banquet, the plates or bowls could not be piled up together, as it might implies a bigamy. The completely cooked fish on the banquet is not to be touched so as to wish and congratulate the host a complete happy year from the beginning to the end. Family members going out far away from home, relatives and friends calling upon from a far away place, celebrating the birthday of an elder, on the wedding, there would be a bowl of peace and tranquility noodle steamed with eggs. There are far more taboos in spoken language: to want a bowl of rice, one should say "come on a bowl of rice" in order to avoid a mistake for begging; short pants must be referred to as "trousers long" or half long trousers, because the word "trouser" is a partial word for the word "store" and short storage is an unwelcome expression. If a person has passed away, he shall be referred to as being born to life instead of being dead. To make mourning clothes should be said as making longevity clothes. To purchase a coffin should be said as "choose longevity board".

The South of Fujian people also have various taboos. Ever since a being is born to this world, he is confined by numerous taboos and commandments that are easily violated. When an infant is about six month old, he is permitted to see six kinds of people: people in mourning period, a bride, a patient, a widower and widow, a stranger and a madman. As a person in mourning period belongs to obsequies, he conflicts a happy event. On the other hand a bride belongs to a happy event that is considered a conflict to another happy event; and the rest of the four kinds of people are considered unlucky for the infant. Gifts for a confined woman must be chicken instead of duck, for duck is regarded to be humid and wet, not to say that among the folk, there are sayings like "a dead duck of hard closed mouth", "a duck in the middle of July does not realize its dead end", reminding people of unhappy things. No one is allowed to stand on the threshold of the door or bring an electric torch into a bridal chamber. On the New Year's Eve and the first day of the New Year, it is forbidden to break furniture especially bowls and plates. If there is some incident happening such as a patient or an accident, there must be always pine tree branches inserted on the door or at home and no stranger entering the house so as to avoid the evil. People who have just attended a mourning event shall not go to attend a red event like a wedding. If there has been a funeral, the family shall not hold a happy event like a marriage within a whole year period. Back home from a trip or a visit, the straw sandals should be put outside the door so as to avoid bringing home the evil spirit on the way. For straw sandal is an object for a mourning event. Gifts for other people shall be in even numbers instead of a single number, for an even number means a pair or a couple of happy or reunion celebration. Some objects are not considerd appropriate to be a gift such as handkerchief, scissor, fan or umbrella. Handkerchief is a souvenir from a funeral ceremony indicating a farewell forever. Scissor may contain a meaning of a thorough break. Giving a umbrella in the South of Fujian dialect is a partial tone for "giving a mourning". A fan is used in summer but put away in Autumn, so it does not stand for a long relationship. Sweet rice cake or Zongzi (a pyramid-shaped rice dumpling made of glutinous rice wrapped a bamboo or reed leaves eaten during the Dragon Festival) are forbidden to give others as a gift, for a mourning home conventionally does not make sweet rice cake or Zongzi. They will be mistaken. When in a mountain, it is forbidden to address people's name as ghosts and spirits will come to haunt around if they know people by name. When in a forest, it is forbidden to howl in order not to disturb wide beasts. When getting down into water, it is forbidden to go alone. When on the roof, it is forbidden to sit on the cornice so as to avoid an accident. It is forbidden to wear a piece of clothes inside out, for it may mean a mourning event at home. It is forbidden to knock the desk or bowls with chopsticks, or the candles with hands or other things, which may hurt God Father of Stoves.

Although it may be in a same region, differential exists in taboos and commandments because of difference in life ways and production ways. For the fishermen along the coastal lines of the South of Fujian, it is forbidden to turn upside down the fish when eating: eat the upper part of the fish first, and then remove the chine bones exposed before starting to eat the other side of the fish, never to turn the fish on the plate up side down, for turning the fish that way is deemed equal to ship turning over, a bad sign. Some fishermen do not like to put the chopsticks on the edge of a bowl, instead they will circle the chopsticks around the bowl several times to indicate the ship is sailing around the submerged reefs and shoals.

V. Parade Arts and Competitions

Parade arts and competitions usually pertain to many folk customs without their own independence. Nevertheless, parade arts and competitions get themselves inherited and characterized by circulation of many regional customs and habits. Fujian regional customs and habit present themselves with spectacular varieties and features, and so do the parade arts and competitions popular in Fujian.

Parade arts and competitions relate to the annual festivals and feast days, and many places go in for activities and programs of their own. Folks in Kengtingding Village of Jinjiang celebrate the Dragon Festival with a uniquely styled parade of "throwing". The word "throw" in local jargon means an activity of demonstrating marksmanship. The performer holds a shotgun in hands, carrying a parcel of fire powder (a horn-shaped wooden tin containing fire powder) and a bag (made from cloth to keep fuse and iron grains) on the shoulder and back. The requirements and regulations of throwing are as following: the performer should overstep all kinds of barriers while firing at goals in different surroundings with various firing postures; the performer should be able to play to the score. The thrower must be trained strictly to follow or master the set footwork for different route, to adopt the fixed firing postures for certain goals. Only in command of the basic footwork, can the performer be able to shoot the targets with high rate of hitting in full charge. The audience can appreciate the work and skills of the arms, legs, back, fingers and sight of the performer. In Hutou Town of

Anxi County, during the Spring Festival, there is a special activity called Dressing up for a Pavilion Show. Build a pavilion of about a double bed in width, install on the two ends of the pavilion two iron poles and put a plank between the two poles, and beleaguer the pavilion with a fence of one chi (a unit of length, one chi= 1/3 meter)in height. Let two handsome lads sit on the plank, fix them to the iron poles with newly woven cloth stripes, put on them theatrical costumes, make-ups and decorative pearl crowns of a dan in an ancient opera, so they may look attractive and secluded. And then hide their feet in the pants and dexterously fix a pair of small shoes of three inches long (commonly called three inch golden lotus) under their pants and attach to their small fingers a piece of handkerchiefs so that they may appear more graceful when they play on the white sandalwood. The pavilion is decorated as a garden with new flower-patterned paper on the surface and paper pots of flowers in the middle. The two lads sing South Tones rhymed by sandal beats. Four strong men carry the colorful pavilion on shoulder and parade the street in the spring-touring procession. They will stop to sing a few lines of the South Tones wherever they think it is necessary. Xiayang Town of Nanping also practices the custom of parading a "pavilion" on the street during the Spring Festival. This kind of pavilion is a movable platform or stage, one square meter in area fend with flower-patterned paper railing. In the middle, there installed an iron framework of two layers that are able to stand on them four or five children dressed up as the dramatis personas such as Nezha Making a Rumpus in the Sea, Mother Instructing His Son in the Spinning Room and Visiting Thatch for Three

Times, etc. Dongshi Town of Jinjiang celebrates their feast day
with "centipede pavilion"(also called dragon pavilion). The pavilion procession is consisted of several dozens of pavilions constructed with wood blocks of two meters long and one meter
wide. The pavilions are connected by movable knots from the beginning to the end, and on the pavilions, there are skillfully installed various animals and beats, and several cute and lovely
children to be dressed up as dramatis personas. At the head of
the procession, a dragon is installed, and at the end of the procession, there is a tail of the dragon, all carried on shoulders by
strong youngsters in uniform. The procession looks extremely
like a centipede or a moving dragon.

In some places of Fujian, annual festivals are celebrated
with particular parade forms. For example, Dongping Villagers
of Zhenghe County do not put on dragon lantern dance in the
first month of the lunar year but they hold a dragon running
competition, which in fact is a dash race in uniform. The competition arena is set on the level ground for solarizing corns. Starting point is at one side of the ground, over it is a bamboo shed
constructed with four bamboos with leaves still on, which is se-
vered as the dragon gate; and the opposite side of the ground is
the finish point, over which is an archway constructed with two
big bamboo poles with leaves on. Hanging from the arch is a big
round shining lantern about three meters above the surface of the
ground, so the lantern is called the gate of pearl. Competition
team is usually made up of seven team members and each member holds a bamboo lantern; and the first member holds a dragon's head lantern and the last member holds a dragon tail's lan-

tern. So the race team looks like a long dragon. Four teams coming from the east street, south street, west street and north street will take part in the round robin competition. Two competing dragon teams starting from the dragon gate each holding a lantern in hand will first run around their dragon gate three circles and then dash for the dragon pearl gate. He who touches the pearl at the gate by the dragonhead first is the winner. On the fourth day, the champion belongs to the one who has accumulated the most winning scores. In some places of the South of Fujian, people do not enjoy the moonlight, but instead they play a game of cake (also called betting on cakes), i. e. to cast six lots into a big bowl and divide the cakes according to arrangement of the points shown on the six lots, just as in a gambling: One Zhuangyuan for one cake; Two Tanhua for two cakes; Three Huiyuan for four cakes; Four Jinshi for eight cakes; Two Juren for sixteen cakes and One xiucai for thirty-two cakes. The game is settled after a whole set is finished. The winner Zhangyuan is considered to be very auspicious. The champion should let off fire firecracker and invite other players to share his cakes to celebrate complacently. People in Luofang and Tanbei of Liancheng County spend the Lantern Festival in Walking Stories that are full of regional flavor. Luofang of Lou Surname used to have nine platforms for walking story, but now there are only seven platforms remained. On every platform, there are two handsome children dressed up in Heaven Official and Officer, and after them stands Lishimin with Xuerengui; and Liubang with Fankuai; and Yangliulang with Yangzongbao; and Guaozhen with Meiwenzhong; and Liubei with Kongming; and Zhouyu with Ganning, all in pair. The Heaven Official stands on an iron pole, and his waist is fastened by iron rings while the Heaven Officer sits on a platform, one of his hands supporting the Heaven Official, which forms a beautiful structure. The platform is actually a square wood framework whose four sides decorated with exquisite picture screens. Every platform weighs about two hundred kilograms with two carriage bars on the left and right sides for twenty carriers to carry on the shoulder. As the walking is a very intense competition, it takes three spells. The walking story divides into two shifts: one shift is performed in the morning of the fourteenth. Carriers surround in the middle, the litter of Bodhisattva, colorful flag and precious umbrella, etc. running on a four hundred meter oval shaped racetrack. They start to run as soon as the blunderbuss is fired, and take a ten-minute rest after finishing every two circles. Till the fifth shift, the running speed reduces, which turns the race into a walk. But the race will not finish until the first platform is out of joint with the second platform, all carriers exhausted. The second walking story takes place in the morning of the fifteenth of the first lunar month. The first part of the race is performed just in the form of the previous day. Till one o'clock in the afternoon, all story platforms step down into the river bed of blue rocks in throngs and walk against the river current as soon as the blunderbuss fired three times. The competition between the platforms are intense and it is judged if the behind platform is able to catch up with the advanced platform, for it indicates that this family or clan will be prosperous enjoying an abundant harvest of all food crops. The carriers try their best to run in the first place in extremely high spirits regardless of cold weather and deep water.

Parade arts and competitions relate to various kinds of temple fairs. Fuzhou used to regard Taishan as the God of the city, so it was grander to greet Taishan than other divinities. Every 23rd of March in the lunar calendar, whatever divinity it is, it must pay homage to Taishan in Dongyue Temple. On the 24th, Taishan parades the city proper and on the 25th, Taishan parades Nantai. The procession is very huge preceded by ceremonial band for the Son of Heaven, eighteen weapons and followed by various colorful operas such as stilt and Dixiaping that are played right on the spot; and strong men carry children who are dressed up in color on their backs to perform Carried on Shoulders; but trumpeters will sit on the rented horse back playing tones to show a Blowing on the Horse Back. All musical instruments play together Shifang and Annanchi; and flower baskets are carried on the shoulders, so as Kangdan, i. e. baskets that are filled with cultural relics; and mini wooden platform pavilions will be filled with little boys and girls that are dressed up in dramatis personae. Among them, the most attractive and noisy performance is Sailing Boats on Land. These are boats constructed with colorful paper and carrying two people who are dressed in Huadan and Xiaosheng. They imitate to row and pole the boat sailing on the water while singing and dancing. Whenever they meet "a summer palace" setting out a banquet or building up a hall on their way, the Huadan and Xiaosheng in the procession will come out to sing some popular songs under the firecrackers. After the colorful opera, there are all kinds of divining officers like Heiwuchang, Baiwuchang, Fork Father, Third Prince of

Nezha. All of them walk in their fixed dancing steps. Following
them are twenty-eight persons dressed up in eunuchs lifting
stoves and color lanterns guiding the way. Another eight great
officers are shielding the carriage while sixteen persons carrying
Taishan's soft statue will walk slowly forward. Tongan area
prevails a parade of "Copying Songjiang" in the greeting god
competition of the temple fair. "To copy" means to imitate or
perform, which is an art of martial art performance. Every sixth
day of the first lunar month for Father Qingshui of Xiangshan,
every twelfth of February for the holy birthday temple fair of
Wang Shenzhi, the Min King of the Northern Mountain, there
are five or six Songjiang teams come to give performance on the
playground; so there are all together thirty-six or seventy-two
performers. All the performers play the part of Lu Junyi, Caijin,
Likui, Sun Erniang, etc. They hold weapons in the hand and
have dragon flag bearers precede in front. The stage is a town
scene put up by two stripes of cloth, and performers charge out
of the town in two dispatches, which is called "wasps charging
into battlefield". After that, there is a single performance of
martial art: Likui using double axes, Guangsheng wielding big
broadsword; and there follows a dual-meet performance: shield
versus hammer, umbrella versus broadsword, falchion versus i-
ron harrow; and group performance of contest; etc. Besides,
there is lion dance: Songjiang team members wrestling with lions
boosted by the drums and gongs and Suona. When performances
are finished, all the troops are withdrawn into the town. Huge
crowd of audience will watch the show.

　　Some folk parade arts display a rather high level of skills.

For example, it is impossible for ordinary people to manage "Paifan", a sort of tier flag show popular in Jianou. The flag is normally a five or six-meter-long bamboo pole painted with oil paint, hung colorful stripes and a tower lantern from the top and decorated with colorful papers or dramatis personas. To manage the pole, the performer first puts the pole on the toe of his foot; and lift it lightly to make the pole rest on his shoulder; and again shake the pole onto the arm or palm. The performer will have to do several jobs in the same time using first one hand and then the other in quick succession, making the pole rest on the shoulder or foot or from foot to hand and arm and then to shoulder, even onto his nose and mouth without falling off. The colorful stripes and lantern dance together in riotous profusion looking as if divining lanterns of the empyrean were waving to and fro in the sky — too many things for the eyes to see.

Ⅵ. Foods and Drinks

Among the eight cuisine systems in China including Beijing, Shandong, Guangdong, Jiangsu, Hunan, Sichuan and Hubei and Fujian, Fujian cuisine has a distinctive style of its own.

Fuzhou cuisine is a representative of the Min dishes, possessing a unique flavor. The materials and seasons for Fuzhou dishes are mainly produced in the locality, and special attention is paid to the proper cutting work, level of attainment, color, smell, flavor and shape for a dish in the operation. Various cooking methods such as stir-fry, quick-fry, stew, steam are utilized dexterously. The main characteristics of Fuzhou cuisine are as following: 1. Good at using sugar. Fuzhou people like to use sugar as a season and make the dishes taste sweet, sour and light in flavor, which is quite different from the Hunan cuisine that is good at using capsicum in dishes. Sugar is able to rid dishes of the smell of fish and mutton while vinegar is tasty and refreshing, a flavor suitable to the brazing hot weather of Fuzhou. Light flavor is able to keep the original taste and fresh taste of a dish. Proper use of sugar, vinegar and other seasons can make the dish taste sweet yet not greasy, sour yet not severe, light yet not tasteless. 2. Frequent usage of grains. Red grains is a native product of Fuzhou. So Fuzhou cuisine utilizes grains in more than ten ways, such as in light grains, drunken grains, etc. Besides, shrimp oil (also called Qi oil) is frequently used as a season. 3. Many soup dishes. Fuzhou cuisine is good at keeping the fresh taste by cooking the dish in soup. It is said that there are one hundred soups of one hundred flavors. Soup dish is the essence of the Min cuisine. Proper auxiliary materials can produce numerous perfectly delicious courses without losing its original taste. There are above two thousand dishes cooked by Fuzhou cuisine, and among them, Fu Tao Qiang, Light Grains Quick-fried Bamboo Razor Clam, Best Crab Holding Oysters are well known dishes at home and abroad.

The formation of Fujian foods and drinks characterized of distinctive regional flavors is connected with the unique geographical conditions, climate and productions of Fujian. Fujian lies on a long coastal line teemed with rich sea products. Consequently, dishes made from sea products constitute the majority like Chicken Soup Stewed Clam, Quick-fried White Fresh of Dried Shellfish and Crisp Sleeve-fish Slice, etc. Some flavored snacks are also made from sea products like "water pellet of deep sea" (Yuwan, in Chinese), Hai Lijiang (Oyster sauce fry), Thick Soup of Fried Crab, etc. Fujian is a mountainous area teemed with mountain products, well known ones like: Dried Sweet Potato made in Liancheng, Dried Pig Liver made in Wuping, Dried Radish made in Shanghang, Dried Meat made in Mingxi, Dried Vegetable made in Yongding, Dried Capsicum made in Ninghua, Dried Mouse made in Qingliu, Dried Bean Curd made in Changting, etc. Some well-known dishes are made up of mountain products as raw materials. For example, Dragon and Phoenix Soup, popular in Wuyi Mountains, is made up of meats of Snake and Chicken cooked together, Winter Bamboo Shoot in Clear Water, Mushrooms in Wine popular in the North of Fujian, and Taiji Mud of Taro made in Fuding, etc. Fujian depends upon paddy plantations, consequently many foods with typical regional traits are made from rice. For example, Shao Rou Zong (Rice dumpling with pork stewed in soy sauce) made in Xiamen, Shi Shi Sweet Rice Cake popular in the south of Fujian, Paogueng (sticky rice pellet covered with powder of fried bean), Bai Ba Guo popular in Fuzhou, Xinhua Fen (rice noodle made in Xinhua) produced in Putian, and Ciba in the west of Fujian (pellet made from steamed sticky rice that is smashed into rice mud). It is humid in Fuzhou, which is suitable for planting fruits of the tropics, subtropics and temperate zones, and Fujian native fruits like orange, longan, lichee, banana, pineapple, loquat, olive and sugar cane are known far and wide. Accordingly, Fujian people are particular about eating fruits. For example, Zhangzhou is known for a kind of Grapefruit Banquet. On the banquet, people light on grapefruit oil lamp, drink grapefruit tea, eat grapefruit meat, and sugar confected skins of grapefruit. Dongbi Dragon Pearl produced in Quanzhou, is a dish that is made up of longan meat (quick-fried through the oil), Kumquat Candy made in Yongchun, Qingjin Fruit made in Xiamen, Wuxaing Olive made in Fuzhou, are all sold well at home and abroad.

Fujian enjoys a profusion of annual precipitation, and much of its land is reddish loess, which provide an excellent natural condition for planting tea trees. Out of the six major teas, the green tea, oolong tea, black tea, jasmine tea, white tea and hard pressed tea in China, five major teas are produced in Fujian in a great amount, except the hard pressed teas (i. e. tea block and tea cakes that are mainly used by the minority nationalities). Besides, almost every county in Fujian produces teas. So Fujian is one of the five major tea producing provinces in China, the other four provinces being Zhejiang, Hunan, Hubei and Sichuan. Some famous best quality teas like Tie Guanyin (a variety of oolong tea) produced in Anxi, Da Hongpao (Scarlet Robe) produced in Wuyi Mountain, Baihao Yingzhen (White Hair Silvery Needle) produced in Fuding, to name only a few, have a good reputation far and near. Tea production in Fujian has a history of long standing. As early as Southern Tang period, there was an Imperial Tea Garden of the North in the North of Fujian. The custom of drinking prevailed more widely than any other provinces in China, resulting in the formation of particular tea drinking custom to such an extent that it might be just as a saying goes that it is not a home if there will be no tea even for one day.

Gongfu Tea (time-consuming tea) is a profound art and

craft of making tea and appreciating tea, which requires a strict operation and a time-consuming labor. To prepare for the making of a cup of tea: first, take out some of the best quality tea of Tie Guanyin, the oolong tea, Wuyi Rock tea; and set out the exquisite tea set with the tea pot being the best if the inner side of it is not glazed and tea cups of a small and cute size being the best; spring water for making the tea is the best, and well water takes the second place; the water should be boiled by charcoal fire. To make a cup of tea: the boiled water must pour into the pot from a higher level and then the water is lowered to a level position so as to dunk the tea. The two overlapped actions are very important because the rushing water can stir the tea leaves to release the juice and fragrance quickly and then lower the pouring to a level position so as to keep the water hot enough and keep the fragrance inside the pot. To appreciate tea: pick up the tiny walnut like tea cup and appreciate to the heart content of the strong and pervasive fragrance, and then gently sip the tea juice into mouth and throat; stop to concentrate on the flavor of the tea; and then feel first in the whole mouth and then in the body a flavor of freshness and sweetness stirring just as what they called "the universe is vast in tea, and the life is long in teapot".

"Tea Contest", also called "Tea Fight" or "Tea Comparison" is to distinguish the winners from the losers according to the quality of tea through concrete procedures of making, tasting and appreciating teas. Fang Zhongyan wrote in his poem entitled An Answer to Zhangmin's Tea Contest Song about the grand occasion of tea contest taking place in the North of Fujian, "… Flavor of the tea coming from the contest disparages the fragrance of the finest cream; and the fragrance coming from the contest weakens the smell of orchid. Under ten eyes watching and ten fingers pointing, to place them on the name list of the contest is no kidding. The winner feels as if he was mounting to a paradise attracting admiration from all; but the losers are downgraded to suffer boundless humiliation". In a tea contest, the contester grinds the tea into tiny powder and put the power into the teapot that has be washed and warmed, and the pour boiled water into the teapot. Lightly stir the tea to compare its tea color and water trace in the pot with those of others. Decide the winner and loser according to the quality of teas. The operation skills and arts are demanded daintily. To pour water, the operation must be accurate and reserved to avoid either result of "too much soup for less tea causing a disperse cloud, yet less soup causing a cloudy surface". The contester pours boiled water by one hand and lightly and rhythmically stir the tea with a bamboo stirring stick by the other hand, two hands cooperating in harmony. If you win the contest, both the market and the price of the tea will raise. So to contest for a champion is a vital event for tea planters and in turn the population of tea contest boosts the improvement of tea quality and the formation of tea drinking habit.

"Fen Cha", also called "Tea Operas", is an entertainment, i. e. to pour boiled water into the tea powder and wait to see the illusive formation of the tea soup into characters or certain patterns. Tea and water mingle with each other by the boiled water. Their soup arteries and veins will show themselves in wonderful and magic changes: there are birds and wide beasts, insects or fishes, grasses and flowers as well as beautiful stretching landscapes or delicate pictures. But all will disappear instantly. Poet Yang Wanli depicted the scene of Fen Cha vividly in his poem Watch Zens Doing Fen Cai on Zhang An Seat: The new jade fingers of Longxin new spring season, ··· "How can Fen Cha be better than cooking tea, yet how can cooking tea be more dexterous than Fen Cha? The aged water steaming zen and spring player, Watch Zens Doing Fen Cai on Zhang An Seat: The new jade fingers of Longxin new spring season, ··· How they are apt to changes in strange forms. Like clouds sailing across the space, shadows in boundless shapes falling off from cold sky; under the silvery cups and heads, out of the pouring water float characters smart and bright. "

"Leicha" (tea that is smashed into mud before being drunk) is a vogue of the West of Fujian and the North of Fujian. The ingredients of this tea are green tea of good quality, white sesames, peanuts, mung beans and sundry Chinese medicines, all of which are put into an earthen bowl to be smashed into tiny pieces and then grinded into mud; and wrap the tea mud in a piece of gauze and sieve the juice; and then dunk juice with boiled spring water. With different additional ingredients, there can be different varieties: sweet, salt, meat or vegetable, etc. Leicha produced in Jiangle is the most outstanding one, which possesses particular medicine functions. To make a Leicha, factors like season, climate, proper people and occasion must be taken into consideration. To produce different curative effects, Chinese medicines of different functions shall be added accordingly into the tea. For example, Leicha may possess the functions of clearing heat and fever, helping digest, stopping cough and dissolving spit. A cup of Leicha that has been made ready for drink looks pour in color, tastes pleasant and sweet and smells fragrant in the mouth. Leicha is also a very grand gift for entertainment, for it is regarded as a way of expressing celebration. Some places practice a custom called "Leicha on Being Admitted into College", i. e. when a high school student is enrolled by a college or university, the parents will entertain the relevant teachers or couches to Leicha. So teachers are the most favorable guests on the entertainment.

Art of tea making is the essence of the profound tea culture. It is a highly poetic amusement pleasing the heart and soul. To appreciate tea, there are some details that might be followed out as well. It would be better if the surrounding looks clearly elegant and classically quaint; the mood and manner remain peaceful and restrained; tea set looks shiny and glossy; clear mountain spring water holding in sandy or copper teapot is boiled by charcoal fire. But the arts and crafts of making a tea and appreciating a tea require more particularities, for there are many proprieties and doctrines to follow: to pour the first teapot, the tea must be slightly given to each cup, and evenly pour round all the cups, which is named "Guangong patrols the town"; when there is little tea left in the teapot, just drop little to each cup, which is compare to "Hangxing musters his soldiers"; to hold up a tea cup, it is better that thumb and forefinger buttress the cup and the middle finger support from the bottom of the cup, which is named as "protect the vessel by three dragons".

Chapter Nine
Education

Fujian started to develop in a comparatively late period, and so did its education. According to the records in literature, in Taikang Third Year of the western Jin Dynasty(282), there set a Jin'an County in Fujian; in Liu Song Period, Ruan Mizhi was Taishou (the highest administrative official in a county from the Han Jin Emperor) to Jin' an County. He started to set up schools. At that time, people a cultural life of "reading poems and books, and not to fight with weapons on the street" (*Famed Officials Fujian Complete History*); when Yuyuan was assumed Taishou to Jin'an, he "set up a school and taught disciples" (*Biography of Yuyuan from the South History*). Furthermore, some scholars who had migrated from the Central Plains set up schools off and on by spells, despite of the limited influence on the whole, which obviously laid a foundation for the educational development later on.

During the Sui and Tang periods, education in Fujian was still at the starting stage, though it had been greatly developed. When Li Yi who was an imperial clansman of the Tang, was the Observer to Fujian, he "esteemed schooling and encouraged learning custom" (*Officials from Three Mountain Records*), and "greatly established learning institutes and persuaded students" (*Officials from Records on Eight Mins*). When Chang Gun assumed the Observer to Fujian, he "set up local schools, engaged famous masters to teach Fujian people who then started to go to school" (*Reconstruct Chang Gun's Epitaph*). Lu Changyuan, who was Cishi (a title of the imperial official) to Jiangzhou, also paid attention to running schools and persuading people to go to school. Chen Yuanguang, Cishi to Zhangzhou, made his son study hard to encourage the local people to attend school. When the son of Chen Yuanguang was in charge of the county affairs, he gathered students and taught them. According to what is described in the book *Picture Scriptures*, "both Li Yi and Chang Gun thought highly of establishing learning institutes alone the coast extending to Zhusi (the ancient name of a place, possibly in today's Shandong province)". In the Five Dynasties, Fujian education began to popularize. On one hand, famous scholars returned to their hometowns in succession and set up schools after the finish of the Tang Dynasty. For example, Huang Qiao, who had been the senior official of the Works Department of the imperial court (in Chinese, the title for the official is called Gongbu Shangshu), returned to hometown and set up a learning institute called "Heping College" and "invited Confucians to give lectures on poesy and verse so as to guide the youngsters". (*Huang Qiao, Founder of the Huang Family in Zhiyun*); on the other hand, Wang Shenzhi, the King of the Min, set up schools over a wide area. He appropriated a special fund for teacher and student's

meal and gave order that all children of study age should go to
school. The records on Tablet of Benevolence of Lang Ya Emperor, which is now kept in Fuzhou Ancestral Temple of the
King of the Min, say about him that "Trying to set up school is
meant for having a source of civilization, that is, to instruct un-
cultivated children to learn to know the courtesy." During the
Five Dynasties, Fujian society was found rather stable, which
provided a good condition for education popularization.

In the Song Dynasty, Fujian education developed further.
Jianzhou State College in Nanping was set up in Tiansheng Third
Year (AD1025), whose teaching system, subject and course setting, teaching stuff and facilities all reached a certain level. After
that, eight military states had built up state colleges, and later,
even counties built up learning institutes. About fifty-six institutes of this kind could be checked up in the records. So in the
Song Dynasty, the quantity and the quality of colleges together
with their influence had been quite infrequent across the country
at that time. According to *Relics Studies on the Idealist School
in Famous Wuyi Site*, there were twenty colleges that had related to some extent to the Idealist scholars such as Zhu Xi, and
fourteen of them were in Jianyang. Some colleges had a reputation over the country. Admirers from other provinces came to
seek for learning in an endless stream. In the Song Dynasty, educational enterprises run by the local people like Righteousness
Room, Study Hall, Private School, were quite popular as well.
To attend school became a common practice. Just as what county
historical records had described in poetic languages that Fuzhou
was seen "the city and its bridge were best remembered under

tranquil and peaceful lamps and lights, the south end and the north end of the lane were heard reading poems aloud"; Nan'an "within a distance of one hundred *li* (one li equals 500 meters), music strings and book reading aloud were echoing each other" (*Records on Confucian Temple Construction*); Tingzhou "Vogues and habits quite like those of Zhongzhou" (*Postscript of Inscription for Learning Field* by Chen Yixin of the Song); Yanping "Five step distance away there is a private school, and ten step distance away there is a school. Sounds of reading aloud and reciting in the morning and playing stringed music in the evening filled the air far and wide" (*History of Yanping*); Shaowu "Reading aloud under the company of stringed music from the neighborhood are filling in the whole ear" (*History of Shaowu*); even in the remote area like Taining "reading aloud under the company of the stringed music from the near doors were heard by each other. Those who do not study poetry and prose would be laughed at by beloved mass" (*History of Taining*).

In the Yuan, Ming and Qing Dynasties, educational enterprises in Fujian developed forward in general and ranked the top in the country in spite of the slight declination in some places caused by chaos of war affairs and Japanese invasion. Take the colleges constructed in the past dynasties as an example. According to imperfect statistics about the colleges of certain influence that can be checked up on historical literatures, in the Yuan Dynasty, there were twenty; in the Ming Dynasty, there were two hundreds; in the Qing Dynasty, there were three hundreds. During the Ming and Qing periods, not only was the native place of the Idealistic School of Confucian in the North of Fujian

densely covered with colleges, but also was Fuzhou that was
then the political and cultural center. It might be said that constructing a college was all the fashion across the whole province.
For example, in the Ming Dynasty, there were ten newly built
colleges in the East of Fujian, there were thirty newly built colleges in the West of Fujian; in the Qing Dynasty, there were one
hundred newly built colleges in the West of Fujian, nearly thirty
newly built colleges in the East of Fujian. In the Qing Dynasty,
Fujian started to have provincial level colleges such as Aofeng,
Fengchi, Zhengyi and Zhiyong colleges, which were capable of
bringing up notabilities like Lin Zexu, Lin Shu and Chen
Baochen. At the end of the Qing Dynasty, there appeared a
number of great provincial collegial institutions run by the government in Fujian: Fujian Vessel Administration Institute run by
Yangwu Party, and some other missionary schools run by foreign churches.

The main reasons why Fujian educational enterprises had
flourished for a long time starting from the Tang Dynasty to the
contemporary time without a decline are summarized as the following:

Support and Advocacy from the Local Bureaucracy. Generally speaking, the attitudes of the local bureaucracy towards education were of pivotal function to the promotion and declination
of the education. It had been fortunate that the majority of senior
officials to Fujian paid attention to the educational course and
took positive measures to push the course forward. Changgun of
the Tang Dynasty, who was then the Observer of the Court to
Fujian, greatly promoted the establishment of schools and en-

couraged youngsters to study making "the Min folks enjoy study
in the Changgun's learning palace in spring and in autumn."
(*Biography of Changgun. A New Book on the Tang Dynasty*);
When Chen Yuanguang took the position of Zhangzhou Cishi (
top official of a prefecture in the Sui Dynasty), he thought much
of the local education. He pointed out in the *Report to Jianzhou*
that" the essential principle lies on the construction of the county
and the crucial points lie on the development of Xiang Xu
(schools run by local forces in the ancient times)". He especially
appointed educational officials to take charge of the educational
affairs. He initiated a countryside school in Zhangzhou, and
Songzhou College as well. When Xiong Mi, who was Bing Bu
Shangshu (Senior Officer of the Imperial Military Department),
was leading an army garrisoning Wengling (today's Quanzhou),
he initiated Aofeng College in Jiangyang and taught children. In
the Five Dynasties, the King of the Min Wang Shenzhi "set up
four higher learning institutions so as to train excellent persons
of the Min" in Fujian (*Spring and Autumn of Ten Kingdoms* by
Wu Renchen). Under his advocacy, there appeared at that time
schools of state, county and village levels to an extent that
"young persons admire and learn from their masters while the
elderly serve for the country's learning institutions." (quoted
from the same source as the previous one). While Liu Congxiao
was the Director of Quanzhou Capital and governed Quanzhou,
he set up the "Autumn Hall". The Song Imperial Court practiced
a policy of emphasizing on literary, and evaluated a magistrate by
achievements in building up schools and social customs. Magistrates of both higher and lower positions all spared no effort to

set up schools. According to some historical records, there were no less than one hundred celebrated magistrates that had tried to run schools. Not only did famous persons like Xin Qiji, who had been Anfushi (minister sent by the court to important place in the Song Dynasty) to Fujian run school but also county administrators of remote counties like Liancheng, Jianning, Gutian, Pucheng, Ninghua went in for education in a large scale. Therefore, the popularization of Fujian education in the Song Dynasty had been unprecedented. Not few magistrates of the Yuan Dynasty contributed to the flourishing of Fujian's education. Magistrates of ethnic origins also tried to promote education by appropriating special fields for school site: Daluhuachi Qieyu in Quanzhou, Daluhuachi Ashilang in Songxi, Daluhuachi Wenshumeiya in Youxi, etc. Magistrates initiated and repaired some of the learning institutions. For example, Jiaochuang College initiated by Tong Zhi Wangbuhua in Shaowulu, Yunyang College initiated by Yi Kuangkui in Guangze, and several big Confucian Colleges repaired by Vice-Youbugong Yao Mo in Fujian. Fujian magistrates of the Ming and Qing Dynasties were concerned about troubles in the rear as well. They either appropriated funds or purchased fields to support the setting up and long growth of a school or college. Remarkably, they often donated their salaries of silver initiatively. In the Song Dynasty, Chong'an County Administrator Zhao Chongcui once donated his salary to buy a piece of wasteland from Kai Yuan Temple for a college; County Chief of Yanping, Chenmi donate salary to buy fields for college students' supply; Zhangzhou County Administrator Li Yinshi donated salary to buy field for school; Administrator of Jianning

County donated two thousand *min* (unit of volume, a string of copper, per *min* containing one thousand cents in ancient time) to increase the size of a school; In the Ming Dynasty, Yinren, Xunfushi to Fujian (minister that was temporarily sent to inspect and supervise the local civil and military administrations in the Ming Dynasty) donated one hundred *liang* (then 1 *liang* equals 31. 25g) of silver to reconstruct Lufeng College; County Chief of Gutian donated his salary in buying land for teaching buildings; Lin Xichun, Jiangle County Head donated his salary for constructing school buildings; Bachelor of Duanming Palace Chen Xianbo contributed money for the reconstruction of Luoyuan Songting College; In the Qing Dynasty, Jinjiang County Head Zhao Tongqi contributed to reconstruction of Meishi College; You Shilang of the Military Ministry and You Qiandu Yushi Chensheng donated a large sum to help repair Zhiyang College; County Head of Songxi, Sun Dakun donated money to reconstruct Nanxi College; Ningde County Head Xu Wenhan donated salary to supplement school's expense on lighting oil; Xu Zhilin, Tongpan (official title taking charge of affairs like grain transportation and agricultural irrigation) of Quanzhou, contributed salary to rebuild Zhuoying Lecture Hall; Sun Erzhun, Xunfu to Fujian, donated silver to support Fengchi College as student's stipends. Sometimes, magistrates called for donations from the subordinates. For example, Lü Rilin, Zhenshou (officer title during the ruling period of Beiyang Warlord, in charge of an army in area of a province) to Haitan called for two battalion soldiers and officers to donate salary to initiate Xinwen College.

A large number of high-level teachers. These teachers were educators that mainly undertook teaching as an occupation. Every dynasty had its educators. In the Song Dynasty, there were Luo Chongyan, Li Tong, Zhu Xi, Li Guangchao, Cai Liding, Huang Gan to name only a few. Zhu Xi undertook educational course for more than fifty years, putting forward famous seven teaching principles. His practical experiences and theories on education exerted a strong influence over the late feudalistic society in China. Moreover, some well-known politicians, philosophers, litterateurs and militarists often went into classrooms to give lectures. Though they might have not been a teacher by profession or accomplished in educational course, their lectures were able to attract many admirers by activating the academic atmosphere and broadening the students' viewpoints. For example, Yangshi discoursed on academic subjects after he forsook his official position and returned to his hometown. His disciples amounted to more than one thousand. The celebrity of the generation, Cai Xiang, who was well known for his identity as a scholar of Shu Mi (the central government of the feudalistic China; in the Qing Dynasty, a respective title for military minister) in Fuzhou, "went to the classroom in person to discourse on lectures and set an example for his students" (*Biographies on Litterateurs of Dongyue*). The historian, Zheng Qiao once taught as many students as two hundreds. Litterateur Yangyi also opened a hall to instruct disciples. The famous militarist and expert of phonology Chendi had given lectures in Zhangzhou and Fuzhou many times and always encouraged students. Famous scholar Huang Daozhou returned to his hometown five times to give lectures with followers of about one thousand; Lin Zexu, an outstanding patriot and national hero, taught in a learning hall before he successfully passed the imperial exanimation and obtained Jinshi. Celebrated litterateur Lin Shu once had been a teacher in a private school and taught Chinese language in Fuzhou Cangxia Refining House. Some outstanding imperial officials of Fujian origin were often invited to give a lecture when they stayed at their hometown paying filial piety to the diseased parents, which had been a way to broaden students' knowledge on realistic society. For example, Chen Luolin, who was Director of Fengtain (probably today's Liaoning province) Department in Xingbu (Ministry of Punishment in feudal China)and returned home because of his mother's funeral affairs, once gave lectures in Danxia College in Zhangzhou; Li Yanzhang who was Zhongshu (cabinet member of the imperial court in the Ming and Qing Dynasty, taking charge of writing, compiling and translating, recording, etc.) of the Cabinet came back for his father's funeral. He gave lectures in Xing'an College in Xinghua for one year; Lin Chunfu who was an editor of Hangliyuan (the Imperial Academy in feudal China) returned home for his mother's funeral and went to give a lecture in Yuping College.

The Long-term Flourishing of the Imperial Examination System. China formally started to practice the policy of selecting officials by examinations in the Sui Dynasty and it came into full play in the Tang Dynasty. Although in the Five Dynasties of the Tang, Fujian was at the beginning of development with a population of only around seven hundred thousand, Fujian had 74 persons successfully passed the examination and were granted as

Jinshi (title for a talented personnel granted through the highest examination which took place in the emperor's palace and the most important qualification for being an official in the feudal China). In the Song Dynasty, there were 7607 persons admitted to be Jinshi, 22 persons to be Zhuangyuan (Number One Scholar), which was a high ratio as far as the population was concerned. Fujian toped the first place in the county, which gave rise to circulation of numerous miracles. Take Putian for an example, from Putian once there were persons admitted as Zhuangyuan of both arts and the military in one examination, three persons admitted as Zhuangyuan out of three successive exanimations, and Putian monopolized number one to number four places in one examination, which was a rarely excellent achievement in examinations unprecedented in the country. In the Yuan Dynasty, there were 76 persons successfully got Jinshi in Fujian, which was a higher number than that of any Han dialect spoken provinces in the South of China. In the Ming Dynasty, there were 2410 people hit Jinshi in the examination, which once again came out to be top in the country. There even appeared a situation in which first three best-result examination takers (called Jidi) were all of Fujian origin on one list of names posted up. It was absolutely a rare thing. In the Qing Dynasty, Fujian had 1337 persons gloriously hit Jinshi, a number higher than the average level in the country. The boost of imperial higher-level examination system greatly pushed forward the popularization of the education. It had long been a tradition that the examination takers encouraged each other. Ou Yangzhan was the first person from Quanzhou in the Tang Dynasty to hit Jinshi and all the Fujian scholars were very proud of him. So increasingly many people followed his way to take the examination. Quanzhou scholar Xuhui sit for the examination but failed, and Ou Yangzhan always encouraged him. Xuhui studied more harder than ever and took a number one in the second year's examination. Many people undertook preparations and passing of the examination as their goal of lifetime. For example, in the Song Dynasty there was a person named Chen Xiu in Min County, who was determined not to get married unless he passed the examination. Unexpectadly, he tried but failed many times. He did not succeeded until he was at the age of seventy-three. Gaozong Emperor of the Song Dynasty gave order that maid-in-waiting surnamed Shi be obliged to marry him. At the night in the bridal chamber under the colorful candlelight, the bride asked the bridegroom how old he was. He answered, "Are you bride asking me how old I am? Fifty years ago, I was twenty-three." Such cases were not few at that time. To help students achieve what they were wishing for, some teachers had tried their best leaving no stone unturned. In the Ming Dynasty, Quanzhou Chen Zifeng spent a great deal of time and energy to translate *"Four Books"* and *"Scriptures of Changes"*, which were two basic classics for the preparation of the examination, into colloquial lectures entitled separately *"Elementary Introduction to Four Books"* and *"General Interpretation to Scriptures of Changes"*. After that, he himself sat for the examination and was granted Jinshi.

Concern from Family on the Education. Most of the Fujian families and clans were concerned about the education of their family members. The famous scholar Luo Zhongyan wrote on

the family hall the following words that were later recorded in
Lou Family Chart of Min Soil and Rich Stream, "From our ancestors passed on to us a spirit of cleanness and purity that shall
be fostered. Though we have a lot of gold and silk, they will disperse in a decade; though we have vast farming land and tall
houses, they will be worn away after decades of generations.
How about if I leave behind me several old books to my sons and
grandsons so that they can study and use them for generations e-
ternally. Again how about if part of my spirits and soul pass on
to my sons and grandsons so that they will get benefit from them
forever. " Thus he expressed his high concern on the education
and built up a family tradition of taking pride on study and feeling disgraceful in neglecting study. Lin Xiyuan of the Ming Dynasty wrote in his Lin Family Chart like that, "Every generation
of the Lin Family regards studies as profession. Whichever member of the family takes other professions instead of study and yet
will not correct his choice will be driven out of the family. " Some
clans wrote in their "family rules" about running family school or
private schools. For example, in Liancheng, a New Spring Chart
of Zhan Surname Family wrote, "Today the discussion is on the
setting up two charity schools: one is Jinshi in Dongshan Building, the other is Mengguan, just inside the Family Temple. " To
ensure that the family members enjoy education, every family
took relevant measures. Many families bought "study fields" i.
e. "fields for books and oil lamp" to provide for educational ex-
penditure. Chen Shengshao of the Qing Dynasty wrote in Records on Asking for Customs, "Book and oil lamp fields are several *mu* of fields left by grandfather to provide sons and grand-

sons with the need on studies". Many families cooperated to build up a private school or different surnamed families joint venture to build a college. For example, in Meihuali of Changle, more than forty surnames lived together and in the Qing Dynasty they initiated a He Geng College. To encourage children to study, some families even lay out regulations about economic encouragement. For example, in Pucheng, stipulated in a Da Surname Clan Chart that "Those who have become Xiucai (that has passed the elementary test and qualified to study in a county-level school) are awarded blue clothes and two liangs of silver. Those who will sit for Xiangshi (test held every three years by the province in the provincial capital) examination will be given four *liang* of silver as traveling expenses. Those who will take Huishi (an imperial test, which could be taken only by Juren who had succeeded in the Xiangshi, every three years held in the country capital in the Ming and Qing Dynasties) will be given eight *liang* of silver as traveling expenses. Those who have Jidi (passed the imperial examinations and got Jinshi title. In the Ming and Qing Dynasties, exclusively indicating the first three best examination takers) and returned to hometown in brocade clothes to worship ancestors, will be awarded flag and twenty *liang* of silver. " Clansmen often appointed those who had high reputations to run school. Chen Zhirou of Quanzhou origin in the Song Dynasty took a leave from his official position and returned to hometown to run a school for his clansmen. His nephews Chen Pu, Chen Mo, etc. passed the imperial examinations one by one, and the family was referred as "eight steeds from one gate" and the county government set up a memorial archway engraved with

words meaning "lane of generations of imperial examination takers". Family's concern on education was highly rewarded by
good achievements and produced marvelous spectacles in the history of Chinese imperial examinations. For example, in the Tang
Dynasty, Putain Lin Pisheng had nine sons, all of whom were Jidi and became imperial officials as Cishi. So there was a saying of
"nine Cishi from one family". Putian Huang Pu stroke Jinshi
listing with his four sons on official positions, which passed on a
story of "five scholars in one gate". A Zhan Family in Pucheng
during the Northern Song Dynasty, twenty-four persons hit Jinshi and one person hit Zhuangyuan. There was a person named
Chen Wan in Minqing in the Northern Song Dynasty, whose four
sons out of five passed the imperial examinations. A Yang family
in Changle in the Southern Song Dynasty, educated four Jinshi in
the same examination. A Ke family in Putian in the Ming Dynasty had one Jinshi successively for five generations. A Lin family
in Min County in the Ming Dynasty, came out eight Jinshi and
five Shangshu from three generations. A Huang family in Putian
during the Ming Dynasty all together came out eleven Xie Yuan
(winning the number one place in the Xiangshi, the provincial
test). Offspring who had stood out from the imperial examinations would not forget to share benefit with the clansmen: either
to give financial support, or to encourage learners in the family
clan to study harder, all of which greatly promoted the educational development to some extent.

   Various Types of Learning Institutions. For the past generations, Fujian had constituted sundry types of learning institutions to meet the demand of social and cultural development ex-

pect for the schools of provincial, prefecture, county, military levels that were entirely run by the governments or entirely by private forces, and various colleges that were jointly run by governmental and nongovernmental forces. For example, the Song Dynasty had opened a sect school for the offspring of Zhao Surnamed princes of the royal blood in Fuzhou and Quanzhou with thousands of students. In the Song period, Quanzhou especially set up a foreign school for the children of foreigners resided in the local. In the Yuan Dynasty, administrative areas like Fuzhou, Jianning, Quanzhou, Zhangzhou, Tingzhou, Yanping, Xinghua, Funing, Shaowu opened schools that taught Mongolia characters. In the Yuan Dynasty, all prefectures and forty counties opened schools of science and technology subjects (this learning institutions were also called as Yin and Yang School or School of Positive and Negative Forces) such as medical science, astronomy, chronometer, Zhou Theories on Changes (also entitled as Scriptures of Changes, one of the Confucius classics) and mathematics. During the three dynasties of the Yuan, Ming and Qing, thousands of schools characterized by primary level and social compulsory education were set up in cities and countryside to popularize ethics and farming techniques. Usually there were one to four schools of this kind in one city zone, ten or more in the countryside. These schools contributed a great deal to the promulgation of basic education. There were numerous dialects spoken in Fujian, thus the Qing Dynasty opened schools to correct local dialects called "private schools of official tone" and schools of "Eight Qi official School" especially for Qi people (one administrative qi in the north part of China equal to one county,

residents within the eight qi were called Qi people) who resided
in Fuzhou. Some clans set up foreign language schools for their
children. Luozhou Private School in Fuzhou outskirt, for example, taught Japanese as well as French. At the end of the Qing
Dynasty, the Yanwu Party (the principle party in Westernization
Movement in the latter half of the 19th century) started up a
"Fujian Ships and Boats Administrative Learning Hall", employing foreign teachers and taught foreign text books according to
the curriculum program and teaching methods used in foreign
countries. The school broke away from the bandage of family
status and its students came from all walks of life. A large number of excellent talented personnel in ship building, navigating
fields were cultivated and trained, which had exerted a far and
wide influences over China's Science and technology development, diplomatic relations, foreign language translation an interpretation and education. After the introduction of Christianity
into Fujian, more schools were set up in every place of Fujian.
These schools opened to doors to the lower levels of common
people and produced unpredicted influence. Some church schools
(as in Fuzhou, Putian and Nanping) were of better quality than
that of those which were run by the government or other private
forces. There appeared in Fujian towards the end of the Ming
Dynasty schools run by overseas Chinese. For example, During
the Daoguang Year of the Qing Dynasty, a Hui'an parent and
son coming home from the overseas donated thousand *liang* of
silver for running of a school that Daoguang Emperor wrote a
praising rescript and granted them an plaque written with "Ready
for goodness and benevolence, Father and son both enjoy favor

and grace". After that it became quite a fashion and a good tradition that overseas Chinese ran a school in the hometown.

Prosperity of the printing industry and large library. The industry of printing books started from the Five Dynasties. With the increasing prevalence of study and examination in addition to Fujian abundant raw material for paper making, the printing industry developed to its top stage during the Song, Yuan and Ming Dynasties. Whether it was official printing, private printing or small mill printing, the quality and quantity all topped the like industry in across the country and lasted for a quite a long time. In the Song Dynasty, Jianyang Masha Book Mill was claimed to be "Mansion of Books", whose books were treasured by latter generations as "Jian Copy" together with the books printed in Hangzhou and Sichuang mills. In the Yuan Dynasty, the number of book printing mills in Fuajin also topped that in the country. Famous mills like Chen Surnamed Yuqing Hall in Jianan, Zhu Surnamed Yugeng Hall, Meiyin Hall, Shuanggui Book Hall, to name only a few, could produce exquisite books. In the Ming Dynasty, Fujian operated the most productive book printing industry. Among the four great printing centers including Jianyang, Jinlin, Hangzhou, Beijing, Jianyang was the most famous center. Only in Chonghua Town, "there were book sellers from one door to the next, and traveling merchants under the sun coming and going busily like weaving spins, and there was a market day every Monday and Saturday." (Third Volume of *Jianyang County History*) The developed printing industry and dissemination of books provided students of Fujian with adequate books to read as well as enriched the fork libraries. Ac-

cording to the records available, around one hundred and thirty
celebrated bibliophiles had visited Fujian for the past dynasties.
When Zhu Xi was assuming the official position of Zhubu (title
of an official who took charge of governmental documents and related affairs) and manager of the educational affairs of Tongan
County, he clear up the library of the county and collected over a
wide scale many collect books from the folks amounting to nine
hundred volumes. In the Song Dynasty, Fuzhou colleges had
constructed libraries printed by governments and catalogued
them into two ancient book pavilions and three modern book pavilions. It is obvious that the collection had reached a certain
scale. Colleges all made effort to collect books. Zhang Boxing,
who was Xunfu to Fujian (title of an official who was sent to the
local by the court, of provincial level) devoted one thousand
books from his own library to Fuzhou Aofeng College, just as recorded in the Seventeenth Volume of Biographies Collections that
"He devoted a thousand collected books from his library to fill
into the college library". In the Qing Dynasty, Fuzhou Yueshan
College had a library storage of five thousand volumes catalogued
in four hundred types kept in twenty large cabinets. Pucheng
Nanpu College kept one hundred and thirty volumes in more than
one thousand five hundred pieces. Many famous teachers in the
colleges kept a large library individually. For example, in the
Qing Dynasty, Chen Shouqi, who was the president of Aofeng
College, kept a library of eighty thousand volumes of books,
from which Lin Changli was able to feast himself with the piles
of the books and lay a solid foundation for the future.

Chapter Ten
Architecture

I. Ancient Pagodas

There are at least one hundred of pagodas of different kinds kept in rather good conditions in Fujian, occupying a big proportion of the surviving pagodas in the country. The appearance of pagodas in Fujian was related to the unique characteristic of Fujian culture. For example Buddhism in Fujian was lasting long and Buddhist temples spread in all parts of the province and the faction of Logos was dominating for a long time in the southeast of the province. Fujian had a long coast line and the marine transportation was flourishing for a period of time and all this had been promoting the building of pagodas in this area.

The ancient pagodas mainly functioned as follows.

1. For keeping the bones of dignitarial monks and worshiping Buddha. Pagodas of this category were closely related to temples with fine cuttings of Buddha statuaries such as the ancient pagoda of Buddha Shijiawen built in 1165, the first year

of Songqiandao, in the Guanghua Temple of Putian, with a height of 36 meters, structured in a style of wooden pavilion with two doors in the ground floor facing east and west respectively and there being niches with images of Buddha on the other six sides, and that of his disciples on the both sides of each niche and each door. There were also niches on the second to the fifth floors with Buddha images inside, too. Built in 1117, the 7th year of Zhenghe of the Song Dynasty, in Tapingshan, west of Changle, the Pagoda of Sanfeng Temple was 27 meters high with seven storeys and eight angles with more than 200 basso-relievo—the most numerous in the first story with more than sixty— of Buddha sitting on lotus flowers carved on the walls. The Buddha Pagoda of Brahman in Fantian Temple in Beidou of Tong'an was built in the period of 1086 to 1094, the first year of the Yuanyou of the Song Dynasty, of which on each of the four sides of the ⊥-shaped base there was on lotus flowers a group basso-relievos telling Buddhist stories and on each of the four corners there was a divinity animal with spreading wings. Zhiti Temple built in 971, the fourth year of Kaibao of the Song Dynasty, had several pagodas of Buddhist monk set up in the Yuan and the Ming Dynasties. The Temple Pagoda of Huguotianhuang Temple in Beidou of Lianjiang County was built in 849, the third year of Dazhong of the Tang Dynasty. It was used for keeping scriptures in the Tang Dynasty. It was 9 meters high. There was a standing Buddha statue on the corner on the stone bar of the second layer of the base and under the eaves there were five sitting Buddha statues solemn and grand on each side. Beneath each statue there was a niche with two green stone Arhat statues inside it. There were divinities of household protector with back towards the door. On both sides of the door it was carved with the scriptures of Dafang guangfu huayan and Dacheng miaofa lianhua and on the forehead there was a seal cutting··· of xida duo-mi dalou. All this revealed the close relationship between pagodas and Buddhism.

2. For navigation. Fujian Province bordered on the sea in the east and there were rivers flowing eastwards and southwards in this area, so there were many ancient pagodas for navigation which stood on the seaside or in the outlet of the rivers, able to be seen from far. Luoxing Pagoda in Mawei of Fuzhou, for example, was first built between 960 and 1127, in the North Song Dynasty and rebuilt between 1621 and 1627, the years of Tianqi of the Ming Dynasty. It was 31. 5 meters high, the body, the door and the windows designed in the south style and there being lot of lantern niches in the body. Obviously it was built for navigation and in the world, navigating map it was marked *Pagoda of China*. The pagoda of the Pagoda Temple in Putian, built in between 1522 and 1566, the years of Jiajing of the Ming Dynasty, was about twenty meters high and had five storeys with a temple-shaped top. It was very solid and became a navigation pagoda. The Aojiang Pagoda, built in 1600, the 28th year of Wanli of the Ming Dynasty, in Tashan Village of Fuqing was twenty-six meters high and had seven storeys. On each layer there was a statuary on the top of which on the right carved the names of the women who donated money to the construction of the pagoda. It was said that there were eighteen husbands went overseas doing business but they died in the sea, so the eighteen widows con-

tributed money to build this navigation pagoda. There was a
sisters-in-law pagoda built in between 1131 and 1162, the years
of Shaoxing of the South Song Dynasty, on the top of Baogai
Hill in Shishi, which was 21. 65 meters high with five storeys.
As the story goes, the two sisters-in-law went to the top of the
hill looking forward to the return of their family members and
died there, so people built the pagoda remember them. And this
pagoda had a a calabash-shaped top supporting a light, which
was a very important navigation signal in the ancient Quanzhou
Port. Liushi Pagoda, built in between 1573 and 1620, the years
of Wanli of the Ming Dynasty, in Liushi Village of Jinjiang, was
20 meters high, opposite to the southern door of Quanzhou
across the river and served as a navigation mark for the sailors
going against the river. Built in 1798, the third year of Jiaqing of
the Qing Dynasty, on the Hill of Kylin of Zhaoan, Xianglin Pagoda was twenty meters high with seven storeys serving as a
navigation mark. Rebuilt in between 1336 and 1339, between the
second and the fifth year of the Yuan Dynasty, in Shihu Village
of Jinjiang, Liusheng Pagoda was thirty-one meters high with
five storeys and eight angles and, because of on the east sea,
served as a navigation mark for Quanzhou's oversea voyage.

　　3. For beautifying scenic spots. Such pagodas are usually
related to geomantic omen, so they are also called Wengfeng pagodas, geomantic pagodas or Wengfeng towers etc. and later
they became man-made marks of certain area. For example,
Dongguan Pagoda on the Dongguan Hill of Zhangping built in
between 1628 and 1644, the years of Chongzhen, is said to be a
fishing rod. It is said that the landform of the county was like a

fish and people were afraid that the "fish" would swim along the river to the sea when flood came, so they built the pagoda, the body like a rod and the top like a hook, so as to stop the "fish" flowing away. In 1786, the fifty-first year of Qianlong of the Qing Dynasty another pagoda was built on the other side of the river, the two pagodas facing each other as a mark of this county. The twin pagodas of Nanping were built in 1605, the thirty-third year of Wanli of the Ming Dynasty, on the both sides of the outlet-joint of Jianxi River and Futunxi River just like protectors of the city, the east one about 30 meters high and the west 20 meters, the bodies carved with such words as "People with abundant wealth"" Literafure with long flourishetc", There is strong wind in Jinmen County, so in the villages of Doumen, Beishan, Xibao, Xiazhuang, Anqi, Dongshanqian, Xishangqian, Pubian, etc. there have been pagodas built to suppress the geomantic power. Such, being built by the sea, or the river or the pond and in the lowland vulnerable to flood, are also called Water-end Pagodas, for people there believed that the pagodas functioned as road signs as well as protectors against demons and ghosts, and gradually they have become scenic spots. Houguan Pagoda with four angles and seven storeys of solid stone and carved on the four sides of the base with the words Pagoda Guarding the Land was built in Shangjie Town of Minhou County on the hill by the Min River meaning to suppress the evil spirit of water, so it is also called Floating Suppressive Pagoda and Defensive and Suppressive Pagoda, and then it served as the sign of Houguan Dock. Built in Nanjin County in , the fortieth year of Qianlong the Qing Dynasty, Wenchang Pagoda was 50 meters high with

seven storeys, with thick walls and a hollow core and with stair-
way on the inner side of the wall. People could reach the top and
looked far into the distance. The North and the South Pagodas
on the mountain range of Yongan were built in 1452, the third
year of Jingtai of the Ming Dynasty and rebuilt many times afterwards. They each stood on the either side of Yan River, facing
each other and they were viewed as the beginning of Yongan
County. Lingxiao Pagoda, built in 1629, the second year of
Chongzhen of the Ming Dynasty, on the top of Qiding Hill in
Jiangjiadu Village in the south of Fuan County, was twenty-four
meters high with seven storeys and eight angles facing Xikou Pagoda (now toppled), both being taken as geomantic omens.

4. Other functions. Tingxiu Pagoda, built in 1581, the
ninth year of Wanli of the Ming Dynasty and modified in 1775,
the fortieth year of Qianlong of the Qing Dynasty, was set up at
the joint of a stream and Longjin River in the east of Longyan
and for slowing the interflowing speed, which was 26 meters
high in pavilion style. Dingxin Pagoda was built in between 1573
and 1620, in the Ming Dynasty, with 4. 5 meters high, eight angles and six storeys the first of which was of stones. In the old
times, Quanzhou was to be enlarged and the pagoda was built in
the center, so it was also called the Center Pagoda.

The architectural features of the ancient pagodas in Fujian

1. Mainly built of stone with some other materials. The
first pagodas in China were built of wood. And later, in order to
prevent from catching fire and to keep solid, many pagodas were
built of brick and stone or brick and wood after the Sui and the
Tang Dynasties, few being entirely built of stone. Fujian was

full of stone and stone and stone technique was long lasting. However, all the pagodas were not built of stone. Ling Pagoda, built in 1610, the thirty-eighth year of Wanli of the Ming Dynasty in Shiqi of Shaowu, Qingyun Pagoda built in 1632, the fifth year of Chongzhen of the Ming Dynasty in Taining both were built of brick, stone and wood. Yuxiu Pagoda built in 1778, the forty-third year of Qianlong of the Qing Dynasty in Zhangping, was built of mixed soil. The White Pagoda, the highest point in the city, rebuilt in 1548, the twenty-seventh year of Jiajing of the Ming Dynasty in Fuzhou was built of bricks. Fired and made in 1082, the fifth year of Yuanfeng of the North Song Dynasty the thousand-Buddha Pagoda in Mount Gu was made of excellent clay. The pagoda of the Shaoming Temple on Mount Aofeng in the west of Fuding County, built in 1534, the thirteenth year of Jiajing of the Ming Dynasty, Yuanjue Pagoda, built in 1602, the thirtieth year of Wanli of the Ming Dynasty in Shuangyang of Zhangping County and the North Pagoda, built in 1452, the third year of Jingtai of the Ming Dynasty in Yong'an were made of brick and wood.

2. Various Forms and Shapes in the history of architecture. It is generally believed that the artistic forms of pagodas built in the south part differ from those in the north part of China. Pagodas built in the south appear exquisite, slim, gentle and pretty while pagodas in the north possess verve of majestic, solemn, grand and decent. But when under a close survey of the hundred pagodas in Fujian, they cannot be generalized by only "exquisite and slim, gentle and pretty", for they display in rich forms and structures. Some are short and strong like a stout built man.

Sister-in-law Towers sitting in Shishi, which were built in 1131—1162, the year of Gaozong Shaoxing of the Southern Song, stand 21m high and 20m wide with five stories; on the eight stone turning corners, there is a big dougong (a system of brackets inserted between the top of a column and a crossbeam); all the eaves are built by protruding and lining bricks and stones in certain patterns. The first and second stories have stone outer frames and the raft eaves can stand or walk on; As the ground floor is comparatively wide in area, it appears a kind of coarse and spacious, short and heavy shape. Some pagodas seem to be slim in structure like a jade column approaching to the sky. Ruiyun Tower in Fuqing city, built in Wanglin thirty-fourth year of the Ming Dynasty, stands 30m in height with seven stories and eight corners. The leaning column at every turning corner is made into Chinese flowering crabapple type; on the top of the columns there are two layers of dougong protruding out of the eaves. The tower is called "Number One Tower in the South Part of the Changjian River". Many pagodas in Fujian have particular structures that are rarely seen in China. For example, Dustless Tower in Xianyou, which was started to be built in the sixth Xiantong Year of the Tang Dynasty (865), stands 14m in height with three stories and eight corners: the tower base sculptured in a lotus flower petals over the water waves, eight tower columns, meridian line pattern on the ground floor, doors open to the South and North, windows open on to the East and West; Its door protectors are not lain on the both sides of the ground floor, instead they are inserted on the stone walls of the Southeast side and Southwest side with a moon platform in the front.

The structure of the stone tower is peculiar, completely different from the styles built after the Song Dynasty. The Stone Temple in Putain built in the time of Wanli of the Ming Dynasty stands 25m in height with seven stories and eight corners, flat square surface of brocks, a rarity in the Ming period. Some small pagodas, small and exquisite, are symbols of some kinds. For example, Doubao Tower in Quanzhou Kaiyuan Temple built in the Song Dynasty, stands 4m in height with a lamp body structure and a square stone platform base. On the platform, there places a seat of eight corners, upon which places a ball shape tower body that is covering with eight-cornered tower eaves. The high-raising tower eaves extend out quite distinctively and exquisitely. Some towers look extremely elegantly slim and beautifully slanting. For example, Yinggeng Tower in Chongfu Temple of Quanzhou built in the Song Dynasty stands more than 20m in height with seven floors. It is said that the side to which the tower is slanting means there will be bumper harvest of five crops in that direction. The tower has been slanting in response to request ever since. Eight Egrets Tower in Zhongchun, Sanyuan District of Sanming city, built in Tianqi first year of the Ming Dynasty (1621), stands 13m in height with seven stories and eight corners, a lotus body and a calabash tower top. Some tower is entirely a column in structure. For example, the Jufo Pagoda within Zhaojiabao of Zhangpu County was built in the Ming Dynasty. Its base is Xumi Seat (also called Buddha's warrior attendant seat, a base for the Buddhist figure in China, a traditional architectural platform base built of stones and bricks with concave and dented decorative patterns), and its top is constructed into three overlapped layers, between which there is a flat seat design. The structure size of the top part of the tower does not differentiates much with that of the lower part of the tower. Yingchao Pagoda in Sanshan Village of Fuqing was built in the Second Jiajing year of the Ming Dynasty (1523). It is 18m in height with seven stories and eight sides and solid body. For several hundreds of years of duration, it has slanted increasingly to about 15 degrees. Seemingly tottery but actually it is as stable as a mountain to such an extent that it may compare beauty with Pisa Slanting Tower in Italy. Fairyland Stone Pagoda in Fairyland Village, Nanpu of Hui'an County, was built in the Song Dynasty. The pagoda has other two sister pagodas in quite the same structure and shape about twenty meters away. The first and second stories are in square size and the third story is oval in size.

3. Exquisite carves and high level of carving art. Many ancient pagodas have exquisite and vivid decorative carves to go harmoniously with the whole pagoda structure, presenting before the eyes a beautiful artistic work. For example, Taojiang stone pagoda in Talin Mountain of Minhou County built in Chentaijian period of the Southern Song Dynasty (569—582), has very clumsy old tower carves. The dragon is shortly built with rough legs, small head and sharp horns and few diverging tail, yet looking very vivid to life. Sakymuni Tower in Putian Guanghua Temple built in Qiandao period of the Song Dynasty (1165) has beautiful modal decorations like lion playing with a ball and flower patterns like peony. The manikins have vivid expressions, the Guanyin statue looks chubby and dignified, and phoe-

nixes, fly beings and double-wing beings can seen vividly. Dong-
wu Stone Pagoda in Zhongmen Village of Putian city was built in
Wangli forty-sixth year of the Ming Dynasty. The facial engraves have dragon, lion, kylin, deer and crane, etc. The tower's stone Protecting Generals stand mighty and sturdy. Inside
the niche, Buddha figures appear in different bearings and manners. Tianzhong Wanshou Tower in Fengting Tadou Mountain
of Xainyou County was built in Jia fourth year of the Song Dynasty (1059). From the second story to the fifth story, there are
exquisite carve decorative patterns of double dragons, lotus and
sea waves. On the fifth story there carved a big Buddha figure
holding a lotus in his palm with Thunder Father beside him, eyes
watching around, and the Cock God's mouth looking like a
hook; on the fourth story, there carved three seated Buddha figures and each close two palms before the chest. "These Buddha
figures are painted in smooth lines and to the details, appearing
vivid to the life in beautiful postures: sitting with two legs crossing under the body, head raising and shoulders bridling; smiling
slightly, angry with glowering eyes, charming and slim, powerful and dignified. No one is not lifelike." (*Appreciation of Chinese Ancient Pagodas* edited by Gu Yanpei, p. 253) Sanfeng Pagoda in Changle County, was built in Shaosheng Third year of
the Northern Song Dynasty (1096). Its base is carved with
strong men and lions and peony flower patterns around the four
sides. On the walls of the pagoda of the first story, there are relievos of Manjusri (one of the figures in Mahayana religion,
known for his wisdom, servant of Sykamuni, standing on the
left of Syka, often riding on a lion) and Samantabhadra (who is

the servant of Sykamuni, known for his realization of wishes, often standing on the right of Sykamuni riding on a white elephant), fifty arhats and sixteen sky flying dancers, and a set of
Buddhist religious stories. From the first story to the sixth story, there carved 200 Buddha figures on lotus in various lively
postures by primitively simple styles. The East and the West Pagodas in Quanzhou were started to be built in Xiantong Sixth
year of the Tang Dynasty (865) and rebuilt later in the Song Dynasty. The two pagodas are 200 m apart from each other and
their carving arts and contents may be ranked the utmost of Fujian. The East pagoda is named Zhenguo Pagoda standing 48.27
m in height while the West pagoda is named Renshou Pagoda
standing 45.066 m in height. The two pagodas are flat-surfaced
and eight-cornered five stories with every story embed with 16
relievos of Buddhist figures. There are 160 figure relievos of
Buddha, Bodhisattva, dignitary, arhat, various deities and Buddha's warrior attendants and strong men decorated within the
two pagodas, as well as 80 statues of Keeping Watching Gods on
the pagoda's eaves and 16 statues of manikins on the small towers. On the Buddha's seat platform, there are about 40 pictures
about the Buddhist story and 48 pictures of flower, bird and wide
beats. These relievos and pictures speak out the development
and merits and virtues of the Buddhist religion and some folklore
in condensed symbols of art. The various figure relievos and
statues represent and display all kinds of bearings and manners
under the sun in such a multitude variety that they well incarnate
the superb level of the stone inscription at that time. The realistic method used in the composition of these pictures and the free-

hand brushwork used in the expressions and bold outlines enrich
the artistic charm of the decoration.

II. Fujian Civil Residence

Fuzhou Civil Residence

Fuzhou is a famous city with rich historical cultures. In the
city proper, there are lanes and alleys stretching all over. In the
ancient time, there were 49 alleys and 60 or more lanes in
Fuzhou, but the representatives of Fuzhou's ancient civil residence architectural styles are the well-known "Three Alleys and
Seven Lanes" in the downtown area of Fuzhou, so named because it is the shorted form for the ten lanes arranging from the
north to the south. The Three Alleys are pronounced in Chinese
respectively as following: Yijin Fang (Clothes in Brocade Alley), Wenru Fang (Confucian Alley), and Guanglu Fang (
Honor and Fortune Alley). The Seven Lanes are respectively
pronounced as follows: Yangqiao Xiang (xiang means a lane),
Langguan Xiang, Anmin Xiang, Huang Xiang, Ta Xiang, Gong
Xiang, and Jipi Xiang. "Three Alleys and Seven Lanes" originated from the East Jin Period, after the extension in the Five Dynasties, preservation in the Song, and experienced through the
Yuan, Ming and the Qing dynasties. In the long duration of construction and reconstruction, they come to have a complete traditional setup of their own typical of lane structure in the Chinese
ancient town. They are one of the most complete ancient city districts existent in the south part of China. The 260 civil residences built in the Ming and the Qing Dynasties within the Three
Alleys and Seven Lanes are referred to as the most gigantically

dimensioned "Ancient Architectural Museum of the Ming and Qing Dynasties" by the architectural circles.

The architectural characteristics of Three Alleys and Seven Lanes are classified as following three aspects.

1. Clear layout of the alleys and lanes. The lane roads are usually paved with stone flags of 3 to 6 meters in width. On both sides the of the road, stand erecting high whitening painted walls which are tied tightly by stones at large. On the entrance of the lane, there is an archway of single rain cover. Some archways are decorated with Chinese ancient script-roll patterns. Every residence alone the lanes and alleys is entirely surrounded by high walls except its gate. The smooth fireproof walls from one house to another form into a fluid curve that is commonly known as "Matao Wall"; The top part of the wall has a warped corner to separate regularly one house from another.

2. Gates, houses and gardens strew at random yet have their original style. The gates in the Three Alleys and Seven Lanes always become an interesting architectural structure by themselves. The archaeologist Yang Binglun classifies the construction of gates into five types:

Type 1. To construct the gate frame with large complete pieces of stone and install right behind the gate thick and heavy gate planks for safety protection purpose;

Type 2. To construct the gate with stone framework and fasten the knob hole by copper wares such as tiger, snake. The door bolt is usually made of iron;

Type 3. To construct the gate into three openings with six door leafs, or three obvious-sighted door leafs yet five to six hidden leafs. In front of the gate, there is spacious porch with arch raft and double sloping roof covering over; beside the gate, there are high whitening walls to back up a very ostensive and extravagant fa? ade;

Type 4. The gate and the compound do not lie on the same axes, and instead they fall into independent units, for behind one side of the gate, there is a door screen leading to the compound;

Type 5. Do not build janitor's room behind the gate. Right behind the gate, there is a cloister for the compound and for the cloister there will certainly be a screen to shun out the direct line of sight to the whole building.

According to customs prevalent in Fuzhou, one gate leads to one house. The main hall usually has three rooms or five, seven rooms with dooryards in front (often large one) and behind (often small one) the main hall. To make best use the space, there are usually side-sheds alone the two sides of the frond and back dooryards with the front yard shed used as a study and the back yard shed used as servant's room or kitchen. The living rooms of the house are usually placed at the rear part. The garden of the house, which is also called flower hall, is arranged on either side of the axes, often modified with rockwork, mini buildings, pavilions on waterside, all in a very elegant and exquisite mini layout and full of sentiments and appeals.

3. Art works of fine carvings go harmoniously with the whole building. The principle parts of an architecture that are to be decorated by carvings are as following:

(1) doors and windows; by hollowed-out engravings and suspended carvings of skillful arts and crafts, in rather rich pat-

terns such as character-makeup, geometric shapes.

(2) the front profiles of the bright rooms in the main hall; over the screen and upon the dougong, there are often engravings of a cigarette basket or a treasure bottle, or books and script rolls.

(3) frameworks and trusses; almost all the frameworks and trusses of the house are carved with beautiful flowers, birds, animals and figures in a clear layout and bold brushworks. All these carvings might be in round carve, basso-relievo, penetrating carve, in a single picture, a group pictures or interlink pictures, the contents of which may be numerous poems and verses inscriptions or patterns about musical instruments, chessboard, book and picture rolls and landscape painting, emitting a strong cultural atmosphere.

Famous civil residences in Three Alleys and Seven Lanes:

Building One: Former residence of Huang Pu belonging to the Tang Dynasty within Huang Xiang. It used to the house of the famous scholar Liang Zhangju in the Qing Dynasty, later it belonged to Chen Shouqi, an imperial official retired at home. Inside the compound, there is a two-storied building surrounded by fire-proof walls and is separated from rooms by two rockworks and snowed-covered mountain cave piled up by materials like white lime and sticky rice juice. From the mountain cave and the two rockworks, there are two divergent paths leading to the east and the west. The east path leads to a booth-typed small pavilion with a Xieshanding (one of the traditional roof constructions in China, formed by four slanting slopes, one horizontal and four vertical beams to construct a triangle wall surface) whose raising corners carved with fine tassel balls. All the poles, columns, beams and eaves are carved and painted with dragons and phoenixes. The windows, doors and screens were all worked at with special care. On the whole, the layout of the house is small and exquisite, clear and classic, obliquely showing a sort of verve of garden arts in the south of Changjiang River. Moreover, the location of the house is very quiet although it situates on the busy streets, for out of the lane, there is the busiest downtown area of Fuzhou. Nevertheless, it is another world in the house. I had been living in this house for many years, so I have personal experiences about this surrounding.

Building Two: Ouyang Tuihua Hall in Yijin Fang. This compound was bought and rebuilt in the Guangxu Time of the Qing Dynasty by Ouyang Bin. The hall of house covers two fifths of the compound that is divided into two front part and back part by wall with small doors on it. The front part is male's recreation hall while the back part is female's recreation hall; Its twenty nanmu door leafs are carved with hundreds of patterns of flowers and birds, all by refined craftworks; The wing-rooms on both sides have eight doors. On these doors, there embedded hundreds pieces of boxwood roots that were carved into flowers and birds. These carvings are removable at any time.

Building Three: Former residence of Chen Chengqiu and his wife Lady Zhang. One of the characteristics of the house is all the doors and windows are decorated with refined and beautiful carvings. The doors and windows of the main hall are engraved with various flower patterns and bronze wares; The doors and windows of the back hall are engraved with imitated Chinese flower and bird paintings and drawings from nature such as chrysanthemum, lotus, peony, pied magpie and water bird. All these engravings are real fine works; Another characteristics about the house is that in the courtyard, rockworks, fish pool and waterside pavilion all in mini size, small and exquisite complement each other; There is a study and drawing rooms in the garden that is separated by wall from the back garden which forms another place of unique scenery.

There are other typical civil residences in the counties administrated by Fuzhou municipality. Such as Honglin residence lies in Xinhu Village, Bandong Town of Minqing County, the design of which was done at one time and was started to be built up in Qianlong sixtieth year of the Qing Dynasty (1795). The residence covers an area of 17000 square meters, possessing 35 large and small halls, 25 gardens, 30 dooryards and 666 lodgings. The whole housing is of earth and wood structure with bird-wing eaves being a flying-bird like, face raising upwards and tail lowering downwards, and the right and left being symmetrical. Three horizontal paths across from the east to west together with winding corridors, gateways, flower walls and street-crossing storied buildings divide the gigantic compound into large and small courtyards. On the both sides of the main hall, there built first, second and third offices and fire protecting walls; on each side of the main hall, there are three studies, and in the middle, there is the central study hall. The main hall, central study hall and study rooms are surrounding to make a dooryard. The main hall and the back hall are separated by a screen. Behind the fire protecting walls, houses and rooms are built in vertical order,

forming a 90 degree angle to the main houses. On each side of
the vertical house, built vertically two halls with their backs towards each other; And out of the vertical houses, built another
vertical house; between the two entrances, there is a street. The
entire architecture and its layout is artfully and skillfully in good
order.

Dongchengcuo in Ta Village of Minqing County is composed
of four courtyards large and small with a gun building in front.
On the sides of the house, there built hill walls with covering
brims so as to integrated into one unit the suspending mountain
top, four sloping top roofs and fire protecting walls. Former Lin
Chunze residence situated in Nanyu of Minhou County is a doub-
le-storied wood structure with high walls surrounding on four
sides. On the left and the right sides of the dooryard are single-
storied wood house. The main building has three rooms; The
second floor is a dressing and making-up room in a style characterized by the Ming Dynasty architecture.

Puxian Civil Residence

Puxian includes Putian County and Xianyou County. These
two counties lie between Fuzhou and the South of Fujian area.
But they are influenced neither by Fuzhou nor by the South of
Fujian area, and becoming to have a style of their own. The distinctive feature of residences in Puxian area is called "full decoration", i. e. to try best to pile up decorations on the outer surface
of a building, no matter it is wood carve, stone carve, brick
carve, clay mold, wall painting or surface material. Even round
carving, relievo and hallowed-out engraving are not spared. The
building, inside and outside walls, is made up extremely magnif-

icent and luxurious and attractive. Mr. Huang Hanming has excellent analysis as he says that the coastal geographical position
of Puxian area and the development of maritime traffic have ena-
bled the local people to leave the past disaster-ridden days behind
when their life goal was only to go abroad to make a living. and
finally returned to hometown after getting fame or money in order to glory the ancestors. But such state of mind of the social
colony is still there and is strongly reflected on the outer wall
decorations of the Puxian residences. Sparing no huge sum of
money to pursue the outer appearance of a building in order to
attract the admiring sights instead of improving the inner functions is entirely a psychological need.

Xianyou folk arrange their houses in a horizontal order,
short distance from the door to opposite side of a compound and
wide layout. Typical of this kind are the residences in Xianglong-
shan Village, Youyang Township. Some residences have a depth
of only 2m, yet 17 rooms stretching horizontally omitting frond
hall and back hall and save a great deal of building materials compared with the deep-compounded and multi-entranced houses.
Besides these Xianyou residences are prone to sunlight and venti-
lation, less interference, convenient traffic and easy for subdivi-
sion of household. The top of the house is usually a combination
of two-sloped xuanshanding and four-sloped xieshanding in five
layers with two sides gradually falling lower. Outer wall decoration starting from the window side is pasted with red colored
bricks, and white and gray colored patterns. Green stone, white
stone, red bricks and white-gray complement each other, making
the house refined and flowery.

Another characteristics of the residences in Xianyou is that several kinds of basic units are usually put together to form a architectural colony. The basic unit is one hall with two bedrooms. To stretch out horizontally, it becomes one hall with four bedrooms; to stretch out backwards, the basic unit may be extended to three buildings. The Guo's House in Lishan Village of Duwei Town is 2m in depth and 13 rooms in width, composing basically one hall, two bedrooms. In addition, upon the two sides of the basic unit there are two smaller units with a protecting wall. All together there are 80 halls and rooms, 17 dooryards. Immortal Water Hall in Xianshui Village of Bangtou Town is a magnificent building colony of the Ming Dynasty: three courtyards, 9 rooms horizontally, 160 rooms in all. This is a gigantic and multi-functioned building colony after many times of integration and reconstruction. Right in the middle, there is the most principle unit of one hall and two bed-rooms, from which build another three buildings backwards, a series of wing-rooms sideward; beyond a side dooryard, there stand another row of attendant's rooms. This kind of colony buildings is combined together by corridors, cloisters and wing-rooms. So it is accessible from the east to the west and from the north to the south within the colony without difficulty in spite of the poor weather. The construction of the building is of earth and wood structure, single roof brim, four-sloped top with thick and strong wood materials, solid and firm.

Putian residences pay special attention to the outer appearance just as what is described by Mr. Huang Hanmin, an architect, who thinks that the walls are treated with unique method, i. e. build the wall with red brick in sequence order and insert vertically the small piece of granite stone regularly to form a red bricked wall decorated with white colored diamond patterns. This is a way of both decorating the wall surface and straightening the entire wall structure (*Old Houses. Fujian Civil Residence*, published in 1994 by Jiangsu Art Publishing House). The Yu's House situated in Hougang Village, Jiangkou Town of Putian is typical of this construction.

Residences in the South of Fujian

The characteristics of the residences in the South of Fujian are as following:

1. Symmetrical Layout. All the residences have an accurate axes and the hall is situated on the center with the left and the right part, the primary and the secondary part stretching out around in a clear symmetry. For the purpose of enlarging the scale, just to increase more halls alone the same axes forming a large-scaled building with several courtyards. The center hall is very important because it shall function as the place to ancestor and god worshipping.

2. Outer materials usually made up of red bricks and white stones while the inner structural materials mostly being wood frameworks. South of Fujian has a long history of firing bricks especially the red brick, which has a high density, glazing surface, bright red colored. The bricks are made in different thickness and size capable of meeting various demands. The South of Fujian is rich with good quality stone resources that can be made into excellent building materials. Fujian is teemed with woods. So the inner structure of the civil residences in the South of Fujian mostly utilize wood truss of pull-through structure; tenons

between dougong and girder is seamless; the girder head is fastened overlapping in good order; the room partition is mostly of wood.

3. Refined engravings. The South of Fujian is the hometown of engravings with the stone carvings made in Huian being the most famous in the country. Its wooden carvings and brick carvings are known far and wide. Therefore, people often carve their columns and paint girders, especially the important parts of the house like girder in the main hall, bracket, window and door, rafter and base of the column. Another parts like white stone porch are inlaid with bluestone relievos of flying birds and animals, the two outer surfaces of the house are inlaid with bluestone hollowed-out carvings of diamond patterns in a window lattices. Even ridge of the house, top part of the two slopes roof, windows are decorated with various engravings.

4. Rich and picturesque shape of the top of a house. As the inner structural heights are not uniform, the single sloped or double sloped roof is covered over or overlapped over the blue-tiled top of the house to form a top shape of one layer upon another layer; or the ridge of the house goes naturally from a smooth and unfolding curve to a flying swallow tail curve. The eaves always have high raising pecks while ridge being warped looking like a sky flying dragon; So ridge and eaves complement each other.

The variety of the residences in the South of Fujian:

1. Large housing. "Cuo" in the dialect of the South of Fujian means "mansion". Though these houses were mostly built by the rich merchants at the time, they were not so magnificent

as civil residences of "official residence type". The former usually has a layout of sanheyuan(three sides are built with house,
one side being a wall, a courtyard in the middle) or siheyuan(
four sides are built with house with a courtyard in the middle),
and xuanshan style, five ridges and two falling layers and a
stone-paved vestibule in the front. Generally the residence has
two courtyards and three halls, sometimes three courtyards and
five halls with every courtyard separated by a dooryard and connected by cloisters. Some residences have a long range of wing-
rooms outside of the cloisters, behind them, there is a dressing
up building used as embroidery room for girls. This kind of
"large housing" is able to provide comfortable and enduring lodg-
ing. The materials are very particular. The floors are paved with
square bricks and dustless. The profile doorframes and window
frames are usually inlaid with green glass stone engravings with
couplet written by a famed figure. For example, "Scholar Village" in Wujiang of Zhangpu was built in the Qing Dynasty, the
main building is composed of three range of bungalows and two
ranges of compounds with each compound having three courtyards, and it is still preserved in very good conditions. The Cai'
s Old Residence in Guanjiao of Nanan County was built between
1864 and 1911. The residence stretches over three kilometers a-
way, having a perfect combination of wood carves and stone
carves. Every carving work is a story. The Cai's House in
Tacahng of Jinjiang County is two-storied watchtower building,
having two courtyards with the first courtyard bringing open pavilions on its left and right sides, and wall materials in bright
colors. Zhuang's Residence in Jinjian is a field-side building,

having horizontal and symmetrical layout in luxurious decoration
of high standard brick and wood engravings. Yang'a Miao civil
residence in Tingdian Village of Quanzhou was built at the time
of Guangxu period in the Qing Dynasty. The residence preserved
in very good conditions, occupies an area of 1200 square meters:
five standard-width rooms, two range of wing-rooms, three
courtyards, a stone-paved vestibule, surrounding by walls to
form a complete set of building. The decoration used in this residence is very exquisite, on which Mr. Huang Hanmin has a com-
ment: It seems that the house has collected every decorative
means popular in the South of Fujian and the arts and crafts are
so perfectly refined just like a museum of the South of Fujian
decoration arts. The most remarkable part is the outer profile
wall: white stone wall base, bluestone column base and the edg-
ed walls; red bricks built in groups to surface the wall and colorful clay sculptured eave mouth; contrasting bright colors for wall
patterns, showing a rich and powerful family's fortune and no-
bility. The bluestone engravings on the main entrance, the gate
case, stele are all rarely seen; The stone hollowed-out carves of
dramatis figures and war horses on the top wall of the porch
might be said as the masterpiece of the South of Fujian stone
carvings. On the large part of the polished bluestone of the wall,
there shallowly carved flower, bird, fish and insect, copied writ-
ings and paintings of the past celebrities like Yan Zhengqing,
Shushi and Zhang Ritu. Besides, the patterns on the windows,
cases and legs of the cabinet are conceived in astonishing idea and
every piece can be rated as the first class art curiosity. The
wooden carvings in the Yang Amiao's residence are also remark-

able and painstaking works: the window frames, partitions are made from Nanmu and camphor; figures and landscapes, precious bids and animals carved on the poles and beams, columns and queti(supporting part for a column and a beam in a traditional building) are depicted in hundred of postures and with refined crafts as beautiful as one can imagine (*Old Houses. Fujian Civil Residence*, published in 1994 by Jiangsu Art Publishing House).

2. Official Residence Type. This type is often seen in the South of Fujian. Officials in the South of Fujian would like to build this kind of residence at their hometowns. In Dongcheng of Quanzhou, there are splendid official residences of the following personages: Jinjiang King Liu Chongxiao in the Five Dynasties, Hong Chengchou who was Shangshu of the Military Department In the Ming Dynasty, Zhan Yangpi who was Shangshu of the Punishment Department of Nanjing in the Ming Dynasty, Caique who was the premier of the Southern Song Dynasty, Liang Kejia who was Zhuang Yuan of the Southern Song Dynasty, Guonan who was the imperial inspection official of the Ming Dynasty, Wan Zhengxie who was Gongbao Tidu (officer title of provincial grade) of the Qing Dynasty, Shiliang who was the navy senior officer to Fujian, Zheng Zhilong who was called "Father of Nan' an" by Longwu Emperor of South Ming period. Moreover there is another range of the official residences of the ten high-ranking military officers under the leadership of Shilang, stretching in a line to form an ancient official building colony. These magnificent official buildings all center on axes, multi-courtyard, multi-room and vertically arranged alone the center in group with por-

ches, dooryards, antechamber, back-halls. After the entrance, there is the porch beside which there are two attendant's rooms with a dooryard in front of them; and beside the dooryard, there are wing-rooms; main house is beyond the dooryard. In the middle, there is usually the hall which is facing the dooryard and is semi-opened. The antechamber is a place fro worshipping ancestor and gods, the back-chamber is the living rooms for dependants. On the right and left side of the hall, there are two sets of four rooms which are commonly called big room and back room. Actually they are living rooms and bedrooms. In addition, there is a back yard or rooms served as a kitchen, miscellaneous room and living room. To enlarge the house, add more courtyards behind and extend from the left and right. Dooryard and open hall go in harmony; the ridge and roof are stretching in a smooth and easy curve appearing natural and graceful. "Zhong Xian House" in Nanan Shijing was built in Yongzheng sixth year of the Qing Dynasty (1728). It is a perfectly persevered complete official building. The house has five compounds of Xuanshan top. The hall is the center of the building, with east and west wing-room, covering an area of 7780 square meters. The study-hall, Martial law hall, dressing room, moon pond, fish pool, waterside pavilion, rockworks, garden, etc. are all annexes in a good and reasonable layout with shallow and deep turnings and paths.

3. Westernized buildings. This is the third ordinary type of civil residences in the South of Fujian, which are mostly built by retired overseas Chinese who have been influenced by the inhabited country's architecture as well as typical residential characters in the South of Fujian. They might be said an integration of

Chinese and Western styles—developing the useful and discarding the useless. They discard the dooryard and open hall centered compound. Instead they center on antechamber and back chamber with four rooms surrounding around and facing to the main hall. Usually they are two-storied. The most distinguish character of this architecture is to surround the building with space instead of surround the space with building as was done by traditional method. Though there are Korinthos (an ancient Greece town) typed round corridor column and westernized leaf windows, their gates and walls are still made from bricks and there are also stone-carved door plague, couplets and colorful porcelain door decorations. Though the westernized buildings start to have flat top roof and ceramic painted pottery baluster, they still like to have dragon ridge and phoenix eaves. There are gardens before and behind the building, and ivy and violet climb all over the house and the roof full of the alien sentiments and appeals. Some small westernized houses in Shishi city are the result of the integration of Chinese and western styles. Granite wall foot, red brick outer wall are local tradition while the structure of the pilasters and window top are made in a western method.

4. Earthen storied building. The earthen storied building in Shajian Village of Huaan County is named "Rixin Building", which is typical of the earthen buildings that contain rich cultural values of the South of Fujian. The building was built during Wangli Period of the Ming Dynasty. The outer wall of the building is made from rammed earth, inside which there are rows of rooms in good order. The building absorbs the characteristics of

the architecture of the Ming Dynasty in the Central Plains and
the traditions of different styles. Rixin Building backs on the
mountain cliffs and sees a thick beautiful bamboo forest. The
building seeks the layout of the whole building colony in the
space instead of the outstanding position of a single building.
The interior room creates an easy, symmetrical, flexible and im-
plicit environment. The series-wound courtyards inlay a time
process in the spatial combination, giving prominence to the architectural aesthetical characters of time and space. "Chang
Yuan Building" in Xiuzhuang Village of Zhaoan County is typical
of the square buildings in the South of Fujian. The building was
built in Qianlong time of the Qing Dynasty, 42m in length, having only one gate facing to the west; two-storied, 65 rooms in
all, beyond the axes, there built an ancestor temple. Outside the
gate, surrounded by a wall is a square front yard. Round shaped
earthen buildings in the South of Fujian have a lot of varieties.
"Qi Yun Lou" in Shajian Village of Huaan County is the most
ancient building that was built in Wanli years of the Ming Dynasty. It has an oval structure and so do the courtyards in the building, smooth and unfolding: two-storied high, courtyard in the
middle, single unit; the ground floor is built up by stones while
the first floor is built by rammed earth, the gates facing the
south; the east gate is "birth gate", used when there is a marriage; the west gate is "death gate", used when there is a funeral; Outstandingly, the outlay of the rooms seem to be the simpli-
fied three hall in one line arrangement instead of an equally divided rooms; the larger room is one time or two times bigger than
the small one; the largest room is near 200 square meters while

the one is about 100 square meters; the internal arrangement is extremely complicated and filled with dynamics and life. Most a-mazingly, every room is not of equal depth with the rooms in the south side having a shorter depth while the rooms in the north side have a longer depth, much to the bewilderment of an ob-server. Living in the same round building, every family has a dif-ferent layout, yet looked around from the courtyard, all the rooms are seem to be under such a harmonious unification with-out one household overgrowing the other that people would feel a comfortable and gentle environment. At present, there are still more than twenty households living in this building that is an ar-chitectural relic of the Ming Dynasty. The most gigantic earthen storied building is Feng Ning Stockade Village in Luxi Town of Pinghe County. The village was started to build in the first year of Kangxi and was finished 40 years later. The diameter of the building is about 77 meters; the main four-storied building of 14. 5 meters high; every floor having 77 rooms lived by 77 house-holds with a population of 250 persons; there had been more than 700 persons at the most. The rooms in the building are nar-row in the former part of the room and wider in the back part like an "ax shape"; on the gate of the building, there installed fire-protecting water tank, groove; the well in he middle of the building is usually covered by stone table with three hole on it for fetching water. What a secure and sanitary design. Er Yi Storied Building in Xiandu Village of Huaan County is round earthen building characterized of architectural arts. It was con-structed in the years of Qianlong in the Qing Dynasty, twelve years of construction period in all. The diameter is 73. 4 meters,

18 meters high, the foundation 4 meters high; the building is composed of two internal rings and two outer rings: the inner ring is one storied, the outer rings are four storied; the inner and the outer bringing out the best in each other so that it is called "mutually appropriation".

The inner ring is a one-storied platform as kitchen and dining room area; the outer four-storied ring is an area of bed-room that is divided into twelve independent units called "shy quarter" with 224 rooms; on the fourth floor there are halls, each of which has a channel of one meter wide near the back wall to connect the twelve units together. Living in this earthen building of 220 years of history are 200 people. Jinjiang Storied Building in Shentu Village of Zhangpu County is another earthen construction with a unique style. It is composed of three ring groups with different height, the outer ring is not a complete ring, cut open at the gate, having 36 rooms; the middle ring is two-storied with 52 rooms; the inner ring is three-storied having 36 rooms, at the entrance of whose second and third floors, there built watching platforms; there is no outstretching eaves on the whole building except for "daughter walls". Umbrella Building in Gaoche Village of Huanan County was built on a hill. It makes best use of the terrain and the outer ring is three-storied lowering in accordance to the landform; the inner ring is two sto-ried situated on the hilltop, having 18 rooms of different size, which are connected by narrow stairs. Shuzi Building in Heping Village of Yunxiao County was built in the time of Qianlong of the Qing Dynasty. It is three storied high; the eaves stretch out of the outer wall very little; 50 meters in diameter; every room is an independent unit.

In the South of Fujian, there are many earthen buildings of mixed shape of round and square, i. e. mainly of a round shape yet square in some part. For example, "Zaitian Building" in Gongbei Village of Zhaoan County has a history of more than four hundred years. It is made up of outer ring and inner ring.

The inner rig is three storied and lays out by a square shape for the back wall go in a curve turning, which is squared shape at front but a round shape at the back; the outer ring is three-storied and lays out in an Eight Diagrams round form, having 64 rooms. The building is 86 meters long, which is the longest building that has ever seen by now. Earthen constructions in Nanjing County account for an important part of the residence in the South of Fujian. The first point is that they are many in quantity for according to recent statistics, there are about three hundred buildings of this kind, each of which is about 30 to 50 meters in length and having 30 rooms on every floor; The other point is their structural features: there are Four cornered building, Round Building, Chair Building and building in an umbrella, fan, folding-ruler shapes. Among them, the best preserved one is Huaiyuan Building in Meilin Kanxia Village, built in Xuantong first year of the Qing Dynasty (1909); the largest one is Shunyu Building in Shiqiao Village, Shuyang Town, for it has five stories with each floor having 72 rooms, 74 meters in length.

Civil Residence in the West of Fujian

Large and medium-sized civil residences are multi-compound-centered buildings situated on the axes with two ranges of houses surrounding on both side. The auxiliary buildings are joining houses. Generally, there are halls in the civil residences with antechamber and back chamber, wing-rooms on both sides, kitchen and dooryard. Its overall layout is extending to the four directions; the left and right sides in symmetry; every unit within the gate is connected to form a well-equipped and enclosed palace setup. To be in detail, there are "three openings" and "eight openings". The so-called "three openings" is a unit whose middle hall is bright and big with He door(two-leafed door); on the left and right of the hall, there are "private school rooms"; there is a screen outside the gate and behind the gate, there is the courtyard; the building is actually composed of hall, chamber and room; door stairs is before the hall, room is behind the hall to which the room is accessible; between the gate and the hall, there is another door behind which the hosts live. The so-called "eight openings" indicates common residence in which there are two halls, four chambers and two wing-rooms, a dooryard in the middle. Some layouts are the extensions of the "eight openings".

According to what are recorded in Longyan Local History and Changting History, the typical residences of the West Fujian area are as following: Eighteen Halls situated in Xiajing Alley of Longyan which was built in Ming Wanli years (1573—1620). It is made up of three buildings of six courtyards, brick and wood structure, every building having six courtyards and bungalows; in every courtyard, there stand three openings with the hall in the middle, living rooms on both sides with side door; alone the dooryard, there are corridor rooms. Every building has six halls, so the three buildings have 18 halls and 18 dooryards in total.

Qiu Cuo built in the Qing Dynasty is situated in Longyan city proper. From the south to the north, there line playground, gate, ante dooryard, middle hall, back dooryard and back hall. There is a cloister alone the two sides of the ante and back dooryards; the main house has three rooms with the middle one is a wooden truss structure, the side two are wing-rooms; the corridor room is connected with the main house. Wu's House, built in the Qing Dynasty is in the south street of Changting County, occupying an area of 600 square meters, made up of side door, low wall, gate tower, dooryard, main hall and back hall. The side door sits on the east facing to the west, of wooden structure; three rooms horizontally nearing the fire protecting walls on both sides; the ends of the main ridge are moldered with double lions playing with ball; the gate tower is single eave of stone structure; the door rafter is painted with colorful figure; the door to the ante hall is a six-leaf partitions; the main chamber is of wooden pulling-on-through frame structure; there are relievo on the girder; three horizontally lined rooms, and four vertical rooms; the front rafters all are hung with drooping balls; the back hall is a pulling-on-through structure with nine-purline canopies, three rooms horizontally, six rooms vertically, a shrine in the center, the back chamber is a two-storied embroidery rooms with beauty's room in the building, typical of the traditional Changting residence.

Farmer's residences like the one in Mujin Village of Yongding County are also representative of the West Fujian residence. It is a one-storied building in u-shape, four-sided compound, two rows of houses on the both sides of the square in the middle of the compound; behind the outer row of house, there is an arc row of houses. The front courtyard is a playground surrounded by wall and the torii like gate; before the house, there is a water pool of half-moon shape. The Zhang's House in Xinquan Town of Liancheng County sits on the north and faces to the south. Its gate is installed at northwest side, which pops out the white stone exquisitely engraved gate from the dark gray bricks of one layer after another.

The most influential and distinguished of the residences in the West of Fujian is the earthen building. The well-known square earthen colony is in Shizhong Village of Longyan. There are preserved till now 242 of three-storied earthen buildings. Those built in the Ming Dynasty in Shizhong Village are simple in outer appearance, flat ridge and eaves, single gate, empty dooryard, every floor having 16 rooms. Those built in the Qing Dynasty have a hall at the back part. Those built in the middle of Qing Dynasty pay attention to the quality and appearance. Their main buildings are mostly in flat square layout: at the front part and at the back part, there are separately one hall with six rooms; on the right and left sides, there are one hall with four rooms separately, or a stair; in the main building, there are 16 halls, rooms as many as 80, every one of which is 12 square meters. Out of the medium-sized earthen building colonies, Shancheng Building covers 15 mu, the largest acreage. Hezhi Building has the widest main building layout, for there are separately four units horizontally and vertically, nine gates, 18 halls, one gate leading to one lane. Dianchang Building has the most

exquisite decorative arts and crafts: piled up structures and flying eaves, painted cloisters and engraved columns , Hechun
Building is famous for its multi-halls, multi-types and multi-win-
dows. The largest square building with the highest main building
in the West of Fujian is Yijing Building in Yongding. The building was constructed in the time of Daoguang of the Qing Dynasty, which is also named Huaxing Building, or Big Mansion for
its gigantic construction scales. Its main architecture is composed
of paratactic three five-storied buildings with 17 meters in
height. On the left and right side of the main architecture, there
connected separately four-storied high buildings in vertical directions that again closely linked with the front four storied "center
hall building" which is paralleled the main building, forming a
big mouth, vigorous and majestic. Inside the big mouth, and before the main building, there is the big hall that is connecting to
storehouses on the both sides; and the ends of the two storehouses connect to a cloister so as to form a smaller "mouth". So
the bigger "mouth" has a side length of 76 meters in a square
shape; the perimeter of the whole building is 136 meters, and 76
meters in width, 10 336 square meters of acreage. Outside the
gate, and connected to the left side and right side of the gate are
two schools; between the two schools, there is a spacious stone
playground; at the anterior part of the playground, there is the
large gate tower which is 6 meters high and 4 maters wide, accessible for a four-ton truck. Fuxin Building, situated in Hulie
Village of Yongding County, is the most ancient square building
in the West of Fujian. Generally, it is thought to have a history
of thousand of years, for it was consider to be built by first an-

cestors of the Hakka who went into Yongding in the Five Dynasties and the Tang period. At first, the building was constructed
by four surnames and later they occupied one corner each. A-
round the building, there surrounds an entrenchment of four meters wide with suspended walls. Yude Building in Hukeng Village of Yongding is another well-known square earthen building
in the West of Fujian. It is a building of a big mouth shape within which there built another square-shaped architecture. Xiang-
zheng Building, Yongfu Building and Yanjia Building situated in
Xiayang Town connect themselves to form a mouth shape, which
encloses two rows of buildings inside. The largest round-shaped
earthen building in the West of Fujian is Chengqi Building in
Yongding, which was built in the years of Kangxi of the Qing
Dynasty. The perimeter is 1915.6 meters with 12.42 meters in
height and 15 meters in width. It is made up of three rings of
buildings with the taller one in the exterior and lower one in the
interior. In addition, a round hall sits in the center of the rings.
Looked from the sky, the architecture seems to have four rings.
The main building is four-storied and each floor has 72 rooms.
From the main building, another two rings of two storied buildings are extending to the interior, every floor of which has 40
rooms; the inner most ring is bungalow having 32 rooms, big
hall in the middle; the whole building possesses 400 rooms in total and occupies an area of 5376.17 square meters; the main
building has three gates; every ring installs six gates and two
wells. At its prime time, there lived in this building more than
80 household with a population of 600 hundred people. As this
Chengqi Building has such a huge scale that a story like that may

sound real to life: at a marriage ceremony, two young women at the same table talked to each other boasting of the largeness of their living quarters. After further inquiry, they found that they both lived in the same chengqi Building yet they knew nothing about each other though they were actually sister-in-laws. It happens that people live on the east part do not know those who live on the west part as there is too large a population. In 1986, Ministry of Posts and Telecommunications issued a stamp named Chinese Civil Residence with the picture of Chengqi Building on the one yuan stamp. It was selected as the best stamp of the year. Shenyuan Building in Guzhu Village of Yongding County is a round earthen building with the longest diameter, for its perimeter of outer ring is 80 meters long. It has three rings of buildings, 328 rooms lived by 80 households with a population of more than 500 people. Jin Shan Ancient Stockade Village in Guzhu Village is the most ancient round building that was built in the second year of Xiangxing of the South Song Dynasty (1279), 2 to 3 meters high, 30 meters in diameter, having a watching tower on the center. Zhencheng Building in Hukeng Village of Yongding County is the most magnificent round architecture in the West of Fujian. The outer ring of the building is four-storied, every floor having 48 rooms that are divided into eight equal parts in accordance to the Eight Diagrams pattern. Between every part there is the fire protective walls that are separating parts into independent units connecting to each other by archways. The roof of the hall can be served as a dancing stage, and inside the building there are schools and gardens. In 1985, on World Architectural Modal Exhibition held in Los Angeles of

USA, Zhencheng Building was one of the architectural modals of ancient China and it became a collector's curiosity together with the modals of Beijing Heaven Altar, Yonghe Palace.

Civil Residence of the North of Fujian

Most of the residences in the North of Fujian are of wooden and earthen structured tiled houses, having a dooryard in the middle, two or three main rooms stand along the sides. On the both sides of the dooryard, there are stone stairs of two or three steps that leads to a big hall in the middle and living rooms on both sides of it; behind them, there is the back room with kitchens beside. Just as what is described in the *History of Mingxi County* printed in the 32nd Year of Minguo, "Most houses were built with woods and walls were built with bricks and mud in a regular system of three halls up and down, wing-rooms on the left and right sides; some people constructed storied buildings, not very gaudy but solid and firm. These houses could be used for very long tome and were easy to be repaired. So they had advantages. " Typical of this kinds of civil residences are as following:

1. Upon the local type, imitating types from those of the other places. As is recorded in *A New History of Chong'an County* that was printed in the 31st year of Minguo, "Residence construction in the Ming Dynasty were rather simple: usually there installed two poles in front of the hall, and the hall is divided into two sections; the upper section was built with bamboo frames that were fastened by thick mud, which is quite the same as the artificial walls used in today; till the Ming Dynasty, the productive procession was changed a little; during the Qian and

the Jia periods, a Zhou of Xiamei, and a Peng of Chaodun went to Guangdong on business and imitate Guangdong's house building and put on luxurious decorations; a Peng people went to Suzhou on business and imitated the housing construction of Suzhou and made his house wide and deep inside; in the Qing period, two people who were named Wang and Zhu in Chengfang built their houses in a large and spacious scale, letting in enough sunshine, ranking number one house in the North of Fujian". In the Qing Dynasty, merchants imitated Guangzhou and Suzhou and Zhangzhou's architectural style and built more than 70 houses in Xiamei Village of Wuyi Mountains, and now 50 houses are existed as ancient civil residence colony. By comparison, residences in the North of Fujian have following characteristics: first, they are spacious as the entire building has gate, gate tower, ante hall, main hall, back hall, study room, pavilion, etc.; every building has three courtyards; the main hall is built by lifted girders with two dougongs connected from the ends of a column; the dougong is engraved with flower and bird patterns; second, they are beautiful as all the brick gate, hallowed-out carved wooden girders, windows and cloister eaves are done with refined and careful works; third, they have complete layout and beautiful top shape of the wall.

2. High Hill Houses. These kinds of houses usually built in the village that is beside streams and hills, in two stories with the second story built of wooden structure while the ground floor lifted by several fir tree trunks as a framework for the hills to protect floods and prevent from snake and other insects; the base of the houses are surrounded by bamboo fence. Some houses

have only one supporting post that is surrounded by walls a-round; the house may be one or two storied according to the height of the wooden post; the space in the building is divided into several rooms on each floor; These houses are quite similar with the architectures of "pole-fence type" discovered in the relic site of the Han's Town in the Wuyi mountains. The pole-fence type is a house lifted up by short posts with the unfenced lower part used as livestock house and store house while the porch used as sun drying platform behind which there are the hall and bedroom of the house.

3. Three courtyards and nine units type. Many retired imperial officials returned home with fortunes and built themselves a large sized tiled house with three courtyards and nine units. Its dooryards, corridors, eave stairs are mostly built of stones; every house is protected by fireproof walls of pottery bricks or clay mud; in the upper part of the third hall, there built a shrine; the house looks magnificent. The most typical of this kind is the residence of Li Chunye who was the senior officer of the imperial military of the Ming Dynasty (1621—1627). The residence situates in the town proper of Taining and was built in the years of Tianqi of the Ming Dynasty. It is often referred to as Shangshu's House, Number One Happiness Mansion, the characteristics of which are as follows: First, magnificent; the whole architecture sits on the west and faces the east; 87 meters long from the south end to the north end; 60 meters long from the east end to the west end; occupying an acreage of 5220 square meters; 5 main buildings, 8 sets of auxiliary rooms, all of which scattering over separately behind the five gates along the corri-

dor; there are 120 rooms in all expect for halls, dooryards and cloisters all in brick and wood structure. Second, reasonable layout; the five units are three courtyards compounds almost similar in structure; the main hall is built with lifting girders and reduced posts with the wooden posts very strong and big; the hall is open to the dooryard; there installed on the both sides of the hall high balusters decorated with exquisite engraves. Third, particular materials; the corridors, courtyards, cloisters and dooryards are all paved with granite slates while the floor of the halls uses square bricks. Fourth, refined arts and crafts; there are as many as thirty types for the base of the posts used in the hall, all engraved with kylin, colorful elephant, flower and tree; stone, brick and wooden carvings of figures, flying birds, growing grass, flower in blossom and bright brocade are used all over gate frame, stele, pole, column, dougong and wall surfaces.

Civil Residences in the East of Fujian

The traditional residences in the East of Fujian are mostly composed of one hall and left and right wing-rooms. Nevertheless, there are other forms and types such as what Mr. Huang Hanmin has found out about: traditional Fuan residence used to have large and huge house tops with increased large size of roof slope; from the huge two sloped top come out two or three layers of drooping eaves, under which the wood structure contrast the white bamboo and clay walls; the tile decoration on the topping roof and the suspended wooden fish can conceive numerous rich pictures. The houses built by the She nationality of Fuan County are mostly "four structure quarters"; i. e. two frame works added to two sides of walls; the three rooms under the roof are partitioned by wooden frame that is named as "partition wall"; the ante part of the wall is the hall, behind it there is the back hall; in the middle of the hall there is often place an old fashioned square table for eight people for entertaining guests on the festivals and offering sacrifices for dead ancestors; there are one or two dooryards with cloisters and the back dooryard is used as a place for stock and a dining room; the left and the right parts are partitioned by wooden boards to make two or three bedrooms. (History of Fuan She Nationality generally editted by Lan Tongjia.) The East of Fujian area is close to the sea side, and in order to protect the strong coastal winds from the sea and make the housing fast, the residences use a great deal of granite stones to build their walls for normally one room needs 14 to 16 stone pieces. After all, the East of Fujian is teemed with granite.

Ⅲ. Ancient Bridges in Fujian

China has a long history of constructing bridges with remarkable accomplishments and it led the world in this filed before the nineteenth century. With a vast mountainous land that is full of streams and rivers running to the east sea, Fujian has been engaged in bridge construction ever since. We find that the ancient bridges built in Fujian had reached very high standards of architecture when we make a study on the length, span, weight, construction speed, construction technology, types of bridge, and bridge foundations. They have a very important position in the history of China's ancient bridge construction. Wang Shimao of the Ming Dynasty honored Fujian bridges in the book *Notes on the Min Capital* as "the best bridges under the sun". Zhou Lianggong of the Qing Dynasty considered the bridges in Fujian, in his work Notes on Min about its Bridges as "the most beautifully gigantic bridges".

It was later for Fujian to start to build bridges. But when it was at the initial period in the Tang Dynasty, Fujian was able to construct good quality bridges. For example, Lianban Bridge in the Lianban Village in Chengmen Town of Fuzhou was built in the sixth year of Dali of the Tang Dynasty (771). The bridge was 15 meters long, 14. 1 meters wide; the platforms on the both ends of the bridge was in rectangle shapes that were set on the wooden posts (40cm in diameter each); over the two bridge platforms, there placed two huge stone girders. Huilong Bridge in Minan Town of Fuzhou was built in the Tang Dynasty, 66 metrs long, 4. 8 meters wide, having four piers and five openings, all built with granite; between the two piers, place five stone girders, the thickness of which is about 0. 8 meters; after many times of repairing and remedy, the piers, girders and fences are still considered to be the relics from the Tang Dynasty. The bride with five openings built in the Tang Dynasty is very rare in the history Chinese bridge construction. One point that should be noted is that some very priceless bridges in the northern part of China have disappeared slowly with the time passes by, and with the south bound immigration of the Central Plains culture, the bridge building technology has spread to Fujian. Some bridges built by Central Plain techniques and types have been preserved till today. For example, Hong Bridge over Bian River built in the North Song period, is built with wooden girders instead of posts, which is convenient both for construction as well as for navigation. This kind of method of using long span wood structure known as "structure of Hong Bridge" occupies a very important position in the history of Chinese bridge building for its rarity. After the perdition of the North Song Dynasty, there has been records about this kind of bridge are built any more. Today, some experts have found that in Pingnan County of Fujian, there is a wooden arch bridge named Qiancheng Bridge that resembles the sample of Hong Bridge. Pan Hongxuan pointed out in *Ten Famous Bridges* that: " This was caused by the south bound immigration of the political and cultural center of the Song Dynasty to Hangzhou, and craftsmen brought the techniques used in Hong Bridge from the Yellow River to the south of China. "This kind of bridge is also found on the boundary area of Fujian and Zhejiang. But judged from the names that are carved on the girders of those who had taken part in the bridge construction, the bridge seems to be built by Fujian artisans. The quantity of bridges built in ancient time in Fujian ranks one of the tops in China. According to the statistical data in the History of Fujian, Fujian had constructed 2694 bridges from the Tang to the Qing Dynasty. The statistical data may not be very accurate, the remote area like Longyan, had built 594 bridges according to what is recorded in the History of Longyan. Yet only by this imperfect data, Fujian's accomplishments in bridge building under such poor conditions are astonishing. Just as Dr. Joseph Li, the British expert of science and technology history had pointed out in China's History in Science and Technology: "especially in Fujian province, there is no place in China or in any other country can be comparable with them. "

Fujian not only has a long history of bridge building with the largest number of ancient bridges but also accomplished in constructing various types of bridges characterized by strong points of different schools. To summarize, Fujian bridges have the following characteristics:

1. Not stick to the length. As far as the length of the bridge is concerned, Fujian has the longest and shortest bridges in China. As to the longest one, Anping Bridge in Quanzhou is about 2300 meters long, which connects five li of sea bay from Anhai in the South of Fujian to Shuitou across which people used to go by boat. The bridge, which was called "the longest bridge under the sun" had been the longest one in China for about eight hundred years before the Yellow River Bridge in Zhengzhou was built up in 1925. Some experts think that Yulan Bridge of 1000 *zhang* (1 zhang = 3. 3 meters) long, situated outside the south gate of Quanzhou and Suli Bridge of 2400 *zhang* long, built in the years of Shaoxin periods of the South Song Dynasty are longer than Anping Bridge. Louyang Bridge in Quanzhou is about 1106 meters long; Yu Bridge in Huian is about 2300 meters, submerged by tides normally, but accessible when tide ebbing; Wangshou Bridge in Fuzhou is 550 meters long. Liugang Bridge in Zhangzhou is 799 meters long. Longjian Bridge in Fuqing is 553 meters long. Hudu Bridge is 614 meters long. The shortest bridge is only three meters long, such as the single opening and stoned arch bridge in Hudi Village, Huafeng Town of Huaan County. Its span is not more than 1 meter so small that it looks exquisite.

2. Using all kinds of materials. As far as the materials used

are concerned, most bridges use wood material with few using
stone and wood materials. There are stone girder bridges like
Hudu Bridge in Zhangzhou which was built in Shaoxi years of the
Song Dynasty (1190—1194). There are stone arch bridges like
Zhengan Bridge in Jianning which was built up in Shaoding first
year of the Yuan Dynasty (1228) with a span of 18 meter long,
capable of passing trucks till now; Bolan Bridge in Fuqing started to be built in Chenghua 19th year of the Ming Dynasty (
1483), is a single opening stone bridge. Its net span is 6. 6 meters long, bridge surface width 2. 15 meters, arch height 3. 3 meters. It is impossible to look through the bridge from one end of
the bridge to other end. Thin Arch Bridge situated on the south
part of Bayiqi Road of Fuzhou city proper is also called "Xiao
Qiao". It was started on in the Yuan Dynasty with a span diameter 7. 2 meters, the thickness of the arch 20 centimeters, much
smaller than what it should have been by modern bridge construction theory. Yet thousands of vehicles pass across it every
day. Experts of modern bridges consider it a miracle. There are
wooden material bridges like Chenzi Bridge in Xiyang Village,
Hetang Town of Gutian County. The bridge was built in De first
year of the Southern Song Dynasty (1275) totally with yew
trunks for the whole bridge still in perfect conditions through
long ages. There are stone and wood structure bridges like Lanxi
Bridge in Lanxi Village, Yijia Town of Jianning County. It was
built in Jiajing 36th year of the Ming Dynasty (1557), bridge
width of 6. 5 meters, height 12 meters, length 75 meters; upon
the stone piers are four wooden layers of framework in a check
pattern; wooden shafts stretch out of the layers; large tree

trunks are used as bridge girders; Dayang Bridge, in Dongliu
Village of the west of Wuping County which is thought to be reconstructed in Xianfeng fifth year of the Qing Dynasty (1855)
has a few *zhang* of length and one *zhang* of width. Upon the
huge stone piers, there are layers of fir frameworks, which are
quite like a dougong, unique in style.

3. With a variety of types. Except for the bridges mentioned
above like Hong Bridge and stone arch bridges, there are still
many other types of bridges. There are float bridges like Dongjin
Float Bridge in Jianyang County which was built in Yongle 8th
year of the Ming Dynasty (1410). The bridge was made up of
thirty big boats combined together by thirty iron chains which
were fastened to the stone posts on the both banks of the river.
The bridge linked the east part and the town. There used to be
many float bridges in Fujian. Nan Bridge in the south corner of
Zhangzhou city proper was a float bridge in Shaoxi years(1131—
1162) of the Song Dynasty, later it was changed into a stone
bridge in the year of Jading. Hudu Bridge on the lower valley of
Bei Stream of Longhai County was called Jiandong Bridge or
Tongji Bridge. It was a float bridge when it was being built in
Shaoxing years of the Song Dynasty (1131—1162). Apart from
these, there are suspended bridges, traffic bridges, single wood
bridges and mark-time bridges.

4. Harmonious integration of utility and arts. It has been
taken into consideration that a bridge shall go well with the surroundings. Those stone pier and girder bridges built in the Song
and the Yuan periods are mostly situated at the seaport. Gusts of
wind lift up the waves surging high into the air over the bound-

less sea. The simple and imposing stone piers and girders stand vigorously and majestically there like a long sea wall to calm down the roaring waves. Just as what Pan Hongxuan had said in Ten Great Ancient Bridges: Anping stone bridge in Quanzhou Fujian, "the longest bridge under the sun" strides over Anhai seaport like a sea stabilizing long wall, displaying a visual impression of " the shy that is spreading down a silky rainbow hundreds of and thousands of zhang long, the straight fence and horizontal cage flies across the vast space" to conceive with the surroundings a beautiful scenery of "over the clear water and bright mountain, a bridge is jumping". Ninghai Bridge in Qiaodou Village of Putian County was built in Yuantong second year of the end of the Yuan Dynasty (1334). It runs across Mulan Stream and pours into the Xinghua Bay. When the morning sun rises, the rosy clouds dyes the water red, the bridge will look like a golden dragon splashing into the sea with waves jumping and dancing against the horizon. The scenery is known as Ninghai Early Sun, one of the twenty scenic spots of Putian. Yanshou Bridge near Yanshou Village of Putian County was under construction in first year of Jianyan of the Song Dynasty (1127). The scenes alone the banks of the bridge look just like those drawn in the pictures. Under the bridge, the green water popples so lively that countless longhairs and refined scholars enjoy the scenery, making pictures and recite poems, sailing in a boat or fishing in the water. It is known as "fishing and boating in Shou Stream" and has been one of the twenty scenic spots of Putian ever since the ancient time.

    5. Refined arts and crafts seen on the auxiliary architectures

and stone carvings. It seems that most of Fujian bridge builders
pay special attention to the visual effects as they always decorate
the bridge with stone carvings, stele inscriptions, pavilion, tower and supporting fence. The stone decorations look either powerful and mighty, vivid and lively or holy and solemn, clear and
bright, no matter it is a stone bridge stabilizing officer or a water
stabilizing animal or a stone lion standing for the national un-
yielding spirits, or memorial figures or religious themes like a
sitting Buddha, lotus. The beautiful lines and clear images serve
as a foil to the magnificent bridge structure and at the same time
emitting a spirit of comeliness under the great momentum of the
bridge. Those decorations on the arm-stretching typed bridge
particularly impress people with a sense of "flying pavilion and
floating boat running down to boundless world". Typical of this
is Luoyang Bridge in Quanzhou. According to the introduction in
History of Luoyang Wan'an Bridge by Liu Haoran, installed
on Luoyang Bridge, there are "Stele of Merit and Faith", which
was placed before Jiang Zhili's Temple of the Ming Dynasty installed in the former middle pavilion; Jinhong Pavilion that was
originally built in the Ming Dynasty; Wind stabilizers on the
south and north ends; Four stone statues of the North Song
characters placed on the south and north ends; Quannan Buddhist Pavilion built in the Yuan Dynasty; The Middle Pavilion
built in modern times; Sweet Rain Stele Pavilion installed on the
west side of the middle pavilion; Reconstruct Cai's Merits and
Faith Stele Pavilion that originally stood on the west side of the
Cai's Temple; Yuqitang Stele Pavilion that stood originally on
the east side of the Cai's Temple; Eight towers on the each end

of he bridge; 28 stone lions of various postures on the fence of
the bridge; 81 Bodhisattvas of various postures that were installed on the tower and pavilions. Though most of these decorations have been destroyed, those stone towers, figures and steles
inscriptions such as Wan'an Bridge Records written by Caixiang
are priceless indeed. How it is like a mini museum! Ancient
bridges that provided rich visual appeals as well as practicability
are to be found everywhere in Fujian. Jinshan Bridge situated on
the high way from Zhangzhou to Huaan, and bestriding Jiulong
River, provides a very high value of artistic appreciation. The
entire bridge is built with well-prepared stone materials, beautiful structure and skillful constructive method. The arch span of
100 meter bestrides the river like a rainbow appearing in the sky;
over the great arch, there built another 28 town gate like arches
in smaller size, and every two the arches is a group installed directly into the end of a big arch. Looked at from a distance, they
seem to be numerous exquisite arch bridges on the rainbow like
great bridge—a splendor scenic spot. On the each end of the
bridge, a bridge head is built and installed beautiful stone fence.
The structure of the bridge is reasonable and artful. Yuchi
Bridge in Jinjiang reconstructed in the years of the Yuan Dynasty
(1341—1368) were decorated with many stone figures and stone
tower on the head of the bridge. Masi Bridge in Dongtong of Datian County was built in Hongzhi 9th year of the Ming Dynasty
(1496). On the top of the pavilions, there are paintings of auspicious dragon and phoenix, and stone decorations like animals,
flowers, figures by refined arts and crafts. Huilong Bridge in
Fuzhou had three stone steles in the pavilions on the bridge.

Longjiang Bridge in Fuqing city has two Buddha towers on the south head of the bridge, and relievo of manikins, lotus and lions. Wanshou Bridge in Fuzhou has wind and rain pavilion, and various stone lions carved on the posts of the bridge fence.

6. Charming house bridges; Among the ancient bridges of varied modals, house bridge (bridge of wind and rain) can be reckoned as the most distinguished one, for it is a bridge that contains a house, a cloister or a building on it. Zhou Lianggong of the Qing Dynasty, described this bridge in Notes about the Min: "Build a house on the bridge, carefully and clearly, making a picture of it from every direction. ··· It is because of the rainy weather in Min, and with the purpose of providing a pedestrian with a place to rest his feet, a wood board framework is built on the both sides of the bridge, covered with wood roofs of several *chi* (1 chi=33.3 cm) high. Looked out from the eaves, the scenery is beautiful, yet inside the eaves, the wondering sight can not reach. It seems that the roof cover is built to shut out the beautiful mountain looks. "

In the West of Fujian, the representative of the house bridge is Yunlong Bridge, which was situated at the entrance of Luofang Village of Liancheng County. The bridge was built in Qianlong 37th year of the Qing Dynasty (1772), 81 meters long, 5 meters wide; the bridge road surface was paved with cobblestones; on the both sides of the bridge, stood 64 pairs of columns in two rows that were covered by two layers of wood rain sails to shut out rains and winds; at the head of the bridge, there built pavilion-gates; in the middle of the bridge, there was a Wenchang Pavilion of ten meters high. Situated outside of the south city gate of Liancheng County was the Wenchuan Bridge that was started to be built in the years of Shaoxing of the Song Dynasty (1131—1164). It was more than 50 meters long, 4 meters wide, installed with 17 rooms, the middle one of which was a hall for Kwan-yin; the hall having two layers of gourd-top.

In the North of Fujian, representative of the house bridge is Banhuatou Bridge situated on Bantao Pan Stream of Zhenghe County. It was built in Zhengde 6th year of the Ming Dynasty (1511), 38 meters long, 10 meters wide, 16 meters high. It was a storied-house bridge with main building was three-storied and two side buildings were two-storied, the east building of which was served as Wenchang Pavilion. The bridge was installed with 80 columns, on each of which there was a couplet. Siqian Shed Bridge (also known as Taian Shed Bridge) was over Siqian Stream of Guangze County. It was built in Qianlong 23rd year of the Qing Dynasty (1758), 100 meters long, 2.5 meters wide, 2 meter high. On the both side of the bridge, there installed with two ranges of benched or chairs for pedestrians to take a rest. Baisha Bridge also called Dragon Gate Bridge situated in the east of Mingxi County was under construction in Chenghua 8th year if the Ming Dynasty (1472), more than 50 *zhang* long, 3 *zhang* wide, covered with 39 houses; a three storied building with six corners in the middle of the bridge; After it was unfortunately destroyed in 1933 by mountain floods, it had no houses built on it any more.

In the East of Fujian, the representative of house bridges is Chenzi Bridge in Xiyang Village, Hetang Town, Gutian County. It was built in Deyou first year of the Southern Song (1275), 55 meters long, 4 meters wide; the upper part is double sloped roof; there are chairs in the side cloisters.

In the South of Fujian, the representative of this bridge is Dongguan Bridge in Dongmei Village of Dongping Town, Yongchun County. It was built in Shaoxing 15th year of the South Song, 85 meters long, 5 meters wide; the bridge had house built on in Hongzhi 13th year of the Ming Dynasty (1500). There are twenty equal sized sets of wood houses in 25 openings; the roof coved by small dark green tiles made from the local clay and the girder built with dark green bricks. Ruiyun Bridge in Jinde Village, Lantian Town, Anxi County was built in Chongzhen 3rd year of the Ming Dynasty (1630), 14.7 meters long, 5.1 meters wide; there was cloister, outside which there were double layers of rain capes; inside the cloister, there were chairs; in the middle of the bridge, there was a Fish Pelargonium Pavilion, and on the wood frameworks of the pavilion, there painted colorful pictures and carved with patterns.

Fujian province has made a great break through in the ancient bridge building technology and has indelibly contributed to the development of the ancient bridge construction of China and even of the world. Technologically, the principle achievements are summarized as the followings:

1. Creating "raft-shape foundation". Bridge foundation is always of crucial importance to bridge construction. Luoyang Bridge is situated on the wide seaport of Luoyang River, the convergent place of river and sea rushed by huge waves. It had been unprecedented to build a bridge in this terra. So the engineering was very difficult and many technical problems should be solved.

In order to deal with the stability of the bridge foundation, "raft-shape foundation" was created, i. e. to throw into the river-bed ten thousand square tons of huge stones in line with the bridge body and built up a stone bank 20 meters in width and 1 *li* in length so as to raise the river bed 3 meters higher, and then to build piers on the stone bank. This is a great creation in the history of bridge construction.

2. Creating a method of "strengthening the foundation by growing oyster". To connect solidly the piers with the foundation without the modernized rapid coagulate concrete had proved to a tough problem. The bridge builders brought into full play their astonishing ability and wisdom and invented a method, i. e. to grow oysters on the foundation and the piers, for maritime animal oyster has a lime quality shell that can adhere to the stones and grow at a fast speed. So the method was used in place of the iron belt method. As the iron belt and its casting pieces would be eroded by seawater very quickly.

3. Creating "float carriage and support" method. In the Song Dynasty, many bridges in Fujian were built in the dangerous waves and billows of rivers and sea. Luoyang Bridge had used 300 stone girders, and every girder was about 12 meters long and no less than 0. 5 meters thick, weighed 7~8 tons. With simple and undeveloped transporting means, bridge engineers and workers invented a float carriage and support method, i. e. to put the stone girders of 7~8 tons on a wood raft and let it float to the position by the flood tide. When the tide ebbed, the raft was lowered and the girder was placed on the pier or lifted by the wood winch and slowly and accurately placed on the pier.

4. Creating "sleeping log and sunk foundation" method. In dealing with the bridge foundation, the archeologists invented a method named "sleeping log and sunk foundation", i. e. in the dry season, clean up the mud and sand to level the foundation of the pier; fix into the pier foundation position a wood raft made up of several layers of wood strips that are plaited and overlapped vertically and horizontally; rampart pier stones on the wood raft; the raft will sink in the bed of the river as the pier stones are piling up. This method is used in the pier construction of Jinji Bridge which is situated at the foot of Jiuri Mountain bestriding Jinjiang River. When in the mountain area, the stream water can be controlled below the lowest level, the raft is placed directly on the pier pit. Sometimes a wood cage filled with stones used as a foundation is also practical. Fuzhou Wanshou Bridge was such a case. It was under construction in Dade 7th year of the Yuan Dynasty (1303). A wood raft was dropped down to its pier pit and a wood cage that was filled fully with stones was placed upon the raft as a foundation.

5. A variety of bridge piers. As far as the structure of the bridge pier is concerned, the stone pier is always built in the following way: first, build a outer curved stone ring with stone blocks or stone stripes and fill into the ring with detritus of different sizes and intensity; the laying method is to lay one stone or brick vertically and the other horizontally to intercross each other; sometimes lime slurry or sticky rice or pig blood is used as glue to fasten the stone and bricks.

Usually, the bridge piers take an outer form of a ship, i. e. the sharp head to face the current while the square part at the

rare. Such are the case with the following bridges: the Wu
Bridge in Yangqi Village, Gaishan Town, Fuzhou built in
Yuanyou 4th year of the North Song (1089); Nieyun Bridge in
Shangjin Village, Fuqing County built in Yunfeng first year of
the North Song Dynasty (1078); Longjiang Bridge in Haikou
Town, Fuqing County built in Zhenghe 3rd year of the North
Song Dynasty (1113); Ninghai Bridge in Qiaodou Village,
Huangshi Town, Putian County built in Yuantong second year
of the Yuang Dynasty (1333—1334); Yunshui Bridge in Lizip-
ing of Huaan County built in Jiajing 33rd year of the Ming Dy-
asty (1554); Yangwei Bridge in the east suburb of Zhaoan
County built in Wanli 7th year of the Ming Dynasty, etc.

Some piers take up a ship shape with two sharp heads. Such
is the case with Huilong Bridge in Minan Town, Fuzhou built in
the end of the Tang Dynasty. Some piers have a combination of
multi-shapes. For example, the famous Anping Bridge in Jinjiang city, had piers built with stone stripes in round, square,
rectangle, single ship head or double ship heads.

6. Creative bridge structure. As to the bridge structure,
wood materials are placed and lined one layer upon the other paralleled or intercrossed and then extend gradually to the middle
part in order to reduce the span length; and then put on the girders. Dayang Bridge in Xidongliu Village, Wuping County was reconstructed in Xianfeng fifth year of the Qing Dynasty(1855).
Its piers had several layers of fir tree to form a dougong —an interesting style. Tongqing Bridge in Shaowu County built in the
period of Yuantong of the Yuan Dyansty (1334). Its four piers
had 11 layers of vertically and horizontally installed frameworks,

and then had the wood girders placed upon the frameworks. Some stone girders had a layer of stone slates paved over them. Longjiang Bridge in Haikou Town of Fuqing city built in Shaoxing 30th year of the Song Dynasty (1160) is such a case. Six stone girders line paralleled on the pier's stone cap, and over the girders, pave stone bridge planks horizontally.

The development and flourishing state of the bridge construction in Fujian in ancient time have closely related to the culture characters of Fujian except for the unique natural environment. The Buddhist religion has been popular in Fujian for a very time without declination, therefore, many Buddhist monks have taken part in the solicit contributions for the bridge building. On one hand, Fujian is the province that has the largest number of monks joining in the construction of bridges, which is a phenomenon rarely seen in other places in China. On the other hand, the flourishing state of the bridge construction can be proved by the monks'active contributions.

Postscript

With people's increasing favor for regional cultures, the treasury of the Min Culture is being opened gradually. The Min Culture differs other regional cultures in that it does not only have influence upon Fujian, it also has influence upon Chinese o-verseas of Fujian origin all over the world. There are about 1,030,000 Chinese residing abroad with Fujian origin, who still keep and practice different degrees of Fujian customs and habits. Many of them have tried to return to their motherland seeking the roots of their ancestors. The unique charm and profound content have attracted the interests and concerns of more and more people. Therefore, to translate the book into English has been our desire for many years, for it can help further introduce to the world the Min Culture and meet the curiosity and concerns of our friends who want to have an idea of the Min Culture. Our initial trial has been understood and supported by the Basic Cour-ses Department of Fujian R TV University, the Min Culture In-stitute of Fujian R TV University, Fujian Provincial Institute of the Min Culture. Our leaders Li Hong, Fan Qiyuan, Ye Wen-hua, Zhao Jie, Liu Shiben, Gao Yangming and Kang Naimei have given the work great concern and useful guidance. We are also grateful for Mr. Niu Yaotian, the editor from the Publishing House of Xiamen University, who has been supporting our researches on the Min Culture for all these years and pouring a great deal of energy in the improvement of the quality of this book.

The book is compiled by Zheng Lixian, who has also translated the Preface and Chapter Ten from Chinese into English. Chapter One to Chapter Nine are translated from Chinese into English by Xie Yanhua. The English part of the book is proofread by Zheng Lixian. Huang Xiaohong, Chen Qing, Yan Chunrong, He Shuixian have taken part in the related translation work.

As the content of this book covers a wide range of fields and the time for English translation work was pressing, we might have neglected many errors and made some mistakes that our insufficient knowledge could hardly prevent and we will be responsible for all of them if our readers and experts will kindly point them out. Readers may notice that few parts of the English version may not be in equavalence with its Chinese version; yet they may not affact in anyway the completeness of the whole book.

Chinese Writer and English Translator
July 30, 2003

引　言

　　随着区域文化热的持续升温,闽文化的宝库正在被缓缓打开,闽文化独特的魅力和深厚的内涵,引起了愈来愈多人的关注和兴趣。

　　福建有"歌舞之乡"之称。山文化、水文化与海文化的熏染,使山歌和渔歌在福建民歌中占有重要位置。此外,劳动号子、唱诗、小调、舞歌、斗俗歌曲、儿歌、生活音调等民歌也异彩纷呈,其中如流传于闽南一带的儿歌《天乌乌》,表现二老在煮泥鳅时为淡咸而争吵,把锅都打破了,妙趣横生,余味无穷。福建曲艺音乐有20余种形式,其中南曲(也称南音)影响最大、最古老,它不仅是唐末五代燕乐杂曲的遗响,还可以从中探寻到宋代南戏的声腔,是我国古代音乐文化最丰富和最完整的大乐种,被称为"活的音乐历史"和"音乐化石"。

　　福建又素有"戏曲之省"之称,莆仙戏、梨园戏、高甲戏、闽剧、芗剧五大剧种饮誉海内外,传统遗产极为丰富。如莆仙戏仅传统剧目就有5 000多个,8 000多本,不仅保存了全国最多的南戏剧目和中原古剧,还是迄今收藏世界戏剧艺术作品最丰富的图书馆和博物馆。莆仙戏和梨园戏的传统剧目、音乐曲牌、角色行当等都与南戏关系密切,其音乐和演奏上与唐宋大曲有一定继承关系,所以被称为"南戏遗响"和中原古剧的"活化石"。

　　福建历代书画以其绚丽多彩的成就,极大地丰富了我国艺术宝库。福建画家能融合各家之长,表现出极强的创造性。宋代建阳人惠崇的画充满江南牧歌式情调,世称"惠崇小景";福唐(今福清)人陈容的《云龙图》开元代以后诗、书、画三位一体普遍化先河;连江人郑思肖以不着地、没有根的《墨兰图》,使"露根兰"成为一种绘画流派而在福建盛行到清末;清代长汀人上官周注重人物传神,开创了"闽派"画风;宁化人、"扬州八怪"之一的黄慎将书法和画法相结合,独步人物画坛。

　　福建书法名家辈出,宋代仙游人蔡襄取法多家后自成一家,明代漳浦人黄道周的书法被称为人品与书风紧密统一的结晶,清代汀州人伊秉绶的隶书被称为清代碑学的开山鼻祖。福建书画传统延绵至今,文化部曾先后命名福建的龙海、同安、晋江、莆田、漳平新桥、诏安、建瓯等为"书画之乡"。

　　福建的民间美术丰富多姿,琳琅满目。福建年画以木版画为主,内容几乎涉及人民生活各个方面。漳州年画善于推陈出新,既有北方年画之粗犷,又兼有江南年画之秀丽;泉州年画往往与乡间民俗结合在一起,深受南洋华人欢迎;福鼎年画别具一格,如《八锤大闹朱仙镇》将美人与武打同出一图,实为罕见。福建石雕饮誉海内外,惠安石雕和寿山石雕为其最著名的种类。惠安石雕有圆雕、浮雕、沉雕、影雕四种,各有千秋,海内外许多地方都可看到惠安石雕艺人的精湛之作,如南京中山陵华表、台湾龙山寺的八对大龙柱、北京人民大会堂的柱座、日本鉴真和尚墓园等。寿山石雕分圆雕、浮雕、镂雕、薄意和印钮五大类,品种已近千种,现陈列于人民大会堂的"求偶鸡"意趣盎然。福建民间木雕也颇为盛行,泉州开元寺24尊雕附在斗拱面的"飞天乐伎",是罕见的木雕珍品。现代著名木偶头制作艺人江加走吸收了民间木雕神像和戏曲脸谱的表现技法,创造了不少艺术珍品。剪纸是福建农村妇女热爱的一种民间艺术,漳浦曾被文化部命名为"剪纸之乡",并两次编辑出版

《中国福建漳浦剪纸集》,发行国内外,有数千件作品在国际展出并销往海外。福建烧制陶瓷历史悠久,宋代建阳水吉建窑的黑釉器颜色亮丽奇特,其最主要的黑釉器"建盏"曾作为珍宝被带到日本,被当做日本国宝级文物收藏于东京静嘉堂文库的"曜变"瓷碗,就是其中一种。元代时间德化窑的白釉器俗称"建白",滋润明亮,滑腻坚实,洁白中微见淡黄,纯净无瑕,光洁如绢。明清时期福建的青花瓷器,主要产于德化窑和安溪窑,皆为珍品。

福建作家以长于文论而称著于世。恐怕没有哪一个省的文学理论有福建这么兴盛过。中国的真正诗话产生在宋代。严羽的《沧浪诗话》是宋代最负盛名、对后世影响最大的一部诗话;魏庆之的《诗人玉屑》是研究宋代诗论不可或缺的诗话集;刘克庄的《后村诗话》和敖陶孙的《敖器之诗话》都是著名江湖派诗论代表作。元代杨载的《诗法家数》、《诗学正源》、《杜律心法》都是当时重要的诗话著作。明代高棅的《唐诗品汇》拉开了唐、宋之争的帷幕,引导了整个文学潮流;王慎中的诗文主张曾被唐宋派奉为圭臬;李贽的"童心说"等文学理论成为明代后期新的文学思潮纲领;谢肇淛对小说戏曲的精辟论述大大提高了小说戏曲在文学史上的地位。这些闽籍文论家的出现,使福建的文论兴极一时,清代和近代,福建的文学评论也毫不逊色,林昌彝的《射鹰楼诗话》、梁章钜的《东南桥外诗话》、陈石遗的《石遗室诗话》、严复和林纾的文论等,都在中国文学批评史上占有重要地位。

福建历来有重视教育的传统,教育由唐至近代久盛不衰。唐代福建处于开发阶段。唐宗室李椅任福建观察使时,"崇学校,励风俗";常衮任福建观察使时。"设乡校、延名师儒以教闽人";漳州刺史陈元光命子弟读书勤学,鼓励漳州人读书。五代时,闽王王审知广设学校,下令学龄儿童均需入学。宋代福建八个军州都办有州学,还办了许多县学。建阳人游酢、将乐人杨时赴中原拜师而有"立雪程门"故事。宋代福建书院之多,质量之高,影响之大,为全国罕见。一些民办义斋、书堂、家塾等也较为普及,读书蔚然成风,不仅福州"最忆市桥灯火静,巷南巷北读书声",连偏僻的泰宁,也"比屋连墙,弦诵之声相闻"。教育的兴盛创造了我国科举史上的奇迹。唐五代福建人口仅70万左右,但已有74人中进士。两宋福建有5985人中进士,22人为状元,按人口比例为全国第一。

元明清各代福建教育仍居全国前列。元代开设有蒙古字学、医学和科技学校(也称阴阳学)。明清在城乡办有千所以上带有义务教育性质的义学,清代开有纠正土语的"官音书塾",为旗人开的"八旗官学",清代洋务派在福州办起了"福建船政学堂"。

宋元明清,在福建学术思想界占统治地位的是闽学。它产生于北宋,至南宋朱熹为集大成者,其思想核心是天理论。在中国历史上,还很少有哪一个学派像闽学这样产生过如此深远的影响:作为闽学核心的朱熹学说其理论价值被统治者所认识后,逐渐成为控制整个国家社会意识形态的官方哲学。闽学还传入日本、朝鲜、越南、新加坡等国家,并和这些国家的社会现实相结合,产生了日本朱子学、朝鲜退溪学等。闽学还传入欧美,近年来西方研究朱子之说极为活跃,开过多次研讨会,朱子学说逐渐成为世界性学说。福建古代科技也大放异彩。仅以两宋而言,就有天文学家、《新仪象法要》的作者苏颂,世界法医学鼻祖、《洗冤集录》的作者宋慈,主编《武经总要》的曾公亮等。

福建宗教在我国宗教史上有着特殊地位。福建佛教自唐五代后,延绵发展至今。福建佛教高僧辈出,特别与禅宗五家关系密切,如曹洞宗二祖本寂为莆田人,云门宗创立者文偃为福州雪峰寺义存(南安人)弟子,法眼宗创立者文益,为王审知所尊礼的玄沙师备(福州人)再传弟子,沩仰宗创立者灵祐为长溪(今霞浦)人,临济宗创立者义玄为福清黄檗山希运(福清人)的法嗣。福建刻经事业也很发达。如宋代全国官私刻印的《大藏经》一共只有五种版本,福州就占了两种,即东禅寺的《崇宁万寿大藏》和开元寺的《毗卢大藏》。福建高僧与海外关系密切,1654年,黄檗寺福清人隐元曾率20余人渡海赴日,开创了日本佛教黄檗宗。福建出名的寺庙,几乎在海外都有廨院。福建道教也很兴盛,《云笈七签》载:闽北武夷山被称为道教三十六小洞天之中的"第十六洞天",道教极盛时有九十九观;闽东支提山(霍童山)被称为道教三十六小洞天之一。福建伊斯兰教在宋代就有相当规模,当时从海上丝绸之路直接到泉州定居的穆斯林修建了一座规模宏大的清真寺(即圣友寺),元代穆斯林在泉州又修建了多座清真寺。基督教于唐武宗时期就传入福建,但影响最大的是开教福州的意大利耶稣会传教士艾儒略,他遍识闽中名士,被称为"西来孔子"。福建民间宗教也极为盛行,护海女神妈祖、临水娘娘陈靖姑、保生大帝吴真人不仅成为福建民间信仰,还成为台湾同胞以及东南亚一带闽籍华侨、华人的信仰。

　　福建的建筑在中国建筑史上有着特殊的价值。福州的"三坊七巷"始建于东晋时晚期,是中国历史文化古城中坊制典型代表和中国南方现存较为完整的古街区之一,至今保存了大量的名人故居和明清时代建筑,被誉为"明清古建筑博物馆"。漳浦县湖西乡的赵家堡完整地保留了宋朝都城开封的格局。福建民居中最典型、最有魅力的是遍布闽西南的土楼。福建土楼被认为是中国乃至世界建筑史上的奇观,"可与万里长城媲美","是世界生土建筑发展史上的伟大奇迹"。福建是我国古代建造各种寺庙最多的地区之一。位于泉州西街的开元寺是闽南现存众多木构建筑中年代最久、规模最大的一处,其大量突破创新,将雕饰艺术与构造技术巧妙地融为一体,在我国建筑史上有着独特的文化价值。位于泉州涂门街的清净寺是我国现存最古老的一所伊斯兰教寺,它以中世纪伊斯兰教寺的建筑风格为主,在许多建筑部位上又融入了中国传统建筑技艺,为建筑史上的珍宝。福建的桥梁建筑也享有盛誉,全国十大桥梁中,泉州地区的洛阳桥、安平桥就占了两个,故有"闽中桥梁甲天下,泉州桥梁甲闽中"之说。

　　福建虽然位于东南之隅,远离全国政治文化中心,却人才辈出,历史上的杰出人物宛如灿烂群星,其中不乏影响中国历史进程的伟人。且不论朱熹等古代杰出人物,仅以近代侯官为例,这个弹丸之地在极短时间内崛起一批重要人物。如林则徐是我国近代史上第一个民族英雄,他主张严禁鸦片、抵抗西方资本主义侵略,被称之为近代中国"开眼看世界第一人",其《赴戍登程口占示家人》中"苟利国家生死以,岂因祸福避趋之"的爱国诗句,已成为以身许国的政治家的座右铭。严复是我国近代著名资产阶级启蒙家、翻译家,是系统地翻译介绍西方资产阶级学术思想的第一人,被誉为"于西学中学皆为我国第一流人物"。此外,还有如林纾、沈葆桢、林昌彝、郭柏苍、陈衍、刘步蟾、林永升、萨镇冰、方声洞、林觉民、林旭等,令人惊叹的是这些杰出人物有政治家、军事家、教育家、文学家、外交家、思想家、翻译家,几乎囊括各个领域。正是这些人物,在中国近代史上演出一幕幕精彩纷呈的活剧。近代侯官文化中强烈的爱国主义精神、对真理的不懈追求、渴望通过变革使祖国强大等优秀传统一直绵延至今。

第一章　闽文化的历史

一、远古及商周时期的闽文化

据 20 世纪 60 年代前的文物普查,福建古文化遗存达 1100 处左右。其中有代表性的如:1. 漳州旧石器、新石器、商周时代文化。漳州旧石器时代文化遗址,在漳州市北郊的莲花池山和竹林山,为1989 年兴建公路时发现,并从原生层中采集到旧石器时代的石制品 27 件,其中出自莲花池山的 23 件,出自竹林山的 4 件,分为石核、石片、砍砸器和刮削器 4 种。漳州新石器时代文化遗址,如漳州市郊的覆船山、龙海的万宝山、漳浦的香山、东山的大帽山和诏安的腊ām山等。其遗物多为陶片、石器、石片、兽骨、贝壳等,可见当时这里的居民有着丰富的物质生活和精神生活。可推知大约在距今 7 000~3 000 多年这个时期里,有一部分原始居民在这里生息。由于自然的原因,他们通常选择能避风的海湾地区,依山面海的小岛或小丘作为聚落居址,过着狩猎、捕鱼、捞贝和采集的生活。(尤玉柱主编《漳州史前文化》,福建人民出版社 1991 年版)漳州商周时代文化遗址,据专家考证,目前全区共发现 274 处,主要分布在河流两岸的山岗、台地和缓坡,以及滨海台地、小岛顶部和河流入海处的三角洲地区,遗物主要有石器、陶器、青铜器三大类。(《漳州史前文化》)2. 平潭壳丘头文化遗址。该遗址在福建最大岛——平潭岛平原乡南垅村壳丘头，为新石器时代文化遗址，距今为5 500～6000年。其出土的生产工具，主要是石器和骨器，如打制石器、磨光的石锛、石斧和骨箭镞，以及大量贝壳和兽骨，可看出当时以渔猎为主。出土的陶器以手制夹砂陶为主，多圆底器形，有釜、罐类和豆、盘、碗与纺轮等。3.闽侯县石山文化遗址。该遗址在闽侯县甘蔗镇，为新石器时代晚期文化遗址，距今5 000多年。共出土陶、石、骨、玉、牙、贝等6类33种，近千件文化遗物。其生产工具，以磨制石器为主，其中石锛为多，还有石镰、石镞、骨镞和陶网坠等。陶器以釜为多，其次是豆、罐、杯、碗、壶、簋等。有专家据其出土的遗物，推断当时人们生活情景是：有比较发达的原始农业、渔业、狩猎和畜牧，有了纺织业和缝纫技术。据考古学家统计，远古及商周时期福建古文化遗址还有：闽江上游及东部沿海地区，如闽侯庄边山、白沙溪头、黄土仑，福州新店浮村，福清东张等；闽江上游及西北山地地区，如浦城石排下、政和铁山、南平漳湖坂、明溪南山塔下等；汀江流域及闽西山地地区，如武平、龙岩、连城、长汀等发现的各类陶器，九龙江、晋江流域及闽南沿海地区，如泉州狮子山、东山坑北、漳浦湄力水库、金门岛富有墩等。（林公务《福建史前文化遗存概论》）从以上遗址可看出，新石器时代福建先民的聚集与江、海、山地关系密切，当时福建居民的足迹已遍及闽江、汀江、九龙江、晋江、沿海及有关山地。

　　福建这一时期文化的典型代表，还如武夷山悬棺葬。武夷山的悬棺葬分布在武夷山九曲溪流两岸的悬崖峭壁上，或置于高耸岩峰的洞穴内，一般距溪面70米。1500年前，曾有史籍谓武夷："半岩，有悬棺数千。"清《武夷山志》统计尚存十六。据1979年8月有关部门的调查，目前尚存的悬棺和遗迹的岩壁有：大王峰升真洞、兜鍪峰、真武洞、白云岩、大藏峰金鸡洞与鸡窠岩、换骨岩、鼓子峰、白岩、幔亭峰北洞穴、王女峰北侧裂隙、仙馆岩东壁、鸣鹤峰仙机洞、观音岩北壁洞、长窠、霞滨岩东壁等，约20余处，但保存完好的已不多了。1978年9月,福建省博物馆考察队从白岩高出地面51米的洞穴内取下一具完整的船棺,通过考察,得知该船棺距今3 445(±150)年,其纺织品残片有大麻、苎麻、丝、棉布4种质料,麻织品工艺水平略高于商代中期;丝织品为家蚕丝,接近商代同期丝织品水平;棉织品是我国目前所发现的年代最早的棉布实物资料。由此可看出,当时先民已有了高超的纺织水平。船棺为船形,可看出当时先民生活在溪河山谷之间,与舟船结下不解之缘。这一时期生活在闽地的先民,被《周礼·禹贡》称为"七闽",有人认为是指闽地的七个小国,有人认为是指闽地七个种族。公元前334年,七闽北部的越国被楚国击败,越国瓦解,部分越人来到福建,与闽人结合,合称闽越人。

二、秦汉时期的福建文化

据《史记·东越列传》载:"闽越王无诸及越东海王摇者,其先皆越王勾践之后也……秦已并天下,皆废为君长,以其地为闽中郡。"这是福建历史上第一次正式列入中华民族统一版图,但秦设闽中郡后,势力并没有进入福建。汉初,无诸为闽越王,建都城于福州。1996年10月29日,欧潭生、黄荣春等专家对福州新店村古城进行了考察,通过对西城墙中段的发掘,得知其一期城墙始建于战国晚期至汉初;二期城墙补筑于汉初,宽达23米,并出土了战国晚期或秦朝的绳纹红砖和汉初绳纹灰砖、板瓦等残件;在中区的遗迹中,出土了汉初方格纹、水波纹、弦纹、席纹、绳纹陶片上千片,其中可复原的有4件:两件方格纹大陶瓮、一件灰色硬陶盒、一件黄色硬陶杯。考古专家们认为新店古城是无诸为闽越王时所筑,即闽越王城,也称中城。当时,福州是福建的政治、经济中心。闽越国前后存在了92年,后因余善反抗朝廷,被汉武帝所灭。为了彻底征服闽越人,汉武帝采取迁其民、墟其地的政策,将部分的闽越人迁徙到江淮。但随后散居故土的闽越人又逐渐聚集,自立冶县。同时,北方南下的汉族人民也与日俱增,汉族和闽越族开始杂居混合,并开始融合。这一时期出土的陶制器皿,如鼎、豆、壶、罐等,已有浓厚的中原文化特征。

关于闽越国文化,目前可查阅到的史籍记载极少,但不断出土的文物,极大丰富了人们对闽越国文化的认识,其中最有代表性的应为武夷山汉城遗址。汉城遗址发掘于 1958 年,近几年又有新的进展和发现。古汉城的面积为 48 万平方米,南北长 850 米,东、西、北三面被崇阳溪环绕。城墙为夯土板筑,周长 2 896 米,至今完好无缺,是我国江南发现年代最早、保存最完整的古城遗址。其建造时间,有认为是汉武帝迁移闽越人之前建造的,有认为是迁移后散居故土闽越人聚拢后所建,但从规模和发掘中遍地瓦砾、处处炭遗和烧痕来看,应认为是迁移前建造,可以看出当时居民在汉军押解下弃城北迁的痕迹。古汉城遗址的发掘,填补了秦汉时期福建文化的空白,如反映了当时建筑业、制陶业和冶铁业的水平。

三、魏晋南朝时期的福建文化

魏晋南朝时期福建文化最显著的特点,就是北方汉人大批入闽,经过长期交融,中原文化与闽越文化融为一体,先进的中原文化开始占主导地位,闽越文化的影响逐渐衰微而最终成为历史遗存。

从东汉末年起,北方汉人开始大批入闽,其主要构成者如:避乱入闽者、随军入闽者、逃户、流放者及罪犯、农民起义军余部、仕宦入闽者等。福建现已发现的近千座魏晋南朝时期的墓葬,可为中原人士入闽的印证。如 1986 年 12 月于建瓯阳泽村发现的东晋咸和六年墓葬,从其出土的钵、碗、盅及墓的形制可看出墓主为中原入闽的士族地主。上世纪 90 年代发掘的将乐永吉东晋 5 座墓葬,其中 3 座分别有"太原廿一年"、"太元廿一年"、"太和四年"铭文砖,纪年砖号有"宁康"、"元嘉"等,可见墓主与中原关系密切。

1982 年在建瓯小桥出土的永和三年古墓,出土瓷器中双唇口罐为北方墓葬常见的随葬品,由此可推断死者应为北方南下入闽的士族。1986 年 4 月在浦城县莲塘乡吕处坞村七坊山发现的 6 座晋代古墓,从其出土墓砖铭文及埋葬习俗等看出:"浦城一带是西晋永嘉之乱后中原士族较早迁徙、居留的地区,他们带来的中原文化传统和习俗在这里得到继续。"(《浦城吕处坞会窑古墓群清理简报》,见《福建文博》1988 年 1 期)"松溪、政和、霞浦、闽侯、建瓯等地发现的猪圈、鸭笼、谷仓、谷斗、水井、狗圈,都带有浓厚的中原文化特征。"(林存琪《福建六朝青瓷略谈》,《福建文博》1993 年 1—2 期)中原北方汉人大批入闽,使福建人口增加,永安三年(260 年)福建设建安郡,郡下有 9 个县。晋代分为建安、晋安两郡,建安郡治所在建瓯,下有 7 县;晋安郡治所在福州,下有 8 县。南朝时,从晋安郡分出南安郡。中原先进的生产技能、生产管理经验和文化知识,大大推动了福建经济文化的发展。

魏晋南朝时期福建造船业发达。三国时期孙吴把福建当做造船基地,在福建设立典船校尉,在今霞浦县设立温麻船屯,负责督造船只。其造船工场规模大、种类多、设备好,使福建成为当时造船中心。晋后期,民间造船取代官府造船。南朝时,福建已能制造远洋木船,驶往印度和南洋。当时陶瓷制造业也有很大发展。魏晋南朝时期福建陶瓷以青瓷为主,各个时期造型特点鲜明,如西晋的扁圆矮墩,东晋的肥壮浑圆,南朝前期的高大圆鼓,南朝后期的趋向椭圆。(林存琪《福建六朝青瓷略谈》,《福建文博》1993 年 1—2 期)一些精心制作的艺术品,表明福建青瓷已在中国青瓷史上占有重要地位。福建的纺织业也有了发展,麻葛织品质量得以提高。

四、隋唐时期的福建文化

隋唐时期大量外来移民进入福建,他们或随军入闽,或避乱入闽,或仕官入闽,推动了福建人口的持续增长。许多出土的墓葬,印证了北方人口南迁历史,如从 1966 年 2 月在永春金峰山发掘的初唐时期墓群的出土文物中,专家推测:"金峰山墓群可能是隋末唐初中原宦贵衍派南迁晋江流域,寓居桃林场(今永春)的家族墓地。"(林存琪《福建永春金峰山唐墓》,《福建文博》1983 年 1 期)唐开元二十一年(733 年),从福州、建州各取一字,名为福建经略使(军区长官职),这是福建名称的第一次出现。唐代相继设置福、建、泉、漳、汀五州,至代宗大历六年(771 年)正式成立福建观察使,成为地方最高长官,形成颇具规模的行省雏形。

　　隋唐福建文化的主要特点,可表现在以下几个方面。兴学热推动了科举。这一时期教育发展与官员的支持是分不开的。唐宗室李椅任福建观察使时,鼓励兴办学府,并鼓励闽人入学,常衮任福建观察使时,也设乡校,请名师教闽人。漳州刺史陈元光认为兴办学校与创建州政府一样重要,并创办了州学;建州刺史陆长源也注重创办学校,劝人入学。教育的发展,推动了科举,据不完全统计,唐代福建进士为 56 人,虽然与中原相比并不太多,但为宋代以后福建文化的繁荣开辟了道路。制瓷业、纺织业、造船业等相继得以发展。制瓷业大部分在闽北和沿海一带,具有鲜明的时代特点,如 1988 年浦城县南部石陂镇梨岭朱塘窑村后山出土了一座唐代窑址,其器物"青灰较为粗糙的窑质、拙朴的造型与简练刻划阴纹、浑厚的釉汁、叠烧的技法特征,均具有唐代风格,明显地表现出产品除了本地工艺外还包含吸收继承唐越窑之技术的历史关系"。(赵洪亲等《福建浦城唐代窑址的调查》,《福建文博》1990 年 1 期)纺织业以泉州为代表,据《新唐书·地理志》载,当时泉州土贡有绵、丝、蕉、葛等,其中绵 200 匹,福州、建州有蕉布各 20 匹。造船业以福州、泉州为中心,天宝年间,泉州等地制造了一批高大华丽的大海船,其长十八丈,面宽四丈二尺许,底宽二丈,为尖圆形,银镶舱舷十五格,可贮货品二万至四万担。当时东渡日本的僧人都设法到福建购买这种海船。

五、五代闽国文化

五代十国之一的闽国,为王潮、王审知所建,首府为福州。盛时辖境为福州、建州、汀州、泉州、漳州,约为今福建省全境。光启元年(885年)光州固始人王潮、王审邽、王审知兄弟在福建南安发动兵变自立,次年攻占泉州,福建观察史陈岩表王潮为泉州刺史。景福二年(893年)王氏兄弟攻入福州,旋又先后占据汀州、建州、漳州。唐朝先后封王潮为福建观察史、威武军节度使。唐乾宁四年(898年)王潮卒,王审知继位。王审知在位期间是闽国的黄金时代。王审知采取保境息民的立国方针,对外称臣纳贡于中原朝廷,对内则勤修政事,致力于发展经济。在拓展水陆交通、扩大内外贸易、鼓励农业生产、大力发展手工业和商业等方面做出了很大贡献。王审知极为重视文化教育,注意延揽人才,曾组织大批知识分子搜集缮写各家遗书,如《琅琊郡王德政碑》所论,"次第签题,森罗卷轴","又拓四门学以教闽中秀士",以至教育较为普及,府有府学,县有县学,乡僻村间设有私塾。当时中原四分五裂,战乱不断,而闽国却成为安定的绿洲,堪称"世外桃源"。因此,地僻一隅的闽国文化盛极一时。王审知积极开拓海外交通,发展海外贸易,促进与东南亚的来往。王审知制定了优待外商的政策,鼓励自由贸易,并开辟了福州外港甘棠港口,极力扩大海外贸易,并在福州港置有榷货部门,专门管理舶货征榷事务,使泉州从原来中转港口变为直接对外贸易的主要港口。闽国对外贸易有着积极意义:与海外官方频繁直接往来,表明闽国对外贸易已具有前所未有的独立自主权;由于统治者的直接参与和倡导,有利于自由贸易氛围的形成;促使对外贸易的扩大,以补内陆贸易不畅通之缺;从事海外贸易的人有的成为海外移民;出现宫廷向海外定货的事例。当时,闽国北与新罗(今朝鲜半岛),南与南洋群岛以及印度、三佛齐和阿拉伯等国家,都有使者和商旅往来。舶来品如象牙、犀角、真珠、香料等应有尽有。一些出土文物对当时的情况作了很好的印证,如1965年2月在福州北郊新店莲花峰南麓东宝山发掘的闽国第三主王延钧妻刘华墓,内有孔雀蓝釉瓶,据陈存洗等专家考证,应为波斯产品,是通过波斯人或经过阿拉伯商人输入闽国的。

六、宋代的福建文化

北宋时期福建路行政区划,有福、建、泉、漳、汀、南剑六州,邵武、兴化二军。南宋时期设一府、五州、二军,皆为同一级行政机构,共八个,故福建号称"八闽"。由于长期北方汉人入闽,福建在隋唐及五代闽国时未受大的灾祸,再由于宋室南渡,政治中心转向东南,故宋代福建经济飞跃,文化发达,正如张守《毗陵集》卷六载:"惟昔瓯越险远之地,为今东南全盛之邦。"福建籍进士北宋时期为2503人,南宋时期为3482人,居于全国之首。北宋元丰时,福建户数居全国第八位;南宋嘉定时,福建的户数仅次于江西和两浙,居第三位。福建人位居宰辅之职的有18人,名列全国第三;《宋史》"道学"、"儒林"列传的福建人有17人,位居全国之首。在闽文化史上,宋代福建文化最为兴盛,其主要特点有以下几个方面:闽学的产生和发展。北宋仁宗时期为闽学发展的萌芽,一批闽地学者注重对儒家经典研究,不重训诂重义理,提倡儒家道德,宣扬儒家"尽天知性"之说,强调儒家伦理常纲,重视个人的道德修养,并热衷于授徒讲学。北宋末与南宋初是闽学的创始阶段,二程洛学入闽,在福建得到很好地传播和阐发。南宋绍兴至淳熙年间,是朱熹思想形成时期,也是闽学成熟发展时期。朱熹对北宋以来的理学思潮进行了一次全面总结,建立了一个客观唯心主义思想体系。闽学的产生和发展在中国文化史上产生了极为深远的影响,它不但属于福建、属于中国,也属于世界。福建刻书业为全国三大中心之一。宋代福建刻书的特点有四:一是地域广泛,其分布地点不但有各州府、军所在地,也有偏僻小县,几乎无处不刻书;其中尤以福州地区和建阳地区刻书最盛,成为全国刻书中心。二是量大,如北宋时期福州雕版印刷的两部大藏经和一部道藏,总数达1.8万余卷,是另外两个刻书中心浙江和四川所无法比拟的。南宋叶梦得在《石林燕语》中言:"福建本几遍天下。"可见福建刻书量之多。三是所刻内容广泛,有较流行的经史百家名著和诗文集,史书节本和诗文选本,时文科举应试之书、字书、韵书、类书、农医杂书等民间日常参考实用之书等。四是编纂形式时有创新,如字体多样,最早使用黑口与书耳、经注合刊等。

海上交通和贸易日趋繁荣。由于福建人多地少,海岸线绵长,长期有人从事海上贸易。宋代在泉州设市舶司,泉州逐渐成为全国最大商港,与世界上40个国家都有往来。据中外关系史专家谢必震先生考证,以泉州为起点的交通航线,有6条以上,如:泉州至占城,泉州至三佛齐、阇婆、渤泥等地,泉州经马六甲海峡至印度、波斯湾,泉州经南海、三佛齐入波斯湾,泉州至菲律宾古国麻逸、三屿等地,泉州至高丽、日本的航线。

七、元代的福建文化

元朝于至元十七年(1280年),在福建设"福建行中书省",虽然这是福建历史上第一次设省,但同时在福建还设立了泉州、隆兴两个行省,所以还不能代表整个福建省。后福建境内设八个路,由江浙行中书省管辖。至正十六年(1356年)成立福建省。元代福建一些重要城市保存相对完好,如掌握泉州军政大权的蒲寿庚弃宋降元,使泉州港不但不因战乱而受创,反而继南宋后走向极盛。元初福建因重兵入境,农村人口锐减,田园抛荒,生产力受到很大摧残,元朝统治者在南方实行分封宗王国戚政策,分封福建的计有9个宗王,两个公主及驸马和1个千户,由于实行分封食邑,又加重了百姓负担。但随着元朝对福建统治地位的巩固,统治者也采取了一些有效措施来促使福建发展。如兴学立教,重视水利建设,发展农业、手工业和商业。

元代闽学凭借天时地利得以发展。元代统治者大力褒奖朱熹学说,朱熹的《四书集注》被朝廷定为科场试士的程式,由于当官要经科举,科举需要朱子学,因此福建涌现出许多研究、继承闽学的人才,他们都从不同方面进一步丰富和发展了闽学。福建再次成为文人士子的理学朝圣之地。元朝积极鼓励海外贸易,泉州港在元代继续得以发展,泉州为元代四大海舶建造基地之一,海上贸易空前繁荣。元代统治者对市舶司的设置几经变动,但泉州市舶司均没有被废或合并,可见元朝统治者对泉州港的重视。与泉州贸易的国家和地区,从南宋时50个增加到100个;到至元末年以后,泉州港被誉为世界最大港之一。意大利旅行家马可·波罗1291年从泉州港启航,他描述当时泉州港为:"刺桐(泉州)是世界上最大港口之一,大批商人云集在这里,货物堆积如山。"1345年来泉州的摩洛哥旅行家伊本·白图泰也说:"该城的港口是世界大港之一,甚至是最大的港口。我看到港内停有大船约百艘,小船多得无数。"

八、明清时期的福建文化

明代洪武元年(1368年),福建全省八路改为福州、建宁、延平、邵武、兴化、泉州、漳州、汀州八府。成化九年(1473年),恢复被废为县的福宁州,直隶于布政司,合计"八府一州"。明代福建造船业、印刷业、制瓷业等在全国继续保持领先地位。教育继元代中落后,又进入一个昌盛时期;虽然王阳明学说的出现冲击了朱子学说,但闽学在福建不但长盛不衰,还有创造性发展。在充满希望的14世纪,福建如果凭借长期发展起来的工商经济机制,凭借其特有的沿海地理条件,应该在全国最早崛起。王世懋在《闽部疏》中记述了明代福建商品经济的情况:"凡福之细丝,漳之纱绢,泉之蓝、福延之铁、福漳之桔、福兴之荔枝、泉漳之糖、顺昌之纸,无日不走分水岭及浦城小关,下吴越如流水,其航大海而去者尤不可计,皆衣被天下。"但明代统治者志在铲除东南沿海已有的城市经济基础,再加上倭祸严重,明代统治者多次在福建沿海实施严厉的海禁,规定濒海百姓不得擅自下海与番国买卖,违者正犯处以极刑,家人戍边充军,并强迫沿海一些岛屿居民内迁大陆。200 年的海禁,极大遏制了福建的发展。

民间走私贸易是明代福建文化一大特点。走私的中心是漳州龙海的月港。其因独特的地理条件,逐渐成为东南沿海最大的走私贸易港口。民间海商用多种方式隐蔽走私,参与走私者与日俱增,大小商船穿梭月港,当地一时成为闽南的一大都会,被誉为"小苏杭"。隆庆元年(1567 年)后朝廷被迫开放洋市,龙海月港贸易更加繁荣,与交趾、占城、吕宋、朝鲜、日本、琉球等 47 个国家和地区有贸易往来。在外贸进出口商品中,输出量远远多输入量,其中手工产品和土特产品的输出量占较大比例。月港出现的意义不仅是它成为与福州港、泉州港、厦门港并称的福建古代四大外贸商港之一,还在于它是适应商品经济需要而出现的;月港的对外贸易一改以往官府对海贸的垄断,成为民间经营的,带有反封建束缚的自由贸易性质,并已具有资本主义雇佣关系的经营方式。它对福建社会文化的影响,是相当深远的。

清代在福建设置闽浙总督和福建巡抚。清初省下辖有福州、兴化、泉州、漳州、延平、建宁、邵武、汀州八府。康熙二十三年(1684 年)增设台湾府。至光绪十二年(1886 年),才分出台湾府设省。至清末,有九府二州、五十八县、六厅。清初朝廷在福建沿海实行海禁,为断绝沿海人民与郑成功的联系,不准本地商船运货出海,后又下诏大规模迁界,凡沿海地区内迁 30 里,给沿海人民带来巨大灾难,往日沿海的繁荣如过眼烟云。后来虽允复界,但又实行闭关政策,沿海一带仍然恢复缓慢。至清政府统一台湾后,才准许商民出海贸易,福建对外贸易转至以厦门为中心,漳州、泉州为两翼。航船到东南亚的最多,冬去夏回。

　　清代福建教育制度发达,学风鼎盛,各府 70％的书院、各县大部分书院都是新修建的。据不完整统计,清代当地新建书院约 300 所。清代福建出现全省性书院,如鳌峰、凤池、正谊、致用四大书院,清末出现了官办的全闽大学堂、洋务派办的船政学堂、外国教会办的教会学校等。教育的兴盛,推动了其他文化事业的发展。如清代福建理学更加兴盛,乾隆皇帝曾称福建为理学之乡,福建一些著名书院如鳌峰书院等,培养了大批理学人才,诸如《濂洛关闽书》等几十种闽学著作风行一时。乾嘉时代,汉学几成一尊之局,但福建理学不但愈趋兴盛,并有发展。清代福建研究理学,卓有成就者人数众多。清代福建还兴起了修纂地方志热潮,现在可查阅到的地方志大多是清代编纂的,以省总志为例,清至民国有代表性的如:康熙二十三年(1684)年郑开极等人修纂的《福建通志》(六十四卷)、乾隆二年(1737 年)谢道承等人编纂的《福建通志》(七十八卷)、乾隆三十三年(1768 年)沈廷芳等人主撰的《福建续志》(九十二卷)、道光年间陈寿祺等人修纂的《福建通志》、民国时期陈衍等人修纂的《福建通志》等。

第二章　闽文化的源流

　　闽文化的形成经过了漫长的时间,其过程是极为复杂的。从总体上看,它的形成与以下几个方面有着极为密切的关系。

一、古越文化的遗风

　　古越族是我国南方少数民族的总称,福建的土著居民是古越族的一个分支,称为闽越人。虽然随着中原汉族人民南迁入闽,闽越人在福建各地主人地位逐渐被替代,但其悠久的文化传统却不同程度地被保存。比如福建闽越人的图腾蛇,《说文解字》云:"闽,东南越,蛇种。从虫,门声。"这里的"蛇种"就是"蛇族",即信仰蛇神的氏族。"闽"字的造字是从虫,门声。"虫"字通"蛇"解,即家门供奉蛇的氏族。闽越人之所以以蛇为图腾,是因为他们的祖先生活在湿温的丘陵山区,溪谷江河纵横交错,许多蛇类繁衍滋生其中,对闽越人的生命和生产造成极大威胁。《太平广记》引《宣室志》云:"泉州之南,有山焉,峻起壁立,下有潭,水深不可测,周十余亩。中有蛟螭常为人患,人有误近,或牛马就而饮者,辄为吞食,泉人苦之有年矣。"因此人们在近山的岩石上刻画蛇形以祈求神灵的保护,并建庙供奉,希望能借助于祈祷来求得好的结果。这种崇拜延续至今,到今天福建还有不少地方保留着蛇王庙,如闽西长汀县西门外的蛇王宫、长汀县平原里溪边的蛇腾寺、福清和莆田等地的蛇王庙等。平和县三平寺与漳浦县交界一带的村民,一直把蛇尊为"侍者公",把蛇当做"神明"加以顶礼膜拜,蛇与人同床共寝和同室共处更是司空见惯的事。南平樟湖板的崇蛇习俗至今还极为隆重,每年六月下旬村民四出捕蛇,七月七日那天组成浩浩荡荡的迎蛇队伍,将蛇送到蛇王庙前的闽江放生。福建武夷山一带闽越人的悬棺葬距今已有3 400年的历史,但这些悬棺并不是每具均有骨骸,有些空棺是为同族死者准备的,这是因为血缘氏族社会的族葬要将同族葬于一处。这种葬俗至今在某些地方仍流行。如武夷山脉松溪县花桥乡狮子崖险峻陡峭,其山崖裂隙中有深达100多米的"万棺洞",历代存放在那里的棺枢达百具,层层叠架在洞内,下层年代古远者已陆续腐朽,上层的棺枢则有些是当世放进的。

二、中原文化的传入

其传入方式以大量移民为主。中原汉族曾四次大规模进入福建,第一次是西晋末年的八姓入闽。这八姓多为中州的簪缨世胄,有较高的文化素养,他们为避"永嘉之乱"而携眷南逃,都带着自己的宗族、部曲、宾客等,大大增加了福建地方人口。第二次是唐代陈元光开发漳州。河南光州固始人陈政于唐总章二年(669年)率府兵3 600多人进入漳州,年仅13岁的陈元光也随父进漳,21岁时承袭父职,定居漳州,并大力开发漳州,使漳州改变了昔日满目狉榛的荒凉状况,促进了地方社会的迅速发展。(也有学者对"八姓入闽"和"陈政入漳"持不同看法,笔者对此已有专文探讨,此不赘述。)第三次是唐末五代王审知治闽。河南光州固始人王审知与其兄一起率中原人马5 000余人入闽,定都福州,后被封为"闽王"。他为治理福建做出了卓越贡献,使福建在中原动乱之际成为东南的富裕之邦。第四次是北宋南迁。宋室南渡前后,北方百姓为避战乱,再次出现南迁浪潮,大批人扶老携幼入闽,使福建地方人口急增。除了这几次大规模入闽外,从"永嘉之乱"前至明清,都有中原人士陆续入闽定居。早期这些入闽者大多为逃亡或流放者,后期多为驻闽将士、赴闽仕宦者、为避乱而投亲靠友者。唐五代时河南固始来投奔王审知的,多不胜数。这四次大移民和陆续进入的大量移民,都不同程度地带来了中原的先进文化,加快了福建的开发和进步。此外,名士南下和闽人北游也或多或少地带来了中原文化。从唐德宗年间常衮任福建观察使起至明清,大批中原名士或慕名前来投奔,或为闽地秀丽山水而至,或前来授课讲学,他们虽然没有在闽定居,有的在闽时间也并不长,却为闭塞的福建吹进了新鲜的空气,活跃启沃了闽地学术文化。宋南渡之后,大批北方名流蜂拥而至,一时成了风气。此外,唐中期之后,闽人开始中进士第,由此纷纷北上,受到中原文化的熏陶,他们宦游归里时带回了中原文化。还有不少闽人北上访学,也将中原文化带回闽地。如理学开创者周敦颐、张载、程颢、程颐、邵雍等都在北方中原一带,不少闽人投奔其门下,深受其影响。建阳人游酢、将乐人杨时亦受业于二程,曾有"立雪程门"的故事。他们返回闽地后大力传播理学,后被朱熹改造发扬为闽学。泉州人谭峭是唐五代的大哲学家,他到北方"自经终南、游太白、太行、王屋、嵩、华、泰、岳,迤逦游历名山"(南唐沈汾《续仙传》卷下)。谭峭提出以虚、气、化范畴为核心的道家哲学,为宋明理学家所吸取和效法,成为唐宋哲学发展中一个承上启下的中间环节。

三、宗教文化的传播

四大宗教在福建极为兴盛,传播速度极快。佛教传入中国约在东汉初年,而西晋武帝太康三年(282年),福州正处开发之际,已有了绍因寺。晋太康九年(288年),南安也有了延福寺。唐代马祖道一禅师入建阳,是闽地禅宗的开端。当时中国佛教宗派林立,主要有盛于北方的"渐悟"和盛于南方的"顿悟"两支,故有"南顿北渐"之说。唐中期因寺院经济与国家利益矛盾日深,武宗发布诏令,废除佛教,当时全国被迫还俗的和尚尼姑约26万人之多。福建虽有所波及,如莆田寺院被毁不少,"洎武宗乙丑(845年)之否,邑之东有敬善寺,民井而居之;乾有玉洞寺,民亩而田之"(《黄御史集》,卷五),但福建毕竟远离政治中心,山高皇帝远,佛教一直很兴盛。"顿悟"一支到唐末能衍为五宗,与福建有极大的关系。如临济宗的始祖义玄是福清人黄檗希运的门徒,沩仰宗创始人沩山灵祐是长溪人,曹洞宗创立人曹山是莆田人,立云门宗的文偃、立法眼宗的文益均出于南安人义存门下。长乐人怀海运用中国儒家的宗法制度,改造印度式的佛教戒律,制定出一套适合中国禅宗特点的清规戒律,称《百丈清规》或《禅门规式》,使印度佛教戒律中国化,成为中国佛教丛林制度的奠基者。当时不少福建人撰写的佛教著作誉满佛林,如莆田释文矩的《博山经》,仙游释叔端的《宗镜边缘》,建州释慧海的《顿悟入道要门论》、南安释义存的《真觉语缘》等。王审知治闽时笃信佛教,在闽地建佛寺267座,闽王发给凭证的出家僧尼,竟有3万多人,故有"山路逢人半是僧"之诗。宋元明清至近代,佛教在福建也始终没有衰竭过,如宋末元初,仅福州府统辖的各县,就有佛教寺庙1 500座以上,这在全国来说也是罕见的。福建名僧不但常奉诏晋京,授经讲法,还常漂洋过海。如唐代泉州超功寺僧昙静,曾追随鉴真和尚东渡日本;元代的明极、楚俊等曾赴日本讲经;明代漳州名僧觉海亦赴日本长崎传法,并在长崎建有漳州寺。道教传入福建的时间较早,武夷山被列为道教"三十六洞天,七十二福地"的十六洞天,称为"真升化玄天",升华元化洞天真人刘少公为武夷山主。秦时,在武夷山修道的有崇安人潘遇、闽清人游三蓬,并在山中建止止庵。西汉时,浦城子期山、福州九仙山、南平衍仙山等都有道士在修炼。唐代时福建出现了道坛庙观和职业道士,福州著名的道士有张林、符契元等人。五代时,王审知敬重道士,不少道士握有大权。宋代福建道教发展很快,不少道士屡受朝廷赏赐,新建道观如雨后春笋,著名的有福州真庆观、延平元妙观、莆田元妙观、闽县崇禧观、沙县宜福观、松溪文昌观等。泉州清源山上巨型石刻李老君像,高约一丈五六,具有很高的艺术价值,由此可看出当年道教的兴盛。宋元之际江西兴起"净明忠孝道",注意符箓禁咒驱邪御瘟等道术,从事服炼斋醮、作仙度人,福建由此出现炼养、符箓两派。前者代表人物如泉州龙兴观道士吴崇岳、长汀人王中兴、崇安人杨万大等。后者代表人物如漳州天庆观道士邱允、沙县人谢祐、长汀人梁野等。到明代,道教被取消"天师"称号,福建出现正一道和全真道。清代因乾隆宣布黄教为"国教",道教被认为是汉人的宗教,所以开始衰落。但在福建,民间祈祷斋醮之事及服饵丹道之术仍旧流行,并逐渐成为民间习俗。公元 7 世纪初在阿拉伯麦加城创兴的伊斯兰教,早在唐中叶就由航路传入泉州。宋元期间泉州跃为东方大港后,数以万计信奉伊斯兰教的阿拉伯人云集泉州,使之成为我国最早的三个伊斯兰教区之一。不仅金、丁、马、铁、郭、葛、黄、夏、蒲等十多姓的穆斯林后裔在这里生息繁衍,还建造了极具伊斯兰教色彩的清真寺、安葬伊斯兰先贤的灵山圣墓等,并留下了许多刻有阿拉伯文、波斯文和中文的墓碑铭文。泉州至今还保存有我国最早的清真寺。元朝时不少伊斯兰教徒跟随西域金吉军队经邵武到福州,因此邵武至今还有不少伊斯兰教徒。福建的伊斯兰教从属于人数最多的逊尼派,在教法上崇尚哈乃斐法律学派。基督教在福建的传播主要是通过传教士进行的。明代时,意大利耶稣会传教士艾儒略等在明大臣叶向高的支持下,到闽北传教,并向福安、闽县等地发展,前后达 24 年,建有教堂 23 所。艾儒略曾被称为"西来孔子",誉为开教福建第一人。明末,菲律宾教省派传教士 11 人抵厦门、福州,开创"圣多明我会"传教区,发展迅速,郑成功还曾聘传教士为老师。清康熙年间,以白伯多禄为首的一批传教士,深入泉州、兴化、福安等地传教,在福建成立"圣多明我第三会"。鸦片战争之后,西方不同派系的传教士在福建展开激烈的传教竞争,基督

教建的教堂、学校、医院、救济机关,几乎遍及城乡各地。无论从传
教和建教堂时间上看,还是从教派、教徒和教会学校数量上看,福
建都较早,也较多。除了以上四大宗教的影响外,福建的地方宗教
也有很大的影响,最有名的是"三一教"。这是将儒、释、道三教合
而为一的教派,由明代正德、嘉靖、万历年间福建莆田林兆恩创建。
林兆恩认为儒、释、道本为一体,但后世的继承者不懂其本源,妄分
三教,越走越邪。倡三教合一的本质是将儒家的纲常伦理与道教
的修持功夫及佛教的涅槃理论合而为一,三者缺一不可。所以林
兆恩认为儒教为立本,道教为入门,佛教为极则。"三一教"在福建
立足后,曾向外省扩展过,清代中末叶曾发展到台湾、新加坡一带。
福建的民间宗教也颇为风盛,其中最著名的是天上圣母、临水夫
人、保生大帝这三神。这三尊神原型都是人,后被逐渐演化为神,
赋予类人而又超人的神力,再借以护佑人们自身。民间宗教虽带
有区域性,但因其有旺盛的生命力而持久不衰,对闽文化产生了深
远的影响。

四、海外文化的冲击

　　福建东临大海,良港棋布,有占全国五分之一长的海岸线,因
此早在南朝时代,就与海外有联系。海外文化的冲击主要通过国
际贸易、外商定居闽地、闽人越洋后归里等几个途径。早在五代王
审知治闽时,福建与海外的商业贸易往来就比较广泛,东起新罗,
中经南洋群岛,西至阿拉伯地区都与福建建立了初步的贸易关系。
北宋时,泉州成为国际贸易港,被称为"涨海声中万国商",与36个
岛国有贸易关系。福建商人由泉州出发前往海外,一般一年往返,
远的二年往返,用五色缬绢和建本书籍,与海外交换所需之物。到
了南宋和元代,泉州发展为世界第一商港。明代统治者厉行海禁
200年之久,但位于龙海的月港依然帆樯如栉,海外客商汇聚,成
为全国最大的走私港。明隆庆元年(1567年)取消海禁,月港每年

孟夏之后,数百艘商船远洋四海。到明万历年间,月港的国际贸易更为繁荣。由于国际贸易的繁华,许多外商定居闽地。特别在宋元两代,数量极多的印度人、波斯人、阿拉伯人、欧洲人为世界贸易大港泉州所吸引,定居当地而不返,被人称为番客,其娶本地妇女所生的孩子,叫做半南番。他们将本国的风俗民情信仰融会在当地居民之中,日长天久,海外文化便与当地文化水乳交融地渗透在一起。与外商定居闽地一样,也有不少闽人定居海外,宋元之后,逐渐增多,几乎遍及日本、朝鲜和整个东南亚。明代数万闽人出海后"往往久居不返,至长子孙"(《明史·吕宋传》)。17世纪前后,东南亚的福建华人已在50万人以上。这些华侨大多与家乡保持程度不同的联系,并时时有不少人回乡里探亲,带来了形态各异的海外文化。

五、台湾文化的交融

台湾人有80%祖籍福建,由于闽台一水相连,地缘相近,血缘相亲,习俗相同,语言相通,因此人们往往将闽台文化同划为一个文化区。但从另一个方面看,由于特殊的历史背景、地理环境和社会经济条件,台湾文化与福建文化,还是有一些差异,这就是台湾文化的独特性。必须看到,既然是交融,除了闽文化对台湾文化产生了深刻和恒久的影响外(这是主要的),台湾文化也对闽文化产生了影响。这些影响表现在多方面,其如:

1. 大量台湾人到闽地任职。《台湾省通志稿》对此有详细记录:"刘其灼,字汉章,号为轩。台湾府东安坛人。清康熙乙末(五十四年,1715年)岁贡,雍正壬子(十年,1732年)选受长泰县学训导,泰邑志称其清修自好,和易可亲。乾隆甲子(九年,1744年)升长汀教谕,告老归,士子钱送盈余。"据杨彦杰《台湾历史与文化》(海峡文艺出版社1995年版)介绍:"在清领台湾期间,全台共有80名科举人物被派往福建任职。其中进士1名、举人18名、贡生

61名。有的在福建连任教职。如进士庄久进,凤山县人,历任泉州、福宁教授。举人李维梓,台湾县人,历任闽县、安溪教谕,贡生林萃冈,台湾府人,历任兴化、清流训导。蔡复旦,台湾府人,历任闽清训导、漳平、永安教谕等等。"台湾赴福建任职者分布很广,足迹几乎遍及沿海及山区各地,带来了台湾的本土文化,有的还撰文介绍台湾的风土人情。

2.台湾本土艺术输入福建,最有代表性的如台湾的歌仔戏输入福建。在台湾18个地方戏曲中,歌仔戏是唯一产生于本土的剧种,它发祥于台湾宜兰县,源自闽南的锦歌,经过台湾艺人不断加工、提高,终于成为完整的大戏,后又由台湾传入闽南,成为福建五大剧种之一的芗剧,至今已有400多个传统剧目,受到漳州、厦门观众的喜爱。

3.访祖探亲。闽籍台湾人返回闽地探亲时,带来了台湾的风俗民情。以饮食文化为例,每当夏季来临时,闽南街头常有人挑卖一种叫石花的食品,形同冰冻的藕粉膏。它是由薜荔藤汁制成,凉爽可口,已成为闽南人解渴消暑的佳品。薜荔性清凉,原产于台湾嘉义山中,由祖籍同安的居民发现制作,后由台湾的福建移民回乡探亲访友时传到福建。

4.经济贸易。台湾与福建早就有经贸往来,台湾历史上最早的郊行为北郊、南郊、港郊,其中南郊主要负责将货物配运闽南。台湾商人不仅将货物运至闽南,还带来了台湾商人的做生意方式和生活习俗。

六、邻域文化的渗透

福建北连浙江,南接广东,西临江西。这几个邻域的文化长期对福建渗透,特别在周边地区产生了很大影响。

1.历史沿革。福建在唐以前称作"七闽",其范围除了福建全境外,还北涉浙江温州,南入广东潮州,西接江西余干。春秋时期的越国为楚所亡后,越国遗民纷纷进入浙江南部与福建境内。秦始皇时期设置闽中郡,这是福建历史上第一个区域建置,其辖地北部仍达浙江温、台、处三府,西部接江西铅山。汉代刘邦设闽越国,其辖地仍跨有赣东、浙东、粤东潮梅等地区。三国时,占据江浙的孙权把福建作为东吴的后方基地,置建安郡。唐玄宗时,取福州、建州各一字名为福建经略使,从此有了福建的名称。从历史上看,福建有不少辖地是今天邻省的辖地,因此与这些邻域关系始终很密切。

2.交通往来。唐中期之后,闽人与外界接触逐渐频繁,因应试、为宦、从商、访学等原因北上外出者增多,浙、赣为外出的必经之路。宋代,建州著名的分水关路由江西抵浙江,然后再北上,因此本地文人与邻域文人来往较多,如黄升深受姜白石的影响,李虚己常与婿晏殊唱酬。明代闽地与江淮流域的交通已很发达,或由建阳往邵武入赣,或由浦城入浙,或由崇安入赣、浙。频繁便利的往来,促进了周边文化的渗透。

3.人口迁移。邻省长期陆续向闽地迁移人口,至明清达到高潮。如江西、浙江有许多农民迁移至闽北山区,为开发山区做出贡献。正如郑丽生《闽广记》卷六载:"延建诸邑深山中,每有客籍贫民,盖茅而居,或治畲田,或种菇,或烧松明,或烧炭,或煽铁,或造纸,或陶埴,因为地利,聚散无常,大抵江西上饶、玉山及浙江之庆元、仁和之人为多。"他们带来邻省文化,使"土著人民效尤垦种者亦复不少,岁加稠密,连岗互嶂"(道光《建阳县志》卷二)。当地人逐步"效尤"垦种经济作物,邻省移民起了重大作用。

4.经济贸易。福建与周边毗邻地区的贸易极为频繁,如明人何乔远在《闽书》卷三八载:"建宁土地膏腴,专有鱼稻、油漆、竹布之利,以通商贾;邻于建昌藩邸,习尚移染,故其俗奢。"可见建宁与江西建昌府之间的密切关系。此外一些边远的小县,也常与毗邻地区展开经济活动。如泰宁牛口牛会,就是每年秋季举行的跨省大型牛会,江西、浙江等周围几省数十个县的牛都被赶往此地交易,远近闻名。

5.互派官吏。闽人热衷科举,不少人被派往浙、赣任职,亦有不少浙、赣官吏在福建供职,促进了文化的互相渗透。

第三章　闽文化的特点

　　闽文化最鲜明的特点是多元性。这种多元性主要表现在以下几个方面：

　　1.各种区域都具有各自的特点，差异鲜明。有人将闽文化分为闽东、闽南、闽西、闽北、莆仙五个文化区，认为闽北文化为典型的山林文化，闽南文化为典型的海洋文化，闽东文化为典型的综合型文化，闽西客家文化为典型的移民文化，莆仙文化为科举文化的模范。(徐晓望主编：《福建思想文化史纲》)有人将闽文化分为闽东、闽南、闽西、闽北四个文化区，认为其差异极大，如闽东求稳怕乱，闽西宗亲内聚，闽南过番出洋，闽北安贫乐道。(倪健中主编：《人文中国》)有人将闽文化分闽东的江营文化、闽南的海播文化、闽北的山耕文化、闽西的移垦文化。(李如龙：《福建方言与福建文化的类型区》)有人将闽文化分为六大文化区，即：福州文化区、莆仙文化区、闽南文化区、闽西文化区、闽北文化区、闽东文化区，每一文化区的精神文化都有其鲜明特点：如福州人便宜行事，莆仙人精明省俭，闽南人热情豪爽，闽西人纯朴好客，闽北人安分吃苦，闽东人勤勉笃厚。(何绵山主编：《福建经济与文化》)但各个文化区再细分，也有不少区别。如闽南指厦门、漳州、泉州三个市，这三个市文化有很大差异。就是泉州市，沿海的晋江、石狮，与永春、安溪、南安仍有明显的差别。

2.各文化区域人的性格特点千差百异。山东人的豪爽,上海人的精明,浙江人的机灵……福建人以什么特点著称呢?杨东平在《城市季风》中援引韩国一家刊物对福建人的评价:"福建人特别小气。下雨时带两把伞,自己用一把,卖一把。"这其实不能代表福建人的性格。福建人性格的差异十分鲜明,如果是闽南人,或许干脆把自己要用的伞也送人,交个朋友,今后也多一条路。如果是福州人,或许多带几把伞,能赚则赚,又不是坑蒙拐骗,何乐不为?如果是闽北人,或许只带一把自己用,认为卖人太俗气,送人没必要,自己有的用就行了。在打品牌做广告投入方面,各个区域的人也有不同看法,如闽南石狮人认为做广告是非常有必要的,在电视台长期打出广告,广告形象是凶猛动物——狼。而且不只是一只,是前奔后窜的七匹狼,让人有"与狼共舞,方显出英雄本色"之感。这种广告并没有点明是什么商品,但"七匹狼"成为著名商标后,服装可以是七匹狼,香烟也可以是七匹狼。如果福州人,可能要算一下这广告要投入多少钱,能不能把本钱赚回来,决不干冒险的事。如果是闽西人,或许没有这个气魄,但可以自己的产品与别人联营,用自己资源(如香烟)打"七匹狼"商标,这样似乎更保险。福州与莆田交界,但福州人与莆田人的性格是大不相同的。如福州女子往往爱当家,爱把夫家东西拿回娘家,对丈夫管束特别严。故福州有"老婆打麻将,丈夫煮点心";"老婆睡懒觉,丈夫倒马桶"之说。有一则笑话或许能表达出福州妻子对丈夫的管束:一对夫妻家中被小偷光顾后,在外地的妻子在电话中急切地问丈夫钱有没有被偷,丈夫回答:"你藏的钱,我找了十年都找不到,小偷怎么可能一下就找到?"据考福州男人很能干活,煮小菜手艺不错,可谓须眉不让巾帼。而莆田女子则特别勤劳节俭,用自己的全部精力和智慧维护家庭,可谓任怨任劳,终身不悔。她们没有更多的侈望,也从来不想管丈夫,而丈夫则推下饭碗就出门,从来不管那些婆婆妈妈的小事,认为男子汉赚钱养家是理所当然的事。

3.方言极为复杂。在我国八大汉语方言中,福建方言就占了三种,如果加上省界交叉地区,仅福建境内流行的就有汉语七大方言,真可以说是全国汉语方言的缩影。而其复杂性还在于同一方言区不同地方的方言,如闽南方言区中的厦门话、龙岩话、大田话、尤溪话之间也有很大的差异。令人惊异的是有的县同时说几种不同的方言,如大田县通行着闽南话、大田话、永安话、客家话;尤溪县通行着闽南话、尤溪话、闽东话。而连城县、清流县、大田县等竟然没有本县通用方言。更令人不可思议的是,有的地方过了一座山、一条河就不能通话,这种现象在全国是罕见的。福建方言庞杂,一方面给交流带来不便,另一方面也使福建方言文化更加丰富多姿。据报载,闽南石狮代表在北方参加某贸易洽谈会时致辞:"欢迎大家到石狮市去投资贸易",由于方言作祟,却讲成欢迎大家"去 CCC 偷鸡摸鸭",与会代表听不明白,还夸石狮代表很幽默。一位不谙莆田方言的领导到莆田某村巡查,村干部用带莆田腔的普通话介绍:"过去村里没有人野蛮,精神文明工作不好搞;现在野蛮的人多了,精神文明工作好搞了。"原来他把"养鳗"讲成了"野蛮"。这类例子不胜枚举。故有"天不怕,地不怕,就怕福建人讲官话"之说。

4.民间信仰的神灵众多。有的同一县内,每个乡、村都有自己特定的神灵为保护神,抬神出游一般不能越出本地界。如旧时泉州就城内就划为 36 埔 94 境,奉有 100 多尊神灵,以致福建民间创造的神灵数量惊人,充斥天上、人间和地府。

5.民俗民风不同。福建历来有"十里不同风,一乡有一俗"之说,它形象地说明了福建民俗的差异。这种差异不是指福建某一区域前后民俗变更、替换的频率(恰恰相反,福建某一区域民俗往往因传承性极强而前后变化不大以至相对稳定),而是指同个区域对同一民俗事象的不同表现。如对一些传统的节日,福建不同区域的表现是有很大差别的。由于民俗不同,各地认识不同,民间谚语也有许多完全相左。仅以男女婚嫁年龄的谚语为例,如上杭谚语:"女大五,赛老母;女大三,抱金砖。"福州谚语:"男大三,门前立旗杆;女大三,井水会吊干。"龙海谚语:"茶要喝厚,某(指妻子)要娶老。"武夷山谚语:"夫大妻,大五不大六。"龙岩谚语:"宁嫁老头,不嫁瘦猴。"武夷山谚语:"女人四十一枝花,男人五十成专家。"再以男女婚嫁相貌为例,华安谚语:"阔嘴查埔(查埔:男方)吃四方,阔嘴查某(查某:女方)吃嫁妆。"福鼎谚语:"男人嘴阔吃天仓,女人嘴阔辅丈夫。"罗源谚语:"男人嘴阔食天饭,女人嘴阔食嫁妆。"

6.各种艺术难以全面交融,始终保持其鲜明地方色彩。福建的戏曲不像其他省市那样,有一种或几种为全省人民普遍接受的戏曲,如北京的京剧,浙江的越剧,安徽的黄梅戏、河南的豫剧、四川的川剧、云南的滇剧、西藏的藏剧、甘肃的陇剧等。在福建省上演的剧种有 29 个,但没有一个剧种能在全省流行,更没有一个剧种能代表福建。其中最有影响的闽剧、莆仙戏、梨园戏、高甲戏、芗剧五大剧种,流行的地区也很有限。这五大剧演出的范围如果变换,即使演员的演技再精湛,也是不可能取得好效果的。再如舞蹈,主要用形体动作表达感情,它虽不用唱,不存在方言障碍,但也难流行。如闽南最著名的拍胸舞,很难在闽北找到知音。因为这与区域差异等有关。闽南人性格粗犷豪爽,拍胸舞极符合闽南人表达、宣泄感情方式;而闽北是理学的故乡,讲究克己谦恭,不可想像闽北人会赤裸上身沿街拍打胸脯表演舞蹈。而闽北的采茶灯舞细腻,规范性强,其独特的采茶步轻盈细碎,当然也不可能在闽南流行。福建民歌难以在全省流传,其原因也是很明显的。正是因为福建各类艺术交融有限,所以福建各类艺术更加绚丽多姿。

造成闽文化的多元性的原因很多,但主要有三个方面:

1.地理环境因素。福建依山傍海,既是"东南山国",又是"闽水泱泱",高山急流把福建分隔成几片自然区域,各区域内又由于山脉河流走向,再被划分为若干个闭塞的小区,因此难以交流、沟通。武夷山的静穆清幽与刺桐港的富庶繁华似很不协调：封闭的山区经济发展缓慢，有时连糊口都成问题，而沿海一带却能常领风气之先，甚至走在全国之前。

2. 构成闽文化的成分极为复杂。闽文化的形成与闽越文化的遗风、中原文化的传入、宗教文化的传播、海外文化的冲击关系密切，而其中各种情况也异常复杂，并不都是集中在某个局部。因此，闽文化不会长期在某区域发展，其发展中心容易转移。如秦汉闽越文化、唐代漳州文化、五代闽国文化、宋代建州文化、元代泉州文化、明代月港文化、晚清侯官文化等都曾各领风骚。因此谁也主宰不了谁，谁也取代不了谁。

3. 中原文化延伸到福建后不同程度受到闽地文化影响，无法形成坚强内核。虽然中原文化一次又一次的进入福建，时间之长久、内容之丰富，是全国其他省所罕见的，但由于中原文化分期分批进入，且闽地又较封闭，中原文化进入后又被隔绝，因此显示出寄居性质，难以一统闽地文化。

第四章 艺术

一、音乐

福建素有"歌乡"之称,人民群众口头代代相传的民歌散发着浓郁的泥土芳香。福建依山傍海,江河纵横,山文化、水文化与海文化的交织,使山歌和渔歌成为福建民歌中最有特色的样式。

福建的山地丘陵地约占 95% 左右,山歌是最为普及的一种民歌。福建山歌受方言区的影响,其调式、音调等都有很大的不同。主要为:1.闽西山歌。闽西山歌旋律高亢,节奏自由,音域较窄,绝大部分是徵调式,不存在商调式。调式主音大部分是全曲最低音,曲调简单、朴素、原始。每首一般为四个乐句,乐段大多由平行的上下两句组成,一般用三个乐音或四个乐音就构成一曲。由于地理习俗的影响,闽西山歌又可分为三种:(1)客家山歌。流行于长汀、武平、上杭、永定等县,以曲调绵长、字少腔多为特色,如《选种》:"凤生凤来龙生(吓)龙嗬哎,田间(吓)选种(哎)莫放(吓)松嗬哎,好种不但多打谷嗬哎,四箩还比五箩重嗬哎。"(2)龙岩山歌。流行于龙岩及漳平山区,多是七字一句,四句一首,结构严谨。曲式结构多为上下句的反复,如《山歌越唱音越高》:"山歌越唱音越高噢,月琴来和九龙箫噢,一节山歌一团火呀,唱得满山烈火烧噢。"(3)连城山歌。流行于连城县及连城、上杭、龙岩三县市的交界区域,节奏急促,字多腔少。如《大风吹来小风凉》:"大风吹来小风凉哎,郎吃甘蔗妹吃(啰)糖,郎吃凌冰妹吃雪,凌冰跟雪一般(啰)凉。"2.闽北山歌。闽北山歌样式多种,主要有刀花山歌、油茶谣、锁歌等。刀花山歌指唱山歌时,以茶刀和竹担互击伴奏而得名,演唱形式有齐唱和对唱两种。油茶谣为丰收时所唱的歌,音调充满活力,节奏丰富多变。锁歌即一人提问一人回答的歌唱形式,问即锁,答即开,环环相扣,节奏时缓时急。此外,闽南山歌、畲族山歌、莆仙山歌、闽中山歌等也都颇有特色。

福建不仅有绵长的海岸线,还有众多河流,其中流域面积500平方公里以上的一级河流有闽江、九龙江、汀江、晋江等12条江,以捕鱼为生的渔民常用歌声表达自己对生活的感受。福建渔歌主要有两种。1.海上渔歌。主要流行于闽东、闽中沿海各县,内容多为直接反映海上捕鱼生活,如福鼎的《海上归来渔满舱》:"哎!朵朵白帆映霞光,海上归来鱼满舱。男女老少齐欢呼,明日风帆又远航。"节奏悠长,音调宽广,充满对生活的热爱和丰收的喜悦。有的海上渔歌是直接配合劳动歌唱的,如福鼎的《拔帆起锭》:"中帆拔起咧咧哮噢,起锭吹螺就开流啰,各个渔民齐齐到噢,船到渔场就要敲啰。""锭"指船锚;"咧咧哮"指扯帆时发出的声音;"敲"指敲特制竹筒,是以强烈声响使鱼震昏然后围捕的一种捕鱼方式。节奏较强,旋律充满浓郁的生活气息。2.水上渔歌。主要流行于江河纵横的闽中、闽南各县。在福州一带的闽江渔歌中,有的歌充满豪情,如福州的《渔歌》"老子自幼在江边,不怕地来不怕天,看不尽青山绿水,吃不尽鱼虾渔鲜。"有的描述了在江上讨生活的艰辛,如福州苍霞的《水上渔歌》:"我是船下讨鱼婆,母女二人去江河;天晴是我好日主,拍风段雨没奈何。我伶使力来拔篷,一篷能转八面风;篷转风顺船驶进,看着前斗好地方。""日主"指日子,"拍风段雨"指刮风下雨,"伶"指现在,"前斗"指前面。这类渔歌节奏整齐,结构匀称,唱词中夹杂着不少地方方言。

　　福建民歌中还有许多样式,如劳动号子、唱诗、小调、舞歌、习俗歌曲、儿歌、生活音调等,其中最有名的为流传在闽南一带的儿歌《天乌乌》:"天乌乌,要落雨,阿公仔举锄头要掘芋,掘啊掘,掘啊掘,掘着一尾旋鰡鼓,真正趣味。阿公仔要煮盐,阿妈要煮淡,俩人相打弄破锅,依哟灰都当叱当枪,哈哈哈。"全曲前一部分唱阿公挖了泥鳅回来,全家高兴;后一部分唱二老争吵,把锅给打破了。每一部分各由两个乐段组成,旋律以第一乐段为基础,慢慢衍化,音域也逐段向上扩展,层次清晰,乐段的结尾处常用衬腔,最后仿佛打破锅的声音,妙趣横生,余味无穷。全曲大多一字一音,与口语相近,语言朴实自然,语调诙谐生动,音化形象朴实无华,极富闽南农村生活气息。

　　福建曲艺音乐有着悠久的历史,其主要形式有南音、锦歌、南词、评话、伬唱、建瓯鼓词、芗曲说唱、大广弦说唱、俚歌、竹板歌、莲花落、俚歌、十音八乐、北管唱、九莲唱、摇钱树、答嘴鼓、唱歌册、说古文、讲故事、说书等20余种,其中影响最大、最古老、最具有浓郁地方特色的是南音。

　　南音也称"南曲"、"南乐"、"南管"、"弦管",从南音所用乐器、演奏特点、曲牌名称等方面看,它与唐、宋、元、明时期音乐关系密切,是保存我国古代音乐文化最丰富和最完整的乐种,被称为"活的音乐历史"和"音乐化石"。南音不仅是唐末五代燕乐杂曲的遗响,还可从中探寻到宋代南戏的声腔,甚至可以从中找到在戏曲史界已无法寻觅的海盐腔、早期弋阳腔、青阳腔及昆山腔、二黄腔的音调,堪称绝响。南音发祥于泉州,流行于福建南部,还被运用于闽南一些地方戏曲,成为它们唱腔和器乐曲的一个重要组成部分。南音的演奏形式分上四管与下四管两种,上四管比较清雅,适合在室内演奏,以洞箫为主奏乐器的叫洞管,以品箫为主奏乐器的叫品管。下四管比较活泼,演奏上较复杂,适合在室外演奏或参与民间行列仪式。南音的乐器有:洞箫、二弦、琵琶、拍板、唢呐、三弦等,打击乐器有:响盏、小铛锣、木鱼、四宝、铜铃、扁鼓等。南音中的琵琶(也称"南琵琶"),弹奏时是横抱着的,用手指头拨弦,不同于北琵琶是竖立着弹奏,用拨器撩拨。南琵琶大弦弹奏发出的声音,深沉如钟鸣,和北琵琶的"大弦嘈嘈如急雨"大异其趣。南音的艺术风格可用"古朴幽雅,委婉柔美"来概括,其曲目分三大部分:1.指,亦指"指套",每一首套曲均有唱词、乐谱和琵琶弹奏指法三个方面,较为完整,有48套,每套又可分为若干节,而每一节都是一首独立的乐曲。2.谱,每一首套曲的乐谱包括工尺谱和演奏技法的标志两个方面,没有唱词,有十六大套,每套内均包括3至8个曲牌,内容大都是描写四季景色、花鸟昆虫或骏马奔驰等情景。3.曲,即散曲,计有1 000多首,其结构简单,词曲活泼,内容多为抒情、写景与叙事之类,曲词大多取材于梨园戏文,也吸收昆腔、弋阳腔、潮腔、民歌等,予以南曲化,融合后自成一格。由于简短通俗,曲调优美,善于抒发感情,长期以来成为闽南民间自弹自唱的乡音。

福建民间器乐遍及城乡,种类繁多,几乎每个地区都有自己的代表器乐,现择其主要评介如下:

1.福州十番。"十番"名称由来说法不一,有认为据清代李斗《扬州画舫录》卷十一记载,此乐种因用笛、管、箫、弦、提琴、云锣、汤锣、木鱼、檀板、大鼓这十种乐器轮番反复演奏而称"十番";有认为福州话"番"与"欢"同音,"番"由"欢"演变而来。福州十番音乐是一种著名的民间器乐演奏形式,它是由当地民间龙灯舞演变发展而来的,原来只是龙灯舞的伴奏打击乐,乐器只有狼帐、清鼓、大小锣、大小钹等,后又逐渐加入笛、管、笙、椰胡等丝竹乐器。十番音乐的曲目有百余首,曲调来源可分四类:(1)曲牌,为流行于当地的民间音乐;(2)小调,为逐渐器乐化的民间小调;(3)哗牌,当地流行的唢呐曲;(4)打击乐,只用打击乐器演奏的"清锣鼓"。最常用的有五大曲牌:《东瓯令》、《西江月》、《南进宫》、《北云墩》、《月中桂》等。演奏形式分室内与室外两种,室外演奏边走边奏,室内演奏乐队分为前堂和后堂,前堂以金革为主,后堂以丝竹为主。演奏时,先由笛子奏出前面的一两个音符,具有引子性质,接着其他乐器全部加入演奏。演奏曲调既粗犷、热烈,又不失悠雅、抒情。节奏明晰,顿挫分明,情绪跌宕起伏,速度变化井然,慢时如高山流水,快时似电闪雷鸣,最后在热烈的气氛中结束。

2.闽南十音。一般认为这一乐种是从北方传入闽南的,在发展过程中,汲取了闽南的民间戏曲、民歌、民间器乐曲中许多精华,形成了浓郁地方风格。其曲调可分成沉静、优美幽雅、欢乐活泼、诙谐风趣、热烈红火、昂扬激烈等六类。乐器分主乐、副乐,管弦乐中以唢呐为主,打击乐以板鼓为主,它们掌握着演奏的起始、结束、力度。演奏时,常以一个基本曲调反复三遍,作慢、中、快的速度变化,从而形成一首完整的乐曲。演奏形式为室内。室外两种,室外多为游行演奏,俗称踩街,打击乐在前,丝竹乐在后;室内演奏俗称坐奏,丝竹乐列前,打击乐坐后。

3.闽西十班。因其由十个人掌握十件乐器组成班子而得名。它是由外出经商者从江浙或汉口一带传入的,然后在闽西流播,并地方化。曲牌可分为三种:(1)大牌,为十班所特有器乐曲牌,音乐典雅优美;(2)小调,为船灯伴奏时所吸收过来的民间小调;(3)戏曲过串,取自汉剧、潮剧的过场音乐。乐器有:笛子、管、头弦、二胡、三弦、月琴、琵琶、鼓板等,演奏形式有坐奏、路奏两种。

4.莆仙十音。这是流行于莆田、仙游两县的民间音乐唱奏形式,因以十人组成一队,奏十件乐器而得名。其主要形式有两种:(1)文十音,乐器有笙、箫、琵琶、三弦、枕头琴、云锣、老胡、二胡、拍鼓和丹皮鼓等,演奏时节奏徐缓,旋律委婉,词少腔多,风格古朴曲雅。(2)武十音,乐器有云锣一,横笛三,碗胡、四胡、尺胡、贡胡、八角琴、三弦各一,演奏时,曲调加花调繁多,气氛热烈。福建民间器乐还有晋江十番、静板、福鼎拾锦、龙溪西壁、闽南笼吹、长汀公嬷嗛吹、连城鼓吹、永春闹厅、京鼓吹、五音吹、漳州十八音等。

二、舞蹈

　　福建民间舞蹈的最主要特点是种类繁多，形态各异，仅已发现的就有 700 多种。其迥异的风韵、丰富的内涵、独特的魅力，真让人大开眼界。现择其主要评述如下。

　　灯舞。如流行于闽西客家人聚居地区的《龙凤灯》，为元宵灯舞。客家人"灯"、"丁"谐音，"出灯"即"添丁"。元宵之夜，村民们从祖祠出发周游村寨，表演者装扮成生、旦、丑等角色，把黄龙、凤凰、雄狮、猛虎、公鸡、白鹤、大象、山鹿等彩灯系于腰间，头在前，尾在后。同时左手还托着一盏诸如鼓子灯、龙头灯、飞蝶灯之类花灯，右手策动马鞭，由两匹大红竹马灯领头。队形变化频繁，花式多样，有"关公巡城"、"围篱笆"、"倒插花"、"扎三门"、"黄龙盘珠"、"退马"、"猴子烧蜂"等，每一场面的转接都以"双龙出水"为间隔，承上启下，层次清晰。再如流行于连江城关一带的《茶篮鼓》，是一种形式活泼、充满吉祥气氛的灯舞。每逢元宵佳节，少男少女手托五彩"茶篮"（即彩灯），游于街市。"茶篮"中插象征生女的红花、象征生男的白花，由新婚或婚后未育的媳妇们挑选采摘，此时，一对俗称"孩哥孩弟"的大头娃娃嬉戏于彩篮花灯之间，专与争相采花的媳妇们捣乱，你进我退，你阻我拦，场面情趣盎然。表演时以走队形、摆场面为特点，主要动作有"单一托篮"、"连接托篮"、"晃篮"、"比花"等，其中少女动作，如"举案齐眉"、"比花"、"观花"、"选花"等，细腻生动，大头娃娃动作则风趣诙谐。有的灯舞不仅以舞队形式走街，还进入厅堂表演。如流行于浦城东乡的《茶灯》，表演者左手托着烛光透亮的茶灯，右手挥舞轻柔飘逸的纱绢，以圆场步表演"托灯"、"举灯"、"盘灯"、"穿灯"等各种舞蹈，进入厅堂庭院后，乐队奏"采茶调"，舞队边歌边舞，最后舞队向主人拜年。流传于福州地区的"龙灯舞"也颇有代表性，表演时，每个龙节为一盏灯,点亮蜡烛,每盏灯由一人执拿,加龙珠一盏灯共为十人。执龙珠者由身材矮小者担任,执龙头者由身材高大者担任,其余前矮后高。舞龙者各节动作各有不同,第一节与第二节以"迈步"为主,第八节舞者以"侧身马步跳"和"跨步跑"为主,龙尾以"阔步跑"为主,其余为"小跑步",在前者小跑,愈后者跨步愈大。其舞法程式有三个特色:一是队形以对称的"太极图"为基础;二是动作有一套规定,如"臂关落"(即龙身各节由前者的头顶正中臂落下而舞)、"转手吞节"(即左右手上下对换,左右变换以及上手的推收演变)、"小跃脚"(即前掌小跑步);三是舞法有一定讲究,如"随前节,顾后节,勿前推,忌后拉,眼光敏捷,顺顺舞来"等。流行于全省各地的灯舞不少,如光泽的《马仔灯》、永定的《竹马灯》、连城的《马灯舞》、长汀的《踩马灯》等,都有一定代表性。

球舞。主要流行于泉州一带。如《甩球舞》,表演者多位于迎神、踩街队伍前面,在人群熙攘的地方,常出其不意地向观众甩去彩球。其彩球用藤条编制而成,直径为14.5厘米,藤条上缠绕着各色彩带,悬挂在一条长230厘米的棉绳上,绳的另一端系垂细线穗子。表演者手握绳索,以大幅度的抛、甩、投、收等动作,上下挥舞,左右环绕,彩球宛若流星,让围观近者自觉回避。表演者或边行进边表演,或让队伍停下围场表演,让彩球上下飞抛,左右甩投,刚柔相济,沉浮参错,洒脱优美。再如《彩球舞》,以数女一婆一男孩为主,男孩将彩球上下左右抛引,使数女手托脚踢、肩碰膝顶,婆婆则运用头、手、身、足逗弄彩球,做出多种诙谐风趣的动作,整个表演生动活泼,妙趣横生。球舞还有多种形式,如《抛球舞》、《滚球舞》、《绣球舞》等。

武舞。如流行于闽东的《藤牌舞》,原是驻扎在福鼎秦屿镇的陆军烽火营会操检阅时的表演,后成为乡民一种游舞活动。藤牌舞队游舞时,分为两列纵队,一队身着全红色的服装扮成陆军,一队身着全蓝色的服装扮成水军,左手执虎头藤牌,右手握大刀,随着击乐队演奏的节奏便步沿街行进,有时亦成陆、水军简单的对打表演。至宽广处,往往停下围场表演,执旗者圆步先舞,接着陆、水军分别由左右侧出场,右手舞大刀,做砍、杀、劈、刺、扫、架等进攻动作,左手握藤牌做抵、挡、顶、阻、架等守卫动作,左右手协调配合,动作干脆有力,勇猛矫健,刀牌相击,铿然有声,显得威武豪迈,气势雄浑。队形变化多以横、竖、斜、圆的粗线条为主,气氛热烈。再如流传于建宁县的《打团牌》,为男性执矛、盾、枪、棍等对舞的表演。枪、棍表演多为刺、劈、挑、撩等进攻性动作,凶猛异常,执盾者多为闪、避、架、顶等抵挡性动作,快速敏捷。

傩舞。这是一种头戴面具表演的舞蹈,流行于闽北地区。"傩"是"除"的意思,当时人们对瘟疫等病束手无策,只好求助神灵佑助,因此戴上由木雕、纸、油布制的几种面具起舞,以驱逐疫鬼,去除邪气。闽北傩舞种类丰富,有"跳幡僧","跳八褐"、"跳弥勒"、"跳五神"等。傩舞的跳法以集体舞为主,个别领舞为辅,舞队一般由开路神清整出一块场地就跳一通。起舞时,动作、程式基本一致,以弓步、跨步转身为主,加以队形变化,也有用后踢跳、狐步的。如流行于邵武大阜岗乡的"跳八褐",为每年农历六月初二日奉祀出巡时表演,由男八人各扮成成对的脸戴木面具的开路神、弥勒、黑脸、绿脸进行表演。开路神执锣,弥勒握铜,黑绿脸腹前挂一扁鼓,分为二组,成单列纵队行进。观者多时,即开始变换队形,由纵队成圆形,再变成四方形,然后以"退弓步"、"转弓步"、"续转步"为主要步伐,配着夸张、优雅敲击着道具的双手动作穿插起舞。

畲族舞蹈。福建畲族分布在40多个县市内,其中以闽东最为密集。畲族能歌善舞,创造了许多丰富多彩风格独具的民族舞蹈。如流行于福鼎的《栽竹舞》,是畲族法师作法时的舞蹈。竹子是畲家吉祥物。畲族人认为,妖魔鬼怪被法师用竹子赶打过后,永世不得翻身重现。法师作法时,分别向东南西北中五个方位,带随意性地翩翩起舞。并模拟栽竹造纸、敬神中的动作程序,从栽、砍、破、下池、舀浆、造纸,到打成纸钱奉给上、中、下三界菩萨而结束。动作流畅、跳跃,柔韧,力度适中,身体和手脚配合协调。舞者按鼓点节奏,左右急旋转时,神裙张如伞形的舞姿,给人以轻快、优美的感觉。流行于宁德漳湾的《猎捕舞》,主要表现猎手的围猎过程,由四名左手执螺号,右手握猎刀的畲族男青年表演。整个舞蹈由"窥探"、"围捕"、"越障"、"吹螺"、"刺杀"、"凯归"等舞蹈场面构成,动作主要运用跑与跳相结合的方式,以强调体现猎手们在险峻的深山老林里猎捕野兽的气概。流行于福安的《雷诀》,是畲族巫师在祭师祭祀活动做道场时,贯串始终谓之"防身打鬼"的成套手势造型动作,由一人表演,共有 46 个手势造型动作,分为"藏身诀"、"打鬼诀"、"吊楼诀"、"罗房决"四类,以"藏身诀"为主,即用指、掌的手势变化造型,模拟观音、哪吒、王母娘娘、鲁班及虎、龟、蛇、鹤等,以威慑鬼怪。雷诀可称为是巫舞中手势造型动作程式的汇集。流行于宁德八都的《铃刀舞》、连江的《迎龙伞》、霞浦的《祈福》及《畲族婚礼舞》等,都是福建畲族舞蹈的经典之作。

宗教舞蹈。在莆田,道士设醮仪式有好多种舞蹈场面,如"迎真走庭",即三日三夜醮典中正午举行的"迎真"时,设一法坛在大庭上,并搭一高栅象征天阙,由 7 个道士从法坛上朝天阙,迎真下降,来回都在大庭上穿花进行,舞蹈场面很壮观。再如"进贡围炉",即法事结束时,将法坛上所有疏封都收叠在一起,捧到大庭的焚化炉中送其"上天庭",道士们围绕焚化炉穿花舞蹈。流行于闽南的《献铙钹》,是道士超度亡灵时的一种舞蹈,目的是使亡灵稳得房子和库银。表演时由一人独舞,动作有"推出"、"照镜"、"云龙过日"、"炒茶跳舞"、"绞刀剪浮铜"、"板钹"等 20 多个,表演时间达两个小时,故通常由两人交替进行。除一些固定顺序外,舞者可以随意选择动作进行即兴表演。表演时动作惊险,表演者把一面飞旋着的铜钹抛向空中,再用另一面钹把它接住,在抛与接的过程中,做出一系列高难度动作,如做"直送如"动作时,右手做"旋钹"向上高抛钹,落下时以中指尖接住钹锥,钹仍旋转,反复三次后,接轻抛呈"抓蒂"接住,再做一次"旋钹",高抛中指接钹锥后,手臂由腋下向上屈时画圆还原,掌面始终朝上,上身随着前俯后仰,最后做轻抛接钹呈"抓蒂"。流行于闽清的《穿花舞》,佛、道两家兼用。在佛教中,是和尚做"普渡",为死者招魂引渡的一种法场舞蹈;在道教中,是道士设坛做"报孝",以超度父母亡灵所表演的一种法事舞蹈。表演时,8人右手执铜铃,左手提托灯笼,在民间音乐伴奏下,脚走台步,身形左右辗转成"S"形,相互沿供桌穿插、绕走,队形变化有致,快慢相间得当,显得飘逸流畅。闽东北的《奶娘踩罡》,流行于三明、永安的《保奏》,顺昌洋口的《仙女洗镜》,闽东的《香花舞》,南平峡阳的《战台鼓》,莆田和仙游的《皂隶摆》等,也都是福建很有代表性的宗教舞蹈。

高跷。如流行于闽西长汀的《高跷扑蝶》,表演时为二人,一扮丑公,一扮丑婆,丑公左手执扇,右手举着系有蝴蝶的竹片。舞蹈以丑婆为主,丑公以蝴蝶逗引丑婆,时而上下,时而左右,迫使丑婆左蹲右转,前俯后仰,时而眉开眼笑,时而歪嘴眨眼,时而娇媚柔态,时而气急败坏。通过"望蝶"、"戏蝶"、"追蝶"、"扑蝶"等情节铺陈,运用"小秧歌步"、"蹉步"、"单腿小跳"、"双腿小跳",以及"劈叉"、"下前腰"等技巧性动作,生动地表现了公戏婆、婆扑蝶等欢乐情景,场面活跃,格调诙谐。

福建民间舞蹈之所以形态各异,其原因是多方面的。如由于受交通、方言等影响,福建民间舞蹈难以在全境交流,没有一种舞种,能覆盖全境。在交通、经济相对发达的区域,如闽南,一些舞种经过长期碰撞、交融,流播的面还相对广些。而在一些较为封闭的区域,则只在一个县,一个乡,甚至一个村流传。如流传于沙县湖源乡湖四村的《打车鼓》,为明代村中青年人为求神灵保佑家族平安而跳,经过民间艺人一代复一代的加工润色,形式日趋丰富,内容愈加完善,但至今也仅在本乡流传。流行于宁化高地村的《走阵

灯》（又名《关刀舞》），是高地村池姓家族世代相传的一种祭祖舞
蹈，虽然早在南宋就已形成，但至今也只在本村演出。流传于闽侯
县荆溪官口村的《扛猫》，生动地展示了猎户猎虎满载而归的过程，
但自产生以来，一直未出过官口村，也是官口村惟一流传的舞蹈。
此外，民风不同也是造成这种情况的原因之一。福建"十里不同
风，一村有一俗"。很难想象，闽西北的人民会接受闽南上身赤裸、
沿街拍打胸脯的"拍胸舞"；而闽西北细腻的《采茶舞》，也难以在闽
南流传。

　　福建民间舞蹈的产生和形成，主要与如下五个方面有关。

　　1.产生于本地的劳动生活中。福建民间舞蹈是生活在八闽大
地上人们抒发感情的一种艺术，它反映了人们的生存、劳作，表达
着人们的欢乐、向往。如流传于闽北的《竹林刀花》，生动地反映了
人民的劳动生活情景。当地农民出工时都要自带柴刀、竹担，开始
只是为解闷而随意敲打，有时和着山歌，变换不同节奏边歌边舞，
自娱自乐。后经过不断加工修改，成为表现当地人民劳动情趣的
一种舞蹈。流传于闽北的《茶灯舞》，其动作也是融各种采茶姿势
而成。产生于闽地的民间舞蹈与闽地特有的民俗有着极为密切的
关系。如流传于闽南的《戏灯》（也称《抢灯》），即由民俗演变而来。
闽南有"送灯"的习俗，女儿出嫁三年内，每逢元宵佳节，都要由父
母购花灯，由家中小孩送给亲家。新婚第一年送一对，一为莲花
灯，表示能生男孩，一为绣球灯，表示能生女孩。第二年，如女儿还
未生，再送一对；如已生，改送"桃灯"。第三年再送一盏"鼓灯"。
《戏灯》演的是：一小女孩，于元宵佳节，奉父母之命，将一盏花灯送
到姐姐的婆家去，有一玩竹马小男孩在半路要抢花灯，女孩不给，
二人你抢我闪，你躲我逐，表现了儿童的天真活泼，嬉戏逗趣。闽
地民间舞蹈的产生和发展也与当地传统有关。如流行于南平峡阳
的《战台鼓》（也称《战斗鼓》、《战胜鼓》），表现了战争中将士们随着
鼓声缓进、速进等进军过程，气势磅礴。这是当年在郑成功军中任

旗手、后退伍回峡阳的一位姓薛的传授的,但所以能代代相传,与峡阳有浓厚的习武传统有关。峡阳多习武世家,考取武进士、武举人及在朝廷任武职的很多,习武成风。闽地民间舞蹈的形成与当地人民要表达自己爱憎和风情有关。如流传于漳州和龙海的《大鼓凉伞》(也称《花鼓阵》),表演时男演员身上挂着鼓边舞边打,若干女演员手拿彩伞,为打鼓的演员遮凉。溯其源,是当年闽南人民为戚家军胜利归来击鼓庆功,戚继光看到人们在炎热的太阳下打鼓(一说在雨中打鼓),个个满头大汗,心里十分感动,就命令战士和侍女撑着伞为打鼓者遮凉,随着队伍走动,形成了这种边打边舞的场面。

2.外地传入。外地传入福建的舞蹈主要有三个方面:(1)中原传入。中原文化多次传入福建,使无数中土舞蹈荟萃于福建,并以得天独厚的历史与地域条件,受到围护而得以积淀。如流传于闽西客家居住区的《龙凤灯》,原为中原舞蹈,距今已有七八百年,流传至今不变。(2)由台湾传入。如流行于南安诗山凤坡村的《凤坡跳鼓》,是由台湾传入凤坡的。200多年前,凤坡村有一人往台湾扎篾衣谋生,在台湾学会了《跳鼓》这一舞蹈,返乡后恰逢家乡谒祖进香,他表演了《跳鼓》,从此每逢迎神赛会、谒祖,凤坡必有《跳鼓》表演。(3)东南传入。如流行于建宁的《打团牌》,是明代由湖南传入的。流行于闽西的《九连环》,就其使用道具而言,实际是苏皖一带的"莲汀"(也称"霸王鞭"、"钱棍")。明末江淮动乱,百姓南逃至闽西,民间艺人在汀州街头操起"莲汀",沿街卖唱,并唱起当地小曲"九连环"。久而久之,就变成了闽西民间歌舞。流行于龙岩的《采茶灯》,其曲谱和战鼓,均为苏坂乡美山村林氏17世祖由广东传入,距今已有250多年。

3.脱胎于戏曲。福建是戏曲之乡,不少戏曲唱做俱佳,其表演程式和科步动作,具有很强的舞蹈性,因此福建舞蹈不少直接源于戏曲。如流传于莆田、仙游的《走雨》,原为莆仙戏《瑞兰走雨》"踏伞"中表现剧中人物瑞兰母女冒雨赶路的情景。流行于闽南的《抬四轿》(即"四人抬轿"),也直接脱胎于戏曲。在梨园戏、莆仙戏中,"抬轿"的动作被发挥得淋漓尽致,备受观众青睐,由此诱发了舞蹈者的仿效,久而久之,经过加工的舞蹈《抬四轿》更加幽默风趣,神情惟妙惟肖:四个演员头戴尖顶帽,身着轿夫装,用身体摹拟抬轿的动作,如上山、下坡、涉滩、过桥等,再伴以闽南原始轿歌,更增添了舞蹈活泼气氛。流行于长汀策武乡的《碟子舞》,则从湖南来策武乡演出的《骂门生祭》戏中某个精彩片断演化而来。有的舞蹈形式被戏曲所吸收,后又独立出来。如流行于闽南的《摇钱树》,最早为乞丐讨饭要钱时跳的,后被高甲戏《大名府》所采用,并加以改造,使其动作更规范,以后又成为人们在春节期间跳的"恭喜发财"的舞蹈。

4.宗教的影响。如流行于仙游枫亭的《簪花轿》,就是由道观传入民间的,所以带有浓重的宗教色彩。流行于莆田的《九莲灯》,以莲花灯象征圣洁的灵光,寓意"照破重重黑地,勋成皎皎青天",以"引灵魂脱凡尘,上西天"。每段舞蹈之间都穿插演唱三教教义,表演时灯随人舞,旋转不息。

5.多方面的影响。福建不少民间舞蹈,既有外地传入成分,又经本地民俗的熏陶,还受到戏曲,宗教等影响,可以说是汲取了多方面精华,因此内涵丰富,令人百看不厌。如流行于闽南的《拍胸舞》,是福建最有代表性的民间舞蹈之一,舞者为男性,头套草圈,上身裸露;动作以趋于单一节奏的击、拍、夹、跺为主;部位集中在胸、肘、肩、掌,并辅以雄健的蹲步和怡然自得的摆头,构成粗犷、古朴、诙谐、热烈的风格。关于《拍胸舞》的来源有多种说法,如:(1)与古闽越族祭祀舞蹈有关,其外在表演形式和内在动律都保留有闽越遗风;(2)与古代中原踏歌有关,其神态、形态与宋代马远"踏歌图"有相似之处,是随中州移民进入泉州的;(3)与古代闽南人劳动习俗有关,闽南人民习惯赤脚劳动,休息时常击掌拍胸,自娱起舞;(4)与宗教有关,唐宋时泉州僧尼云集,"拍胸"是在迎神赛会上出现的一种舞蹈形式;(5)与戏曲有关,即梨园戏《李亚仙》中郑元和与乞丐为伍行乞时所跳。这些看法并不矛盾,《拍胸舞》在长期演出过程中,受到各种因素影响,也由此汲取了各方面精华,很难说它仅源于此而无缘于彼。也正是因为其广博的包容性,才使这一舞蹈表现出多方面的内容,并由纯朴的民间舞蹈形式生发出较高层次的舞蹈审美意义。

三、戏曲

　　福建虽然在唐代才得以全面开发,但戏曲形成的时间却几乎与全国同步。唐咸通二年(861年),福州玄沙寺住持宗一法师"南游莆田,县排百戏迎接"(宋道原纂《景德传灯录》卷十八)。至宋代,宋杂剧传入福建莆仙,与盛行在民间的古乐和百戏结合,并用莆仙方言演唱,形成具有莆仙地方特色的杂剧。因宋时莆仙属兴化军,故名兴化杂剧。南宋莆田诗人刘克庄大量记载了莆田戏曲的盛况,如"抽簪脱袴满城忙,大半人多在戏场"(《即事三首》)。宋时杂剧在漳州也很流行,以至宋庆元三年(1197年)陈淳在漳州写了《上傅寺丞论淫戏书》,一方面反映了道学家对民间戏曲的鄙夷,另一方面也可看出当时漳州戏曲的兴盛。宋末元初,南戏开始传入福建,逐渐与莆田的兴化戏、泉州的梨园戏、漳州的竹马戏相结合,并从剧目、表演和音乐上促进了这三种戏的发展。福建戏曲萌芽于唐,形成于宋,成熟于元。其因素,一是晋末至唐五代,北方人民南移入闽,使中原古乐传入福建;二是唐五代福建相对安定繁华,不仅官邸宴舞为常事,民间也出现歌楼;三是福建唐五代佛教兴盛,寺院林立,庙会成了演出场所;四是宋代福建中举及在外居官者甚多,他们返乡时,常带家伎随侍娱乐;五是宋南渡后,大批皇族入闽,且闽人多官于浙,而浙人多官于闽。皇族和官员多蓄养家班,他们入闽后,即将盛行于杭州的温州杂剧带进福建,皇族家班开始流入民间。

明代是福建戏曲的发展时期。弋阳腔、昆山腔、四平腔等相继传入福建,为福建各地戏曲声腔所融合吸收,不仅产生了许多新的声腔剧种,还对已有的剧种在程式、行当、服饰、脸谱等方面产生了较大的影响,各种新旧剧种争奇斗胜,异彩纷呈。据有关文献记载,从城市到乡村,各种演出极为频繁,且剧目丰富多彩。如在泉州演出的有《西厢记》、《陈三五娘》等;在莆田演出的有《范蠡献西施》、《潘必正》、《霍小玉》等;在福州演出的有《鸣凤记》、《彩毫记》、《采茶》、《出塞》等。此外,明万历间,福建戏班还曾到琉球国演出,深受欢迎。

明代福建戏曲发展的原因有四方面:1.外来声腔传入途径多样化。一是随商人入闽,如徽池一带戏班,曾随徽商入闽,将弋阳高腔、昆腔、徽州腔、青阳腔等传入福建;二是外任官员返乡,如曾任江苏嘉定县令的陈一元,喜昆剧,返乡后在福州家中蓄昆曲"歌童一部",以演出娱宾。2.传入路线多方面。如"稍变弋阳"的四平腔,曾分三路传入福建,一路从赣东经闽北传到政和、屏南和宁德;一路经浙江东路沿海流传到了闽中沿海的福清、长乐、平潭等地;一路从赣南流传到闽粤交界的平和、漳州、南靖等地。3.涌现了一批戏曲作家与作品。如福州陈轼的《续牡丹亭》、陈介夫的《异梦记》,福清林章的《青虹记》及何璧撰校的《北西厢记》等。4.涌现出一些在戏曲评论方面有见地的学者,如长乐的谢肇淛、莆田的姚旅、泉州的李贽、连江的陈弟、福州的曹学佺等。

清代是福建戏曲的繁荣时期。其标志:1.戏班众多。如据清莆田人陈鸿《莆靖小纪》载,1693年,莆田戏班已有28班。福建官吏常蓄家班演戏,甚至连厦门海防厅都设有戏班,专为官衙内部演出。2.流播国外。1685年至1688年,福建戏班曾到泰国王宫、大城等地演出喜剧、悲剧等;1840年至1843年,高甲戏"三合兴"班曾到新加坡、马来西亚、缅甸等国演出《三气周瑜》等戏;1843年至

1844 年,高甲戏"福金兴"班曾到泰国、新加坡、马来西亚、印度尼西亚等国演出《白蛇传》等戏。3.演出更加普及。各地方志对演出的盛况多有详尽记载,如清康熙《平和县志》卷十"风土志"载:"诸少年装束狮猊、八仙、竹马等戏。"清乾隆《长泰县志》卷十"风俗"载:"锣鼓喧天,旌旗蔽日,燃灯结采,演剧连朝。"清道光《龙岩州志》卷七"风俗"载:"自元旦至元夕,沿家演戏,鸣锣索赏。"清道光《永定县志》卷十六"风俗志"载:"迎神申敬,演戏为欢,亦不可三五日而止。"清道光《罗源县志》卷二十七"风俗"载:"他邑梨园子弟,惟是月有至罗者,演唱庙中匝月。"清代侯官人聂敦观在《观剧》中,对福州戏曲演出的盛况有过生动的描述:"就中闱门粗识字,听词能诵《鸾凤记》。香车逐队无猜忌,搭棚一丈为标识;棚前众目不相识,歌声未起人声沸。……流连竟夕都忘寐,但觉歌词有情致。"清代福建戏曲的繁荣,最主要原因是大量的外地戏曲进入福建后,与当地的民间艺术融为一体,成为各具特色的地方戏。如从清中叶至 20 世纪 30 年代,湖南祁阳班经江西到龙岩、连城、宁化等地,许多艺人就地落籍,并吸收融合了闽西木偶戏、民间的中军鼓乐和西秦戏,形成了"外江戏"这一地方剧种,后又称"闽西汉剧"。以吹腔为主要唱腔的"乱弹",于清中叶经浙江、江西传入闽东北的寿宁、古田、屏南、福安等地,并吸收了当地民间艺术,形成后称"北路戏"的剧种。徽班由浙江经江西传入闽西北泰宁县梅林乡一带,吸收了当地道士音乐和民歌小调,后称"梅林戏"。江西戏班传到闽北浦城一带,后称"赣剧"。

　　福建剧种中,最主要的有闽剧、莆仙戏、梨园戏、高甲戏、芗剧这五大剧种。

　　闽剧俗称"福州戏",流行于福州方言区及宁德、建阳、三明等地。闽剧是明代末年的儒林戏和清中叶以来的江湖戏与平讲戏这三种不同艺术风格的剧种,互相渗透融合,并吸收了徽戏和昆曲而形成的以唱"逗腔"的儒林戏为主的综合性多声腔剧种。闽剧传统剧目很丰富,据统计有 1500 多个。著名的如《女运骸》《双玉蝉》、《甘国宝》《陈若霖斩皇子》《伍老与周良显》《红裙记》等。今人改编整理的如《桐油煮粉干》《钗头凤》《炼印》等。闽剧的音乐曲调富有浓厚的地方色彩,它由典雅婉约的"逗腔"、粗犷激越的"江湖"、通俗流畅的"洋歌"和清新活泼的"小调"这四类曲调构成。伴奏乐器分软片、硬片两类,软片伴奏以丝竹为主,主要乐器有京胡、三弦、笛、笙、唢呐等;硬片伴奏以金革为主,主要乐器有清鼓、堂鼓、大小锣、大小钹、鱼鼓、清水磬等。角色行当早期只有生、旦、丑,后来日渐完整,分有正生、小生、老生、贴生、武生,正旦、青衣、花旦、小旦、武旦、老旦、丑旦、小丑、三花、武三花,大花、二花、武二花,末、外、杂等。闽剧表演动作激烈、粗犷,如舞台上常有三赶三追、扁嘴憋脸、抖手颤腿、耍发甩须等表演程式。但也有部分生、旦表演较为细腻、典雅,尤其是一些旦角的表演,十分细腻柔美。闽剧对身段要求严格,有"有脚才有手,有手才有身"、"脚动手动,手动身动"和"一动百动"之说。

莆仙戏主要流行于莆田、仙游二县及邻县的兴化方言区,因宋时莆田、仙游隶兴化军,明、清时隶兴化府,故又称"兴化戏"。莆仙戏历史悠久,早在 700 多年前,莆田著名诗人刘克庄曾在其诗中大量描述过当时演戏的盛况。莆仙戏传统遗产极为丰富,仅传统剧目就有 5 000 多个,8 000 多本。刘念兹在《南戏新证》(中华书局 1986 年版)中指出,莆仙戏剧本之多,"全国以至全世界,还没有别的剧种可以与之相比。它是迄今收藏世界戏剧艺术作品最丰富的一个图书馆和博物馆"。著名的传统剧目如《目连》《叶里》(又名《叶里娘》《翁懿娘》)、《张洽》《春江》《商辂教书》等,今人整理改编的如《团圆之后》《状元与乞丐》《春草闯堂》《琴桃》《嵩口司》等。莆仙戏音乐属兴化语系的兴化腔,唱腔结构形式为曲牌体,有谱可传的曲牌不下千支,男女同腔同调,行腔委婉缠绵。乐器伴奏早期只有锣、鼓、笛,后又陆续增加了横笛、大胡、二胡、月琴、三弦、文鼓、单皮鼓、钟鼓、碗锣等。据称,锣鼓总共有500种以上,有谱可传者现有200余种。脸谱用色为红、白、黑三种。据《莆仙戏传统舞台美术》介绍,目前收集到的脸谱有300多个。角色有生、旦、靓妆、末、外、贴、丑等七个行当,以生、旦为主,表演讲究优美细腻,富有舞蹈性,特别以表现古代女子"行不动裙"的蹀步为最优美,走时两膝夹紧,双足靠拢,足尖着力,一跷一落,蹉着行进。练时需在膝头夹个铜板,以走时铜板不掉算成功。

梨园戏流行于泉州等闽南方言区。宋末元初,当时流行于泉州一带的民间优戏杂剧,吸收了传入泉州的温州南戏的剧目和表演艺术,形成了以闽南地方语言演唱南音为主的戏曲。梨园戏分"上路"、"下南"和演员为童龄的"小梨园"三种不同艺术流派。各个流派都有各自的专有剧目和专用唱腔曲牌。梨园戏剧目有100多个,"上路"中著名的传统剧目如《王十朋》、《王魁》、《刘文良》、《朱文走鬼》、《朱寿昌》等,大都为夫妻悲欢离合的家庭故事,表演风格较为古朴。"下南"中著名传统剧目如《刘大本》、《吕蒙正》、《郑元和》、《苏秦》等,以讽刺封建社会的世态炎凉为主,也有部分公案戏,剧本文词较粗俗,表演风格较为明快、粗犷。"小梨园"中著名的传统剧目如《陈三五娘》、《郭华》、《董永》、《蒋士隆》、《韩国华》,剧文结构严密,文词典雅,内心描写细致,表演风格柔雅精致,多载歌载舞。梨园戏音乐由南音、笼吹、十音和部分潮调等组成,唱腔结构属曲牌体。"上路"曲牌较为刚劲有力、淳朴、哀怨;"下南"曲牌较为明快、粗犷、诙谐;"小梨园"曲牌较优美、纤细、缠绵。角色沿用南戏旧制,"小梨园"分生、旦、净、丑、贴、外、末七个行当,"上路"和"下南"则增加老旦和二旦。表演细腻优美,规范严谨,有"一句曲子一科步","举手到眉毛,分手到肚脐,拱手到下颏","进三步,退三步,三步到台前"等舞台术语。

高甲戏流行于闽南方言区,渊源于明代泉州地区民间街头妆扮游行,最早因多表演《水浒传》里宋江故事,故被称之为"宋江戏"。清中叶时,"宋江戏"与南安岭兜村"合兴班"互相吸收融化,突破了只演宋江故事的框框,受到弋阳腔、徽调、昆腔、四平腔以及后来京剧的影响,使自己在兼收并蓄中日趋成型为今日高甲戏。高甲戏传统剧目约 600 多个,大部分来自木偶戏、布袋戏和古典小说,也有部分来自民间传说,著名的如《大闹花府》、《织锦回文》、《詹典嫂告御状》、《管甫送》,今人改编整理的如《连升三级》、《真假王岫》、《桃花搭渡》、《许仙谢医》、《凤冠梦》等。音乐曲牌以南曲为主,兼收木偶调和民间小调,传统曲调有 200 多首,唱字行腔雄浑高昂,也有清婉细腻的音韵。乐器分文乐和武乐。文乐以唢呐为主,配以品箫、洞箫、三弦、二弦等;武乐有百鼓、小鼓、通鼓、大小锣、大小钹等。角色行当有生、旦、北、丑、杂,以丑角戏的表演最有特色,有男、女丑。男丑又分文丑和武丑。文丑有"长衫丑"和"短衫丑";武丑有"师爷丑"和"捆身丑"。女丑有"夫人丑"、"媒人丑"、"老婆丑"等。表演时身段动作优美细腻,表情幽默诙谐活泼,夸张性大,妙趣横生。

芗剧也称"歌仔戏",流行于闽南漳州地区。明末清初,随着郑成功收复台湾,漳州地区的锦歌、车鼓弄等民间音乐也传入台湾,并与当地民间艺术相结合,又吸收了其他剧种技艺,发展成为一种新的戏曲——歌仔戏。1928 年,台湾歌仔戏"三乐轩"班首次回闽南演出,受到漳州、厦门等地乡亲们的喜爱,于是又在闽南故土迅速发展。芗剧传统剧目有 400 多个,题材多取自民间传说、神话、公案、传奇和历史演义,如《山伯英台》、《火烧楼》、《安安寻母》、《杂货记》、《李妙惠》等,今人改编整理的如《加令记》、《三家福》等。芗剧唱腔多,说白少,腔调主要有七字调、哭调、台湾杂含调、内地杂碎调及来自民歌和其他地方剧种唱腔共五大类。乐器分为文场和武场。文场乐器有通鼓、竖板、板鼓、木鱼、小钹、大钹、大小锣等;武场乐器有月琴、台湾笛、二胡、唢呐等。角色行当一般分生、旦、丑、净;生又分为老、少、文、武;旦分青衣、老旦;净分文武大花脸和二花脸；丑分男、女、文、武、粗思丑。表演讲究夸张,用语幽默诙谐,有一整套表演要求,如指法有"小旦到目眉,小生到肚脐",眼功有"指出手中,眼随指从"、"眼出情,指出神"等要领。

　　除了这五大剧种外,福建较为有名的地方戏还如:1. 竹马戏。流行于长泰、南靖、龙海、漳州、厦门、同安、金门等地,发源于漳浦、华安等地,由民间歌舞"竹马"发展而来,因表演者身扎竹马进行歌舞表演而得名。2. 潮剧。也称"白字仔戏"、"潮音戏",流行于诏安、云霄、东山、平和、漳州、南靖及龙岩等地。明中叶前形成于广东的潮州、汕头一带和福建南部的潮语方言区。3. 大腔戏。流行于三明、永安、大田、龙溪等地,因"大嗓子唱高腔,大锣大鼓唱大戏"而得名。4. 闽南四平戏。流行于漳州、平和、漳浦、诏安、云霄、南靖等地,因演出戏台大,照明灯火大,锣鼓声响大,亦称"大戏"、"老戏"。5. 词明戏。流行于福清、平潭、长乐等地,刚由浙江传入时,唱白均用官话,为了让当地人听懂,强调"词句唱明",故有此称。6. 平讲戏。流行于屏南、古田、宁德、福安及闽侯、长乐等地,因用当地方言演唱戏文而有此称。7. 闽西汉剧。流行于龙岩、三明及龙溪等地,因其主要声腔属弹腔南北路,故称"乱弹";又因其声腔来自外省,亦称"外江戏"。8. 北路戏。流行于闽北和闽东,因主要乐器为长膜笛,故又名"横哨戏"。9. 梅林戏。流行于三明、泰宁、明溪、将乐等地,因其发源于泰宁县朱口乡梅林村,故有此称。10. 三角戏。因只有生、旦、丑三个角色,故又称"三子戏"、"三小戏"。流行于邵武、光泽、泰宁、建宁等地。11. 小腔戏。因由赣东传入,故又称"江西戏"。流行于龙溪、永安、大田、沙县等地。12. 打城戏。因是在宗教作法事"打城超度众生"基础上发展起来的,故又称"法事戏"、"和尚戏"、"道士戏"等。流传于泉州、晋江、南安、龙海、漳州等地。13. 山歌戏。因是在闽西山歌的基础上发展形成的,故有此称。流行于闽西各县。

　　福建地方戏的主要特点有五个方面。

1.保存了全国最多的南戏剧目和中原古剧,被称为"南戏遗响"和中原古剧的"活化石"。特别莆仙戏、梨园戏在传统剧目、音乐曲牌、角色行当等方面都与南戏关系密切。莆仙戏有存本的传统剧目中,有50多个与《南词叙录》"宋元旧篇"著录的南戏剧目相同或基本相似。莆仙戏保存了大量古南戏稀有曲牌,而且其部分曲牌的名目、音韵、词格等,亦与唐宋大曲和宋词调相同。莆仙戏的表演和舞曲,也与唐宋大曲有一定继承关系。梨园戏不仅保留了大量宋元南戏剧目,在音乐和演奏上也都保留了唐代古乐的结构特点和演奏遗风。

2.剧种的形成过程复杂,汲取营养丰富。福建戏曲之所以难以明显区别外来剧种、本地剧种,是因为它所受的影响是多方面的,是各种艺术、各种剧种互相融会的结果。以潮剧为例,似乎纯属外来剧,其实它固然形成于广东潮、汕一带,但其早期称"正音戏",是用中原音韵的"官话"演唱的,属宋、元南戏的一支。后又受到梨园戏的影响,如潮剧传统剧目《荔镜记》,曲文即以泉州方言杂潮语写成。潮剧主要乐器,也与梨园戏基本相似。此外,潮剧还受到畲歌疍舞影响,许多潮剧传统剧目中还保存有斗畲歌的形式和疍民船上歌舞的形式。

3.保留不少稀有剧种。这是福建的封闭性所致。如过去许多戏剧史家们认为,四平腔作为一个独立的剧种已经绝灭。但1981年夏却发现宁德洋中乡的眉岈和屏南县熙岭乡的龙潭这两个偏僻小山村中,有四平戏的遗响。

4.赴东南亚演出频繁。据《福建戏曲志》统计,从明万历年间至1948年,福建戏班赴东南亚演出,有资料可查的有30个左右,共35次,剧种为高甲戏、闽西汉剧、莆仙戏、梨园戏、闽剧、芗剧等。赴外演出时间之悠久、戏班次数之多、剧种之多,为全国地方戏中所不多见。

5.演出习俗繁多。福建各剧种演出习俗之多、之细、之繁,实为罕见。开演前、演出中、演出后各剧种都有一套详尽程序。如闽西汉剧在首场演出时，必须先由一演员扮唐明皇，口念“风调雨顺，国泰民安”。潮剧在开演前，先要演一出《团圆》后才入正剧。新戏开演，新戏棚落成等，也有各自规定的习俗。如芗剧在新戏台演出时，必须洗台。洗台仪式极为繁褥。莆仙戏在新戏开台时，都要先演《田公踏棚》。有的剧种连什么日子该演什么，忌演什么，怎么拾礼（拿东道主红包）等，也都有规定。各剧种都有自己所供奉的保护神，如莆仙戏供奉田公元帅，大腔戏和小腔戏都供奉田清源、窦清奇、葛清巽三个戏神。各剧种也都有自己行话和口诀，如梨园戏称演员唱每一句曲白都要选用能准确表达其含意的表演程式为“一句曲一步科”，称演员在舞台上滥动为“歹戏多科步，歹傀儡多线路”，称鼓一响即要上台为“军令不如赌令，赌令不如戏令”等。

福建戏曲以其独到的表演艺术而令人赞叹。福建各剧种虽然都用方言演唱，却屡屡在上京晋演时，倾倒外地观众，并多次得奖。即使观众听不懂演员的唱白，也能从演员那出神入化的动作表演中得到美的享受。虚拟是中国戏曲的主要特点之一，而身段和动作，又是虚拟凭借的主要方式，“通过演员的身段和动作，把没有实物的实物意象传递给观众欣赏。舞台空无所有，演员心中却一切具有”。（参见拙文《中国古代戏曲的民族特色》，《中国文学导读》，北京大学出版社 1990 年版）。

福建各剧种都注重基本功的训练，讲究步、手、肩的配合，但各剧种又有自己独特的要求。以步法为例，莆仙戏有三步行、蹀步、摇步、拖步、挑步、云步等。闽剧的步法有正步、平步、快步、慢步、叠步、抬步、雀步、错步、趋步、云步、拖步、颠步、摸步、老步、膝步、转步、退步、迈步、弓箭步、跳步、矮步、分水步、探步、滑步、跨步等。芗剧有贴步、碎步、叠步、磨步、垫步、踢裙、跑步、蹉步、上楼步、迈步、颠步、八字步、弓步、勾步、踢步、矮步等。梅林戏有踏步、跺步、蹉步、蹭步、跪步、云步等。各个角色行当，所用的步法也不同。如莆仙戏旦角最主要的是"蹀步",两足并立靠拢,足尖一翘一落,膝头夹紧,足尖着力,不断搓着行进,表现了古代女人婀娜走步的形态;生角最主要的是"三步行",举步时足尖稍抬起,踏地时膝盖稍曲即又伸直,表现了儒雅稳重的风度。再如北路戏,表现花旦欢跃情态时,多用"金鸟步",即脚尖落地用碎步跳跃前进,身躯与头部紧密配合,一俯一仰轻巧自然;表现成年妇女稳重大方时,多用"后跟步",即用脚跟着地,轻移莲步,一进一退,或三进一退。

再以手法为例,闽剧的手法有兰花手、菊花手、弧形手、抱拳手、山膀手、背拦手、哭介手、遮雨手、云手、抖手、翻手、穿手、握手、指手、拦手、背手、拱手、摊手、拉手、上下摆手等。各剧种的手法也都有严格的程式,如竹马戏中的"指手",是将右手从小腹前弯弯划至胸前,向正前方指出,掌心朝外,指尖朝上,高度齐鼻,左手同时插在腰上;"分手"即两手以螃蟹手姿势,从两侧向腹前翻转;"啄手"即左手插腰,右手以观音手姿势划至胸前,然后再着力指出。各种手法作用也都有明确规定。如梨园戏中"指手"是指人、指事、指方位;"啄手"是用于表示羞怯、偷看、探视或在远处暗自思忖;"拍手"是表示欢喜、赞美或庆贺团圆;"提手"是表示疑惑、惊讶或反问;"分手"表示没有、发问或不解;"拱手"表示尊敬等。

福建戏曲属于地方剧种,虽受方言限制,却有不少被全国各地方剧团移植,如莆仙戏《春草闯堂》被全国100余家剧团移植,高甲戏《连升三级》被全国30余家剧团移植。其高超的表演艺术是主要因素之一。如莆仙戏《杀狗记》"迎春牵狗",表现女婢迎春,奉主娘之命,到王婆家买狗后将狗牵回。全出没有唱词和道白,靠迎春的手势、台步、身段、眼神,表现了一只虚拟狗的存在,据《福建戏曲志》载,其层次为:1.迎春运用长短手牵狗,跑圆场;2.狗往回跑,迎春三拉三拖;3.迎春紧拉狗索,与狗对面连续长短手三下翻;4.狗迎面扑来,迎春麻利地作三下跳躲闪过去;5.迎春跌坐在地上,用臀部将狗索压住;6.迎春抚摸狗头,用动作表示狗不再调皮了;7.

迎春对面逗弄狗,走小圆场;8.迎春用绳索向狗作"三下扑",重打绳索套在狗头上;9.迎春左手抓狗,用绳索打狗,狗蹲地,迎春又抚摸狗,从袖中拿饼给狗吃;10.狗吃饼,迎春双手提索牵狗走"雀鸟步",欢欢喜喜下场。这一表演形象细腻地表现了牵狗的过程。再如高甲戏《骑驴探亲》,亲家母是一位麻利的农村老妇人,她挥鞭跑驴时,打一鞭,驴跳一步退两步;打两鞭,驴跳两跳又退回;再重抽一鞭,驴突然向前飞奔。打两个圆场后,驴才慢慢恢复正常。演员运用腿、肩、颈及眉、眼、嘴的表演,使观众感觉到一头难以驾驭的驴之存在,表现了人急驴不急的有趣场面。

福建各剧种还常借扇、伞等砌末中的套数,形象地表现角色性格和思想感情。据《福建戏曲志》载,莆仙戏《百花亭》"百花赠剑"中,生、旦同时慢慢打开扇子,向左边作"乌云盖顶",然后双方把台位拉开,打开扇向左右搭,作"双飞扇"。再扇叠扇,作"双宿"扇法,三上三下,再转换台位,叠扇为"阴阳扇",左掀右翻,慢慢蹲下,相对照面,再次接连作"三托扇",然后双扇如蝴蝶翩翩起舞,若即若离,构成"花鱼戏水"的扇舞。高甲戏《笋江波》中,官宦公子吴世荣未出场先伸出手中扇子上下盘旋,接着以扇遮面;扇向右拉,露出半个脸;扇向左拉,又露出半个脸;扇又向下拉,才逐渐把脸露出来亮相。再将扇子架在脖子上,头向前伸,活脱脱一个花花公子形象。各剧种的扇功五花八门,如芗剧扇功有:持扇、捧扇、点扇、转扇、开扇、托腮扇、瞅视扇、遮羞扇、反夹扇、腰扇、拱扇、背扇、扑蝶扇、卧鱼扇、打风扇等。潮剧文生也注重扇功,各种扇功都有一定程式,当欣赏风景或表示激动时,就以右边扇,托左袖颤扇来表达;当发现近处景物时,结合唱词运用左指扇;表现端庄大方的形象,用反花扇亮相。再以伞为例。梨园戏有"十八雨伞科",如《孟姜女》"送寒衣"中,以张伞、撑伞、顶伞、施伞、升降伞、飘伞、放伞等动作,形象地表现出人物顶风冒雨艰难行进的情景。《高文举》"玉真行"中,王玉真以捧伞、托伞、停伞、荷伞、掷伞、拖伞、开山伞等动作,真切地表现出孤身行路时的惊惧、疑虑而又坚强的心情。《陈三五娘》"留伞"演陈三愤然而去,婢女益春苦苦挽留,通过陈三和益春对一把伞的争夺,表现了一个要去,一个要留的心理:陈三拾伞、荷伞欲走,益春追上挽伞,两个拉、挽各持一端;益春夺过伞,并置地下,陈三捡伞,益春踩伞,陈三手被压而缩,益春歉疚,陈三再拾伞、挟伞而行,益春夺伞,两人握伞绕圈,最后陈三将伞夺回,益春抢前握住伞柄,道出缘由。

福建戏曲常用身段动作来表现虚拟的实物,使观众如同身临其境。如表现"撑船"时,演员牢记"人在船上,船在水中",通过身段动作来表现本不存在的船(参见拙文《中国戏曲鉴赏》,《语文导读》,中国经济出版社1994年2月版)。如闽剧《渔船花烛》,玉珍上船时摇摇晃晃、小心翼翼地一步一步往前挪,表现出跳板之险;在船上,玉珍脚步趔趄,头碰船篷,表现出船的窄小和倍受风涛颠簸。竹马戏《搭渡弄》中,旦角左手模拟扶桨,身子微微倾斜,捧桨的手缩回胸前时,左脚垫在右脚跟下,左手推桨向外伸时,右脚跟垫在左脚跟下,表现了船在水中的动荡。再如表现坐轿行走,演员通过一系列动作,惟妙惟肖地表现出本不存在的轿,梨园戏《商辂》,演吴丞相乘轿上殿时,家院作掀轿动作,丞相双腿下蹲入轿,端坐轿内,家院则绕着四周忽快忽慢地行走,表现轿子以不同速度在行走。最为人称道的是莆仙戏《春草闯堂》"问证"中,知府让春草坐轿,自己步行相随,春草、知府、轿夫分别采用踏步、双跳步、双踏步、踩步、跕步、矮步、抽步、颠步等步法,逼真而生动地表现了上坡下坡、直跑转弯、涉水过沟等情形,使观众强烈地感受到轿子的存在。

四、绘画

福建画家可查考的主要在唐以后。据清代浙江海盐人黄锡蕃编撰的《闽中书画录》载,福建画家,计唐4人,五代1人,北宋五

12人，南宋24人，金2人，元20人，明408人，清188人，女画家24人，僧19人，道士18人，流寓7人，游宦35人，总802人。黄锡蕃曾游闽十年归，所引书籍327种，五易其稿而成此书，其记载当较为可靠。但黄锡蕃编此书时为嘉庆六至十二年(1801—1807年)，故之后的画家未编入。据有关资料考查，清代福建画家约300人，与明代相近。福建画家在分布上有两个特点，一是面广，几乎所有的县都出画家；二是画家群体只集中在几个主要县市。近人孙鼒所著《中国画家大辞典》(神州国光社1934年版)收入福建画家350人，据其载，福建画家最多集中在莆田，约50人，其次集中在福州(即侯官与闽县)，约40人，再次为晋江，约20人，邵武、诏安、沙县、建阳等各约15人。

福建画家最鲜明的特点是能融合各家之长，表现出极强的创造性。他们不墨守成规，敢于创新的特点，在中国历代画家中是很突出的。

宋代福建画家人数虽不多，却特点鲜明。建阳人惠崇擅长花鸟和山水，其画荒率虚旷，世称"惠崇小景"，充满江南牧歌式的情调，与南方山水画派同宗而异趣，其特点是作者将学禅妙悟后的神遇，借"小景山水"表达，别具灵寄，意境虚和萧散。传为其作的《溪山春晓图》，山峦朦胧，江水清澈，渔舟初放，飞鸟啼鸣，展示了江南水乡山村春天早晨时的秀丽景色。在构图上运用了平远法，山林连绵起伏，沙渚溪水相接。福唐(今福清)人陈容善画龙，或全体，或一爪一首，隐约不可名状。其《云龙图》中巨龙自高而下地盘旋于画面中，龙头昂仰，双目惊视，利爪奋攫，周身云翻雾滚，一片迷蒙，形象地表现出巨龙气吞万物、叱咤风云的气概。画幅右下角自题四行三言六句，可称诗、书、画三绝。这种三位一体的再现形式和手法，在南宋文人画中已开始出现，但为数很少，陈容则开元代以降普遍化的先河。

元代最著名的福建画家是由南宋入元的连江人郑思肖。入元后,他隐居不仕,其《墨兰图》花叶萧疏,画兰而不画土,寓意国土被异族践踏,兰花不愿生长其上。短茎小蕊的兰花,借助舒展之姿和浓重水墨,体现出刚劲和清雅之质。这种不着地、没有根的墨兰,是一个新的创造。"露根兰"由此成为一种绘画流派,在福建一直盛行到清末。

明代,许多福建画家以自己的创新丰富了中国绘画的宝库。沙县人边景昭精画禽鸟、花果,师南宋院画中工笔重彩一体,又有所创造。他注重对象的形神特征,其《竹鹤图》描绘溪水之畔,翠竹之间,两只丹顶白鹤悠闲而处的情景,神态生动自如。其《三友百禽图》绘入冬季节,百禽栖戏于梅松竹之间,它们或飞或鸣,或嬉或息,呼应顾盼,各尽其态。如此繁复的构图、众多的禽鸟在作者笔下穿插掩隐,多而不乱,这在南宋院体画派中是罕见的。莆田人李在吸收各家之长,又有创新。他的画细润处接近郭熙,豪放处似马远、夏圭。他在继承两宋院体画基础上又吸取元代文人画技法,对戴进和吴伟的画法也悉心学习,融会变化,自成风格。其《琴高乘鲤图》描绘神话故事中赵国人琴高欲离水中时和学生揖别的情景,虽然是以人物为主,但对自然环境也作了精彩描绘,在河水翻腾、野风狂裂、山动水跃的环境中,衬托了琴高乘鲤仙去的情景。因此,它也是一幅精妙的山水画。李在与明初画家马轼、夏芷根据东晋陶渊明的《归去来辞》一起创作了《归去来兮图》,其《抚孤松而盘桓》、《临清流而赋诗》等画,展示了广阔超脱的精神境界,在明初院体画中具有鲜明的特色。莆田人吴彬善画人物,擅长佛像,形态怪异,与前人迥然不同,自成门户。美国哈佛大学高居翰(James Chahill)教授将吴彬一些作品与17世纪初传到中国的一些西洋版画对照,认为吴彬的画必然受到西洋画的影响(参见 The Compelling Image,哈佛大学出版社1982年版),是有见地的。吴彬所绘的山水画是一种想像的主观世界,是梦境、幻影的综合,自然形态在他笔下都被夸张,改变了原形。其《仙山高士图》奇峰突起,云雾蒸腾,巨石团团,欲腾空而去,幻景般的世界,不存在人间。其《文杏双禽图》风格奇诡,他将水中鸳鸯画在树上栖息,文杏树情状奇特古朴,款印都署在最高的一枯树间,与明末文人画的习惯相异,具有强烈的个性。晋江人曾鲸对肖像画有独到贡献,能突破成法,创造出一种新的表现方法。《国朝画征录》说:"写真有两派:一重墨骨,墨骨既成,然后敷彩,以取气色之老少,其精神早传墨骨中矣,此闽中曾波臣(曾鲸)之学也;一略用淡墨勾出五官部位之大意,全用粉彩渲染,此江南画家之传法,而曾氏善矣。"前者为曾鲸始创,后者为传统与写真结合。据《无声诗史》载,曾鲸"每图一像,烘染数十层,必匠心而后止,其独步艺林,倾动遐迩,非偶然也"。这种创新的画法富有立体感,人称"凹凸法"。

清代,闽西出现了一些杰出的画家。长汀人上官周把他认为值得称颂的古人,创作了120幅人物白描,工夫老到,各具神态,于唐寅、仇英之外,另辟蹊径。其《晚笑堂画传》中的"王子安像",把王勃绘成眉目端秀、面颊丰满的形象,他身着宽袖长袍,赤足站在一片大芭蕉叶上,左手拿一柄大纨扇,右手托一只大酒杯,双眼似微睨。诗人似乎已喝了不少,但犹未尽兴,仍要喝下去。上官周抓住诗人恃才、嗜酒的特点,表现了诗人的放浪形骸和恃才傲世,将诗人仕途上不得志又不愿受羁绊等情感细腻含蓄地表达出来。上杭人华嵒绘画"无不标新领异,机趣天然"(秦祖永《桐阴绘画》),具有别开生面的绝技,在画坛上独树一帜。华嵒山的山水画由于注入了超脱尘世的思想,画面清净无尘,清明爽朗,有一种可望而不可即,可爱而不可求的境界。他的花鸟画具有意在其中,情见于外的艺术魅力,自成特色,达到了"并驾南田,超越流辈"(秦祖永《桐阴绘画》)的境界,开拓了由恽南田开创的、以北宋徐崇嗣没骨法为基础的新花鸟画创作道路,为清代中期花鸟画的新发展做出了贡献。其《山水图》,左方危崖屹立,其上林木扶疏;右方巨坡横卧,坡下拖沙垒石;崖坡之间江水萦回,远处山峦层叠。峻拔与舒缓,险与夷有机地统一在画面空间,了无痕迹。其《天山积雪图》描绘了一位牵驼的旅客在冰山雪岭间缓步行走的情景,一只孤雁横空而过,雁鸣声引起旅客和骆驼皆举首仰望。画面绝大部分布置高耸雪山和暗淡愁云,又使人感到在旅客寒驼脚下,长年积雪的天山是不足畏惧的。其《春水双鸭图》,描绘了两只游鸭在清碧见底的春水中嬉戏的情景:一鸭探身水中,瞪目求食;一鸭浮于水面,缩颈静观,双鸭动态新颖生动,神情活灵活现,生活情趣饶足。其《红叶画眉图》,将一只啭鸣枝头的画眉鸟表现得工致而又细腻,作者汲取了五代孟蜀宫廷画家黄筌工细写实的手法,却注入了自己淡泊、空疏、闲逸的气息情调,手法空灵巧妙而不失闷窒。其《鸟鸣秋树图》描绘一只画眉鸟栖止在秋树干上,引吭高鸣,表现出不畏秋霜的气概,下面的坚石和劲竹进一步强化和深化了这种豪迈气氛。小鸟和秋树以没骨法画成,别有一种柔和、蕴藉、闲逸的韵味。宁化人黄慎以人物画为最,早年以工笔为主,中年以后运用狂草笔法作画,把书法笔法和画法相结合,粗笔挥写,以简驭繁,形成于粗犷中见精练的艺术风格,独步画坛。其《驴背诗思图》为"减笔"之作,作者以枯笔干墨,以"柴笔描"画法,描绘了一个骑在驴背上的老诗人,左手捋着胡须,聚精会神地沉浸在构思中,人物形象简练生动。其《醉眠图》将人、葫芦、包裹和铁拐堆在一起,构成一个三角形。大葫芦仅用几笔线条勾出,化实为虚;铁拐李头部前额凸出,头发和眉毛用秃笔点刷,自然逼真,下垂的眼睑和肥大的酒糟鼻,淋漓尽致地表现了铁拐李于沉醉中的特有形象。其《苏武牧羊图》用半工带写笔调,以伤痕瘢剥却坚劲无比的老树、冰天雪地的恶劣环境,烘托鬓发、眉须尽白的苏武,造型极为写实。其《渔父图》中,一位身躯微曲、携着钓竿的渔父,手中拎着一尾活鱼,似在求人购买。作者用笔具有草书意味,笔法粗犷,挥洒自然。处理人物衣褶时连钩带染,渗透着笔情墨趣。

　　福建画家这种勇于创新的特点,主要与以下三个方面原因有关。

1.福建画家大多有外出的经历,生活阅历丰富,眼界开阔,故能融百家之长,独立机杼。福建画家的外出,主要有这几种途径:(1)应选。如明代遴选天下画家入京任职,福建画家应选者不少。沙县人边景昭曾任武英殿待诏,为宫廷作画,故有机会师南宋画院体格,最终成为明代早期画花鸟画高手。莆田人李在应召入京后,与戴进、谢环、石锐、周文靖同值仁智殿,互相学习,取长补短,甚至日本画僧雪舟亦与他切磋画艺,论者谓"当时戴进以下,一人而已"。闽县周文靖于庭试《枯木寒鸦图》,获第一而历官鸿胪序班。闽县的郑昭甫、邵武上官伯达、浦城詹林能等均曾应召到宫廷作画。(2)游历。福建人从山清水秀的南国,浏览异地,往往有自己特殊的发现,故能以独到的视角来表现所见景物。如北宋瓯宁(今建瓯)人徐竞曾遍游名山大川;南宋道士、闽清人葛长庚15岁后就遍游名山;上官周晚年曾游粤东。(3)任官。外出任官,丰富了画家们的生活,拓展了他们的视野。宦海无常,也加深了他们对事物的理解。如陈容曾为国子监主簿,出守莆田;吴彬曾任工部主事,后被捕入狱;明代晋江人张瑞图曾擢武英殿大学士,后被罢官。他们的绘画,都打上这段生活的印记。(4)流寓。特别明代之后,福建画家流寓外地不少,使他们有机会汲取各种营养。如明代莆田人宋玉、曾鲸都曾流寓金陵;华嵒曾流寓杭州、扬州,以卖画为生,黄慎也曾流寓金陵、扬州,他们被称为"扬州八怪"中的"二怪"。

2.家族、同乡、师生之间的承承相袭,有时青出于蓝,由此形成各类流派。福建画家中,有许多是父子、弟兄画家,如宋代莆田人林希逸、林泳父子,欧宁(今建瓯)人徐竞、徐德正兄弟,陈容、陈珩兄弟,明代建安人苏坤、苏钲父子,莆田人陈元藻、陈元衮兄弟,将乐人郑时敏、郑文英父子,福清人郑麟、郑环父子,闽县人周文靖、周鼎父子等。再加上同乡之间、师生之间的互相促进提携,形成了各种流派。如明初沙县人边景昭是明代花鸟画的鼻祖,其子楚祥,女婿张克信、外甥俞存胜，及同乡邓文明、罗织、刘琦、卢朝阳等都学他的风格，形成一股有影响的“沙县画风”。曾鲸（字波臣）的肖像画独步艺林，他收徒甚多，其弟子谢彬、金谷生、徐易、郭巩、沈韶、廖若可、刘祥生、张琦、张远、沈纪、徐璋等，都继承了他的画法，形成盛极一时的“波臣派”，至清康熙、乾隆之际，“波臣派”几乎一统肖像画坛。清初长汀人上官周注重人物传神，开创了“闽派”画风。其弟子黄慎不囿于老师的画技，认为“吾师绝技难以争名矣，志士当自立以成名，岂肯居人后哉？”志在创新，受到上官周的称赞。清道光、咸丰年间，诏安人谢颖苏、沈瑶池继承了上官周等闽人画法，以工笔画为基础，糅合写意笔墨，以孤冷淡雅自成一格，影响了福建画坛数十位画家，人称“诏安画派”，也称“闽派”。至近现代，福州林纾，仙游李耕，诏安马兆麟、林嘉等，都深受其影响。

3. 各种画论的流行。福建有文论兴盛的传统，画论也不逊色。福建画论内容驳杂。一是对福建画家的评议，如明代徐𤊹所编《闽画记》，清代林家溱、林汾贻所编《闽画记》等，对闽地画家的作品皆有精到的评议。二是为福建画家作传，如清代黄锡蕃所编《闽中书画录》。三是评论画理，如梁章钜的《退庵金石书画跋》，对画境有精到评论；四是将诗画合一评述，如李贽《焚书·诗画》，将诗画互相印证。五是各种文集中对绘画的评论。福建许多文人对绘画有独到的见解，这类文章大都收进他们的文集中，仅评宋代画家的就有李纲的《梁谿全集》、张元干的《芦川归来集》、朱熹的《朱文公文集》、刘克庄的《后村先生大全》、林希逸的《竹溪鬳斋续集》、陈旅的《安雅堂集》、黄镇成的《秋声集》等。

第五章　工艺

一、年画

　　除了装裱成卷轴或册页的"中国画"外,我国还有一种以工艺形式制作的年画,它主要供民间逢年过节新婚之用,有时也用于冥事活动,可以直接粘贴在土墙粉壁或门窗柜橱上。福建年画产地主要集中在泉州、漳州、福安、福鼎等地,以木版年画为主。雕前先将梨木、红柯木、石榴木等木板浸泡一个月,而后晾干制成平板,并将粉本反贴于平板上,干透后用墨鱼草将稿纸磨薄,使画稿反面线条清晰可见,然后再以刀刻之。福建年画内容丰富多彩,几乎涉及人们生活的各个方面,如神像门画、历史戏文、劝善讽世、男耕女织、添丁进财等。

　　漳州的年画最为有名,它既有北方年画之粗犷,又兼有江苏年画之秀丽,用色追求简明的对比,简朴遒劲,用线则根据内容和颜色,粗细迥异,印刷上采用"饾版印刷法",即分版分色来套印。在程式上先印色版,后印线板;并按时令用途,分红黑两种表现喜哀以应喜庆或丧事的不同需要。漳州年画口诀有"画一行,像一行,画中才有好名堂"之说,注重抓住人物身份的主要特征,不仅能栩栩如生地表现单张的内容,还能多张地演绎各种人物故事和民间故事,如八幅《孟姜女前本》年画,将孟姜女与丈夫成亲、丈夫被抓、她历经千辛苦寻夫的过程,生动地表现出来,画面深沉而又富有变化。如丈夫被抓之时,五个人物神态各异:孟姜女从家急步追出,双手向前,似要拽住已被扣住的夫君,脸呈焦急和哀愁;其夫双手被木枷枷住,但还频频回头,流露出对家庭的无限眷念;一差役一手提棍棒,一手牵住梏住孟夫的木枷,回头张望,显然是被孟姜女的叫声惊动;县官高举一令旗,以示不可违抗;另一差役在远处牵马,也回头张望,显然也被孟姜女的哭叫声打动。漳州年画还善于推陈出新,源于传统题材,但又有新的拓展。如《老鼠娶亲》是我国常见的年画题材,但漳州年画《老鼠娶亲》则又有一番风味:图中老鼠有捧鱼的、抱鸡的、吹喇叭的、吹笛子的、敲锣的、躺地以腿击鼓的、抬轿子的、拿仪仗开路的,个个尖腮细腿,憨态可掬。有意思的是新郎不是骑马而是步行,它头戴清朝官帽,手拿摺扇,急不可耐地回头顾盼新娘;新娘身着红装,坐在轿中,往新郎方向张望,神态极为可爱。

泉州年画则往往与乡间民俗结合在一起,如泉州李福记堂印制的《累积资金》图,以墨、绿、黄、红四色套版印制。中间有一黄古钱,上刻"累积资金"四字,由各身着云纹黄衣和绿花锦衣的两童子合捧。传说这两童子为"和合二圣",祀之可使人在万里之外,亦能回家。泉州人多远赴南洋,故最喜此图。再如李福记画店印制的《福禄寿星》图,以大红色为底,套以紫、黄、绿、粉红等各种颜色,中间为一手捧如意的天官,两仙女各擎障扇分立于左右;天官左方为怀抱一子的禄星,右边为手托仙桃的老寿星;前有一头戴紫金冠、手举绣球的童子。全图给人以吉祥和睦、喜意盎然之感,故深受南洋华人的欢迎。福鼎的年画也别具一格,如取材于《说岳全传》的年画《八锤大闹朱仙镇》,图中岳云、何元庆、狄雷、严正方各举双锤围战手持双枪的陆文龙,金兀术头戴夏帽,斜披马褂,在后观阵。间隙中,露出王佐半个脸。全图外缘,画一簪花美人斜倚于一琴几之上,后有盆景,碧草茂生,这种美人与武打同出一图的处理,为其他各地年画所罕见。福鼎年画《小上坟》取材于民间传说：刘禄敬入京应试中举后未归，其妻萧素贞疑已亡为其上坟，后刘任县令返家途中遇一孝服女子哭祭于荒冢间，审之才知是妻。图中刘禄敬戴团纱，穿官衣，萧素贞穿大襟清装，头扎素巾，手举香烛祭盘，后有二衙役，绘刻精美，为年画中的孤本妙品。

二、石雕

　　福建最著名的石雕是惠安石雕和寿山石雕。惠安石雕包括建筑装饰、人物、动物、用具等。海内外许多地方都可看到惠安石雕艺人的精工之作：南京中山陵前的华表、台湾龙山寺的八对大龙柱、厦门南普陀的装饰石雕、集美陈嘉庚陵园的石雕人物、北京人民大会堂的柱座、台湾鹰灵山的庙宇和五百罗汉、日本鉴真和尚墓园、太湖大型壁画、福州西禅寺全国第一高的报恩塔……包罗万象。惠安石雕共分四大类：1. 圆雕。即将石头上下左右镂空成型，再用其中的碎石雕成附件，如口含可滚动石珠的狮子，人称南狮。还如日本式的石灯笼，大小不一，有几百种样式。圆雕中许多精品令人叹为观止，如《鹰蛇搏斗》，鹰的利爪钳住蛇腰，蛇的后半身缠住鹰腿，而头对峙，利爪凝聚铁的力量，舌头吐出火的气势，倚在云片上，给人以凌空、惊险之感。2. 浮雕。即在石板面上精雕细刻，使形象凸起，有立体感，主要用于建筑物的装饰，如门窗、柱、墙面塔等。厦门集美鳌园内建筑雕刻，均采用浮雕技法刻成，各种花鸟虫鱼、飞禽走兽、花卉树木、山水风光、历史人物……姿态纷呈，栩栩如生，琳琅满目。名雕《剑舞》，刻画古代少女舞弄宝剑的神态，舞姿轻盈，横空劈出的利剑长半尺许，宽不过半公分，两条蝴蝶结式的镂空缨带飘逸在剑柄下。3. 沉雕。即形象下凹，线条分明，大多用于雕刻文字、花卉、图案，作为碑类、建筑局部装饰处理。著名的如《四季小屏》，由一块青石加工并连在一起的四块小屏，刻下四季花纹和文字，图文并茂，小巧玲珑。4. 影雕。即将精良青石锯成

1厘米多厚的薄石片,磨光上灰后使其变成黑色,然后再用大小不同的锋利钢针,在石片上精心雕琢。凭借钻点的疏密大小、深浅将图像显示出来。影雕既能再现摄影细腻写实的效果以及体现中国画用墨浓淡枯润的特点,又能较好地表现原作的意境。一些作品,如雄伟的万里长城,古朴的泉州东西塔,徐悲鸿的奔马、齐白石的对虾等,都细腻逼真,具有传神之趣。

寿山石雕因所用石材产于福州市郊寿山而得名。寿山石石质脂润,斑斓多姿,颜色有朱、紫、青、黄、黑、白等,也有一块石上五彩皆有。寿山石雕在1500年前就已问世,南朝墓葬中出土的寿山石雕"卧猪"形象逼真,雕工简朴。唐代已用寿山石刻制佛像、香炉、念珠等宗教用品。宋代由官府组织作坊刻制各种寿山石俑,供官僚贵族作殉葬品。元明之际,石雕艺人创造出独具一格的印钮雕刻艺术。清代是寿山石雕的鼎盛期,各种艺术流派争奇斗艳,或纯朴深厚,或精巧玲珑,精品多为宫廷所收藏。在北京故宫博物院秘藏的寿山石雕中,著名的如九龙章:在一块印钮上端,雕刻了神态各异、变化多端的璃龙、黄龙、亢龙、烛龙、蟠龙、虾龙、鳌龙、夔龙,图的四周又雕了博古图案。寿山石雕分圆雕、浮雕、镂雕、薄意和印钮五大类,有花果、人物、动物、古兽、山水等陈列品,也有印章、文具、烟具、花瓶等用品,品种近千种。其中以具有闽南特色的荔枝、雪藕、佛手、蟹篓、葡萄等为题材的装饰品最为有名。寿山石雕艺术特色是"石",即根据石质、石纹、石形和石色来选择与之相适应的题材,也称"因势造型",有"一相抵九工"之说。现陈列于人民大会堂福建厅的"求偶鸡",利用石料的红色部分刻一雄踞在竹笼上的垂翅的公鸡,笼内母鸡跃跃欲动,四周小鸡唧唧觅食,惟妙惟肖,意趣盎然。

三、木雕

福建盛产林木,民间木雕颇为盛行,最早源于建筑装饰、神像、日用家具雕刻。如泉州开元寺 24 尊雕附在斗拱面的"飞天乐伎"，是罕见的木雕珍品；在许多住宅完全外露的梁架、托架、椽头、门窗、隔扇等处，精雕刻细的故事图案随处可见。一些用具，如永春銮轿，与雕刻技艺融为一体，将分块的雕刻进行整体拼装，轿围上刻满的人物、动物栩栩如生，木雕正面巧妙地用浮雕衔接，虚实疏密得当。闽东的床雕，常以戏文故事为内容，床内有柜，一个柜面就雕一幅图案，有的一张古式床就近 30 块木雕图案，构图与情节均为连续性的戏文。福建木雕以后逐步发展成为独立的木雕工艺品种，龙眼木是主要木雕材料之一。由于龙眼木质地略脆，纹理细密，故适于雕刻。龙眼木雕作品磨光后用皂矾水洗净树脂，晾干后可染成龙眼核、荔枝核、古铜、桔柚黄等颜色，涂上漆后永不退色。此外，还有樟木、楠木、红木、杉木等，也多作为雕刻材料。明末清初长乐人孔氏，利用一些年深日久、沉入溪底被流水冲刷，或暴露地面、经风霜雨露侵蚀而形成的形态怪异的树根，制成天然根雕作品。之后，根雕技艺渐有发展。艺人根据天然疤树的自然疤、纹、凹、凸、弯曲、线条等各种形状，构思主题，因材施艺；艺术上讲求斧痕凿韵，并饰以原漆，使作品达到天然与人工的统一，古拙、质朴、简练，富有意境和神韵。清代福州木雕有三个主要流派：以大坂村艺人陈天赐为代表的大坂村派，约 30 多人，主要雕刻弥勒佛、十八罗汉、八仙、观音、仙女、仕女、动物等；以雁塔乡王清清为代表的雁塔派，主要擅长雕刻图案花纹，以及与漆器相结合的浮雕花鸟；以象园村柯庆元为代表的象园村派，擅长创作虫草花卉、果盘等。前辈艺人柯世仁，擅雕佛像，善于根据黄杨、红木等材料特性，运用劈、削、雕、剔等各种手法，集传统技法之大成。艺人陈望道，在人物眉、眼、鼻、手足、衣褶、服饰等雕刻技艺上，又有进一步的发挥创造。

四、木偶

福建木偶戏的精华所在是木偶头,它不仅是舞台演出用品,也是一种精致的民间工艺品,可供案头陈设。福建木偶头,有采用"梨园戏脸谱"的泉州木偶头,采用"京剧脸谱"的石码木偶头,采用和以汉调"客家调脸谱"的漳州木偶头这三大类,其中以泉州木偶头最为出色。泉州木偶头的制作工艺颇为复杂,要先将樟木锯成木偶头大小的木坯,划出面部中线,将两颊削斜,定出五官,雕成各种人物形象的白坯;接着裱褙棉纸,磨光,彩绘脸谱,盖腊;最后上发髻、胡须等。早期泉州木偶以"西来意"的佚名工艺师、"周冕号"的黄良师、黄才师等最为出名,他们的作品形象逼真、性格突出,面谱造型、粉彩都具有鲜明的民族特色。青年男女两颊丰满,正派人物龙眉凤眼,颇有宋画风格。现代著名木偶头制作艺人江加走住泉州北门花园头,故人称他木偶为"花园头"。江加走创造了二百几十余种不同性格的木偶形象,数以万件,他吸收了民间木雕神像和戏曲脸谱的表现技法,融"西来意"、"周冕号"长处于一体,并将雕刻与绘画巧妙地结合起来,用绘画的加工与渲染来反衬人物的性格。他常用夸张变形的手法来表现人物形象,如第一号丑角"大头"的额头比脸部的下半段大了近三倍,额头上半部涂以朱红,下半部绘以对衬的飞扬皱纹,黑森森、圆滚滚的眼珠与眼白、眉毛形成强烈的黑白对比,再配上粗黑的胡须,一幅凶神恶煞的模样。江加走善于创造富有个性特征的人物形象,如他认为媒婆的笑是言不由衷的,其内心是痛苦的,所以他创造的媒婆,两片薄嘴能开能合,嘴角上有个长毛黑痣,面容消瘦,额头眼角浮现几道皱纹,太阳穴上有两片头晕膏。这个整日用心良苦,善于随机应变的媒婆是个既被鞭挞,又值得同情的形象。江加走创造的"白阔"头,额头部皱纹上下左右各两条,有嘴唇般粗。不这么粗,传不了神。整个头部细眼睛、大鼻子、银白色的长眉沿脸颊而下,一幅慈祥、安宁而又充满智慧的老者形象。一些丑行人物,多是"缺嘴"、"斜目"、"黑阔"等,使人一见便知是狡猾、愚笨的角色。根据剧情需要,他制作的某些木偶头,眼珠能够上下、左右移动,嘴巴、鼻子、舌头能转动,做到忠良、权奸各有性格。

五、剪纸

剪纸在福建甚为普遍,各地都有剪纸的习俗。它是农村妇女所热爱的一种民间艺术,也有其广泛的用途:它用作节日的窗花、墙花、门头花,婚娶陪嫁物品上的喜花,节日敬祖求神祭奠物品上的供花,孝敬长辈礼物上的"寿花"等。其手法多种多样,主要的如平铺式、对称式、多折式、网络式等。福建剪纸比较突出的有泉州、漳浦、柘荣、浦城等地。

泉州剪纸相传始于唐代而盛于宋代,春节时流行刻"红笺",如"福符"一般贴在厅门上楣,五张一堂,宽四寸,长六七寸,刻成麒麟、鲤鱼跳龙门或"福"、"寿"字样,四周饰以古钱图案,"长金"则宽二寸,长六寸,刻作喜鹊登梅、五谷丰登等,一般贴在房门上楣;有的剪纸还作为灯花带雅入俗。漳浦剪纸在北宋时就流传于民间,史志有"元夕张灯烛,剪纸为花,备极工巧"的记载。剪纸在漳浦被称为"铰花",它以"鸳鸯"、"龙凤"、"牡丹"、"鱼草"、"蝙蝠"、"鹿"等组成鞋花、肚围花、猪头花,表示吉祥如意。它具有浓厚的生活气息和乡土情趣,内容也多取之于人们喜闻乐见的题材,如花鸟、走兽、民间故事、戏剧和历史人物等。其最鲜明的特点是风格纤细秀丽、典雅大方。剪纸艺人运用"排剪"将细若发丝的线条成排成组排列,由此表现孔雀的羽毛、龙的麟片、牡丹的花瓣、松树的松针,以及其他动物的毛、羽等,精巧生动。柘荣剪纸风格粗犷而抽象,常用夸张的手法表现一只虾、一尾鱼、一朵花、一片叶等。鞋帽花是柘荣剪纸中常见的一种形式,剪法明朗、简洁,用做刺绣的底样。柘荣剪纸的随意性很强,几种技巧综合应用,如以猪蹄形状为外廓,内剪各种花卉的"蹄包花"剪纸,既采用对折式,又应用多折式,将所剪之物表现得恰到好处。浦城剪纸也有多年历史,清梁章钜曾任浦城南浦书院讲席七年,他在《归田琐记》中描绘了所见的浦城剪纸:"常见人家馈赠果品,无论大盘小盒,其上每加红纸一块,或方或圆,必嵌空剪雕四字好语,如长命富贵,诸事如意类,其婚娶喜庆之家,所用尤繁。"浦城剪纸样式多样,大小不拘,或方或圆,或菱或长,大则盈天,小则一寸;常常是画中有物,物中有字,具有独特的风格。

六、陶瓷

福建烧制陶瓷历史悠久,在商周时代,福建先民已烧制原始青瓷。崇安汉城发掘出的具有闽越风格的原始青瓷,可看出战国至秦汉福建闽越古国烧制陶瓷工艺已有一定水平。福建境内出土的宋以前的士族墓葬中的精美瓷器,反映出魏晋南北朝至隋唐五代福建陶瓷已达相当高的水平。宋元明清,福建瓷器名声鹊起,不仅走向全国,并大量出口到世界各地,成为收藏家注目的珍品。福建瓷器是在本土发展起来的,无论原始瓷、青瓷、青白瓷、黑白瓷、白瓷、青花瓷,都极具福建地方特色。在长期的发展过程中,也受到外地烧制工艺的影响,使其日臻精美。福建地下古窑址几乎遍布全省,其数量之多,在全国名列前茅。

福建陶瓷最有代表性的是宋代建阳水吉建窑的黑釉器,元明间德化窑的白釉器和明清时期德化窑、安溪窑、平和窑的青花瓷器。

宋代建阳水吉建窑的黑釉器颜色碧丽奇特,其釉色变化有纯黑色釉、兔毫釉、鹧鸪斑釉、油滴釉、曜变釉和杂色釉六种,质感温润晶莹。最主要的黑釉器,是一种底小口大、形如漏斗的小碗,有敞口和弇口两种,以弇口为多,俗称"建盏"。其造型优美,釉色润净,乌光发亮,漆黑的釉上闪现出一条条银光闪闪的细毫,状如兔毫,故也称"兔毫盏"。釉下毫纹,是利用酸性釉料所生成的酸化痕迹作装饰,因建窑瓷皆仰烧,釉水下垂,成品口缘釉色浅。由于器壁斜度不同,流速快成纤细毫纹;流速稍慢则粗,就成兔毫之状。"建盏"另一特征是沿口较薄,而器身较厚重,特别从腹部至圈足底周最厚,有的器物胎厚达1厘米,有的底足内有"进琖岠"、"供御"等字,是朝廷贡品。"建盏"曾作为珍宝被带到日本,目前作为日本"国宝"级文物而藏于东京静嘉堂文库的"曜变"瓷碗,高6.8厘米,口径12厘米,造型厚重,外壁釉色黑而发亮,在碗内圆圆的黑色盏体上,环列着大大小小的油滴斑点,散开或汇成的形如云朵或卵形的蓝色结晶体。体周生晕,闪闪如同天上的群星,少数还放出微弱的射线。

元明间德化窑的白釉器俗称"建白",其滋润明亮,滑腻坚实,洁白中微见淡黄,纯净无瑕,光洁如绢。胎、釉浑然一体,温润晶明,无须任何色彩和装饰,却典雅隽永,饶有余韵,美如脂玉,又似奶油、象牙。在光线映照下,通体呈乳黄或牙红半透明,故又被称为"奶油白"、"象牙白"、"中国白",为当时中国白瓷的代表作品。产品以宗教塑像最为突出,如观音、释迦牟尼、弥勒、达摩等,面部刻画细腻,衣纹深而洗练,能很好地表现人物性格。其他产品还有梅花杯、八仙杯、仿青铜香炉、花瓶、文具等。用低铝高硅的"象牙白"制作的观音,有一种特殊的恬静美感,造型端庄慈祥,使信徒自愿敞开灵魂心扉,皈依于她足下,具有非凡的艺术魅力。如现藏于广东博物馆、明代何朝宗制的白瓷观音坐像,高22.5厘米,观音左手持经书,姿态随意地倚坐在山石上,略微俯首,双目稍合,形态极为慈祥;头挽高髻,素洁的长衣广袖垂拂于盘曲的左腿之上,右腿竖曲,双手随意放在竖起的右腿膝上,衣纹疏朗流畅,姿态自然悠闲。现藏于泉州市海交史博物馆的渡海观音塑像,亦为明代何朝宗制,身高46厘米,观音发结髻,项披巾,衣褶深秀,带作结状,双手藏袖作左拱势,露一足踏莲花,另一足被水花掩盖,双目低垂,嘴角深晰,紧闭双唇,浮现一丝若隐若现笑意。1980年人民美术出版社出版的《中国古代雕塑百图》中,收有一尊流落国外的明代德化窑的坐岩观音,观音身披白衣,坐在岩石上,左肘撑着岩石,双臂相抱,头微俯,闭目凝思,面庞丰满秀润,低垂的双眼显得端庄、娴静、凝重。作者将传说中观音温柔的性情、贤淑的品格、善良的心地、高尚的德操形象逼真地表现出来。

　　明清时期福建的青花瓷器,主要产于德化窑和安溪窑。德化窑青花瓷器品种有碗、盘、杯、碟、瓶、炉、尊等,其特点是青花中有深蓝色的线痕,胎体坚白细腻,釉色或幽青淡雅,或明快浓艳。青花瓷器的图案题材丰富,如山水人物、花卉鸟兽、草木虫鱼等,纹饰运笔婉转自如,自然洒脱,疏密有致,构图简洁舒展,画风朴实,图案活泼清晰,充满生机,具有淳朴、浓郁的生活气息。福建博物馆收藏的一件清代德化窑山水瓶,上绘古树参天,小楼于起伏山峰边隐出一小部分,远处重峦叠嶂,显出深远的意境。德化青花瓷器的人物题材也细腻传神,福建省博物馆收藏的一件清代德化窑青花山水人物盘,图案中小姐右手臂曲起掌心托住下颌凝思,眼望远方,像在期盼着什么;贴身丫头双手捧琴回头顾盼;湖岸杨柳依依,湖心半岛宝塔玲珑,远处山峰耸峙,浮云堆积。安溪窑青花瓷器常见的有碗、盒、盘、碟等,碗的造型有模印成菊瓣状的,也有外印重叠菊瓣纹、内刻缠枝花卉的。盒子有大小各种式样,盒外多模印纹样,有的在盒外底印有花卉纹,印纹线条比德化窑同类产品粗。青花蓝色较浓,釉里泛黑,常见的图案为植物中的牵牛花、菊花、兰、竹、梅、松等,也有山水,如溪山、舟楫、树石等,还有少量的"福"、"禄"、"寿"文字。

　　福建陶瓷业的繁荣,除了与生活所需有关外,还与以下几个方面有关:1.得天独厚的资源。福建瓷土矿藏丰富,林木茂盛,燃料充足,且溪河交错,便于利用水力资源陶洗瓷土,也便于外运,具有发展各类瓷器的优越条件。2.民俗的影响。如名冠全国的建阳

"兔毫盏"的研制,就与宋代士大夫品茶赋诗消遣的斗茶习俗有关。
椐北宋蔡襄《茶录》说"茶色白,宜黑盏。建安所造者绀黑,纹如兔
毫,其坏微厚,烧之久热难冷,最为要用。出他处者,或薄或紫,皆
不及也。其青白盏,斗试自不用。"可见,斗茶者最看重的是建窑的
"兔毫盏"。3. 信仰的影响。如泉州在宋元被称为"泉南佛国",因
此德化窑、安溪窑生产了大量的佛教人物瓷器,一些观音、如来、达
摩、罗汉等佛像成为传统产品的代表。像德化窑,仅观音就有72
种姿态造型,大小规格 200 多种,千姿百态,各具特色。4. 对外贸
易的需要。福建泉州宋元时期为贸易大港,明代万历时期是闽南
国际贸易全盛时期,目前东亚、东南亚等地区不少国家都发现了大
量的福建陶瓷。陶瓷大量出口,它成为产瓷地区人民的重要经济
来源,不仅满足了国外的需要,也直接推动了制瓷工业的发展。

第六章　民族

福建省是以汉族为主体的多民族散杂居省份。全省有 50 多万少数民族人口，有 53 个少数民族成分，占全省人口总数的 1.54%，为华东地区少数民族人口比例最多的省份。世居福建的少数民族主要有畲族、回族、高山族、满族、蒙古族等。全省少数民族万人以上的县有 14 个，千人以上的乡有 85 个，民族乡有 17 个，少数民族聚居的行政村有 444 个。

畲族是福建省少数民族主体，人口 38 万，为全国最多，占全国畲族总人口的 57%。福建省 17 个民族乡中，有 16 个是畲族乡。福建畲族居住为大分散，小集中，主要分为四大社区，即：闽西社区，包括现在的龙岩和三明市南部的畲族社区，这是最古老的畲族聚居地；闽南社区，主要指漳州畲族社区，这是畲族早期聚居地，也是历史上畲族活动最活跃的地区；闽东北社区，指现在宁德市和福州北部的畲族社区，是目前福建主要的畲族居住地，其中宁德市畲族人数占全省畲族总人数的 60%，他们都完整地保留了畲族文化习俗；闽中社区，指莆田市和福州南部的畲族社区，这是畲族迁徙的中转站。

畲族是福建一个古老民族，迄今已有千余年历史。畲族宗族活动是以血统关系和族缘关系为基础的，正如畲谚所说："山哈，山哈，不是同宗就是叔伯。""山哈"是畲族人的自称。畲族村寨乡以血缘相近的同姓聚族而居,一般同姓不婚,都在本民族内部盘、蓝、雷、钟四姓中自相婚配。畲族没有本民族文字,通用汉文。畲族民间盛传盘瓠传说,把盘瓠描绘成神奇、英勇的民族英雄,尊称"忠勇王",推崇为畲族始祖。畲族把盘瓠传说按情节绘成40幅左右连环式画像,称为祖图,每逢祭祖时必悬挂出来,以供祀奉。

福建畲族服饰具有浓郁的民族特色,其中以畲族妇女的"凤凰装"最具特色:畲族妇女喜爱用红头绳包扎头髻,高高盘在头上,称为"凤凰髻";衣裳、围裙上刺绣着各种彩色花边,镶绣着金丝银线,象征着凤凰的颈、腰和美丽的羽毛;后腰随风飘动的金黄色腰带,象征着凤凰的尾巴。畲族的许多工艺品也具有浓郁的民族特色。

福建畲族民间文学绚丽多彩,畲族民间流传着许多富有民族特色的民间故事,著名的如:"畲族祖宗的传说"、"高辛和龙王"、"三公主的凤冠"等,叙述畲族祖先怎样创家立业和反抗侵略者,内容简单却又朴素优美。畲族是个能歌善舞的民族,山歌是畲族人民最喜爱的一种音乐形式,闽东畲族聚居区经常举行盘诗会("盘"为反复之意,一般为二人可唱),每逢良辰佳节、喜庆盛会、客来客往时,多有歌会,畲族男女盛装赴会盘歌。畲族人民在唱山歌时无须伴奏,最常见也最精彩的是对歌,往往由男女双方对唱,对方可以各唱一条,也可以各唱多条。盘唱活动常在庭院、山野、村头、大厅和宗祠内举行,有来客对歌、拦路对歌、摆擂台对歌、做表姐和做亲家伯对歌、喜庆对歌和歌节歌会对歌等多种形式。福建畲族人民擅长于二声部重唱的唱法,人们称它为"双音"。这是1958年我国著名音乐家郑小瑛在闽东畲族区发现的,郑小瑛称这种唱法为我国民歌中一颗"稀有的明珠"。畲族的传统舞蹈与祭祀活动、婚丧节庆、生产劳动关系密切,许多舞蹈都由习俗性舞蹈和祭祀性舞蹈发展演变而来。

畲族独有的民族节日为每年三月三举行的染乌米饭祭祀祖先,每年农历夏至后的"辰"日举行的"封龙节"等。一些社区也有节日,如闽东的畲族同胞,每年农历二月二都要到福鼎双华村和福安后门坪的鼓楼山上举行庙会,称为"会亲节"。

回族在福建有 10 多万人,目前有惠安百崎回族乡。福建回族来源广泛,居住相对集中的有四个社区,即:闽南泉州社区,包括泉州、晋江陈埭、惠安百崎等地的回族社区,其先辈大多从海上丝绸之路而来,人称"海回",以区别陆上来的回民,为中国回族发祥地之一;闽南厦门社区,其先辈主要为明清两代全国各地移居来此经商的回民;闽北邵武社区,其先辈主要为外省来福建任职的回族将领及所带的兵士;福州社区,其先辈主要为全国各地因受聘、投亲、居官等迁移来福州的回民。福建回族分布广,居住分散,多次迁移是一个最主要原因,或因避难,或因垦殖,或因从商而不断迁移,不仅大大削弱了原聚居点的力量,而且由于迁移面过广,也不可能形成强大的聚落。

党中央和各级领导高度重视民族政策在福建的落实。十一届三中全会以来,叶飞、曾志、李岚清、温家宝、司马义·艾买提、布赫等领导都曾深入民族社区调查。福建省委、省政府高度重视民族工作,多次召开专题会研究解决福建民族工作中的问题,推进了福建民族地区各项事业的发展和进步。

民族地区发展的关键在于当地劳动者素质的提高,在于拥有急需的建设人才,"教育先行"至关重要。福建省教委制定了一系列措施来促进保证少数民族教育发展,各级政府也多次拨出专款支持民族教育。有效的措施使福建民族教育空前发展。全省现有民族中学 12 所,民族小学 800 多所,少数民族学龄儿童入学率达 97%,普及率、巩固率、升学率与当代汉族地区水平基本接近。民族地区的职业教育也粗具规模,培养了大批经济建设急需人才。宁德地区民族中学至今已有 40 年的历史,目前成为可直接向高校保送新生的省级重点中学。近年来,民族中学每年都有 150 多名高中毕业生被高等院校录取,录取率占应届高中毕业生总数的

80％左右,几乎所有全国重点大学毕业生都有民族中学的校友。宁德市从村到市委、市政府一级的少数民族干部有90％是从地区民族中学毕业的,他们已成为各条战线的骨干力量。

改革开放以来,民族地区医疗卫生条件有了很大改善,17个民族乡都兴建了卫生院,一些民族村办起了卫生所,民族地区共有各类医务人员350名。福建省两次召开民族医药工作会议,专门为有关民族乡卫生院病房改建拨款,进一步推动了民族乡卫生院基础设施的配套和完善。福建省民委和福建省委统战部联合组织了省民主党派医疗专家到福安、宁德两市少数民族聚居乡村义诊,义诊人数达4000多人次。民族地区注意挖掘传统医药,闽东畲族总结出一套富有民族特色的治病方法,如擅长用"捏"、"抓"、"排"、"刮"和针刺疗法治痧症,用草药秘方治不孕症,以及正骨疗伤和食物疗法等。近几年整筛选出畲族单验方300多帖,积极推进了当地畲汉人民的医疗保健。

福建民族地区的文化生产丰富多彩。全省曾多次举办少数民族文艺调演,各民族代表队登台献艺,观众大饱眼福,闽东还多次举办畲族歌会和畲族艺术节,以歌以舞会友。闽东畲族歌舞团北上南下,饮誉北京、广东、澳门、新加坡等地,经文艺工作者的多年挖掘、抢救、整理、创作的畲族民间音乐舞蹈节目共100多个,其中畲族舞蹈《丰收喜》、《欢乐的鸭姑》、《晨曲》、《织裙带》、《走嫁舞》、《山哈带》等多次在全国和省、地文艺演出中获奖。民族地区的文化站开展各种娱乐活动,为民族地区的精神文明活动做出了贡献。民族地区的文化得到进一步的挖掘整理,近几年先后出版了畲族歌谣、畲族故事和畲族谚语,一些民族地区的县市和乡镇编撰了志书,有的志书以其鲜明的特色获省社会科学优秀成果奖。由福建省民委创办的《福建民族》至今已出版46期,发表了大量有独到见解的文章,受到广大读者喜爱,进一步推动了福建省的民族工作。

为了推动民族地区体育活动,福建省以省民委为主体,成立了省少数民族体育协会。近几年来,曾多次举办全省民族运动会。
1995年11月,福建省派出畲族、高山族、回族、满族等少数民族共
114人组成的代表团赴昆明参加全国第五届民族运动会,进行了
龙舟赛等5个项目的竞赛和畲族打枪担、高山族竿球等6个项目
的表演,获得多项奖,取得华东地区最好成绩。民族地区群众体育
活动开展得十分活跃,如流行于闽东畲族村寨一种以木棍击竹条
的体育活动"打尺寸",成为人们喜爱的体育项目。福鼎市番溪乡
的棍术"盘柴槌",罗源县八井村畲族的"井拳"术,福安县金斗洋的
"畲家拳"等,都得到进一步挖掘和整理,成为中华武术百花园中的
奇葩。

要使民族地区经济腾飞,培养少数民族干部至为关键。福建
省多次召开专门会议,研究对少数民族干部的培养和选拔。1995
年,福建省委组织部、统战部及省民委共同制定了《福建省1995
年——2000年培养选拔少数民族干部工作规划》,对培养少数民
族干部提出了具体目标和要求。这一系列有力措施不断加强了少
数民族干部培养选拔力度,逐步形成了一个有利于少数民族干部
队伍健康成长的良好环境。各级部门积极选拔民族干部赴京和到
省内有关县、乡挂职、交流,从培养、选拔、使用三个环节使少数民
族干部队伍建设落到实处。全省17个民族乡基本配备了少数民
族领导干部,20个民族工作重点县县级领导班子大多配备了少数
民族领导干部。全省现有少数民族干部近8 000人,占全省干部
总数的0.96%,有48位少数民族同志当选为省级人大代表和政
协委员,分别占代表、委员总数的5.01%和3%。

"发展才是硬道理"。为了促进民族地区的经济发展,福建省
委、省政府于1994年4月提出了《关于加强民族工作的若干意
见》,要求全省各级领导从政治、经济和社会稳定发展的战略高度,
充分认识发展民族地区经济的重要性和迫切性。省委省政府还成
立了少数民族地区工作协调委员会,成员由省里有关厅局领导组

成。各级领导在制定本地发展战略规划时，都把少数民族地区发展摆上重要位置，逐步增加投入，在使用安排事业费专款时按"同等优先"原则，向民族地区倾斜。

改革开放以来，福建民族乡经济发生了根本变化。如 1997年，17 个民族乡工农业总产值达 39 亿元，农民人均收入 2 596 元。福建民族经济结构，初步形成了以工业开发为主、以农业开发为主、工农结合开发等三种经济模式。以工业开发为主的经济模式，如惠安百崎乡以制鞋业为主，兼有橡塑制品、机械制造、化工、模具加工、纸制品、交通运输业等，现有企业 138 家，年产值超过 1 000万元的有 15 家，人均产值居全县第一。福安市坂中畲乡以建立电机电器工业小区为龙头，共发展企业 237 家，1996 年产值达 3 亿多元。宁德市金涵畲族乡以发展工业为突破口，大力发展集体、个体、股份合作企业，建立两个小区，形成了以建材加工为龙头，其他各业并举的产业结构。1996 年乡镇企业产值达 2.16 亿元。漳浦县湖西畲族乡开发了金鲤工业区，引进了 7 家外资企业。目前外资企业已向食品加工、农产品加工、石板材加工、矿山开发等多元化发展。以农业开发为主的经济，主要重视发展多种经营，改变传统以种植业为主的内部结构，大搞农业综合开发。如永安市青水畲族乡利用山区生态环境，培育反季节蔬菜，在稳定粮食产量同时，发展农作物制种业和庭院经济。漳浦县赤岭畲族乡创办高优农业开发区，大面积种植荔枝、龙眼等名优果树，逐步形成高产优质的水果基地，目前已实现人均 2 亩的目标，水果产量达 1.5 万吨。

在经济大潮冲击下，一些民族地区建立了民族经济开发区。如福安西部的穆阳民族经济开发区，发挥民族特色，开发出民族风情商贸街、闽东最大茶叶交易和木材交易中心，形成了茶叶、餐饮、服装、日用品等系列贸易市场，发展了一大批股份合作制企业，全区脱贫率达 98.7%。福安在城阳乡铁福民族村建立了铁福经济开发区,引进汽车配件、修车、住宿、饮食、加油等综合配套一条龙服务的汽车旅馆项目,辐射带动了整个区的经济发展。晋江陈埭四境回族村是全省著名的亿元村,也是著名的鞋乡,商业区中的鞋材两条街,经营者高达 200 多户,300 多个店面。越来越多民族乡的少数民族开始弄潮商品经济,他们走出山区跑买卖,足迹遍及中国。昔日封闭的民族社区走出一批颇有现代经营意识的商人。

民族社区注意利用人文资源开发旅游业,并逐渐使其成为新的经济增长点。1995 年 11 月在闽东举办的闽东畲族风情旅游节,进一步引起民族地区对旅游业的关注。如龙海市隆教畲族乡利用本乡 1920 年前喷发的古火山口、素有“闽山第一峰”之称的南太武山、保留完好的明代镇海卫古城等,投资 150 万元开发“天下第一滩度假村”、“古火山口乐园”、“镇海卫古城风景区”、“南太武山风景区”等四大景区,并成立了“旅游开发办”、“旅游公司”、“双海公司”等管理机构和经营实体,新发展旅游服务第三产业 100 多家,年产值 1 200 多万元。旅游业将成为隆教畲族乡的支柱产业。一些民族乡开发旅游资源也获得可喜成就,如宁德市金涵畲族乡建造的“中华畲族宫”,连江小沧乡淳朴的畲族风情和秀丽的湖光山色,惠安百崎回族乡的伊斯兰建筑一条街,漳浦湖西畲族乡的赵家堡,蓝鼎元、蓝廷珍府第建筑群,上杭红土地文化等。

要想致富,科技为要。各级领导十分重视在民族乡加强科技应用的指导和科技的投入,多次举办各种类型的科技培训班,千方百计地把针对性强的实用技术推广到各民族乡。在省科委的大力支持下,全省积极开展了民族科技示范乡工作,已有 8 个民族乡被列入省科委的科技示范乡系列,进一步促进了少数民族和民族地区的脱贫致富。为了增加经济发展的后劲,民族地区各级部门都倾注了大量资金加强基础设施的建设,使民族区水、电、路等方面有了很大改观。民族村通路率达 78.5%,通电率达 100%,有 20 多万少数民族群众饮用上清洁水,近一半民族村开通了程控电话。

一些先富起来的民族乡更是重视基础设施的建设,如惠安百崎回族乡仅 1997 年就投入 180 万元兴建自来水厂,共投入 200 多万元改造拓宽乡中的公路。漳浦湖西畲族乡近几年投资 560 万元,铺设了本乡的水泥和柏油路面,投资 270 万元建了 500 门程控电话,投资 75 万元建了 3.5 万伏的变电站。基础设施的建设大大改善了投资环境,使民族乡的建设插上翅膀。

为了解决民族地区人口温饱问题,彻底挖掉穷根,福建省委提出了异地开发、异地脱贫致富的"造福工程"。1994 年,福建省委省政府发出《关于加强民族工作的若干意见》,明确要求各有关地市县积极组织实施,按群众自愿原则,有计划地将一些山高路远、生存条件恶劣、零星分散的少数民族村集中搬迁到地理条件较好的地域,改善生产生活条件,形成新的有利于民族乡经济社会发展的格局。并提出了一系列实施"造福工程"的优惠政策和措施。1997 年,省委省政府把解决闽东畲族世代居住茅草房问题列入为民办的 15 件实事之一,当年就投资 722 万元,帮助 719 户 2 859 名少数民族群众完成茅草房改造工程,从此结束了福建省少数民族群众世世代代居住茅草房的历史。

第七章　宗教

　　佛教、道教、天主教、基督教、伊斯兰教等五大宗教在福建有着悠久的历史和广泛的群众影响。目前可统计的教徒共有 100 万余人,宗教活动场所近 7 000 座。

　　福建佛教目前共有寺庙 4 300 多座,僧尼 12 000 多人,居士约 13 万人,无论寺庙数还是僧尼数都居全国大陆汉族地区首位。福建经国务院批准的全国汉族地区佛教重点寺庙有 14 座,约占全国汉族地区重点寺庙的 10%,它们分别是:福州鼓山涌泉寺、怡山西禅寺、金鸡山地藏寺、瑞峰林阳寺,闽侯雪峰崇圣寺,福清黄檗寺,厦门南普陀寺,宁德支提山华严寺,莆田南山广化寺、梅峰光孝寺、襄山慈寿寺,泉州开元寺,晋江龙山寺,漳州南山寺。

　　佛教在三国时期传入福建,至今已有 1700 多年的历史。福建历史上高僧辈出,曾来福建传法的外省高僧和福建籍高僧著名的有:来建阳建寺的唐代四川人道一,制订了"百丈清规"的唐代福建长乐人怀海,与弟子共创沩仰宗的五代福建霞浦人灵祐,创建雪峰寺的五代福建南安人义存,鼓山涌泉寺开山祖师五代渤海人神晏,主持鼓山涌泉寺 23 年的明末曹洞宗最有影响的禅师福建建阳人元贤,弘法闽南 14 年的近代浙江人弘一,曾任厦门南普陀寺住持兼任闽南佛学院院长的近代浙江人太虚,中国佛教协会首任会长福建古田人圆瑛等。

　　福建佛教与台湾地区及日本、东南亚关系密切,源远流长。明末清初,福州鼓山涌泉寺、怡山西禅寺,福清黄檗寺与台湾僧侣交流极为频繁,香火远播台湾。唐代,日本真言宗祖师空海在福建霞浦县赤岸登陆,经福州(住开元寺)北上长安求法。清初,福清黄檗寺高僧隐元率20余人东渡日本,开创日本佛教黄檗宗。福建许多寺院在菲律宾、新加坡、印尼、马来西亚等国有众多下院。直至现在这些国家的佛教领袖仍然多为闽籍僧人,同福建佛教界保持十分密切的联系。

　　福建寺院刻经历史悠久。宋代福州东禅寺所刻《崇宁藏》和开元寺所刻《毗卢藏》,是中国历史上最早的两部寺刻大藏经。福州鼓山涌泉寺曾成为刻印佛典经书的中心,直至"文革"前,尚存明清及近代各种佛典板片11375块,弘一大师生前曾称其为"庋藏佛典古版之宝窟"。其他一些著名丛林也珍藏了各种佛典,如泉州开元寺就藏有宋元版佛典12部。历史上福建因寺院众多和远离战乱,一些佛教文物保存相对完整,有代表性的如摩崖石刻、碑文经幢、稀世佛像、各类佛塔等。

　　福建道教现有宫观600多座,道士2 600多人。道教在福建的产生与名山有关,武夷山被称为道教三十六小洞天之中的第十六洞天,霍童山被称为道教三十六洞天中的第一洞天,闽东的太姥山、闽南的清源山、福州的于山等,都与道教关系密切。福建现存著名道教宫观,有福州的九仙观、裴仙宫,福清石竹山道观,泉州元妙观,武夷山桃源洞道观,莆田东岳观等。

　　道教在东汉时传入福建,宋代有炼养派和符箓派,明清时有全真道和正一道。全真道主张"出家修真,炼气养神",至近代后开始衰落。正一道画符降妖,祈福禳灾,为人驱邪超度等,其道士人称"师公"。福建道教法事名目繁多,科仪完整,其驱妖镇魔的一些动作,有时具有很强的技艺性和观赏性,因此常被借用到舞蹈中。

　　福建道教与台湾道教同源同流。福建南部移民入台湾开发,将家乡宫庙香火带入台湾,所供奉的神灵为两地共有。东南亚的闽籍先民对家乡的神祇特别虔诚,视为他们在海外生存、发展的保护神,在建立庙宇时,总要冠上故乡的地名或祖庙的名称,并经常回到故乡祖庙进香。

福建天主教目前有教堂 300 多座,神职人员 130 多人,教徒近 30 万人。著名教堂有:福州泛船浦天主堂,长乐城关天主堂,厦门鼓浪屿天主堂,漳州东坂后天主堂,龙海岭东天主堂,福安城关天主堂、穆阳天主堂,宁德三都澳天主堂、城关天主堂、岚口天主堂,邵武东门天主堂,建瓯腊子坪天主堂,上杭城关天主堂等。

天主教早在元代就传入泉州,是全国天主教传播最早的省份之一。公元 1313 年,泉州成立了刺桐教区,为当时全国仅有的两个教区之一,负责包括杭州、扬州等通商口岸在内的东南教务。现存于泉州海交馆中的元代十字架墓碑石中,有 5 方是元代泉州天主教方济各会传教士墓葬的遗物。明代,通晓中国传统文化的意大利耶稣会士艾儒略到福建传教,因善于将其教义与中国传统习惯相结合,因此传教顺利。明末,传统文人和僧人联合反教,纷纷著文"辟邪",由漳州人黄贞将其汇编为《破邪集》。清初,福安人罗文藻成为历史上第一位中国籍主教,在官方规定外国传教士不得传教的年代,罗文藻成为全国惟一能公开传教的天主教神职人员。1696 年福建正式成立天主教福建教区。

福建基督教目前共有教堂 1 700 多座,教牧人员 1 200 多人,教徒 47 万,另有慕道友 14 万人。较有影响的基督教堂,有福州花巷堂、铺前堂、天安堂、苍霞堂,福清城关堂,莆田城关堂,南平梅山堂,晋江金升堂,泉州南街礼拜堂,厦门三一堂、新区堂、新街堂等。

基督教传入福建的时间约在 1840 年前后。1848 年,厦门建立第一座教堂新街礼拜堂,解放前被中华基督教会全国总会称为"中华第一堂"。基督教由此开始从厦门、福州向全省各地辐射。基督教在福建创办了医院、学校,出版报刊、书籍,并促使了闽南白话字的产生。

　　伊斯兰教在福建目前有代表性的清真寺有5座，最有名的是建于北宋年间的泉州清净寺，也称圣友寺，它是我国现存最古老的一所伊斯兰教寺，它以中世纪伊斯兰教的建筑风格为主，在许多建筑部位上又带有中国传统建筑的技艺。其他四座为厦门清真寺、福州清真寺、邵武清真寺、晋江陈埭清真寺。全省教徒有3 000多人。

　　伊斯兰教在唐代就传入泉州，当时有不少阿拉伯、波斯穆斯林商人进入泉州，以后有部分定居下来。许多海外来的穆斯林在当地娶妻生子，代代相传。穆斯林为了满足自己过宗教生活的需要，开始建造清真寺。

　　元代随着泉州继续成为世界贸易大港，穆斯林在泉州有很大发展，又修建了许多清真寺，只是今天已不存在了。明代，穆斯林在开始在邵武发展；清代，由于泉州港的没落，海外穆斯林已不再来，而福建地处东南一隅，与内地穆斯林联系也多不方便，所以福建伊斯兰教不如宋元时期兴盛。

　　福建穆斯林来源广泛，除了宋元时代从海上丝绸之路直接定居以外，还有由北方南下经商的，外省来福建任职的，由于受聘为阿訇、投亲、居官等种种原因从全国各地来的。因多次迁移，福建穆斯林居住分散，除极少数几个点外，只见大分散，难见小集中。

　　在众多的福建地方神中，最著名的是天上圣母妈祖、临水夫人陈靖姑、保生大帝吴夲。妈祖原名林默，宋代莆田人，相传逝世后经常显灵护佑过往船只，救助海难，因此被渔民视为航海保护神。陈靖姑为唐代福州人，18岁时嫁古田人刘杞为妻。相传因福州大旱，陈靖姑脱胎祈雨，不幸劳伤而亡，临终前曾发誓扶胎救助难产，成为救难产的神。吴夲为宋代同安白礁人，是一位信奉道教的民间草药医生，以高超的医术和高尚的医德闻名于闽南一带，因救人采药而不慎坠落深谷身亡。人民群众为纪念他，将他奉为健康保护神。福建还有许多地方神,如广泽尊王、清水祖师、萧太傅等。随着福建人赴台湾和东南亚谋生,这些地方神也成为台湾地区和东南亚国家华人供奉的神祇。

摩尼教是公元3世纪中叶波斯人摩尼创立的宗教,在唐代武宗会昌年间由呼禄法师传入泉州,元代在泉州十分盛行。明代后,逐渐与其他宗教融合。元代在晋江建造的摩尼草庵是国内仅存的摩尼教遗迹,庵中的摩尼光佛被首届世界摩尼教学术讨论会作为会徽图案。三一教是莆田人林兆恩于明代创建的,它主张释儒三教合一,注重三教义理的融会贯通。清朝由于朝廷的查禁而逐渐走向衰微。

改革开放春风吹拂福建大地以来,福建省各级领导高度重视落实党和政府的宗教信仰自由政策。1981年春,当时的省委书记项南亲自抓这项工作的落实,省委、省顾委、省人大、省政府、省政协、福州军区等六大机构联合组成了落实宗教政策检查团,地市也相应成立了检查分团,在全省范围内进行了大规模的深入、持久的检查工作。项南等领导带头分工,直接挂钩抓福州涌泉寺、泉州开元寺、漳州南山寺等寺庙的落实政策问题。项南同志高度重视海外人士对省内宗教界落实政策的反映,对海外宗教界人士来信反映的问题,多次亲自做了批示。领导的率先垂范,极大推动了全省宗教信仰自由政策的落实,使福建在落实宗教信仰自由政策上起步早、力度大、进展快,走在全国前列。

全国宗教界领袖也都极为关心重视福建宗教工作的开展,全国政协副主席、中国佛教协会会长赵朴初曾多次来福建指导工作。全国政协副主席、中国基督教三自爱国会主任丁光训,中国天主教主教团宗怀德主教、金鲁贤副主教,原中国道教协会会长谢宗信,中国伊斯兰教协会副会长马贤等宗教界著名人士,都先后来到福建考察宗教工作,进一步推动了福建宗教工作的顺利开展。

福建各级领导在政治上关心宗教界人士,宗教界的冤假错案已全部得到平反。全省现有各级宗教社会团体 211 个,有 405 名宗教界人士担任各级人大代表或政协委员。广大宗教界人士无不认为近 20 年是进入历史上贯彻执行宗教信仰自由政策最好的黄金时期,他们心情舒畅地开展宗教活动并积极奉献社会。福建省各级领导狠抓宗教房产政策的落实,曾对全省各地宗教房产政策的落实进行了全面的检查,使一些“老大难”问题得以解决。到 20 世纪 80 年代末,已有 95% 的宗教房产归还宗教团体。广大信教群众和海外华侨有感于党和政府落实宗教政策的诚意和决心,慷慨解囊,捐款捐物。如泉州承天寺、福州西禅寺都是因海外华侨捐资而得以修复。

尊重和保护宗教信仰自由,是我国政府对待和处理宗教问题的一项长期的基本政策。福建各级领导排除各种干扰,切实使宗教信仰自由落实到实处。在政通人和的今天,各宗教团体和广大信教群众心情舒畅地按各宗教仪轨开展了各种宗教活动。

各宗教团体根据自治、自传、自养、独立自主办教会的方针,开展自传活动,发展宗教教育出版事业。福建省佛教协会和福建省道教协会分别创办了会刊《福建佛教》和《福建道教》。省佛教协会为了满足广大佛教徒与信友的需要,还先后开设了莆田广化寺经书流通处和省佛教协会经书流通处,一些重点寺庙也相应成立了佛经流通网络。莆田广化寺翻印了大量的佛教经典,福建省佛教协会佛教基金委员会翻印了大量的佛学论著。福建基督教三自爱国会编印了许多阐释教义的书籍。这些都受到信徒的欢迎。

省市各级有关部门为宗教政策的落实,提供了种种方便,1985年初修建泉州承天寺时,在海外捐款尚未汇到情况下,为保进度,泉州市政府支持贷款 150 万元先购买大量木材。为解决进占厂家的搬迁,市委书记、市长又带领五套班子成员到现场办公。1995年,天主教福州教区在长乐古槐镇龙田村买下一块山坡地,建造了融宗教朝圣、宗教旅游和宗教文化交流于一体的系列宗教建筑玫瑰山庄。省、市有关部门不仅在山庄审批手续上提供诸多方便,还本着特事特办的精神给教会减免了各种税费40多万元。天主教福州教区郑长诚主教曾对来访的美国广州总领事说:"今天的中国公民所享有的宗教信仰自由权利不会比美国人差。特别是在照顾宗教界困难,为宗教减免税方面可能美国还不如中国。"

办好各类宗教院校,有计划地培养年轻一代爱国宗教职业人员,是对党和政府宗教信仰自由政策的进一步贯彻和落实,对福建宗教界将来面貌具有决定性的意义。这既是长远大计,又是当务之急,是一件极为重要的基本建设。1983年以来,福建宗教界先后创办或复办了福建佛学院、闽南佛学院、福建神学院、福建天主教修院及各类宗教培训班,培养了1 500多名中高级年轻的宗教教职人员,逐步实现了教职人员的年轻化、知识化。

福建佛学院分为男众部和女众都,男众都在莆田广化寺内,女众部在福州崇福寺内。福建佛学院创办于1983年,是全国最早的省一级佛学院。福建佛学院男众部毕业了五期培训班、七期预科班、三届研究班,毕业、结业学生共600人,现在校男众150人,课程60%为佛学,文化课占了30%,政治课占10%。办学理念是要培养爱国爱教、热爱社会主义、有知识的接班人。福建佛学院定期评比优秀学生,并引入了新的教学设备,学生们学习认真刻苦。福建佛学院女众部开设预科和附设半日制培训班,学生主要来自全国近20个省市。福建佛学院男女众学员以道风严谨闻名全国,赵朴初会长誉其为全国模范丛林,并欣然为广化寺男众学员赋诗:"一入山门在道心,南山风范见传承。威仪秩秩斋堂里,粒米思量大众恩。"

闽南佛学院创办于1925年,1985年复办后强调"学修并重,学用结合"。学院分男女众两个院部,男众部设在南普陀寺内,女众部设在厦门紫竹林。中国佛教协会副会长、闽南佛学院院长、南普陀寺住持圣辉法师说:"闽南佛学院学生来自全国各省市,在校生人数也最多。因为南普陀寺与闽南佛学院同为一体,办学有后盾。现在佛教教育存在一些问题,要靠管理跟上。办学和管理有很深的内在联系。在厦门市委、市政府领导下,我们取得很大成绩。下一步提高办学质量,主要抓三件事:一是师资建设;二对学生宗教情操培养;三是提高学生佛教知识。要搞素质教育。"闽南佛学院有条件很好的办公室、太虚图书馆、教学楼等。优秀学生继续送往高一层学府深造,至今在北京大学东方系当博士后的湛如法师,就出自闽南佛学院。女众部所处的紫竹林环境清幽,教学设施齐备,教学条件在国内居前列。除了佛学院外,一些寺院也举办了各种类型的培训班,提高了宗教界人士的文化水平和宗教学识。

福建神学院创办于1983年,优秀毕业生送往金陵神学院深造,神学院学生学习认真,规定每星期利用一定时间进行爱国主义教育,并经常开展文娱活动。福建天主教修院十多年来培养了修生、修女58人,累计向上海佘山修院和全国神哲学院输送修生67人,选送了5名神职人员出国留学深造。各级教区也都注意培养神职人员,闽东教区1983年以来,培养、输送了十几个神职人员到中国神哲学院深造,已毕业回来的有7人,在外留学两人。

福建各宗教院校培养的大批年轻一代爱国宗教教职人员,大部分已成为各级宗教团体和宗教活动场所的骨干力量,大大缓解了"文革"造成的宗教教职人员青黄不接、严重老化的困难,逐步实现了新老交替,部分教职人员还应聘到美国、菲律宾等东南亚国家及香港地区办理教务。

为了落实依法对宗教场所的管理,省、市各级领导多次深入宗教活动场所检查工作。1998年,福建省宗教局部署了对全省宗教场所的检查清理工作,以福州开元寺为试点,采取了一系列有效整改措施,并派出优秀青年僧才充实管理队伍,使开元寺面貌焕然一新,受到开元寺僧人、信徒的欢迎和社会的好评。各宗教团体也高度重视对宗教场所管理的有关规定,宁德支提山华严寺根据中国佛教协会颁布的有关规定,结合寺务管理具体情况,制定了《支提山华藏寺管理暂行办法》,使寺务管理逐步规范化、制度化。泉州道教协会和元妙观根据中国道教协会有关规定,建立、健全各项规章制度,完善了管理机构,对驻会驻观人员提出严格要求,使工作秩序井然。

党的十一届三中全会以来,福建宗教界在与社会主义相适应方面迈出了重要的步伐,取得了可喜的成就。

为了更好地探讨、研究福建宗教界存在的问题,1993年11月,由福建宗教部门干部、各宗教团体代表、宗教研究者在福州成立了福建省宗教研究会,召开了各种类型研讨会和活动,创办了《福建宗教》刊物,编辑了三本会议论文集。福建省宗教局也多次召开多种表彰会、工作会、研讨会等,这些都为宗教更好地与社会主义相适应做出了积极的努力。

在政府各部门的大力支持下,福建宗教界坚持自供自足的方针。武夷山桃源洞道士的重要生活来源靠种岩茶、开发旅游纪念品等,可劳动自养。福安万寿寺靠生产各类香自养,这两年年产值60多万元,老人退休后每月可分80多元,产品已从内销转为外销。宁德支提山华严寺以农业为主,田产收回后,生产自足。许多寺庙基本靠农业生产,如连城中华山性海寺、闽侯雪峰崇圣寺、莆田广化寺、福州林阳寺等。一些寺庙推出有特色的服务,如厦门南普陀寺、福州西禅寺、福州源泉寺推出素菜服务,受到人民的欢迎。福建宗教界积极为社会提供无偿服务,创办了多所义诊室,受到社会各界的欢迎。天主教三自爱国会创办了医疗卫生所、诊疗所、安老院。

福建宗教界积极推动与台湾的交流,据台湾“行政院陆委会”调查,近年来海峡两岸宗教交流多集中在福建省。早在20世纪80年代末,台湾台北临济寺、台南大仙寺、高雄弘化寺的法师或参观团就开始频频访问福建。20世纪90年代初,台湾法师开始到福建讲学。至 90 年代后,台湾佛教界与福建佛教界往来更加频繁。原福建省佛教协会会长界诠法师曾访问台湾中华佛学研究所,现任福建省佛教协会会长的学诚法师也于 1998 年 7 月赴台参加两岸僧教育研讨会,并应邀在台湾师范大学做了演讲。福建省佛教界还于 1994 年赴台举办"弘一法师书画展",受到台湾人民的欢迎。福建道教宫观每年接待台湾各地道教进香朝圣团达 1000 团以上,超过 20 万人次。1997 年 3 月,以林舟为团长的泉州道教协会赴台交流访问团,与台湾 40 多个道教宫庙和道教会进行了交流。林舟道长认为台湾人民对两岸血缘、神缘有强烈的认同感,林道长说:"中华道教与我们交往,他们也请不少宫观到台访问,但国内仅请中国道协和福建道协。到福建,就说我们回家了,因为语言相通。道教在台湾都赞成统一的。"福建省基督教三自爱国会在全国最早组团赴台访问,福建省天主教三自爱国会也派人赴台访问,双方进一步增加了了解。

福建宗教界与海外交流频繁,通过互访,促进了友谊。福建佛教界与海外交流时间早,早在 1979 年,日本佛教黄檗宗访拜团 18人就到福清黄檗山拜塔谒祖,并在福州鼓山涌泉寺大雄宝殿内,与福建僧人共同举行盛大的华语诵经佛事活动。日、韩等国佛教界多次派出参拜团到福建交流。东南亚一些著名佛教领袖也多次访问福建。如新加坡佛教总会会长宏船法师曾五次访问福建,菲律宾佛教协会会长瑞今法师、马来西亚佛教总会会长寂晃法师等都多次访问福建。福建佛教界也多次出访东南亚诸国。福建伊斯兰积极开展对外活动,省伊斯兰教协会会长曾多次出国访问,增进了与伊斯兰世界的友谊。驰名中外的泉州伊斯兰教古寺清净寺,近几年先后接待了世界上 130 多个国家和地区的来宾,其中包括来自 37 个伊斯兰教国家的宾客,他们在留言簿上题写了歌颂友谊的词句,伊朗、巴基斯坦、伊拉克、阿曼、沙特阿拉伯等国家还向清净寺赠送了精美的《古兰经》。福建基督教三自爱国会、天主教三自爱国会也都多次接待海外来宾,莆田基督教牧师郑金灿说:"我们基督教堂与东南亚关系密切。东南亚华侨许多是基督信徒,希望能到莆田大教堂参加聚会,我们对他们加以引导,使他们更好地安心投资,顺利开展工作,使教堂成为对外开放的窗口。"

在社会主义两个文明建设中,福建宗教界涌现出许多先进单位和个人。福建省宗教局在1997年11月召开"福建宗教界为四化服务先进典型表彰大会",对宗教界为四化服务做出突出贡献的先进单位和先进个人进行了表彰。先进单位有:努力使石竹山被评为省级十大风景区的石竹山道院、架设中阿友好桥梁的泉州清净寺、将寺院建成模范丛林的莆田广化寺、农禅并重的宁德支提山华严寺、热心社会公益事业的邵武市基督教两会等共22个单位。先进个人有17个,最典型的是为保卫国家文物与歹徒搏斗而献出生命的将乐县博物馆原馆长、天主教徒廖国华。

福建宗教界近20年走过的路程充分说明,宗教完全可以与社会主义事业相适应,福建宗教界已成为社会主义两个文明建设、维护社会稳定的一支不可忽视的力量。

第八章 民俗

人们常用"百里不同风，千里不同俗"来形容中国民俗的丰富多彩，但福建民俗的绚丽多姿却可用"十里不同风，一乡有一俗"来形容。福建荟萃了中国民俗的精华，堪称中华民俗的展览馆。外地有的民俗这里有，外地没有的民俗这里也有；外地古时有之现已消失的民俗这里有，外地早已演变得面目全非的民俗，这里仍然可以看到其原来面貌。福建民俗之所以极为丰富多姿，有着多方面的原因。1. 多种文化的兼容并蓄。古越文化的遗风、中原文化的多次大规模传入、原始宗教和现代宗教的广泛传播、海外文化持续不断的冲击、邻地文化的长期渗透等，都使闽地文化极为斑斓多彩。2. 地处僻壤的自然环境。民俗的传承对自然环境有很强的选择性。福建地僻东南一隅，远离政治文化中心，被称为"东南山国"，因交通不便使无数分散的自然村落互不往来，也不易受外界的影响，有时"不知有汉，无论魏晋"。这种独特的环境是各种民俗沉淀的极好温床。3. 极强的家庭观念。民俗的传承是靠人们的口头和行为方式，一代代延续下来，是一种历时持久的、由集体所传递的文化形式。福建村落的居民长期休养生息在同一地缘之内，逐渐形成了村落的集体意识。聚族而居、血缘村落更使福建人有极强的家庭观念，千方百计地保证祖先遗留下来的东西不被遗弃，这就使一些古老民俗有极顽强的生命力。

一、岁时佳节

　　岁时民俗是一种极其杂的社会文化现象。福建的岁时民俗，一方面是闽地人们生产和生活经验的体现，另一方面也与闽地独有的自然环境有着密切的关系。

　　除夕是旧历年的最后一天，也是全年最繁忙的一天。福州话"年盲兜（年终）连没跤灯马也会跑"。福州人要蒸好白米饭贮在饭甑中，供于案前，俗称"隔年饭"。晚上要烧竹竿，后改为烧松柴，烧时撒些盐花，让其发出响声，以扫除晦气。福州还称"除夕"为"做晦"，在门缝里夹上金银箔纸，以示金银多到从门缝里盈满溢出，象征明年能发大财。闽南人在除夕夜将打扫灰尘的旧扫帚丢在火里烧掉，然后全家老少用闽南话说声"今年好过年"，挨个跳过火堆，以祝愿新的一年快乐与吉利。漳州除夕之夜围炉，宴席佳肴有其象征意义，如鱼象征生活富余，鸡寓意家运昌兴，豆腐表示发财致富，韭菜代表幸福长久。漳州人特别看重蚶，除夕宴绝不能少。古时贝壳象征财富、华贵，所以漳州人视蚶壳如金银，食后蚶壳不得扫入垃圾，而要郑重地放置门后或床下，预兆来年发财致富。此外，还须在房门后竖放两连根带叶的甘蔗，称"靠壁硬"，取家运坚实牢固之意。闽西除夕在中庭置方桌，以大米斗置桌上，插上冬青树叶，以银圆、银镯系于冬青树枝上，又以红蛋置米上，叫"上岁饭"。

　　春节是闽俗中最重要的节日，福州俗称"做年"，主要有五项活动：1.饮屠酥。初一清晨汲上井水调和黄酒，家中人按长幼为序各饮一杯，以避瘟疫。2.序拜。先拜天地，然后按辈分向家中长老祝寿。3.却荤食。正月初一吃素，类似今天吃以线面配鸭蛋的"太平面"。4.上冢。祭扫祖先坟墓。5.入学。正月初五送子弟入学拜老师。闽南对过春节的日程有严格的规定，一首盛行的歌谣唱道："初一荣，初二停，初三无姿，初四神落天，初五隔开，初六打囡仔的脚川(屁股),初七七元,初八团圆,初九天公生,初十地公生,十一请子婿,十二返去拜,十三食唵糜配介菜,十四结灯棚,十五上元暝。"大意是:初一决定一年的吉凶祸福,所以家里一定要打扫干净,箱橱里还要放几文钱;初二没事干,妇女们归宁贺新正,并带红包及糖饼散给小孩;初三新聚的妇女归宁未回;初四沐浴焚香将三牲果品排在神前,表示欢迎神降临本家;初五告一段落,各行各业就位;初六可以打不听话孩子的屁股(初一到初五不许打骂孩子,以图吉利);初七将一些蔬菜混合煮食(名七宝汤),可解百病;初八一家人须团聚在一起共享天伦之乐,如妇女未归,家中人要到女方家中兴师问罪;初九、初十是天公、地公的生辰,要排列九牲五果六斋,演戏并请道士和尚念经;初十一女婿到来,岳父、岳母要无微不至地招待,但女婿也需带些红包给岳父家的孩子;初十二贺新年的客人都回家去了;初十三人民没有敬神可食家常便饭;初十四扎结很高的灯棚;初十五过元宵。

闽俗重元宵,前后长达20余天,闽南尤盛,大街小巷张灯结彩,一路舞龙,舞狮、踩高跷,至深夜都极为热闹。家中除了要煮"嫩饼菜"供祖先外,还有几件事是必定要办的:一年内出嫁的女儿,娘家要在元宵节前买绣球灯、莲花灯各一对,差遣男孩送到女婿家中,祈祝早日"出丁"(生孩子)。已出嫁女儿在元宵节后走娘家,要备办"面前"(线面、鸡蛋之类的礼品),孝敬爹妈。有的地方未出嫁的姑娘还需在晚上"迎紫姑"(亦称"迎厕姑娘"),即吃几碗"嫩饼菜"后,三五成群到村边厕所作祷语,青年小伙子也常三五成群到厕所边偷听。

福建有许多独有的年节。农历正月二十九,福州要过拗九节,(也称"后九节"、"孝九节"和"送穷节")。这天清早,家家户户都用糯米和红糖,再加上花生、红枣、桂圆、荸荠、红豆、胡桃、芝麻等配米煮成"拗九粥",用来祭祖和馈赠乡邻、戚友。已嫁的女儿要送上一碗"拗九粥"回娘家孝敬父母,福州俗语"逢九必穷",认为人年龄

上逢"九"或"九"的倍数,要交穷运,必须设法送穷。每年夏历夏至
过后逢辰的一天,闽东要过"分龙节"。此日禁止动用铁器和粪桶
等出门,并祈求各龙王不作水患,各地畲民普遍歇工,携山货到福
宁府进行自由贸易,彼此交流生产技术和生活情况,男女青年通过
盘歌,为自己寻找终身伴侣。

二、婚嫁生育

　　人类的延续,家庭的发展,与婚嫁生育关系最为密切。因此,
这一环节历来都受到个人、家庭和社会的高度重视。从民俗诸礼
的演变传承来看,其形式最为丰富,传承最为悠久。福建传统的婚
嫁生育习俗,也极为丰富多彩。

　　历史上福州婚嫁的程序很繁杂。1."问字",男家请人到女家
说合;2."合婚",双方交换生辰八字,由算命先生测算是否犯冲;3.
"下大帖",选良辰吉日定聘;4."上半礼",男家在定聘时,将鸡、鸭、
酒、礼饼等和龙凤帖,用红拜盒送往女家;女家也用红拜盒盛拜帖
及衣服裤料回男家;5."下半礼",男方在婚前一月把酒肉礼品和礼
金等一齐送到女家,女家以衣帽文具和糕点回赠;6."办亲",女家
收到男家聘金后办好妆奁,于婚前一日鼓吹送往男家;7."试妆",
婚前一日,新娘由伴娘梳洗打扮;8."接亲",结婚之日,新郎由媒人
带领,用花轿去女家迎娶新娘;9."坐床",花轿到男家时,新娘由伴
娘导入洞房,与新郎并坐床沿,新娘悄悄将新郎衣襟压于臀下;10.
"见面礼",升厅拜堂后,新娘按辈分拜见众位亲戚,长辈要送红包
给新娘;11."合卺",新夫妇在洞房喝合欢酒;12."闹房",宴后,亲
友聚集新房请新郎新娘表演节目;13."庙见",第二天谒家庙和六
亲;14."试厨",傍晚新娘亲自下厨做菜,以考验其烹饪手艺;15.
"馁女",第三天女家父母来饷食;16."请回门",女家派亲家舅(新
娘弟弟,无弟须借一男孩代替)来请新夫妇俩回女家;17."撮食",
女家设宴招待亲客,女家的平辈亲友要新郎出钱请客,或设宴、或

说评话。在操办这些程序时,各地做法又有所不同。比如福清在"迎亲"时,有"拦花轿"的独特习俗:迎亲回来路上,人们可以用条椅等拦住花轿;只有让拦路者满意,才让通过,新郎新娘不得生气。一路上拦的人越多,越说明新娘的才貌闻名远近,新郎也就越光彩。有的地方有"避冲"之习:新郎迎新娘到自己家门口时,男家放鞭炮迎新。新娘需由男方亲戚或邻居中福贵双全的年长妇女和喜娘扶进门,此时男家的其他女眷应暂时回避,并熄灭堂内柴火,新娘进大厅后才能见面。还有"关新人房"之习:男家挑一聪明伶俐男孩将嫁妆中的新马桶先接进新房,旋即与预先呆在新房内的男女孩关紧房门。新郎、新娘拍门要求开房门,与门内人讨价还价。时间越长,表示新郎新娘越有耐性,意味今后夫妻恩爱日子越长。

昔日闽南一带婚嫁,很重视"六礼",即:1."问名",托媒人到对方家求"生月";2."订盟",定下婚事;3."采纳",送盘担;4."纳币",送聘礼;5."请期",呈送红帖;6."迎亲",男到女家迎新人。但闽南各地对"六礼"的具体做法并不完全一样。有的地方在"问名"时,用红纸写明男女双方年庚八字,由媒人传给双方家长,将红纸置在神前香炉内,三天内如果家中有打破碗碟瓷器或家中有人走路不小心踢到石头,这项婚事便作罢。在"订盟"时,有时由媒人陪同男方到女家,女的捧茶三巡后,男方要有压茶红包给女的,压的钱双数表示相中,单数表示没相中。有一些讲客家话的地方,男方来相亲时,女方如果煮米粉、红蛋相待,炒"米香"相赠,表示答应婚事。如果煮了米粉不加蛋,不炒"米香",即暗示不中意。

过去闽南"迎亲"有许多独特的习俗。迎亲那一天,新郎必须坐在轿上,无论寒暑,手多执白扇,以"避邪"。新郎轿后还有二轿,坐着新郎的朋友,俗称"炮嫁"。至女家时,新郎不下轿,女家接"炮嫁",将二人请到隔壁邻居家敬茶。"炮嫁"可伺机拿取茶杯两个带回男家,置于新郎床下,说这样会速生男孩。女家荐以线面鸡蛋给轿中新郎,男方则备猪脚、米团送女家,敬孝岳母,说是报答她在生养女儿时的腹痛之苦。新娘出女家时,有的地方有"一对带路鸡,两棵连尾蔗"之俗,即要伴娘护送一只即将下蛋的母鸡和一只刚会啼的公鸡做"带路鸡"到男家,新娘入洞房后,将"带路鸡"放进床下,然后往地下撒米。公鸡先出来,"头胎生查埔"(生男),母鸡先出来"先生阿姐再招小弟"。婚后第三天,新娘由娘家返回时,必带两根带尾的粗壮甘蔗,蔗叶苍翠欲滴,将之放在新房门后,寓意夫妻两人日后生活像甘蔗一样,"甜头好尾",恩爱绵长。

福建一些少数民族的婚嫁程序与自己本民族习俗关系极为密切。闽东的畲族爱唱山歌,因此其婚嫁也离不开唱歌。如"做表姐":在婚礼前,姑娘的舅母要请姑娘和她的母亲去做客,次数不拘,姑娘要穿上最漂亮的衣服,到舅村,村里青年都陪她唱歌。姑娘唱得好,会获得人们的夸奖;唱不好,将遭讥讽。"做亲家伯":娶亲前两天,男方请一个好歌手做全权代表,俗称"亲家伯",与媒人一起把礼物送到女家。晚饭后开始连唱两个晚上的歌。唱得好,男方有面子,女方妇女不敢为难,一切以礼相待。如果不会唱或唱不好,将被妇女奚落,甚至让他扎犁做牛,男方大丢面子。泉州一带流行的"撒金豆",是古代回族婚俗。回族先民中的阿拉伯、波斯巨商结婚时,于婚礼当天在女家由阿訇念完尼卡哈后,向新郎、新娘身上撒黄金豆粒,意为喜庆日子散天课施舍贫民,贫苦的穆斯林拾之均分。后民间改为撒核桃、枣、花生、白果等四果,让围观的大人小孩拣食,意为感谢真主赐结良缘,祈求真主赐生贵子。

福建有的地方的婚俗极为奇特。如过去闽南惠东妇女在婚后三天就要回娘家长住,只有逢年过节及农忙时才到夫家住几天,一年总共时间不过六七天,而这几天到夫家也要天黑后才到,且头戴黑布遮面,到熄灯后才去头布,所以有的甚至结婚多年夫妻之间还不认识。惠东妇女必须在娘家住到怀孕生孩子时,才能回到夫家安定住下。住娘家多的两三年以至于十几二十年。当地人称长住娘家的媳妇为"不欠债的",称住夫家的为"欠债的"。

由于对生育的重视,所以福建各地的生育习俗都很繁多。福州从孩子在娘胎里到周岁,每一阶段都以"喜"称:"带身喜",指妇女身怀六甲;"临盆喜",指妇女分娩后,要向近房亲戚和左邻右舍分送一碗太平面报喜,接受者则要回赠几粒鸡蛋或鸭蛋,以及数量不等的线面;"汤饼之喜",指孩子出生三天时,办"三旦"酒,宴请亲友,娘家必须置办孩子的用物和产妇的食物,于当天送达男家;"弥月之喜",指孩子满月时办满月酒,赴宴的客人除送红包外,还可送些小孩礼物;"坐舆之喜",指孩子四个月时,可以坐竹木车了,为此办酒请客;"做晬之喜",指孩子周岁时办酒请客,规模最大,客人除送"红包"外,还可送童装、玩具。

闽南生育习俗的每个阶段与福州大同小异,但叫法和做法不一样。孩子出世当日,叫"落土",请至亲至友吃喜饭。孩子出生三日,叫"三段",以油饭遍送亲友近邻,并把鸡蛋、鸭蛋和香饼、油饭送往舅家。孩子满月,叫"汤饼会",以油饭、肉、面、酒等物品祀祖宗,敬后分赠亲友,并宴请诸亲。请有"福气"的老人为孩子摸摸头,说些吉利的祝贺话,再背孩子到大路上走,叫"游大街"。背孩子探井,旨在让孩子能顺利成长。孩子四个月时,叫"面桃",周岁时,称"枕头包",皆以油饭、鸡蛋(染红色)、猪肉还礼于前来祝贺的亲友。

福建重男轻女现象较全国其他地方严重,历史上曾有"溺女婴"的陋俗。不少地方生男生女的习俗是不一样的。闽南惠安北部男孩满月时,宴席远比女孩隆重。男家要做大量的圆面包,盖上"囍"字大红印,分送全村。此外,再挑一担给岳母,由岳母家分送邻居。还要煮十几个染红的熟鸡蛋,浸在盆中水里,让孩子去摸了吃。闽西有些地方凡生下男孩,几天后就要请家里辈分最高的长者取名,并用一张长方形的红纸竖写"新丁取名某年某月某日",俗称"写丁榜",一份贴在祠堂,一份贴在家中正厅右边最显眼的地方,使人知道房主新添男孩。如生女,不仅不贴丁榜,而且连名字都不取。

三、寿诞丧葬

　　福建重视给长辈祝寿。福州传统是男庆九,女庆十。比如男人六十大寿,必须提到59岁那年做,因为"九"与"久"谐音,象征长寿。此外,在正寿前一天,必须先做"襄寿"。即寿诞前一天,把小辈们送来的寿烛在祖先灵前全部点燃,然后摆上三碗寿面,分别插三朵纸花,族内小辈对过寿者叩拜,然后落座喝酒赏乐。小辈如有钱,可请佛道设坛念经,替过寿者向北斗星求福寿,称"拜斗"。更有钱的可邀请业余民乐队,在坛前弹奏,称"夹罐"。正式庆寿时,家中华灯齐放,亲朋好友汇聚一堂。赴宴者可送红包,也可送寿烛。有身望的家庭往往事先由其子孙出面,发出"寿启",向各方征求"寿序"及"寿诗",以为纪念。

　　闽南通常以51岁(虚龄)才开始庆寿,称为"头生日"。过了"头生日"后,越往后寿诞越隆重,称"大生日"。每年寿诞之日早晨,全家老少都先食"甜寿面",表示托长辈之福,儿孙自能长寿。之后,儿孙辈开始向过寿者祝寿。女儿、女婿、外甥等也要携带祝寿礼品前来祝寿。寿礼一般为寿面、寿桃(面制品)、寿龟(面制品)等,但要成双数,意为"好事成双"。第一次做寿(51岁)时,寿桃是必送的礼品,取其"蟠桃献寿"之意。所送礼品都必须贴上红纸或染上红色,表示"见红大吉"。祝寿的礼品,事主只能收其部分,余者让送礼人带回,意为彼此福寿。

　　福建有些地方对祝寿有自己的规定。仙游统一以正月初三为"祝寿日"。这一天,路上行人多手提或肩挑着清一色用红布袋或红篮子装着的寿礼,前往寿庆者家里祝寿。过寿者则在这一天宴请前来祝寿的亲友。这一习俗由来,据传是因为春节各家多少都备有些年货,较平时方便;同时,春节期间人们也较往日清闲,可以借此热闹一下。有的地方还时兴"女婿寿",即岳父岳母给年满30

岁的女婿过生日。这一天,岳父岳母携带寿纸往婿家祝寿,寿礼有:鱼,取"有余"之意;米酒,取"粮足"之意;面条,取"长寿"之意;衣物,取"有依靠"之意;枣子,取"早生贵子"之意;桔子,取"吉利"之意等。女婿收下礼品后,要以长寿面、果品、糕饼之类回敬岳父岳母,恭祝岳父岳母长寿。这种寿仪不摆寿堂,仅以寿酒款待前来祝贺的人。

丧葬是一种独特的仪礼。一般民间认为,死对活的人是悲痛的,但对死者却意味着与尘世的解脱,因此,民间常将婚礼和丧礼并称为"红白喜事",把丧事办得和喜事一样热闹。作为一种文化传承,丧葬习俗实际上是一种精神创造,在长期延续过程中,各地都形成了自己独特的程序。

福州丧葬习俗,十分繁琐而奢侈。当逝者弥留之时,亲人必须将其床上蚊帐拆卸掉,据说是为了让死后灵魂好出窍;逝者断气后,必须雇"张穿"杂工为死者更衣(也有由亲人为其淋浴更衣),并在大门口"贴白",放炮,告诉人们这个住宅×府××人丧事(字数须奇数)。然后派人四出报丧,再备好装满土沙的大脚桶,将素烛点燃后插在桶内(或置灯十余盏分数层于架上轮转),将其放置在逝者床前地上,仿佛为死者在奔赴黄泉路上照明。逝者脸上需盖上白纸,以示阴阳有别。请僧或道在厅堂上诵经念咒,孝男孝孙围着七层环形油灯架打圈、号哭,此谓"跋襀抬",也称"搬药梯"。

"做七"在福州丧俗中最为重要。福州话"七"与"漆"同音,所以福州富人棺材要上七道漆。人死后每七天就要一"祭",称"做过七"。至四十九天止,一共要做七次。死亡第七天,称"过头七",也称"孝男七",由孝男出资主持,请道士搭坛诵经,擂锣鼓和钟磬,向城隍爷报亡。"二七"是"内亲七",由族内六亲九眷出资延道诵经。"三七"又是"孝男七"。"四七"是"亲友七",由朋友出资延道诵经。"六七"是"孝女七",由出嫁女出资延请尼姑诵经。"五七"或"七七"是规模最大的活动,届时发讣告遍告亲友,请其参加唁吊。吊唁者向亡灵叩拜,孝男孝女在旁陪祭。酒席后开始出殡,棺柩后紧跟一队手持"哭丧杖"的孝男孝孙,尾随女眷和其他人,一路啼哭。安葬完毕,"哭丧杖"插在墓头。送葬回来的队伍叫"回舆",灵堂供上逝者像后,所有送葬者都必须逐个向亡灵拜别,孝男孝女在一旁伴灵志哀。结束后,逝者家属须向亡灵早晚供奉食物,到百日前才停止。

闽南的丧葬习俗也很繁杂,主要有:"搬铺",死者弥留之际,置床于厅左;"诵经",人死后,子女延道在死者铺前念"往生咒";"路哭",出嫁女闻丧即返,至闾巷破声而哭;"接祖",如死者为已婚女人,其娘家兄弟被称为"祖",死者家人必须接"祖"来验明是否被害;"套殓衣",孝男孝妇所穿孝衣下裾不缝,孝巾用手撕而不用剪,孝男给死者殓衣之前,要头戴斗笠,脚蹬竹凳;"请水",孝男手捧"请水钵"至溪边或井边,钵中放一块白布和 12 枚铜钱,投钱于水中,并跪舀一点水回家,替死者洗身;"大殓",入殓前办 12 碗菜由道士献给死者"辞生",一般三日后入土或火化;"敲棺材头",如死者父母尚健在,入殓时父母将手持木棒敲击棺材头,表示对其未尽养老送终孝道的谴责;"启灵",出殓时用纸糊的高丈二、面目威武狰狞的"开路神"先导,以稻草束"草龙"殿后;"跳过棺",夫妇二人,如死者为女方,男方拟再娶,则背上包袱,手持雨伞,从棺上跳过。闽南有的地方丧葬习俗中还有一种与死者断绝关系的仪式称"割阄",即在入殓前,将长麻丝一端系于死者身上,另一端则由直系亲属各执一段,由道士念吉语,并将丝一一斩断,然后各人将手中麻丝包在银纸中烧掉,以表示与死者断绝来往而不被缠扰。

福建各地还有许多相沿已久的葬俗。闽东畲族丧葬习俗有很多特别之处,如"拣遗骸":每至冬至,家中若有亲人去世后土葬已满三年以上者,须在此日到葬地开棺捡骨,然后置于瓮中,移放在遮风之处,以后再选吉日埋葬。闽东寿宁有称为"金瓶位"的葬俗:将死者的棺木烧后拾取骨灰置瓶于厝,这些置放骨灰瓶的处所通常在居所后,主要用以安置亲族骨瓶,如有余位,可卖与他人。福建客家人丧葬也很特别,如"倒寿":一般以60岁为寿,老人年逾六十而去世,称为"倒寿"。因"寿"和"树"谐音,故在其祖宅屋后或山林,选砍一大树,作为治丧燃料之用。

四、信仰禁忌

　　信仰民俗源于对自然界万物的崇拜,远古时期传下的"万物有灵"观念对后世的信仰有着根深蒂固的影响。信仰具有鲜明的区域性,它的产生与人们的居住环境、生产方式、生活方式有着极为密切的关系。福建各地有各种各样的崇拜,但对蛇的崇拜最为突出。福建闽越族以蛇为图腾,产生于史前的华安许多岩画,均与蛇有关。如华安草仔山岩画图案为两条既不相交也不相连的曲线,之间有一不甚规则的半椭圆形,画面迎向小溪。图案酷似蛇形,长者代表一条母蛇,短者和半椭圆形代表幼蛇和蛇蛋。华安蕉林花岗石刻有蛇形,或似两条交叉的蛇,一个蛇蛋、一条刚刚破壳而出的幼蛇;或似一条盘曲的小蛇;或似纠结在一起的两条蛇;或似首尾相连的蛇;或似结群游动的蛇群。武夷山市发掘的汉城遗址中出土的西汉瓦当,就有类似蛇形的图案。闽越族之所以把蛇作为图腾,是因为其祖先生活在温湿的丘陵山区,溪谷江河纵横交错,许多蛇类繁衍滋生其中,对闽越族人的生命和生产无疑有极大威胁。住在泉州以南的华安一带的闽越族先民,正是因为水患和蛟螭之害,才刻画以祈求神灵的保护。人们由害怕、恐惧到求拜、信仰而建庙供奉,希望能供助于祈祷来获得好的结果。南平樟湖板地方的崇蛇习俗极为隆重,有些遗风一直延续到今天。每年六月下旬开始,村民四出捕蛇,捕到后交给蛇王庙中的巫师,巫师将蛇放入小口陶瓷或木桶中养着,并发给交蛇者一张证明。到了七月初七,凭证明领养一条活蛇参加迎蛇活动。迎蛇队伍浩浩荡荡,前有旗幡招展,鼓乐开道,紧接着是蛇王菩萨舆驾,后面跟着几百人的迎蛇队伍,每人都拿着蛇,或挂在脖子上,或抓在手里,或挎在肩上,千姿百态,颇为壮观,最后送到蛇王庙前的闽江放生。

福建民间还有许多对其他动物的信仰。如闽西南的一些客家人信仰"龟"和"獐"。客家人居住的山村多河谷,洞中多长龟。客家人把龟看成能带来幸福的圣物,用猪肉、田螺等好食品养龟,以求"富贵"。他们把人活百岁称"龟龄";庆寿用的糯米粿上也要印上"龟印"。客家人对獐也爱护备至,认为它心地善良,能帮助百姓消灾免病,抵御邪恶,是"圣物"。闽南畲族以狗为图腾崇拜,今天依然完整流传下来。他们对狗不打不骂,不杀不吃,顶礼膜拜,狗死后,脖子上套上"银钱"纸放入水中漂走。福建是猴子的昌盛之地,早就有崇拜猴的习俗,闽南曾有过许多猴庙,今天在南靖、平和、永泰仍有百姓祀猴王庙。

福建民间还普遍存在着对树木山石的崇拜。凡是较为古老的树木,都被看做是有灵气的神木。如枫神、榕神、樟王、松公等,其中榕树作为吉神化身而更受信仰。无论城镇乡村,大凡在浓荫蔽日的著名古榕下,都会有神龛安放,人们在树下敬香,祀求平安。一些村庄前后或村里的自然石,往往被认为是土地公的神位,是超自然的神灵,受到很好的保护和敬奉。

福建民间被崇拜、受到信仰的神不少,其中最著名的是天上圣母、临水夫人、保生大帝这三神。这三尊民间神原型都是人,后被逐渐演化为神,赋予类人而又超人的"神"力,再借以护佑人们自身。

"天上圣母"也称为"妈祖海神",原名林默,是五代闽都巡检林愿的第六女儿,生于宋太祖建隆元年(960年)农历三月二十三日,宋太宗雍熙四年(987年)农历九月初九日在莆田湄州岛羽化升天。相传她逝世后经常显灵护佑过往船只,救助海难,因此被渔民视为航海保护神,在民间被尊称为"妈祖"、"娘娘",从宋元到明清,多次被统治者褒封升级,从"夫人"、"天妃"、"天后",直到被尊为

"天上圣母",妈祖也成为民间信仰的神祇。每年农历三月二十三日妈祖生日,到湄州岛祭祀妈祖海神的真是人山人海,全岛香火缭绕,有时水泄不通。湄州岛渔民每逢三月二十三日的前后数日内,不敢下海捕鱼或垂钓,以示对妈祖的纪念。莆田一带因崇拜妈祖有许多习俗:因相传妈祖穿朱服,故湄州岛妇女常穿一条上半截为红色的外裤,以此保平安;因据传妈祖生前梳船帆型发型,湄州岛妇女也都梳此型,以求庇护;据传菖蒲为妈祖所赐,莆田一带端午节必于大门顶上悬挂艾草菖蒲;因妈祖殁于九月初九,所以莆田一带在九月初九必蒸"九重米"。此外,凡出海的船员三角旗上都绣着"天上圣母"四字,借以避邪。

"临水夫人",原名陈靖姑,一般认为她是福州南台下渡陈家之女,生于唐大历元年(766年)正月十五日,卒于唐贞元六年(790年)七月二十八日。相传她因身殉产厄,故立誓"吾死后不救世人产难,不神也",灵魂赴闾山恳请许真君再传救产保胎之法,以救女界之难产,因此她具有"护胎救产,催生保赤佑童"的神力。妇女临产时,常供临水夫人神像于家中,婴儿生下第三日,要煮糯米供于神像前。陈靖姑后被越奉越神,凡无子之妇向她请花亦可得子。婚后几年不产的妇女到庙中临水夫人像前膜拜祈祷后,跪下将衣襟牵着拱起,由老妇将注生娘娘头上插的或神座前别人还的花,拿来放在她衣襟里说:"生了后,来拜临水夫人为干妈。"接着将花插在少妇头上。取来的花,红的象征生女,白的象征生男。每年临水夫人诞辰日,要预先由多福长寿的老太太数人为庙中神像更换新衣,女士焚香膜拜,夜晚抬临水夫人神像巡行街市。每年祭日要在"灿斗"中置"童子"代替孩子,由师公吹牛角号将"灿斗"放置小孩床上。临水夫人终年24岁,因此女性忌在24岁结婚。

"保生大帝"也称"健康保护神",原名吴夲,也称吴真人,宋代泉州府同安县白礁人,生于太平兴国四年(979年),卒于景祐三年(1036年)。吴夲是一位信奉道教的民间草药医生,医术高明,所治之疾,无不痊愈。治病时不论病人贫富贵贱,皆济世为怀,以其高超的医术和高尚的医德闻名于闽南一带,赢得百姓的敬仰和崇拜。他因治病救人,攀崖采药不慎跌落深谷身亡。人们在他的出生地和炼丹施药处分别修建了"真人庙"(慈济宫),历代朝廷九次追封其谥号,直到明代的"万寿无极保生大帝"。由于吴夲的医术、医德符合黎民百姓的切身利益,所以对他的崇拜久盛不衰。百姓凡有病痛都要求吴夲保佑。正月迎神赛会中,吴夲作为出巡诸神,乘八人抬轿,灯牌以千数。每年三月十五日是吴夲的诞辰日,"社人鼓乐旗帜,楼阁彩亭前导,浩浩荡荡,至慈济宫传香以归"。

禁忌是一种信仰习俗中消极防范性的制裁手段或观念,它包含两方面意思:一是对受尊重的神物不许随便使用;二是对受鄙视的贱物,不洁、危险之物,不许随便接触。一切禁忌,都不可违反,否则被认为迟早会受到制裁和惩罚。福建的各种禁忌五花八门,千奇百怪,有的甚至因互相矛盾而显得更加扑朔迷离。其广泛性和复杂性已渗透在人们生活和生产的各个方面,伴随人们一生。

福州的生活禁忌可谓无所不在。主人请吃饭时,往往将饭盛得山般高,客人尽可以表示吃不了这么多,将饭往主人饭碗里拨,但千万不要犹豫不决,更不要顺手将筷子插在饭碗上,这样极不吉利。因为福州在供奉灵堂棺头时有一碗装得爆满的"丧食",上面直插一双筷子。除夕年饭后,必须用手纸擦小孩嘴巴,说明孩子所说"死了"、"坏了"等不吉利的话不算数。赴结婚宴席时不能将盘碗重叠,否则就意味着重婚。席间上的全鱼不能动,借以祝主人家全头全尾食有余。家人出远门、亲友远来、长辈做寿、新婚初嫁等必吃两只鸭蛋和一束线面泡的"太平面"。说话禁忌更多,"要碗饭"应称"来碗饭",避"要饭"之意;"短裤"应称"裤长"或"半长裤",因"裤"与"库"同音,要避"短库"之意。如某人死了,则不直呼"死",而称"生";"治丧衣"称"做寿衣";"买棺材"称"选寿板"。

闽南禁忌也很繁多。人一诞生到世上就有许多规定,动辄犯忌。如新生婴儿未满月时,忌见六种人:戴孝的人、新娘、病人、孤寡、陌生人、疯子。因为戴孝的人是丧事,与喜事不能相冲。新娘是喜事,双喜亦不能相冲。其他四种人会给婴儿带来不幸。赠送坐月子的妇女应为鸡,忌送鸭,因鸭阴湿,且民间有"死鸭硬嘴闭"、"七月半鸭,不知死期"之说,会令人想起"死期",不吉利。结婚时禁忌人站门碇,也禁忌人带手电入新娘房。除夕、初一禁忌打破用具,特别是碗盘。家中出事,如病或发生意外,常插松枝,并禁忌生人进家,以避邪。凡参加丧事的人,禁忌再参加红事(如结婚),家中死人,一年内禁忌办喜事(如结婚)。出门回家或外出访友,如穿草鞋,要放在门外,不然会被认为把路上"煞气"带进来,因为草鞋是孝子带在身上行孝的东西。赠送人礼物禁忌单数,一定要双数,取成双成对、喜庆团圆之意。有一些东西禁忌赠人,如手巾、剪刀、扇子、雨伞等。手巾是办丧事时主人家送吊丧者的纪念品,意在永别。剪刀有"一刀两断"之意,闽南方言雨伞与"给丧"同音。扇子夏用秋丢,不很长久。禁忌以甜粿、粽子赠送人,因为丧家按惯例要蒸甜粿、粽子,送这二物,犹如把对方当丧家。上山忌叫名,因为鬼魂知道名字后会前来纠缠。入林忌呼啸,因为怕惊动野兽。下水忌单身,上屋忌坐瓦檐口,因为这样会失事。衣服忌反穿,因为反穿是表示家中有人去世。忌用筷敲打桌面和碗盘,忌用手或器物敲打烛,因为这样会伤害"灶君公神"。

虽然处于同一区域,由于生活方式和生产方式不同,禁忌也不同。闽南沿海一带渔家,吃鱼禁"翻"。上面的鱼肉吃完了,得先把露在上面的鱼脊骨夹掉,然后再吃下面的鱼肉,千万不能将鱼从盘底整条翻转过来。因为翻鱼等于翻船身,是倒霉晦气的兆头。有的地方渔民饭后不能把筷子放在碗沿,而是要把手中筷子在碗上绕几绕,以示渔船绕过了暗礁和浅滩。

五、游艺竞技

　　游艺竞技往往附属在许多民俗事象之中,缺乏独立性,但也正是这些游艺竞技使许多民俗事象更好地流传下来。因此,游艺竞技也有着明显民族特色和地方特点。福建的各类民俗绚丽多彩,游艺竞技的各类花样也不胜枚举。

　　游艺竞技与岁时佳节有密切的关系,不少地方都有自己独特的活动节目。晋江坑亭顶村过端午节时,有别具一格的"投递"习俗。"投递"在当地土语叫"练星",是一种表演枪法的活动。表演者手持鸟枪,身背药囊(即牛角形的木制枪药罐)和药袋(布制装导火材料和小铁子的小袋),按规定谱式,逾越不同障碍物,临阵之中随机应变,按不同环境、地势,以不同姿势进行瞄准发射。"投递"的脚路操练必须严格按不同谱路,其握枪姿势和脚路步法,都必须严格按程式规制进行。只有熟练掌握这些基本脚路,才能在冲跑之间取得较高的命中率。观看者可以看到表演者的臂功、腿功、腰功、指功、目功等。安溪湖头镇每逢春节,都要举行盛大的"扮阁"活动。双人床宽的"阁台"周围有一尺高的栏棚,台的两端各竖一根铁杆,绑上一块木板,让两个美少年坐在上面,并用新织的裹脚布将他们绑在铁杆上,为他们穿上花旦戏装,涂脂搽粉,戴着珠冠,使其窈窕动人。两人将脚缩在裤管里,裤管下巧妙地装上一双三寸金莲。他们左手小指上结一条丝巾,使其在敲檀板按拍子时韵致优雅。"阁台"用新的花纸裱糊,纸扎的盆花置于中间,将全台布置得像一个小花铺。两个花旦手执檀板,唱着南曲,四个壮汉抬着彩台,跟着游春队伍游行。每到一处,就停下来唱一两支南曲。南平峡阳镇也有春节抬"台阁"上街游行的习俗。这种"台阁"是一种活动舞台,有一米见方,四周装有镂花小栏杆,台中央钉一根弯曲成上下两节的铁架,分别站着四五岁小孩,各自打扮成戏剧中人物,如哪吒闹海、机房教子、三顾茅庐等。晋江东石镇逢节日则以

"蜈蚣阁"（也称"龙阁"）形式庆贺。阁队用几十块长二米、宽一米的木板组成阁棚，头尾打活隼相连接，能够灵活转动，连成长串，阁棚上装置各种制作精巧的禽兽，再选美丽活泼的孩童装成各种戏曲人物。阁棚前装上龙头，末尾装上龙尾，由身强力壮、穿戴统一的小伙子肩扛着游行，极像蜈蚣或游龙的形状。

　　福建一些地方岁时佳节的游艺有着独特的表现方式。政和东平乡正月里不是舞龙灯而是跑龙赛，实际是一种化了装的短跑运动。比赛在晒谷坪上进行，起点在谷坪一侧，用四根带叶的大毛竹搭成两座相交的拱门称为龙门；终点在与龙门相对的另一侧，用两根带叶大毛竹搭起一座拱门，拱门中间距地面三米处，悬挂一盏红光耀眼象征龙珠的圆形灯笼，叫作珠门。跑龙赛的队伍由七人组成，他们手中所举的篾制笼第一盏扎成龙头，最后一盏扎成龙尾，七盏连结形成一条长龙。东、南、西、北四街各制一条龙灯，用循环赛形式，每次两队，以龙门为起点，两队队员手举龙灯，各自绕龙门转三圈，然后以最快速度向珠门冲去，以龙头先碰上珠门的龙珠者为胜。赛期四天，积胜者为冠军。闽南有的地方在中秋节不是赏月，而是进行"戏饼"（也称"赌饼"）的游戏，即将六颗骰子在一大碗中投骰，其方式与赌博投骰子差不多，每个骰子有六面，有一、二、三、四、五、六点符号，所投根据不同符号分饼：状元饼1块，对长榜眼探花饼2块，三红会元饼4块，四进进士饼8块，二举举人饼16块，一秀秀才饼32块。"戏饼"的赢输，必须等到所有的饼都有归属才能定局。最后夺取状元，是很吉利的。夺冠者喜气洋洋放炮庆贺，饼大家分吃。连城罗坊、北团一带元宵节以"走故事"来闹元宵，具有浓郁的地方特色。罗坊罗氏原有九棚（组、台）故事，后减为七棚。每棚故事由俊童两名分别扮天官、护将，作戏曲装扮，其后人物的扮相依次为李世民、薛仁贵，刘邦、樊哙，杨六郎、杨宗保，高贞、梅文仲，刘备、孔明，周瑜、甘宁。两两一对。天官直立在一条铁杆上，腰身四周以铁圈固定，护将坐在轿台上，以手托天官，形成一上一下优美造型。轿台由木柱镶成方形框架,四周饰有精美画屏。每台轿约400斤,左右各一轿杠,须用20余名扛夫,因竞走激烈,要三班轮替。"走故事"分两次进行。第一次在十四日上午,扛夫们将三太祖师菩萨轿、彩旗、宝伞等围于中间,在400米椭圆形跑道上奋力奔走,每跑两圈就休息十分钟,土铳响过一声就又开始跑。五轮时速度有所减缓,改"跑"为"游",直到扛夫精疲力竭,第一棚与第二棚脱节,才告结束。第二次"走故事"在正月十五日上午进行,开始依前一日走法,到了正午一时,各棚故事步下青岩河床,土铳响三声后,个个蜂拥下水,逆水行走。各棚竞争激烈,若后棚能超过前棚,则视为吉利,这一族房必五谷丰登。扛夫们不顾天寒水深,拼命争先,跌倒了再爬起,情绪非常高昂。

游艺竞技也与各种迎神庙会有着密切的关系。福州曾将泰山当做全市性的神,因此迎泰山要比迎一般神隆重。每年农历三月二十三日无论各种神,都要到东岳庙中参拜泰山神。泰山神二十四日游城内,二十五日游南台。出游队伍极为庞大,前有天子仪仗,十八般武器,继而是各种彩戏,如:就地演唱各小戏的"高跷"、"地下坪";壮汉肩驮小孩扮成彩童的"肩头驮";吹鼓手坐在租来的马上吹奏曲子的"马上吹";各种乐曲一起吹奏的"十番"、"安南伬";有肩挑着鲜花的"花担";装有文物担子的"看担";童男童女在木制小戏台上装扮成戏中人的"台阁"。其中最热闹、最吸引人的是"陆地行舟"。这是以彩结扎成的花船,舟中所载二人扮花旦、小生,舟前舟后各一人扮成舟子作摇船撑篙状,如船行水中,载歌载舞。迎神沿途遇到有排堂设宴的"行宫",只要放一串鞭炮,舟中花旦、小生就要来一段表演,唱些时新小调。彩戏后是黑无常、白无常、叉神爷、哪吒三太子像以及各种神将,皆扭动各自的一套舞步。再后是由活人扮成的28名太监提炉、彩灯引导,8名大将护驾,16人抬着泰山软身神像,缓缓而行。同安一带盛行在迎神赛会上进行"套宋江"游艺。"套"是模仿、表演的意思,这是一种武打艺术的表演。每逢农历正月初六日香山清水祖师和二月十二日北山闽王王审知的圣诞庙会，都有五六队的宋江队到场操演，人数一般有或72人。所扮人物为卢俊义、柴进、李逵、孙二娘等，手持兵器，由正副旗手举龙旗前导。表演地用两面布条搭起一座城面，队伍分两路出城，叫"黄蜂出阵"。之后，便开始单人武术表演，有李逵使双斧、关胜舞大刀等，再接着进行对打，如盾牌对锤子、雨伞对大刀、踢刀对铁耙等，也可以三至五人进行群斗表演。表演时还加上舞狮，宋江队员与狮子格斗，外有锣鼓、唢呐助威。表演完毕，收兵入城。围观者人山人海。

有的民间游艺要有较高的技巧。如建瓯的排幡一般人便难以操作。幡用一根长达五六米的大竹杆制成，涂上油漆，杆顶悬彩带，上扎一宝塔形的彩灯，缀以五色纸花或戏剧故事人物，配上丝料。表演时将杆扶起，放在表演者的足尖上，轻轻一挑，使幡落在人的肩上，再一拦，落在手上。表演者往往左右开弓，由脚到肩，由肩到手，舞将起来，甚至嘴咬鼻顶，幡并不倒歪。杆上彩灯彩绸闪烁，五色缤纷，仿佛九天神灯在半空飘拂急转，令人目不暇接。

六、饮食与饮茶

在我国京、鲁、闽、粤、苏、皖、川、湘八大菜系中，闽菜别具一格。

福州菜是闽菜的主要代表，有着独特的风味。福州菜肴用料和调味均以地方材料为主，操作注重刀工、火候，色、香、味、形俱佳，烹调上擅长炒、熘、煨、炖、蒸、爆诸法，其主要特点是：1. 善用糖。福州人煮菜，喜用糖调味，偏于甜、酸、淡，与川菜、湘菜多用辣椒形成不同风格。用糖可以去腥膻，用醋使酸能爽口，适合福州炎热气候口味；淡是为了保存本味和鲜味。由于用得恰到好处，所以甜而不腻，酸而不峻，淡而不薄。2. 常用糟。红糟是福建特产，福州菜肴有炮糟、淡糟、醉糟等十余种用糟法。此外，在调味品中也多用虾油（鲑油）。3.多汤菜。福州菜善于以汤保味，有"百汤百味"之说。汤是闽菜的精髓，在汤中加上适当的辅料，可使原汤变化出无数益臻佳美的味道来，而又不失其本味。福州菜花色品种有2 000种以上，其"佛跳墙"、"淡糟炒竹蛏"、"一品蚌抱蛎"等都是名扬海内外的名菜。

　　具有鲜明地方风味的福建饮食的形成，与福建独有的地理、物产、气候有着密切的关系。福建海岸线长，海产丰富，因此以海产类为主的菜居多，如著名的有"鸡汤川海蚌"、"白炒鲜干贝"、"酥鱿鱼丝"等，一些风味小吃也以海产类为多，如"深沪水丸（鱼丸）"、"海蛎煎（蚝仔煎）"、"炒蟹羹"等。福建山多，盛产山货，著名的有连城地瓜干、武平猪胆干、上杭萝卜干、明溪肉脯干、永定菜干、宁化辣椒干、清流老鼠干、长汀豆腐干等，一些名菜也多以山货为原料，如闽北山区的"清水冬笋"和"酿香菇"、福鼎的"太极芋泥"等。福建以种植水稻为主，许多具有地方特色的食品也以米为原料，如厦门的"烧肉粽（好清香）"，闽南一带的"石狮甜粿"，福州市的"抱滚糌（豆粉糌）"、"白八粿"，莆田的"兴化粉"，闽西的"糍粑"等。福建气候温暖，适合种植热带、亚热带和部分温带水果，以柑桔、龙眼、荔枝、香蕉、菠萝、枇杷、橄榄、甘蔗等闻名，因此对各类水果的食用也较为讲究，如漳州有著名的"柚子宴"，宴席上点"柚灯"，喝"柚茶"，吃柚果和柚皮蜜饯。泉州的"东壁龙珠"，将馅填入去核的龙眼肉中炒炸。永春的"金桔糖"、厦门的"青津果"、福州的"五香橄榄"等，都声名远播海内外。

　　福建雨量充沛，多红黄壤土，具有种植茶叶的优越自然条件。绿茶、乌龙茶、红茶、花茶、白茶和紧压茶是我国六大茶类，除主要为少数民族饮用的紧压茶（即茶砖、茶饼等）外，其他五大茶类福建都有大量生产，且几乎每县都产茶，与浙、湘、皖、川并列为我国五大产茶区，其中一些珍品，如安溪"铁观音"、武夷山"大红袍"、福鼎"白毫银针"等闻名遐迩。福建茶叶生产历史悠久，南唐时闽北已有"北苑御茶园",饮茶风俗为全国最盛之地,已成"家不可一日无茶",形成了独有的饮茶风俗。

功夫茶,是以严格泡茶艺术门道进行泡茶与品茶的高深技艺,它有许多讲究,极具功夫。它要求茶叶为铁观音、乌龙茶、武夷岩茶中的上品;还要求有精致的茶具,茶壶以内壁无上釉为好,茶杯以小巧为佳;水以山泉为上,井水溪水次之;煮水必须用炭火,冲泡时必须"高冲低泡",高冲可以翻动茶叶使汁味迅速释出,低泡水不走香,不生水泡。品茶时,端起核桃般小巧的茶杯,先尽情领略茶的馨香味,而后徐徐将茶啜入嘴喉,再专注细尝茶的滋味,只觉嘴生甘味,顿感回肠荡气,真所谓"茶里乾坤大,壶中日月长"。

斗茶,亦称"茗战",或称"比茶",具体内容有点茶、试茶,以品评茶质高低而分输赢。范仲淹《和章岷从事斗茶歌》写出了闽北斗茶盛况:"……斗茶味兮轻醍醐,斗茶香兮薄兰芷。其间品第胡能欺,十目视而十手指。胜若登仙不可攀,输同降将无穷耻。"斗茶时将茶碾为细末,搁入涤烫过的茶盏中,再注入沸水,轻轻搅动,以比试茶的汤色和在盏中的水痕来决定品种的优劣胜负。斗茶的操作技艺很讲究,注入沸水时,要准确而有节制,不然"茶少汤多则云脚散,汤水少则粥面紧"。一手注水时,另一手须执茶筅,旋转拂动茶盏中茶汤,轻重缓急要得当,要与注水配合默契。斗茶得胜后,其茶之销路与茶价必定大增,所以争冠夺魁是茶农的一件大事,而斗茶的兴盛,又进一步促进了茶质量的提高与饮茶之风的盛行。

分茶,亦称"茶百戏",即以沸水冲茶末,使茶乳变幻成图形字迹的一种游艺。茶水交融,汤纹水脉成物象,呈现奇妙变幻,有如鸟兽、虫鱼、花草,有时似悠远美景,又似纤巧之画,但须臾即散。诗人杨万里《澹庵座上观显上人分茶》诗,生动地描绘了分茶的情景:"分茶何似煎茶好,煎茶不似分茶巧,蒸水老禅弄泉手,隆兴元春新玉爪。……纷如劈絮行太空,影落寒空能万变,银瓶首下仍尻高,注汤作势字嫖姚。"

　　擂茶是风行于闽西、闽北的习俗,它用上好的绿茶加白芝麻、花生、绿豆各种佐料及多种中药配在一起,放进擂钵里用擂棒擂碎后,再研成烂泥状,用纱布包裹,扎口滤筛,用烧好的山泉水冲泡。擂茶有不同种类,根据加入佐料不同,可分为甜、咸、荤、素等多种。其中最著名的是将乐擂茶,其特点是讲究药效。制作时针对不同季节、气候,不同的人和不同的场合,加入不同功效的中草药,制出有各种疗效的药用擂茶,诸如清凉解毒的、帮助消化的,止咳化痰的等等。制成后的擂茶颜色纯净,味道清香,甘醇爽口,喝下后满嘴生香。擂茶还是款待客人的隆重礼品,也是表达喜庆的方式。高考制度恢复后,有的地方多了一个"上大学擂茶"的习俗,老师成为最受欢迎的客人。

　　茶艺是博大精深的茶文化的精髓,是一种极富诗意雅兴的赏心乐事,也是一种高层次的精神享受。品茶有许多讲究,如要有清雅古香的环境、平和矜持的心境、光泽油亮的茶具、清冽的山泉、以砂壶或铜壶盛水、以木炭炉煮水,但更讲究冲泡技巧和品尝艺术。冲泡有许多规矩和门道,如斟头道茶时,各杯先斟少许,然后均匀巡回而斟,喻为"关公巡城"。茶水剩少许后,则各杯点斟,喻为"韩信点兵"。端茶杯时,宜用拇指和食指扶住杯身,中指托住杯底,喻为"三龙护鼎"。

第九章　教育

　　福建开发较晚，教育起步也较迟。据文献所载，西晋太康三年（282年）福建设晋安郡，刘宋时期，阮弥之任晋安太守时开始兴办学校，当时社会出现"家有诗书，市无器斗"（《福建通志·名宦》）现象。虞愿任晋安太守时，"初立学堂，教授子弟"（《南史·虞愿传》）。此外，一些中原人士移居闽地时，断断续续地办过学堂，虽然影响都不大，但为以后教育的兴盛奠定了基础。

　　隋唐时期，福建还处于开发阶段，但教育已有较大发展。唐宗室李椅任福建观察使时，"崇学校，励风俗"（《三山志·秩官》）并"大启府学，劝诱生徒"（《八闽通志·秩官》）。常衮任福建观察使时，"设乡校，延名师儒以教闽人，闽人始知向学"（《重修常衮墓志》）。建州刺史陆长源也注重创办学校，劝人入学。漳州刺史陈元光命子弟读书勤学，鼓励漳州人读书。陈元光之子陈珦曾代州事，聚徒授课。据《图经》所说："李椅、常衮皆以崇重学校为意，于时海滨几及洙泗。"五代时，福建教育开始普及。一方面是唐代名士于唐亡后纷纷回乡创办学校，如原工部尚书黄峭归乡创办了和平书院，"聘请宿儒，讲授诗书，诱掖后进"（《紫云黄氏的开山祖黄峭》）；另一方面，闽王王审知广设学校，拨出专门经费供师生膳食，并下令学龄儿童均需入学。现存福州闽王祠的《琅琊郡王德政碑》记载："尝以学校之设，足为教化之源。乃令诱掖蒙童，兴行敬让。"

五代时期福建社会较为安定,也为教育的普及提供了条件。

宋代福建的教育有了很大的发展。南平剑州州学创办于天圣三年(1025年),体制、学田设置、教师配备等皆达到一定水准。之后,福建八个军州都办有州学,后来还办了许多县学,可查的就有56所。宋代福建书院之多,质量之高,影响之大,亦为全国罕见。据《武夷胜境理学遗迹考》所载,仅与朱熹等理学家有关的书院就达20所。其中建阳县境内,就有14所,一些书院在全国都有影响,慕名而来的外省学子络绎不绝。宋代福建义斋、书堂、家塾等民办教育也极普及,读书蔚然成风。如福州"最忆市桥灯火静,巷南巷北读书声";南安"百里之间,弦诵相闻"(《番建夫子庙记》);汀州"风声气习,颇类中州"(宋陈一新《跋赡学田碑》);延平"五步一塾,十步一庠,朝诵暮弦,洋洋盈盈"(《延平府志》);邵武"比屋弦诵之声,洋洋盈耳"(《邵武府志》);甚至连偏僻的泰宁,也"比屋连墙,弦诵之声相闻,有不读诗书者,舆台笑之"(《泰宁县志》)。

元明清福建教育虽因战乱、倭患等原因在某些地区间有衰微,但总的还是向前发展,并在全国名列前茅。以各代新建书院为例,据不完全统计,可查到的有一定影响的书院,元代有20余所,明代近200所,清代300余所。明清时书院已不仅仅密布于闽北理学之乡和政治文化中心福州,而是遍及全省。如明代闽东新建10余所书院,闽西新建30余所,清闽西新建书院100余所,闽东新建书院近30所。清代福建开始出现全省性书院,如鳌峰、凤池、正谊、致用四大书院,培养出林则徐、林纾、陈宝琛等著名人物。清末福建出现了官办的全闽大学堂、洋务派办的船政学堂、外国教会办的教会学校等。

福建教育由唐至近代久盛不衰,主要原因有以下几点:

地方官吏的支持和倡导。地方官吏对教育是否重视,对教育的兴衰起着最为关键的作用。所幸的是,主福建的地方长官,大都对教育都很重视,对推动福建的教育采取了积极措施。唐代,常衮任福建观察使时,大兴学校,鼓励生员读书,使"闽人春秋配享袞于学宫"(《新唐书·常袞传》)。陈元光任漳州刺史时,非常重视教育,他在上《请建州县表》中指出:"其本则在创州县,其要则在兴庠序。"他在州治行政机构中设专司教育的官吏,并在漳州首创乡校,还创办了松州书院。兵部尚书熊秘领兵入守温陵(泉州)时,在建阳创建了鳌峰书院,以教子弟。五代时,闽王王审知于福州"建四门学(高等学府),以教闽中之秀者"(吴任臣《十国春秋》)。在他倡导下,当时州有州学,县有县学,乡村设有私塾,"幼已佩于师训,长者置于国庠"(吴任臣《十国春秋》)。泉州都指挥使留从效统治泉州时,兴设"秋堂"。宋朝实行重文政策,办学成绩与社会风尚成为地方官员考绩的内容之一。福建大小地方官都倾力办学,据有关史籍所记,有名有姓的不下百余名,不仅诸如福建安抚使辛弃疾一类著名人物兴教办学,一些偏僻小县,如连城、建宁、古田、浦城、宁化等知县,也大兴学校,使宋代福建教育空前普及。元代,也不少地方官对福建教育兴盛有过贡献。泉州达鲁花赤契玉、松溪达鲁花赤阿思兰、尤溪达鲁花赤文殊每涯等入主福建的少数民族地方官都大兴教育,拨出专门学田。地方官还纷纷创办、修建书院,如邵武路同知万不花创办樵川书院、光泽县伊况逵创办云岩书院、福建右布政副使姚镆修闽中诸大儒书院,明清两代许多福建地方官吏不仅关心各种学校的创立,还注意解决学校的后顾之忧。他们或拨专款,或购买学田,采用多种方式解决学校经济上的困难,以期学校有长久的发展。值得注意的是,福建历代地方官吏常常主动捐俸银。如宋代崇安知县赵崇萃曾捐俸请买开元寺废寺田以充学廪,延平郡守陈宓捐俸购田以赡延平书院生徒,漳州知府李音石捐俸置学田,建宁知县捐俸二千余缗增新邑学。明代福建巡按使尹仁捐俸银一百两重建庐峰书院,古田县令捐俸买民地以广学舍,将乐县令林熙春捐俸造新学舍,端明殿学士陈显伯出资修建了罗源松亭书院,兵部右侍郎兼右金都御史陈省倾资捐修紫阳书院。

清代晋江县令赵同岐捐俸倡修梅石书院,松溪县令孙大焜捐资重修南溪书院,宁德县令徐文翰捐俸为学校灯油之资,泉州通判徐之霖捐俸重建左营讲堂,福建巡抚孙尔准捐银为凤池书院学生助学金。有时,有的地方官还带领部下捐俸建校,如海坛镇守吕瑞霖率手下两营官兵捐俸创建兴文书院。

有一批高水平的教师。这些教师主要是一些以教书为业的教育家。每个朝代都有这样一批教育家,仅宋代,就有罗从彦、李侗、朱熹、李光朝、蔡立定、黄干等,其中朱熹从事教育50多年,提出了七大教学原则,其教育实践和教育思想,对中国后期封建社会都产生了极大的影响。此外,一些著名政治家、哲学家、文学家、军事家也常到课堂讲学,这些人虽然不是终身从教,其成就也不以教育显,但他们的讲课却活跃了学术空气,扩大丰富了学生的知识,因此吸引了不少学子。如宋代,杨时晚年丢官返乡后讲学,学生千人。一代名臣蔡襄曾以枢密学士知福州,"亲至学舍执经讲问,为诸生率"(《东越文苑传》)。史学家郑樵曾授徒200人,文学家杨亿也开馆授徒。明代著名军事家、音韵学家陈弟曾多次到漳州、福州讲学,对学生多有勉励;著名学者黄道周曾五次回乡讲学,从学者近千人。清代杰出爱国者和民族英雄林则徐在中进士前也教过馆。著名文学家林纾曾做过塾师和福州苍霞精舍的汉文教习。一些在朝廷任官的闽籍杰出人物常因丁父忧或母忧而返乡守孝,其间也常应邀讲学,大大开阔了学生的视野。如清代刑部奉天司主事陈若霖因丁母忧,曾主讲漳州丹霞书院;内阁中书李彦章因丁父忧返乡,曾主讲兴化兴安书院一年;翰林院编修林春溥因丁母忧回乡,曾主讲玉屏书院。

科举的久盛不衰。我国正式开始以试策取士,始于隋,唐代开始大兴。虽然唐五代福建还处于开发阶段,人口仅70万左右,但已有74人中进士;宋代共有7 607人中进士,22人为状元,按人口比例,为全国第一,并创造出不少奇迹。以莆田县为例,曾同科文武两状元,连科三状元,囊括一榜前四名等,均为全国前所未有。元代福建有76人中进士,高于南方汉人各省。明代福建有2 410人中进士,在全国仍名列前茅,其中竟然出现一榜三及第皆闽人这种绝无仅有的事。清代福建有1 337人中进士,仍略高于全国平均水平。科举制的兴旺,大大推动教育的普及。考生中互相勉励,早有传统。欧阳詹是泉州唐代第一个中进士的,福建士子感到莫大光荣,参加科举的人日益增多。泉州士子徐晦首次赴考落第,欧阳詹对他多有勉励,使他加倍苦读,翌年考取第一。许多闽人以考上进士为终身奋斗目标,如宋代闽县陈修曾下决心不考上进士不成婚,不料屡试屡败,至73岁时才被录取,宋高宗下诏赐宫女施氏嫁他。洞房花烛夜,施氏问他几岁,他答曰:"新人若问郎年几?五十年前二十三。"类似这种终身在科场上奋斗的士子当时为数不少。为了使士子能如愿以偿,一些教师也千方百计想办法,如泉州明代陈紫峰费了很大精力将《四书》、《易经》这两部士子登科的基本经书译为白话讲稿《四书浅说》和《易经通典》。之后,他自己也中了进士。

家族对教育的重视。福建的家族大都注意族人的教育,《闽沙茂溪罗氏族谱》曾记有著名学者罗从彦在罗氏家族书堂上写的话:"吾家自祖宗流传以来,一段清白之气不可不培。盖金帛虽多,积之数十年必散,田宇虽广,遗之数十代亦亡。孰若残书数卷,贻之吾子吾孙,世世可以习读不朽,又孰若灵心一点,传之吾子吾孙,可以受用不尽。"表示了对教育的高度重视,并形成了以读书为光荣,以不读书为可耻的族风。如明代林希元撰《林氏家谱》中记道:"林氏世代以读书为业,有不为此业而又不改者,赶出家门。"有的家族把开办族学、族塾写进族规,如连城《新泉张氏族谱》记道:"今议设义学二所,经师一所,在东山楼;蒙馆一所,即在祠内。"为了保证族人能受教育,各家族都采取了许多措施。在经费上,不少家族都置有学田,即"书灯田"。如清陈盛韶《问俗录》中所记:"书灯田,祖父分产之始,留田若干亩,为子孙读书之需,后有入学者收其租,捐纳者不得与其租。"不少地方若干家族还携手共同创办私塾,各姓合资修建书院。如长乐梅花里,共有40余姓相处,清代共议创办了和羹书院。为了激励族人弟子的学习,一些家族还作了经济奖励等规定,如浦城《达氏宗谱》规定:"入泮者,给蓝衫花银二两,凡赴乡试者,给程银四两;凡赴会试进士者,给程银八两;及第衣锦祭祖者,给旗杆银二十两。"族人还注意选派族中有名望人办学,如宋代泉州进士陈知柔辞官返乡后,为族人办起学堂,他的侄儿陈朴、陈模等都先后登第,"一门八骏",县府为之竖立"世科坊"。家族对教育的重视收到了很大成效,创造了中国科举史上的奇观。如唐代莆田林披生有九子,都明经及第,皆官刺史,故有"一家九刺史"之说。五代莆田黄璞举进士,与其四子同列馆职,故有"一门五学士"之说。北宋浦城章氏家族,一门二十四进士,中有一状元,北宋闽清陈玩五子四登科,南宋长乐杨家一门同榜四进士,明代莆田柯家五世进士,明代闽县林氏三世出了八个进士、五位尚书,明代莆田黄氏家族共出十一个解元。子弟靠科举出人头地后,又不忘荫蔽本族,或出资赞助,或激励族中士子苦读,大大推动了教育。

多种类型的学校。福建历代办学有多种形式,除了官办的府学、州学、军学、县学,或官,或民,或半民半官的各种书院、私塾等外,还有多种类型的学校,以满足各种不同阶层人的需要。如宋代在福州、泉州两地特为赵氏皇族子弟开办了宗学,人数多达数千。宋代泉州是海外贸易中心,泉州特为外国侨居者设立了番学。元代在福州、建宁、泉州、漳州、汀州、延平、兴化、福宁、邵武诸路均开设了蒙古字学,元代福建各路和40个县还开设了医学和教授天文、历算、周易、数学等课的科技学校(也称阴阳学)。元、明、清还在城乡创办了千所以上的具有小学和社会义务教育性质的义学,主要是普及伦理和农桑技术,大多数城区一至四所,乡间十所左右,对普及城乡基础教育起了很大作用。福建方言复杂,所以在清代还开设了纠正地方土语的"官音书塾"。还为常住福州的旗人开设了"八旗官学"。有的家族为子女前途开设了外文书塾,如设在螺州的螺江乡塾,除了学日语,还学法语。清末洋务派在福州办起了福建船政学堂,直接聘请洋教习,使用洋课本,按洋式课程设置和教学法教学,并打破门第观念向全社会公开招生,培养了大批优秀的造船、航海和其他方面人才,在我国科技、外交、翻译、教育等方面产生深远影响。基督教传入福建后,在各地创办了许多学校。这些学校对下层平民敞开大门,有一定影响。有的地区(如福州、莆田、南平等)教会学校,竟超过公立、私立学校。清末福建还出现了华侨办学。如清道光年间惠安归侨郭用锡父子捐银千两办学,道光皇帝嘉封诏书,并授予"乐善好施,父子恩荣"的横匾。之后,华侨办学之风越来越盛,成为良好传统。

刻书业的繁荣和藏书的丰富。闽刻书业始于五代,后随着读书应试风气与日盛行,再加上福建造纸原料丰富,所以刻书业鼎盛于宋元明,无论官刻本、家刻本、坊刻本都在同行业中独占鳌头,长盛不衰。宋代建阳麻沙书坊,号称"图书之府",与当时杭州、四川书坊并称全国三大刻书坊,所刻之书被后人称为珍贵的"建本"。元代书坊也以福建地区为最多,如建安陈氏余庆堂、朱氏与耕堂、梅隐书堂、双桂书堂等,都刻了很多精美的书籍。明代书坊福建更盛,在建阳、金陵、杭州、北京这四大书坊中,建阳书坊最为著名。仅崇化镇就"比屋皆鬻书籍,天下客商贩者如织,每月以一、六日集"(《建阳县志》卷三)。刻书业的发达,使书籍普及,福建士子有书可读,也使民间藏书极为丰富。据查,到过福建的历代著名藏书家,就有130多人。朱熹任同安县主簿兼管学事时,曾整理县学藏书,并大力收集民间藏书,共900余卷。宋代福州州学建有收藏官颁书籍之稽古阁二、今书阁三,可见有一定规模。书院都注意收集藏书,清代福建巡抚张伯行,在建福州鳌峰书院时,"出家所藏书千卷,充于其中"(《碑传集》卷十七)。清代福州越山书院有藏书20

大橱,400 多种,5 000 多册。浦城南浦书院藏书 130 余部,1 500
多册。不少书院著名教师个人也有丰富的藏书,如清代福州鳌峰
书院山长陈寿祺家中藏书 8 万余卷之多,林昌彝正是借此得以饱
览群书,为今后在各方面的发展打下了基础。

第十章　建筑

一、古塔

　　福建目前保存较有名的各种塔至少在百座以上,这在我国现存的古塔中占有很大的比例。福建古塔的出现与闽文化独有的特点有关。如福建佛教长盛不衰,佛寺遍布八闽;福建民间历来有重风水习俗,其"理法"一派长期左右东南方域;福建省因有绵长的海岸线,海运事业盛极一时。这些都大大促进了福建的造塔技术。

　　从功能上看,福建古塔的用途主要有以下几个方面:

　　1.供奉舍利、礼佛拜佛。这类用途的古塔多与寺有关,且大多雕有精美佛像。如莆田广化寺内建于宋乾道元年(1165年)的释迦文佛古塔,也名舍利塔。塔高36米,仿木结构楼阁式,一层东西两面开门,其余六面设龛,龛内均有佛像。门和龛两旁都雕有佛弟子菩萨、罗汉等图案,其中迦叶和阿难两弟子,老少分明。第二层到第五层四面都设有佛龛,龛两旁也雕有菩萨像。建于宋政和七年(1117年)的长乐城西塔坪山的三峰寺塔,高27米,七层八角,塔壁上浮雕莲花坐佛,全塔共有坐佛200多尊,第一层最多,有60多尊。建于宋元祐年间(1086—1094)的同安县城北梵天寺波罗门佛塔,第二层工字形座的四面各有一组莲花坐佛浮雕,塔身的四角各有一个展翅神兽,四面浮雕都取材于佛经故事。宋代开宝四年(971年)创建的宁德县支提寺内有元、明建造的多座禅师塔。建于唐大中三年(849年)的连江县城北兜护国天皇寺寺塔,为唐代藏经阁,总高9米,塔基第二层条石转角刻出立佛,塔檐下各边雕有肃穆庄严的五尊座佛,下设佛龛,每龛嵌有两尊青石刻的罗汉像。门神背向塔门两边刻有"大方广佛华严经,大乘妙法莲华经"。门额有"悉达多密怛罗"篆刻,可看出当年与佛教的密切关系。

2.导航标志。福建东临大海,省内江河纵横,因此许多古塔成为航标塔,这类塔都耸立于海边江口,远处便能眺见。如建于北宋年间(960—1127年)、复建于明天启年间(1621—1627年)的福州马尾港罗星塔,高31.5米,塔身门窗均为南方设计手法,塔身保存大量灯龛,显然是为导航之用。在世界航海图上,此塔被注明为"中国塔"。建于明嘉靖年间(1522—1566年)的莆田县塔寺塔,高约20米,五层,塔顶为石宝刹,构造十分坚固,成为航海船只的标志塔。建于明万历二十八年(1600年)的福清县塔山村鳌江宝塔,高26米,七层,每层都有雕像,而雕像右上方镌刻捐银建塔的妇女姓氏,传说十八家男子出洋经商遇难,十八寡妇捐资建造了这座航标塔。建于南宋绍兴年间(1131—1162年)的石狮市宝盖山巅的姑嫂塔,高21.65米,五层,相传因姑嫂二人盼远洋亲人登高而死,人们为此筑塔建念。此塔顶为葫芦宝刹,顶头点灯,为古泉州港的重要航海灯标志。始建于明万历年间(1573—1620年)的晋江市溜石村的溜石塔,高约20米,与泉州南门隔江相对,为后渚港溯江而上的航标。建于清嘉庆三年(1798年)的诏安县麒麟山的祥麟塔,高约20米,七层,过往船只常以此塔为航标。重建于元至元二年至五年(1336—1339年)的晋江市石湖村的六胜塔,高31米,五层八角,因濒临东海,故为泉州海外交通的航标。

3.点缀名胜。这类塔大多与风水有关,故也称文峰塔、风水塔、文风塔等。后往往成为某地区的人文标志。如建于的崇祯年间(1628—1644年)的漳平城郊东关山上的东山塔,据民间传说,因此县城地形似鱼,洪水爆发时,恐"鱼"顺江出海,故建此塔以为钓竿,塔尖呈钩形,宛如一把钓鱼钩,把鱼钩住。清乾隆五十一年(1786年)在江对岸又修一塔,两塔相望,为漳平县城标志。始建于明万历年三十三年(1605年)的南平建溪、富屯溪汇流处两岸的南平双塔,东塔约高30米,西塔约高20余米,塔上均刻有"民财永阜"、"文运遐昌"等字样,双塔隔江相望,俨然为南平守护神。再如金门县因风大,故斗门、北山、西堡、下庄、安岐、东山前、西山前、浦边等村庄,皆有筑造与镇压风水有关的塔。由于在海边、河边或池塘边,以及低地易洪水泛滥之处,故一般称之为"水尾塔"。民间认为水尾塔具有收水怪、镇风煞、剋路箭作用,久之,也成为当地的人文景观。闽侯县上街乡的侯官塔为四角七层檐实心石塔,塔座西面题铭"镇国宝塔",在濒临闽江山岗上建造此塔,意在镇水妖,故也称"浮镇塔"、"护镇塔",后被视为侯官码头标志。建于明万历四十七年(1619年)的南靖县文昌塔,高50米,七层,为厚壁空心式楼层结构,内壁设夹道以通上下。可登高远眺,为别具一格的文风塔。始建于明景泰三年(1452年),后又多次重修的永安岭男山南北塔,拱立燕江之滨,遥遥相对,被认为是永安开县塔。建于明崇祯二年(1629年)的福安县城南江家渡村旗顶山上的凌霄塔,高24米,七层八角,与另一座溪口塔(已崩)成双对峙,共控乾阳门户,故也称"风水塔"。

4.其他功能。如建于明万历九年(1581年)、重修于清乾隆四十年(1775年)的龙岩市东城龙津河和小溪合流处水中的挺秀塔,高26米,楼阁式,纯为阻缓河口合流水速而建。建于明万历年(1573—1620年)的泉州西街定心塔,高约4.5米,六层八角,底层为石砌。建塔实衷,因古代泉州子城欲扩建成罗城,以此塔为中心,故也称"城心塔"。(另一说时泉州瘟疫流行,建此塔以镇邪。)

福建古塔的建筑特点如下:

1.用料以石材为主材,兼有其他。中国早期塔是木料所造,为了防火和保持坚固,隋、唐之后建造了许多砖石结构或砖木混合结构的塔,但全部用石料建造的塔还不是很多。福建各地出产石材,自古以来流传石工技术,因此广泛使用石材造塔,被古建筑学家称为"石塔之乡",被誉为全国石塔之冠。但也有的塔并不全用石材建造,如建于明万历三十八年(1610年)的邵武石岐灵塔,建于明崇祯五年(1632年)的泰宁青云塔,皆为砖、石、木混合构成;建于清乾隆四十三年(1778年)的漳平毓秀塔,则用三合土建成。重建于明嘉靖二十七年(1548年)的福州白塔,即为砖塔,目前仍然是全城最高古建筑物。烧制于北宋元丰五年(1082年)的福州鼓山千佛陶塔,则为上等陶土烧制。重修于明嘉靖十三年(1534年)的福鼎县城西鳌峰山的昭明寺塔、建于明万历三十年(1602年)的漳平县双洋圆觉塔、建于明景泰三年(1452年)的永安北塔等,都为砖木结构。所以认为"福建各县的塔全部使用石材建造"是不妥的。

2.丰富多样的造型。在建筑史上,一般认为塔的造型艺术按南、北两地各具不同特点,南方的塔给人一种玲珑瘦巧、轻灵秀丽的感觉,北方的塔则具有雄伟稳重、庄严大方的气魄。但细细考察福建的上百座古塔,却很难以"玲珑瘦小,轻灵秀丽"来概括。福建古塔除了普遍带有平座、栏杆外,其造型丰富多彩,形态各异,难用某种模式来形容。有的塔粗矮胖壮,像一个低矮的大汉,如建于南宋高宗绍兴年间(1131—1162年)的石狮市姑嫂塔,高约21米,底宽却20米见方,五层八角转角石柱顶上为大栌斗,檐子均砌出鼓楞排檐。一至二层各面还做出石造框架,排檐之上平座可以供行人眺望。因第一层尺度宽大,故造型奇拙,构成一种又粗、又大、又矮、又宽的笨重的形态。有的塔造型纤巧,犹如凌霄玉柱,如建于明万历三十四年(1606年)的福清市瑞云塔,高约30多米,七层八角,每层转角的倚柱成海棠式,柱顶斗拱二层,迭涩出檐,有明代"江南第一塔"之称。福建不少塔造型极为独特,在国内罕见。如始建于唐咸通六年(865年)的仙游县无尘塔,高14米,三层八角,塔基为莲花舒瓣和波浪式雕刻,塔柱八根,底层设子午,南北开门,东西设窗。特别其护门将军不置底层门的左右两旁,而镶在底层东南、西南两个方向石壁上,前有月台。这与宋以来的石塔结构迥然不同,是一座形制特别的石塔。建于明万历年间的莆田市石宝塔,高25米,七层四角,为砖砌平面方形,这是明代塔所少见的。有的塔小巧玲珑,常成为一种象征性标志,如建于宋代的泉州开元寺中的多宝塔,高约4米,为灯式塔,塔基下部为一个方形石台,台上置八角须弥座,其上置球形塔身,顶上覆以八角形塔檐,塔檐伸出较长,八角高翘,十分轻巧。有的塔瘦秀欹斜。如建于宋代的泉州崇福寺内的应庚塔,高20余米,七层,传说塔斜向某一方,即预兆某方五谷丰登。此塔虽然倾斜,却历久不坍。建于明天启元年(1621年)的三明市三元区中村乡八鹭塔,高13米,七层八角,石塔各层形似莲花,塔尖如葫芦。有的塔整体如一根石柱,如建于明代的漳浦赵家堡内的聚佛宝塔,塔座为方形须弥座,塔顶作三层相轮,各层之间设平座,上下收分不大。建于明嘉靖二年(1523年)的福清三山乡的迎潮塔,高18米,七层八面,为实心塔。此塔几百年来逐渐倾斜了约15度,似摇摇欲倒,又稳如泰山,足可与意大利的比萨斜塔相媲美。建于宋代的惠安县南埔仙境村里的仙境石塔,共三座,相距20米,形制相同,第一、二层为四方形,第三层为椭圆形。

3.塔雕工艺术精美,雕刻艺术高超。福建许多古塔塔雕精美,造型栩栩如生,与整座塔和谐地融为一体,成为精美的艺术品。如建于南朝陈泰建年间(569－582年)闽侯县塔林山上的陶江石塔,塔雕古拙,其中龙的体态身短脚粗,头小角尖,尾少分歧,形态生动。建于宋乾道元年(1165年)莆田广化寺内的释迦文佛塔,其狮子滚绣球和牡丹花等图案造型优美,侏儒力士表情生动,观音像丰满圆润,形象优美,凤凰、飞天和双翅羽人栩栩如生。建于明万历四十六年(1618 年)的莆田市忠门乡东吴石塔,人面浮雕有龙、狮、麒麟、鹿、鹤等,神情惟肖,护塔将军石像威武雄壮,佛龛内佛像神态各异。建于宋嘉祐四年(1059 年)的仙游县枫亭塔斗山上的天中万寿塔,二至五层分别镌刻着双龙、莲花、海浪等精美图案,五层刻大佛手持莲花,旁边雷公鸡神嘴如钩,展视四方,四层刻坐佛三尊,每尊双掌合十,"此塔佛像线条流畅、细腻,形象生动逼真,体态优美,或盘膝端坐,或昂首挺胸,或微微含笑,或怒目横视,或娇柔窈窕,或威武庄严,无不栩栩如生"(顾延培主编《中国古塔鉴赏》253 页)。建于北宋绍圣三年(1096 年)的长乐县三峰塔,塔座雕有大力士,八面环饰狮子、牡丹等石刻图案,底层塔壁浮雕为文珠、普贤、五十罗汉、十六飞天伎及一组佛经故事,一至六层共雕有莲花坐佛 200 尊,造型生动,风格古朴。始建于唐咸通六年(865 年),后又于宋重建的泉州东西塔相距约 200 米,其塔雕艺术与内容,堪称福建之最。东塔名镇国塔,高 48.27 米,西塔名仁寿塔,高45.066 米。东西塔作平面八角五层形制,每一层嵌有佛教人物浮雕 16 尊,两塔共有浮雕造像人物 160 尊,包括佛、菩萨、高僧、罗汉、诸天神将、金刚力士,还有 80 尊塔檐守望神将和 16 尊负塔侏儒,须弥座上有佛传图 40 方,花卉鸟兽图 48 方。这些浮雕把佛教的发展、佛教的功德及某些传说凝缩在象征性故事中。浮雕人物造型各臻其妙,百相纷呈,体现了当时石刻艺术的高超水平,在构图上运用写实手法和写意手法,更加丰富了艺术魅力。

二、福建民居

福州民居

福州是一座著名的历史文化名城,市内坊巷纵横,古代福州有四十九坊,60 多条巷,但真正能代表福州古代民居建筑艺术的是位于市中心的"三坊七巷",这是由北到南依次排列的十条坊巷的简称。"三坊"是:衣锦坊、文儒坊、光禄坊;"七巷"是:杨桥巷、郎官巷、安民巷、黄巷、塔巷、宫巷、吉庇巷。"三坊七巷"源于东晋时期，经唐、五代拓展，续于宋，历元、明、清，在长期的修建中完整地形成了自己传统格局，是中国历史文化古城中坊制典型代表和中国南方现存较为完整的古街区之一，保存至今的 260 多座的明清民居被建筑界喻为一座庞大规模的"明清古建筑博物馆"。

"三坊七巷"的建筑特点，主要有以下三个方面。

1. 坊巷格局鲜明。巷内一般由 3 至 6 米宽的石板铺路，两侧高耸白粉墙，门墙普遍用石砌勒脚，入口门楼两侧有插拱支撑的单坡雨罩，有的入口大门扇外还有作书卷饰的镂空"六离门"。每宅皆由高墙环护，整个宅院除门头房外，都围上封火墙，形成流畅的曲线，俗称"马头墙"；墙头构成翘角，重重封火墙极有规格地将座座民居隔开。

2. 门、院、园错落有致。"三坊七巷"的大门往往独成一组建筑，考古学家杨秉纶认为门的处理方式有五种，即：(1)用规整巨石架设门框，在石框后安装厚实版门，主要用于防卫。(2)用石门框，配以厚实的版门，门上装铜铺首，门后用铁栓。(3)大门"三开间六扇门形式或明三暗五六扇门"，门前有宽敞门廊，廊的顶棚用弯椽，双坡顶，门两侧是高大马头墙，门面十分排场。(4)门与院落不在同一轴线上，大门与门房组成单独单元；大门内一侧，有通院落的屏门。(5)大门内不设门房。大门后即是院落前回廊，回廊必有一道插屏门，遮住直对整座建筑的视线。其院落，按福州习俗，一院落为一进。主建筑正座厅堂通常三开间，或五开间、七开间，前后均有天井，前宽后狭。为利用场地，前后天井两侧往往兼有披舍，前作书斋用，后为厨房或佣人用。院中楼房往往安排在最后面。其庭园，也称花厅，往往安排在宅轴线的另一侧，并配以假山、楼阁或水榭。布置典雅，小巧玲珑，情趣盎然。

3. 精美的雕刻艺术与整座建筑有机地融为一体。那些被修饰的部分主要在四个方面：(1)门窗，漏花镂空悬雕，工艺精巧，图案丰富,有拼字、几何形等。(2)厅堂明间正立面,屏门上襻间斗拱常雕刻为香篮形、宝瓶形、卷书形等。(3)构架都刻有精美花卉、人物、鸟兽等。所雕刻形象大多鲜明生动、立体起伏、层次清楚。这些雕刻艺术形式,有圆雕、浮雕、透雕,有单幅雕、组雕、连环雕等,内容除了以上所介绍外,还有大量的诗词题刻、琴、棋、书、画等图案,有较浓的文化氛围。

"三坊七巷"中较著名的民居如:1.黄巷唐代黄璞故居(曾归清朝著名学者梁章钜所有,后又归御史陈寿祺所有)。厅内有一双层小楼,底层封火墙与房屋之间有两个由假山与白石灰、糯米汁堆塑的雪洞,可直通鱼池和假山,假山洞分东西二路,东可登上一亭式小阁,阁为歇山顶,柱头转角有雕刻精细的垂花球,整个布局小巧玲珑,清幽古雅,颇有江南园林神韵。柱、架、檩、檐雕龙画凤,楠木制窗槛、门扇、壁风精雕细刻。在此居住的另一个好处是闹中取静,一出巷口即为福州最热闹街市,但家中却一点听不到闹市的喧哗。笔者曾在此故居住多年,故有切身体会。2.衣锦坊欧阳推花厅。此院于光绪年间由欧阳宾购买重修。其花厅所占面积为整个大院的五分之二,前后隔墙,有小门可通,前为男人娱乐厅,后为女人娱乐厅;其20扇楠木门扇,雕有几百种图案,几百幅花鸟,均雕工精细。左右厢房的八扇门,镶入100多幅用黄杨木树根相形雕琢而成的花鸟图案,不仅极为精致,还可随时拿出再嵌入。3.文儒坊陈承裘与夫人张氏故居。其特点一是各类门窗等均雕工精美。正厅门及窗精雕有各种花卉图案及青铜礼器,后厅堂门窗户扇仿中国花鸟画阴刻的菊花、荷花、牡丹、喜鹊、水禽等写生图案,皆为雕刻精品。二是院落内假山鱼池和临水楼阁皆小巧玲珑,相映成趣,花园有书房和客厅,并有墙将后花厅隔开,别有天地。

在福州市辖的各县,也有许多有特点的民居。如位于闽清县坂东镇新壶村的宏琳民居,为一次性设计而成,始建于清乾隆六十年(1795年),占地面积17 000多平方米,大小厅堂35间,花圃25

个,天井 30 个,住房 666 间。全厝为土木结构,翼檐卷仰,鸟革翚
飞,前高后低,左右对称,以廊庑、门洞、花墙、过街楼分隔成大小不
等的院落空间。厝内正厅两边各建一、二、三官房和火墙衕,左右
书院各三间,中为书院厅,两旁为书房。正厅、书院、回照围为天
井,正厅与后厅以屏风相隔。火墙外左右两旁隔沟建筑横厝,朝向
与正厝成九十度,横厝两端正反方向各开横厝厅一间,横厝之外又
建外横厝,两进之间为横街。整个建筑结构精巧,布局井然有序。
位于闽清县塔庄的东成厝,由大小 4 个庭院组成,前侧有一座炮
楼,住宅侧面除拉弓山墙外,又做出披檐,巧妙地将悬山、四坡顶与
土封火墙结合为一体。位于闽侯县南屿的林春泽故居为双层木构
建筑,四面高墙,天井左右两侧为单层木屋,主楼为三开间,楼上是
梳妆楼,具有明代建筑风格。

　　莆仙民居

　　莆仙指莆田县和仙游县。这两个县位于福州与闽南之间,但
却不受福州和闽南影响而自成一体。莆仙民居最鲜明的特点是
"满装饰",即千方百计堆砌外装饰,无论木雕、石雕、砖雕、泥塑、壁
画、贴面都一起上,且圆雕、浮雕、空透雕并存,将整个墙面弄得
极其富丽堂皇,具有明显的炫耀性。对此,黄汉民先生有精到分
析,他认为:莆仙沿海的地理位置及海上交通的发展,使得当地人
在过去多灾多难的年代,为生活所迫而出洋谋生,出洋之后能衣锦
还乡以荣宗耀祖是他们最高的追求,这种社会的群体心态,强烈地
反映在莆仙民居的外墙装饰上:衣锦还乡新修屋宇而不惜巨资,但
并不着力于内部使用功能的改善,而是竭力追求建筑规模的气派,
注重炫耀给别人看的外表装饰,以达到一种心理上的满足。

　　仙游民居多为横向布局,浅进深,宽开局。最典型的如游洋乡
龙山村的宅屋,有的仅 2 进深,面却宽达 17 间,与多进式深宅相
比,这种建筑省却了正厅和后厅,也就省却了大量的建筑材料,并
易于采光通风,相互干扰也少,交通便利,也利于分户。其屋顶一

般为两坡悬山顶与歇山顶相结合,顶分五段,两侧逐渐迭落。其外墙装饰常在窗两侧的土墙以红砖贴面,与白灰构成红白相间花饰。青石、白石、红砖、白灰相互映衬,使住宅精致、绚丽。

仙游民居另一特色是以几种基本单位组合拼接成建筑群体。最主要的基本单元为一厅二房,向横向发展即为一厅四房,向纵深发展即为三坐落。度尾镇砺山村的郭宅为 2 进深,面宽 13 间,由一个一厅二房的基本单元在两侧各加两个小的组合单元,再加一列护层组成,共 80 多间厅房,17 个天井。榜头镇仙水村的"仙水大厅"是一组规模宏大的明代建筑群:3 进深,面宽 9 间,共 160 余间房。这是一个因多次组合而建成的宏大而又功能明确的建筑群:正中是由其最基本单元一厅二房向纵深发展成三坐落,两侧也是三坐落,再往两侧是一列套间厢房,隔了一个侧天井后,又是一列护屋。这种组合拼接的建筑群将甬道、回廊和连幢的厢房连接起来,因而东西南北贯通,无论刮风下雨,内部都畅行无阻。建筑物皆为单檐歇山顶土木结构,用材粗壮,宏大坚固。

莆田民居讲究外观装饰,建筑家黄汉民认为:其墙面处理有独到之处,即墙体用红砖顺砌,并规则地丁砌小块花岗石,形成红砖墙,面上点缀呈菱形布局的白石图案,丁砌的小石块起到拉接作用,既装点了墙面,又增加了墙身结构的整体性。(《老房子·福建民居》,江苏美术出版社 1994 年版)位于莆田江口镇后港村的余宅,就是这种典型的代表。

闽南民居

闽南民居的主要特征为:1. 对称的布局。闽南民居都有明确的中轴线,以厅堂为中心组织空间,左右对称,主次分明。规模大时则纵向延伸或横向发展;规模更大时,则多厅堂组合,或并列数条轴线,形成多院组成的大型宅第。因为带有祭祖、敬神的功能,因而厅堂的中心地位是很重要的。2. 外部材料运用以红砖、白石为多,内部材料以木构架为主。闽南有悠久的制砖历史,特别红砖烧制有很高水平,其质地缜密光洁,色彩红润鲜亮,厚薄、大小尺寸繁多,能适应组砌各种砖花的要求。闽南有丰富的质地极好的石头资源,可以制成各种上乘的建房材料。福建盛产木材,闽南民居内部多采用穿斗式木构架,斗拱与梁架接榫无缝,梁头用藤条加固,重叠有致,室内隔墙亦多以木板镶嵌。3.精巧的雕饰。闽南是雕刻之乡,尤以惠安石雕为全国首屈一指,木雕、砖雕也颇有名气。因此,常在屋中饰以雕梁画栋,特别在屋中重点处,如厅堂的梁坊、托架、门窗格扇、橼头柱础等,都雕满了花饰,精巧细腻。其余地方,如白石门廊镶满飞禽走兽的青石浮雕,两旁屋面嵌着衬有青石透雕窗棂的方形图案砖雕,甚至连屋脊、山墙顶部、门窗上头也布满了各类雕饰。4.丰富生动的屋顶轮廓。由于建筑内部空间起伏较大,单坡或双坡屋面上覆以青瓦屋面,形成层层叠叠、高低错落的屋顶轮廓;或屋脊由抒展、平缓的曲线向燕尾自然过渡。屋宇一般有高啄的檐身,长龙似的凌空欲飞的雕甍,屋脊飞翘,首尾相接,交错叠映。

闽南民居有多种类型,其如:

1.大厝式。"厝",在闽南方言中是"大厦"的意思。这类民居不如府第式有气派,但也是当时的富商所建。这种"大厝"通常为三合院或四合院的格局,多数是悬山式五脊二落水的建筑,前有石铺的前庭。一般是二进三开张者居多,也有三进五开张,每进用天井隔开并以回廊相连。有的两边回廊之外有长列厢房,后面还有一列雅致的梳妆楼,多为闺女的绣房。这类"大厝"坚固耐用,居住舒适,用料极讲究,地板铺方砖,一尘不染。厅房正面的门框、窗框多用光滑的青草石镶嵌,上刻名家书写的对联。建于清代的漳浦浯江的"秀才村"主体建构为三排平房(户厝)抱着两排各三进的院落,至今保存完好。建于1864年至1911年的南安官桥蔡氏旧居,连绵3公里,其木雕、石雕完美地结合在一起,一个雕刻作品,就是一个故事。晋江县大仑的蔡宅,两层角脚楼,两进宅院,头进左右有敞亭,墙面材料鲜明。晋江县的庄宅为横向布局,对称严谨,并有垾头楼,装饰华丽,砖木雕有相当水平。建于清光绪年间的泉州亭店乡的杨阿苗民居是至今保存较完整的宅院,占地1 200多平方米,为五开间双护三进,前有石铺前庭,绕以围墙,组成一完整建筑。杨阿苗宅的装饰艺术极为精美,建筑家黄汉民先生对此有精到论述:宅内几乎集中了闽南所有的装饰手段,而且工艺精巧绝伦,活像一座闽南建筑装饰的博物馆。满装饰的正立面外墙是最精彩的部分:白石墙基、青石柱础和墙面镶边带饰,红砖组砌贴面和檐口"水车堵"的泥塑彩绘巧妙组合,构成鲜艳的色彩对比,组成华丽的墙面图案,显耀荣华富贵之豪门气派。其主入口"塔寿"和大门框斗、匾额的青石雕亦属罕见,尤其是门廊侧面顶墙上镂空人物戏剧石雕,堪称闽南石雕的杰作,人物战马形状生动,雕刻玲珑剔透,叫人叹为观止。墙身中大量磨光青石阴雕花鸟鱼虫,飞禽走兽,还摹刻颜真卿、苏轼、张瑞图等历代名人墨客的诗词墨迹作为装饰。此外,窗洞、槛框、柜台脚上的青石雕更是构图奇特、巧夺天工,件件都称得上艺术珍品。杨阿苗宅的木雕也是刻意求精的上乘杰作,宅内槛窗,隔扇多用楠木、樟木制作,窗花雕刻精细,檐下梁枋、枓栱、雀替、垂柱等部位上雕刻的人物山水、珍禽异兽更是千姿百态、争奇斗艳,极尽华美之能事。(《老房子·福建民居》,江苏美术出版社1994年版)

2.府第式。府第式是闽南民居中常见类型。闽南为官者都喜欢在家乡修筑居室,如泉州仅东城一隅,就有五代晋江王留从效、明末兵部尚书洪承畴、明代南京刑部尚书詹仰庇、南宋丞相蔡确、南宋状元梁克家、明代监察御史郭楠、清代官保提督万正鋬、清代福建水师提督施琅、被南明隆武帝封为南安伯的郑芝龙等显要府第。此外,还有一字排开的施琅手下十员猛将的府第,组成一群古官邸群。这些府第式大院气势宏伟,平面呈中心对称,是多进深、多空间的纵向组合形式,由下厅、天井、前厅、后轩组成中心序列。

进了大门后就是下厅,下厅两旁有两间下房,前面是天井,天井两旁有厢房,过天井就是主屋。中间是厅堂,厅一般为面向天井的半开敞式。前厅为祭祖、敬神的地方,后厅是内眷起居的地方。厅的左右各有前后两房共四间,俗称大房、后房,是住宅和起居间。一般还加后院或两侧,作为厨房、杂间、住房等。更大型的则在此基础上,组合成前后多进,左右平接的大院落。天井、敞厅互为融合,屋脊舒缓有致,显得从容不迫,雍容大度。位于南安石井的"中宪第"建于清雍正六年(1728年),是保留较为完整的府第式建筑。宅第为悬山式五进大院,以厅为中心,东西各列厢房,占地为7 780平方米,附属建筑还有书院、演武厅、梳妆楼、月亮潭、鱼池、水榭、假山、花园等,布局严谨,曲折深邃。

　　3.洋楼式。洋楼式是闽南民居的第三种常见类型。这种民居主要是归国华侨受侨居国建筑形式影响而建筑的,但也保存了闽南典型民宅中的一部分,可谓中外结合,是一种扬弃。它抛弃了以天井、敞厅为中心的合院形式,以前后厅为中心,四周围似四个房间,均向正厅开门,一般为二层建筑。其最大特点是由传统的建筑围合空间,变为空间围合建筑。虽说出现了科林多式圆形廊柱、叶窗等西式屋饰,但门庭垣墙却仍然是砖石结构,仍然有石刻的题匾、门联,以及彩瓷门饰,顶屋开始出现了平顶,而围以釉彩陶瓷栏杆,但也有不少依旧有龙脊风檐。楼前屋后,多有花圃,屋顶墙壁还爬着藤和紫萝兰,充满侨乡情调。石狮市一些小型洋楼,为中西合璧产物,其花岗石勒脚,红砖拼贴的外墙等都是地方传统的做法,而壁柱的造型、窗眉的处理都是西式的。

　　4.土楼。闽南最富有文化意蕴的方形土楼是华安县沙建乡的"日新楼"。此楼建于明代万历年间,建筑的外围是夯土墙体的楼房,楼里是一行行整齐的平房。"日新楼"吸收了中原地区明式建筑风格的特点,又融会了客家文化的传统,方楼背靠悬崖,下面是一片深窈秀美的竹林。整座楼不着眼于单体建筑形象突出,而追求群体布局的空间意境。内部空间创造出平易近人、对称方正、灵活有序、内向含蓄的境界。一进进串联的院落,给空间的组合揉入时间的过程,突出了建筑美的时空特性。闽南最典型的方形土楼是诏安县秀篆乡的"长源楼"。此楼建于清代乾隆年间,边长约42米,只设一个朝向正西的大门,楼高二层,约有房间五六个,轴线正中后方设有祖堂,正面大门外用照壁围成一方形前院,南边前院因"风水"而错开一个角度。闽南的圆形土楼形式多样,最古老的是华安县沙建乡的"齐云楼"。此楼建于明代万历年间,总平面呈椭圆形,楼中院落也是椭圆形,平缓舒展。楼高二层,当中是天井,为单元式结构,底层用石块垒成,二层夯土,大门朝南,东门为"生门",嫁娶由此出入,西门为"死门",殡葬由此出。其与众不同处是房间布局似为三堂横式简化,且不像一般土楼那样将房间平均分割,一般大小,而是大套面积比小套大一至二倍,最大的一套面积近200平方米,小的则不足100平方米,楼内布局异常复杂,充满动感和生机。最令人赞叹的是:从总平面看,各个单元的纵深不相同,设在南侧的单元纵深浅,北面的单元次之,而东侧的单元最深,费人揣摩。虽同住一座圆楼,各家的布局却不相同。但站在院子中间向四周望去,又是那么统一、协调,看不出哪家大哪家小,使人感到温润舒适。目前,这座明代建筑中仍住有20余户居民。闽南最大的圆形土楼是平和县芦溪乡的"丰宁寨",此楼建于康熙初年,历经40年才告竣工。楼的直径77米,主楼高四层,为14.5米,每层77个房间,现住有77户250多人,最多时住过700多人。楼内房间前窄后宽,呈"斧头形",楼门上安放有防火的水柜、水槽,楼中央水井用石板覆盖,上凿三个圆孔供打水,安全又卫生。闽南圆形土楼中最有建筑艺术特点的为华安县仙都乡的"二宜楼"。此楼建于清代乾隆年间,前后工期12年,直径为73.4米,高18米,底高4米,分内外两环,内环一层,外环四层,内外相得益彰,故称"二宜"。内环为一层的平台,为饮食生活区,外环四层均为卧室,分成

12个"透天厝"式的独立单元,共有224个房间。第四层都设有厅堂,厅背后靠外墙有1米宽的室内环形通道,把12个单元联系起来。这座历经220年的土楼中,现仍有200余人居住。漳浦县深土乡的"锦江楼"也别具一格,它由三个高低错落的圆环组成,外圈一层不交圈,在大门口外断开,有36间房;中圈为二层,有52间房,里圈有三层,有36间房。二、三层入口顶部均设瞭望台,整座楼没有出檐,只设女儿墙。华安县高车乡的"雨伞楼"建在小山顶上,巧妙结合地形,外环顺应山势,内环两层,立于山尖,有18个大小不等开间,小楼梯上下。云霄县和平乡的"树滋楼"建于清代乾隆年间,楼高三层,外墙出檐极小,直径50米,每一开间即一独立单元。闽南有许多方圆混合土楼,其一种是主体为圆形,但圆中有方。如诏安县宫陂乡的"在田楼",约有三四百年历史,此楼由内外两环共同组成,内环三层,按方形平面布局,后面两边呈弧形转角,形成前方后圆平面;外环3层,按八卦形状布局呈圆形,共有64间房。该楼外径达86米,是至今发现直径最大的土楼。南靖土楼在闽南民居中也占一定地位。其特点,一是数量多,目前据统计有300多座,其直径多在30至50米间,每层有30来间;二是造型有特点,有"四角楼"、"圆楼"、"交椅楼",还有雨伞形、扇形、曲尺形等多种形状,其保存最好的是建于清宣统元年(1909年)、位于梅林坎下村的"怀远楼",最大的是书洋乡石桥村的"顺裕楼",直径74米,高5层,每层72间。

闽西民居

闽西大中型民居以横向护厝式合院布局为主,以中轴线上的多进合院与两侧的护厝组合而成。护厝为连排的房间。一般民居则屋中设上下厅堂,左右设厢房、厨房、天井等。总体布局四向延展,左右对称,大门之内各个建筑单体相互贯通,形成设施配套的殿堂式、封闭式格局。按其类型,主要有"三开间"和"八间头"。所谓"三开间"即中一间为明间和门,左右各一间为"塾"。门外有屏,门内为庭,主体建筑由堂、室、房组成。堂前有阶,室在堂后,要入室必先过堂。门与堂之间,还有二门,二门以内是主人起居之处。所谓"八间头",指普通民居,有二厅四间两厢房,中为天井,一些"三栋厅"和几披横屋,都是"八间头"的扩展(林国平主编《福建民俗志》)。

据《龙岩地区志》、《长汀县志》等载,闽西有代表性的民居如:明万历年间(1573—1620年)建,位于龙岩中城下井巷的"十八堂",为3幢并排六进式,砖木结构,每幢由六进平房组成,每进面阔三间,中为厅,左右为房间,两边开边门,天井的两则各有廊屋。每幢6个厅,3幢共18个厅,18个天井。清代建造、位于龙岩城内的邱厝,由南向北依次为灰坪、长门、前天井、中堂、后天井、后厅。前、后天井两侧为廊庑,主房面阔三间,中堂为穿斗构架,主房两侧为厢房,廊屋与主房连成一体。建于清代,位于长汀县南大街的吴宅,占地约600平方米,由边门、照壁、门楼、天井、正堂、后堂组成。边门坐东朝西,木架结构,面阔三间,两侧连接封火墙。正脊翘角为双狮戏球。门楼为单檐见山式,砖石结构,门椽画有人物彩绘。前厅正门是六扇隔扇门,正堂为穿斗式木构架,梁架上有浮雕,面阔三间,进深四间,前椽均有垂球。后厅为穿斗式九檩卷棚,面阔三间,进深六间,中间设神龛。后堂系双层绣花楼,楼间设有美人座。为长汀传统典型民居之一。

闽西民居有特色的还如永定慕荆乡的农宅,这是一种单层住宅类型,平面呈马蹄形,中央为四方形四合院,两侧双道护厝,外厝后面为弧形围厝。前院由围墙和牌坊式大门围合成晒场,屋前有半月形风水池。连城县新泉镇的张宅主体建筑坐北朝南,大门倒置西北侧,在层层叠落的青灰砖立面中突出雕饰精美的白石大门。

闽西民居在外界影响最大、最有特色的是土楼。闽西最著名的方形土楼群在龙岩适中村,目前仅三层以上的大土楼仍存242座。适中村方形土楼凡建成于明代的,大都外表简单,屋脊平檐,楼门单一,天井空旷,每层设房 16 间。清初所建的在后座正中设置一厅。清中叶所建的则讲究质量和美观,主楼多为扁方形,前后两端各有六房一厅,左右两侧各有四房一厅或一梯道,主楼厅 16 个,房间多达 80 间,每间面积为 12 平方米。适中村的这些土楼群中,"善成楼"占地面积最广,达 15 亩;"和致楼"主楼结构最宽,横竖各四落,九门十八厅,一门一条巷;"典常楼"装饰工艺最精,叠档飞檐,画廊雕栋;"和春楼"以多厅、多样、多窗著称。闽西规模最大、主楼最高的方楼是永定的"遗经楼"。此楼建于清道光年间,又名"华兴楼",因建筑规模特大,当地人也称为"大楼厦"。其主体建筑是并列的三座五层楼房,高 17 米,主楼左右两端分别垂直连着一座四层的楼房,再前面又同与主楼平行的四层"中厅楼"紧紧相接,组合成一个大"口"字形,气势雄伟。大"口"字形之内的主楼前面是大厅,两边连着仓库,仓库前端又与横廊连接而成一个小"口"字,形成一个"回"字形的整体造型。"回"字外墙的四边各长 76米,呈正方形。全楼周长 136 米,宽 76 米,占地面积 10 336 平方米。大门外,左右连着对称的两所学堂,学堂之间夹着一块长而宽的石坪,石坪前面的大门楼高 6 米,宽 4 米,4 吨的载重汽车可顺畅进出。闽西最古老的方楼是永定县湖雷乡的"馥馨楼",一般认为它有上千年历史,为唐五代时首批进入永定的客家先祖所建,早期由林、易、周、章四姓合建,各据一角。楼周有约 4 米宽的壕沟,设吊墙。闽西较著名的方形土楼还有永定湖坑乡的"裕德楼",在大"口"字形的主楼中间又建了一座方形建筑;下洋镇的"襄正楼"、"永福楼"、"衍嘉楼"等三座"口"字形大方土楼并列相连,各自独立,又组成一个"目"字形整体。闽西最大的圆形土楼是永定的"承启楼",此楼建于清代康熙年间,圆围长 1 915.6 米,高 12.42 米,楼墙宽 1.5 米,从外到里有三圈外高内低的环形建筑,加上中心圆形大厅,空中俯视有四个圆。主圆楼为四层,每层有房72 间;主楼内依次向内筑建两圈圆楼,外圈二层,每层 40 间,里圈单层,为

32间,中央为大厅。全楼共计400间房,总面积5 376.17平方米,主楼设3个大门,楼内各圈设巷门6个,水井2口。全楼最盛时,曾住80多户,600余人。由于"承启楼"建筑规模宏大,便有"姑嫂夸楼"的故事:某村一次婚礼上,两个年轻女子在同桌吃饭时,都极力夸耀自己的楼屋如何之大,等到双方问清对方所夸之楼时,才知道都住在"承启楼",且为姑嫂。因为一个住楼东,一个住楼西,而楼中人多且常有进出,所以并不相识。1986年邮电部以"承启楼"作为图案的1元票额的"中国民居"邮票发行后,即被评为当年最佳邮票。闽西直径最大的圆楼是永定县古竹乡的"深远楼",外环楼直径达80米,为三环建筑,共有房间328个,住80户,500多人。最古老的圆楼是古竹乡的"金山古寨",南宋祥兴二年(1279年)所建,有2至3米高,直径约30米,中心有一望台。闽西最富丽堂皇的圆楼为永定县湖坑乡的"振成楼",此楼外环楼高4层,每层48个房间,按八卦图造成辐射状八等分,各等分之间有防火墙,既自成院落,又有拱门相通,连成整体。厅顶可作舞台,楼内有学堂和花园。1985年,在美国洛杉矶世界建筑模型展览会上,"振成楼"作为中国古建筑的代表模型之一,和北京天坛、雍和宫一道被视为展览会中的珍品。

闽北民居

闽北民居多为土木结构瓦房,中有天井,两侧为二间或四间正房,天井两旁设二三阶台阶,中有大厅堂,两旁各有两间正房,后阁两边为厨房。正如《明溪县志》(民国23年铅印本)记:"屋多木建,墙以砖泥筑之,规制普通为上下三厅,左右辅以厢房,间有构层楼者,建筑虽不甚华美,而坚致牢实,堪垂久远,且易修理,实有足取者。"但当地也有以下几种有特色的民居。

1.在本地模式上,模仿外地样式。如《崇安县新志》(民国31年铅印本)记:"住,明时,屋制颇卑,庭前多设二柱,厅壁分两段,上段用竹篱附灰,与今日假墙同。至清制作稍变。乾、嘉时,下梅邹姓、曹墩彭姓经商广东,仿广式构屋,藻饰华丽。岚谷彭姓经商苏州,仿苏式构屋,栋(栋)宇宏深。清季,如城坊万朱二姓之屋,规模宏敞,光线充足,闽北当首屈一指。"清代,商人在武夷山下梅村模仿广州、苏杭建筑样式,造房屋 70 余栋,现仍存 50 余栋,为古民居群。与闽北传统民居比,其特点有三:一是宽敞,整座建筑有大门、门楼、前厅、大厅、后厅、书楼、香阁等,每栋均为三进,大厅堂用扛梁造法,柱头挑出二支斗拱,斗拱镌有花鸟饰案。二是精美,无论细砖雕砌的门楼,镂空雕花的木梁,精美的缕窗典雅的廊檐,都经过精工细雕。三是布局统一,墙帽造型优美。

2.“高脚厝”。这类房一般建在闽北一些依山傍溪的村落,为二层木楼房,下层以若干杉木柱为支架形如高脚,既可防洪,又可避虫蛇,下层往往用竹篱圈围。也有的全座楼只用一根木柱,四面围墙,视木柱高度,可建一至二层。楼上楼下隔若干间。这类住房与武夷山汉城遗址中的“干栏式”建筑有相似之处。“干栏式”即用矮柱将整座房屋架起,下部空敞部分往往用作饲养牲畜和堆积杂物之所,上层前为廊及晒台,后为堂屋与卧室。

3.“三进九栋”式。闽北明清时不少告老还乡的官员或在外发财的大户修建“三厅九栋”式大型瓦房,其天井,走廊、檐阶一般为石板,每幢四周以陶砖或泥土筑造防火墙,第三进大厅上方正中设神龛,整座建筑显得富丽堂皇。最有代表性的为位于泰宁城关明朝兵部尚书李春烨建于明天启年年间(1621－1627 年)的府第,人称“尚书第”、“一福堂”,其主要建筑特色有四:一是气势宏伟,整座建筑坐西朝东,南北长 87 米,东西宽 60 米,占地面积 5 220 多平方米,主宅 5 幢,辅房 8 栋,分五道门沿甬道一字排开,除厅堂、天井、回廊外,有房 120 多间,全为砖石木构。二是布局严谨。五幢主体建筑为三进合院,结构大体一致,中厅堂用减柱扛梁造法,木柱粗大。其大厅对天井开敞,厅前两侧设雕饰精美的高栏杆。三是用材讲究。如甬道、庭院、走廊、天井全用花岗石板铺设,厅堂采用方砖地。四是雕工精细。如厅堂内的柱础式样多达 30 余种,都雕刻有麒麟、锦象、花卉等装饰图案,门廊、匾额、梁柱、斗拱及墙面布满石雕、砖雕、木雕装饰,精工雕刻人物、飞鸟、卷草、团花、仿锦等图案。

闽东民居

闽东一带传统民居结构多为一厅,左右为厢房。但也有多种形式,如:黄汉民认为福安传统民居的屋顶高耸而且巨大,屋顶坡度增大,高大的山墙面上挑出两三层披檐,檐下的木构架与竹泥白粉墙形成鲜明的对比。山尖的壁瓦装饰与细长的木悬鱼相互衬托,形成福建木构民居中最富有变化的山面构图。福安畲族的房屋多为"四榴厝",即两榴木料加左右两侧土墙,厝里空间为三透。正中用木板隔障,称为"中庭壁",前为厅堂,后为后厅。厅堂常放一张八仙桌,用于待客或过年过节祭祖,走廊处有 1 至 2 个天井,后厅用于放农具或作餐厅,左右两透用木板各隔成 2 至 3 间卧房(蓝炯嘉总纂《福安畲族志》)。宁德一带用料大多为花岗石,墙均用条石砌成,一间房约需 14～16 层条石。这与闽东沿海风大,需要牢固住房,且闽东富产花岗岩有关。

三、福建古桥

我国古代桥梁建筑历史悠久,成就卓越,在 10 世纪以前一直处于领先地位。福建地形多山,江河纵横,又东濒大海,所以桥梁建造一直兴盛不衰。福建古代桥梁无论在长度、跨度、重量、建造速度、施工技术、桥型和桥梁基础等方面,都达到很高水平,在我国的古桥建筑史中占有重要地位。明人王世懋的《闽都疏》中有"闽中桥梁甲天下"之誉。清人周亮工的《闽小记·桥梁》中称:"闽中桥梁最为巨丽。"

福建的桥梁建造起步较晚,但在唐代福建还处于开发阶段的时候,已建造出高质量的桥梁。如建于唐大历六年(771 年)的福州城门镇连坂村前的连坂桥,全长 15 米,面宽 14.1 米,两座岸边的桥台呈长方形,均用条石叠砌在直径 40 厘米的木桩上,两桥台之间架两条大石梁。始建于唐代的福州闽安镇的回龙桥,长 66 米,面宽 4.8 米,四墩五孔,全部用花岗石砌造,墩间各铺五根石梁,厚度均达 0.8 米左右。桥虽经多次修缮,但墩、梁及栏柱等,仍多为唐宋遗物。这种五孔以上的唐桥在中国建桥史上是罕见的。值得注意的是,一些北方极有价值的桥梁随着时间的推移在北方被湮没,但由于中原文化的南移,造桥技术在福建沿播,一些中原样式的桥梁在福建保存至今。如北宋汴梁的虹桥不用支柱,用木梁相接而成,既易架设又便于通航。这种被称为"虹梁结构"的跨长径木桥建筑不仅在中国桥梁史上占有极其重要地位,在世界桥梁史上也是十分罕见的。但北宋灭亡后,再也没有发现汴河虹桥的任何记载。而当今有关专家学者在调查时发现福建屏南县的千乘桥正是类似虹桥的木拱桥。潘洪萱在《十大名桥》中指出:"这可能是随着宋朝政治文化中心南移杭州,匠人们把建造虹桥的技艺从黄河之滨传到了南方。"在与福建交界的浙江地段也发现这类桥梁,但从一些桥屋梁桥上所写工匠名字来看,是出于福建匠师之手。福建古代桥梁之多,居全国前列。据《福建通志》统计,自唐至清代,福建共建造桥梁 2 694 座。这里统计显然不完全,因据《龙岩地方志》载,地处偏僻的龙岩地区古桥就有 594 座。但仅此数目,也是令人惊叹。这在当时技术条件差的情况下,确实是了不起的成就。正如英国科技史专家李约瑟博士在《中国科技史》中指出:"特别是福建省,在中国其他地区或国外任何地方,都找不到和他们相比的。"

福建古桥不仅历史悠久,数量众多,而且风格各异,博采众长,取得了很大的成就。其特点主要有以下几个方面:

1.长短不拘。从桥的长度上看,福建古桥有全国最长的,也有全国最短的。属长桥的,如泉州安平桥长 811 丈(约 2 300 米),把闽南的安海和水头之间原来以舟渡往来的五里海湾连接起来,被认为"天下无桥长此桥",在 1925 年郑州黄河大桥建成之前的七八百年间,它一直是我国最长一座大桥。(也有专家认为,南宋绍兴年间所建的泉州南门外长 1 000 余丈的玉澜桥和长 2 400 丈的苏埭桥的长度均超过了安平桥。)泉州洛阳桥长 360 余丈(约 1 106 米)。惠安屿桥长五里许(约 2 300 米),潮平时淹没,潮落时可行人;福州万寿桥长 174 丈(约 522 米),福清龙江桥 180 丈(约 553 米);漳州府流冈桥长 260 丈(约 799 米),虎渡桥长 200 丈(约 614 米)。短的桥,如华安华丰镇湖底村的单孔坦弧石拱桥,总长 3 米,跨度不到 1 米,小巧玲珑。

2.用料多样。从用料上看,有以石料为主,有以木料为主,也有石木结合。有石梁桥,如始建于宋绍熙年间(1190—1194 年)的漳州虎渡桥;有石拱桥,如建于宋绍定元年(1228 年)的建宁镇安桥,最大跨径 18 米,至今仍通汽车。始建于明成化十九年(1483年)的福清波澜桥,是一座单孔石拱桥,净跨 6.6 米,宽 2.15 米,拱高 3.3 米,站在桥的一端看不到桥的另一端。位于福州八一七南路的薄拱桥(也称"小桥"),始建于元代,跨径 7.2 米,拱圈厚度仅20 厘米,比按现代桥梁设计理论计算要小得多,至今每天经过桥上车超千辆而无恙,被现代桥梁专家称为奇迹。以木料为主的桥,如古田县鹤塘乡西洋村的沉字桥,建于南宋德祐元年(1275年),桥梁全用水松木架设,经久不腐,保存完好。石木结合的桥,如建宁县伊家乡兰溪村的兰溪桥,建于明嘉靖三十六年(1557年),桥宽 6.5 米,高 12 米,长 75 米。石墩上井字形木架四层,"木轴条层出尺许,亘以大木为梁"。再如武平县西东留乡的大阳桥,始建时间不详,今存为清咸丰五年(1855 年)重造,桥身长数丈,宽 1 丈,巨石砌成的两座桥墩上有数层杉木架构,形似斗拱,风格别致。

3.样式多种。从样式上看,除了以上提到的虹桥、石拱桥外,还有其他各种样式。有浮桥,如建于明永乐八年(1410 年)的建阳县东津浮桥,用三十几根铁索将三十几只大船联为一体。铁索固定在两岸石柱上,使水东与城坊连为一体。福建有许多桥早先都为浮桥,如位于漳州市区南隅的南桥,宋绍兴年间(1131—1162年)始建时为浮桥,于嘉定年间(1208—1224年)才改为石桥。位于龙海市北溪下游的虎渡桥(也称江东桥、通济桥),于宋绍熙年间(1190—1194年)始建时亦为浮桥。此外,还有样式各异的吊桥、交通桥、独木桥、踏步桥等。

4. 将实用与艺术和谐地融为一体。福建古桥建造注重与环境的协调。如宋元时期建的石墩石梁桥,这些桥梁大都地处入海口,江面开阔,风大浪高,古朴凝重的石墩石梁,一如压海之长堤,气势磅礴,雄伟壮观。如潘洪萱在《十大古桥》中所言:"福建泉州'天下无桥长此桥'的安平石梁桥,凌跨于安海港海湾上,如压海长堤,具有'玉帛千丈天投虹,直栏横槛翔虚空'的观感,与四周环境形成了'水秀山明桥跨海'的美景。"再如始建于元末元统二年(1334年)的莆田县桥兜村的宁海桥,横跨木兰溪奔注兴化湾的入海处,每当旭日东升之时,霞光映照江水,犹如金龙下海,跃浪腾波,景象壮观,被称之为"宁海初日",为莆田二十景之一。始建于宋建炎元年(1127年)的莆田县延寿村附近的延寿桥,两岸风光如画,桥下碧波荡漾,为历代文人雅士赏景赋诗,泛舟垂钓佳境,被誉为"寿溪钓艇",自古就是莆田二十景之一。

5. 附属建筑和石雕作品雕刻工艺精湛。福建古代桥梁建造者多注重观赏性,桥上往往以石雕、碑记、亭、塔幢、扶栏等艺术品来装饰。点缀在福建古桥之上的石雕作品,无论是镇桥的石将或镇水兽,还是象征民族不屈精神的石狮子,无论是具有纪念意义的人物造像,还是表现宗教题材的坐佛、莲花,或威武庄严,或生动自然,或神圣肃穆,或清新秀丽,线条优美,衬托出长桥结构的雄伟,又在气吞山河的气魄中透露出一股清秀之气。特别是建在伸臂式桥上的建筑,更给人"飞阁流丹,下临无地"的感觉。泉州洛阳桥最为典型,据刘浩然《洛阳万安桥志》介绍,洛阳桥上有原位于中亭处明代姜志礼生祠前的"功侔忠惠"坊,原建于明代的镜虹阁,位于南北两端的镇风塔,位于南北两端的北宋石介士四尊,元代所建的"泉南佛国亭",今人所建的"中亭",位于中亭西侧的"甘雨碑亭",位于蔡忠惠祠前西侧的"重修蔡忠惠祠碑亭",位于蔡忠惠祠前东侧"舆庆堂去思碑亭",桥两侧石塔8座,两边扶栏分别有形态各异石狮子28只,塔亭等建筑物上姿态各异菩萨81尊等,虽然今天有的已被毁坏,但仅保存下来的石塔、雕像、碑记及蔡襄书写的《万安桥记》碑等,已令人赞叹,真酷似一座小型博物馆。这种融观赏性和实用性为一体的古桥,在福建比比皆是。如坐落在漳州至华安公路干线上,横跨九龙江的金山大桥,具有很高的艺术欣赏价值。全桥采用精制的石料,优美的造型,以奇巧的构筑方法建造而成。净跨100米的大拱如长虹下凡横跨江面;大拱上面又筑有28个城门式的小拱,这28个小拱每个小拱每2拱为一组,从大到小,直插大拱拱端,从远处看像一座座小巧玲珑的小石拱桥,架设在长虹式的大拱上面,形成了桥上的壮丽景观;桥两头各筑一座桥头堡,两边安上精美的石栏。全桥整体结构严紧、造型轻巧、宏伟壮观。元至正年间(1341—1368年)再造的晋江市御赐桥,桥端有附属的石人雕刻及石塔。建于明弘治九年(1496年)的大田县城东通马四桥,桥上亭阁,顶部绘有龙凤呈祥,雕饰动物、花鸟、人物等,工艺精细。福州的回龙桥亭内有三块石碑。福清市龙江桥南端建有两座镇佛塔,浮雕有佛像侏儒、莲花狮子等纹饰。福州万寿桥建有风雨亭,桥栏石柱雕有形态各异的石狮。

6.极富魅力的屋桥。在福建各种样式的古桥中,最有特点的要算是屋桥(也称风雨桥)。即在桥上有桥屋、桥廊或桥楼。正如清代周亮工在《闽小记》中所记:"桥上架屋,翼翼楚楚,无处不堪图画。……闽地多雨,欲便于憩足者,两檐下类覆以木板,深辄数尺,俯栏有致,游目无余,似畏人见好山色故障之者。"在闽西,最有代表性的屋桥,如位于连城县罗坊村口的云龙桥,此桥建于清乾隆三十七年(1772年),长81米,宽5米,桥面用鹅卵石铺面,两旁排列64对楹柱,木栏杆外有上下两层木篷雨盖,用以遮风挡雨,桥两端有亭阁式门楼,桥中央建有高10米的文昌阁。位于连城县城南门外的文川桥,始建于宋绍兴年间(1131—1162年),长50余米,宽4米,桥上架屋17间,中间正殿祀观音大士,殿顶为二层式葫芦顶。在闽北,有代表性的如位于政和县坂头蟠溪的坂花头桥,建于明正德六年(1511年),长38米,宽10米,高16米,为楼阁式屋桥,主楼三层,两侧偏楼双层,楼东面为文昌阁,有柱子80根,每根柱上都有楹联。位于光泽县司前溪上的司前棚桥(又名太安蓬桥),清乾隆二十三年(1758年)始建,桥长约100米,宽2.5米,高2米,桥廊两边列椅,可供休息。位于明溪县城东的白沙桥(也称龙门桥),始建于明成化八年(1472年),长50余丈,宽3丈,桥上盖有39间桥屋,当中有一座三层六角楼阁,可惜1933年春毁于山洪,再建后未盖桥屋。在闽东,有代表性的如位于古田县鹤塘乡西洋村的沉字桥,建于南宋德祐元年(1275年),桥长55米,宽4米,上为双劈屋顶,两廊有长椅。在闽南,有代表性的如位于永春县东平乡东美村的东关桥,始建于南宋绍兴十五年(1145年),桥长85米,宽5米,于明弘治十三年(1500年)建桥屋,共有20套整齐划一的木屋架,分25开间,屋顶用当地出产的粘土小青瓦铺面,青砖砌脊。位于安溪县蓝田乡进德村的瑞云桥,建于明崇祯三年(1630年),桥长14.7米,宽5.1米,桥上建廊,廊外两边各设两层雨披,廊内陈设坐椅。中有天竺亭,梁架均雕花彩绘。

福建古代桥梁建筑在技术上取得了重大的突破,为发展我国以至世界古代桥梁技术做出了不可磨灭的贡献。其突出技术成就主要表现在以下几个方面。

1.创"筏形基础"。桥梁的筑基向来是建造桥梁的关键。洛阳桥位于洛阳江入海口,江面开阔,江水与海水交汇,水急浪高,在这样的地段上建桥是史无前例的,工程艰巨,而且有许多技术上的困难。为了解决桥梁基础稳固问题,建造时首创了"筏形基础"。即在江底沿桥位纵线抛掷数万立方米的大石块,筑成一条宽20多米,长1里的石堤,提升江底标高3米以上,然后在这石堤上筑桥墩。这在桥梁史上是一大创新。

2. 创"种蛎固础"法。在没有现代速凝水泥的条件下,要解决桥基和桥墩的联结稳固问题是一大难题,建桥工匠们发挥了惊人的才智,巧妙地发明了种蛎固基的方法,在桥基和桥墩上养殖海生动物牡蛎,利用牡蛎依靠石灰质贝壳附着在石块间繁殖生长的特性,使桥基和桥墩的石块通过牡蛎壳相互联结成一个坚固的整体。这种方法顺利解决了石灰浆在水中不能凝结,而如用腰铁或铸件等办法连结石块,铸铁很快就会被海水腐蚀等难题。

3. 创"浮运架梁"法。宋代福建的许多桥梁都是在波涛险恶的江海中用石块造成的。洛阳桥的石梁共有300余块,每根石梁长约12米,宽厚均在0.5米以上,重7~8吨,在宋代科技尚不发达,运输工具简陋的情况下,建桥工匠们发挥聪明才智,创造了"浮运架梁"法。即把重达七八吨的石梁,置于木排之上,利用海潮的涨落进行运送、砌筑和架设。趁退潮时砌筑桥墩,趁涨潮时将载有石梁的木排驶入两个桥墩之间,待潮退,木排下降,石梁即被装在桥墩上的木绞车吊起,再慢慢放置在石墩上,并用木绞车校正好石梁的位置。

4. 创"睡木沉基"法。在桥梁基础方面,创造了一种"睡木沉基"法。即:在水位干枯时,将墩基泥沙整平,用几层纵横交叉的木条编成的木筏,固定在墩位处,再在木筏上垒筑墩石,随着墩身逐渐加高加重,木筏也随着下沉江底。如位于九日山下、跨越于晋江之上的金鸡桥便是采用这种沉基方式。在山区,河流降至最低水位以下时,则直接置于坑上。也有用木笼填石为基,如始建于元大德七年(1303年)的福州万寿桥,在桥墩处先下木笼,然后在笼内密填石块为基。

　　5.桥墩形式多样。从桥墩结构方面看,石墩桥往往是外圈砌块石或条石,中间用大小不等和强度不一的碎石块作填充料,其砌筑方法是采用一丁一顺交叉叠置。有的还用石灰浆或糯米猪血等胶凝嵌砌。一般桥墩的形式大多为船形墩,即上游尖下游平,如始建于北宋元祐四年(1089年)的福州盖山乡阳岐村的午桥,始建于北宋元丰元年(1078年)的福清县上径乡的蹑云桥,始建于北宋政和三年(1113年)的福清县海口镇的龙江桥,始建于元元统二年(1334年)的莆田县黄石镇桥兜村的宁海桥,始建于明嘉靖三十三年(1554年)的华安县梨仔坪的云水桥,始建于明万历七年(1579年)的诏安县城东郊的洋尾桥等。也有两头尖的船型墩,如始建于唐末的福州市郊闽安镇的回龙桥。也有以多种墩形组合而成的,如著名的晋江市安海安平桥,桥墩以条石砌成,或四方形,或长方形,或单边、双边船形。桥墩在石梁支座处,将顶上三四层条石,均向左右排出20至30厘米,用以承托石梁,使石梁跨径缩短,提高石梁强度。

　　6.桥梁结构有创意。从桥梁结构上看,或用木材在墩上层层平排或斜插,逐渐向跨中伸出,以缩短跨径后再承托大梁,如重建于清咸丰五年(1855年)的武平县西东留乡的大阳桥,在墩上铺以数层杉木,形式如斗拱,风格别致。建于元元统年间(1333—1334年)的邵武乡铜青桥,在4个墩上纵横架木11层后承托木梁。或在石梁上加铺石板,如建于宋绍兴三十年(1160年)的福清市海口镇龙江桥,6条石梁并排铺设在墩顶帽石上,石梁之上再横铺石桥板。

　　福建古桥的建筑的兴盛,除了与福建独有的自然环境有关外,还与福建文化的特点有关。如佛教在福建长盛不衰,许多僧人都积极参加了桥梁的募建活动,僧人修建桥梁之多,是全国罕见的。僧人在修建桥中的作用,也可看出当时福建修建桥梁的兴盛。

后　记

　　随着区域文化热的持续升温,闽文化的宝库正在被缓缓打开。闽文化与其他区域文化不同之处是它的影响已不仅仅在福建。祖籍福建的海外华人、华侨有 1030 万,他们不同程度地保持着闽地习俗,并千方百计返回故里,寻根问祖。闽文化的独特魅力与深厚内涵,引起了愈来愈多人的关注和兴趣。将闽文化译为英文,是我们多年的愿望。它不仅可以进一步向世界介绍闽文化,也可以使对闽文化有兴趣的朋友在了解闽文化的同时提高英语水平。我们的肤浅尝试,得到了福建广播电视大学教学管理处、福建广播电视大学闽文化研究所、福建省闽文化研究会的大力支持,并得到了李红、樊祺泉、叶文华、赵捷、刘士本、高扬明、康乃美等领导的关心和指导。我们要感谢厦门大学出版社的编辑牛跃天先生,他多年来一直支持我们研究闽文化,这次为提高本书的质量又倾注了大量的心血。

　　本书由郑立宪主编。前言和第十章由郑立宪翻译,第一章至第九章由谢燕华翻译,全书由郑立宪审校。王小红、陈晴、严春容、何随贤也参加了翻译研讨工作。本书中文由何绵山撰写。

　　由于本书内容地域性强,翻译时间紧迫,译者水平有限,所以翻译工作难免有粗糙、疏忽之处,请专家学者给与批评指正。读者可能会注意到译文中有些地方与中文不是那么完全一致,但整本书的基本思想并不会受到影响。

译著者

2003 年 7 月 30 日

图书在版编目(CIP)数据

闽文化/郑立宪主编. 一厦门:厦门大学出版社,2003.8
ISBN 7-5615-2179-0

Ⅰ.闽…　Ⅱ.郑…　Ⅲ.文化史-福建省-汉、英　Ⅳ.K295.7

中国版本图书馆 CIP 数据核字(2003)第 078721 号

厦门大学出版社出版发行
(地址:厦门大学　邮编:361005)
http://www.xmupress.com
xmup @ public.xm.fj.cn
三明日报社印刷厂印刷
2004 年 3 月第 1 版　2004 年 3 月第 1 次印刷
开本:850×1168　1/32　印张:15　插页:2
字数:371 千字　印数:0001-2100 册
定价:28.00 元
本书如有印装质量问题请直接寄承印厂调换